Weave of the Dream King

Weave of the Dream King

John Olson

BLACK
WIDOW
PRESS

BOSTON

Black Widow Press is an imprint of Commonwealth Books, Inc., Boston, MA. Distributed to the trade by NBN (National Book Network) throughout North America, Canada, and the U.K. Black Widow Press and its logo are registered trademarks of Commonwealth Books, Inc.

Joseph S. Phillips and Susan J. Wood, Ph.D., Publishers
www.blackwidowpress.com

Cover artwork: *The Dream King* by Gina Kerr. Ink illustration. 2020.
Cover design by Gina and Robbie Kerr

ISBN-13: 978-1-7338924-8-3

Printed in the United States of America

for Roberta

Acknowledgements

The author would like to thank the following publications in which some of these prose poems first appeared: *Alligatorzine, The Dalhousie Review, KYSO Flash, Surrealists and Outsiders, SurVision, Positive Magnets, Ecopoetics* and *Resist Much Obey Little: Inaugural Poems To The Resistance.*

Contents

Welcome

You're welcome, very welcome here. It's good to see you. Do you like butter? Is that a yes? How about government? We hold these truths to be self-evident: butter is a lisping vulnerability of greasy halibut garnished with cowboys, and my tongue is a subcontinent of hockey. The dawn is loveliest when the body of a woman glides through water, language is mostly breath, dirt is prehistoric, mimicry is a coin that we pay to the gods of combination, and age is not my friend. Some things are transparent and some things are not. Everything else is either a sensation, or golf.

I must say it's much nicer to have a smaller bottle of juice in the refrigerator than that enormous bottle of grape juice we brought home from Costco. We have a small refrigerator. You can only put small items in it. Meadows, puppets, clouds. Puppets are creepy, but they make a good dinner. They go with anything: crustaceans, iPods, fondue. Here's a smear of poetry on a glass slide: little microbial words create sugar. Look what happens when you stay alive this long. Eating turns dark and editorial. The tyranny of hunger is enough to bring a government down.

What is it to think? It is to fill the brain with worries, apprehensions, judgments, anxieties, regrets and hot dogs. I can't possibly know what you're thinking. But if you're thinking what I'm thinking you're having a conversation with yourself. People who think mathematically have mathematical thoughts. If X is an integer then what is Y? Y is cliffs and sea lions. Crashing waves. The Queen is an afterthought. She arrives later in your life, when your brain has become a kingdom of unicorns and broccoli. Pharmaceuticals packed in cotton. Chimeras stitched by hand.

Yesterday I discovered a city of elves beneath the bed. I write during a period of immense crisis. Maybe this is why none of my words seem to preserve anything. Words are ice. They melt in the mind and become rivers and reeds. But they won't save the world. Nothing can save the world now but Superman. And yet I keep putting words down, putting words out there, pushing words into existence. Georges Braque rattling a shape at a palette of paint. Elves drinking coffee in weightless papyrus, ancient and holy. Yet no one is satisfied, least of all me. It's crazy. Why does anyone do art these days? Day after day. My neighbor pounds the dirt. Conjuring more elves.

If you ask me mysticism is celestial softball, poker is a waste of television and matter is a form of energy periodically manifested as a tape measure. Is it literary to have more than one metaphor in your pants? Myriad virilities jiggle on a bar of python soap. I'm wiggled by ninety protoplasmic mops, like the janitor in the Nirvana video. My spirit smells of semantic shellac. Merriment ensues. There will be licorice and root beer in our conversation from now on, and together we will thread the air with rattlesnakes. I could leave now walk right out the door but instead I'm going to offer you a ticket to our large stemmed glass parade. BYOB.

Memories are hives of strange honey. Ghosts seated at an absurdly large table where rumination is served in vinegary regret, grilled plums and smoking resentment. Dumb jobs, the chaos of one's 20s, the kindness of strangers punctuated by bouts of violence. Getting punched and tossed into a Xmas tree stupidly drunk at age 18, followed by numerous psychedelic journeys. Hitch-hiking across France to a gypsy festival at Saintes-Maries-de-la-Mer. Living in a bus for several months with three other guys until one morning the owner of the bus wouldn't let us into his house to use the bathroom and kitchen. Is that normal? I don't know. But I'm glad the brain is plastic.

I still feel the heat of the king's forge, the insufferable chatter of elves. I shave in men's rooms along the highway. If you tell me what you want, I will write it down, and it will become a small village. It's radical getting dressed in rocks. I find a universe in the fuchsia and wear a shirt of sugar. Think of me as a man storming in his teeth. I come to a door and open it to a narwhal sitting on a harpoon smoking a plumber. The cave is dyed in its own darkness. This is the color of oblivion. The aromatic piece of night we all carry in our hearts. Add the clatter of absence and you've got a hawk swooping by. The rustle of feet in the grass. Nature overflowing with wind.

Tiny Balls Of Sound

Have you ever laid awake at night writing and rewriting scripts for things you plan to say and do the next day? And then the day comes and it all comes out forced and weird because your acting isn't that great and the lines you wrote in the liquid of night got stuck in the clay of day. It's like having Tennessee Williams in your head night and day. Ava Gardner chopping the shit out of a lobster in a Mexican kitchen. Richard Burton walking barefoot over broken glass. Who, or what, weaves the narratives of our lives? Is it one big sweeping novel or a collection of short stories with no particular theme holding it together other than our own privately weeping selves?

Things have their uses. Jacks are for lifting. Chairs are for sitting. Mouths are for globules, tiny balls of sound. Ceilings are for alternate realities, the rain that I babble after feeling the implications of floating around in a bucket of words. The world demanded technique so I got naked and cleaned the purpose of it with unctuous concern. We are nascent who hammer out an identity and fill it with syndication. We're stirring a perversity machine. Subtlety is a battle fought with sequins. I pick a sidewalk and whisper ropes of sunlight for the mosaic at the end of the block. Back home, the parlor swells with conversation & Proust gets entangled in adjectives.

We have a stuffed Viking in our kitchen. He hangs from a hook on the wall. I don't know where he came from. When I consider the facts external to existence, I wonder if time works by squirting tiny drops of ink onto the surface of the paper creating sonnets of timely import, or if feelings do this. What's it like being Paul McCartney? The purpose of this mission will be to investigate the origin and nature of cosmic dusts, which are key sources of organic compounds on Earth, and therefore intrinsic to Paul McCartney. Every day we see our lives play out in miniature what the universe does at large. Nothing rational can explain it. There's also the narrative arc of our lives. My life has been a hoot. Bits of pessimism bouncing around in a nervous system made of junkyards & coffee.

Feelings are big mushy things to carry around. They're onions. Complications. Ethical considerations. Moral dilemmas. Guilt. Remorse. That stuff. Anger is an odd one. Dark energy, to be sure, but accelerant, gasoline, diesel, kerosene, butane. Despair is even weirder. It makes you empirical, a pair of hands reaching out of the darkness. Twinkle like a lip. With a word on it. The appeal of mindfulness is in its crumpled beer cans. String theory states that all matter in the universe is composed of tiny vibrating strings of energy and in the long run will redeem us if we can get right by doing nothing. I like to put my fingers on the warm pages of a book and feel the world that way sometimes. I'm a whispering gun. Black engine of opium thundering reality.

Let me show you a frog. We will discover the importance of this later when we share this endeavor, this amphibious journey together, you will help to fulfill that reverie, the dream of finding a frog, attaining frogness in a few words, brain waves, fugues and images. There is nothing either good or bad but thinking makes it so, said Hamlet. But what did he know, besides fencing and madness? Wikiri manager Lola Guarderas holds a glass frog whose translucent skin reveals its organs and beating heart. Think of this as a sentence created by a tongue. This mud will be our beginning, winking slippery ideas like a Florida clitoria. And the rest is silence.

Spinneret

It's true. I like to walk on the ceiling. But please. Don't hold it against me. The ceiling is cold. Nobody lives there. Just a spider. A curious arachnid. She lets herself down sometimes. If I'm on the bed, trying to sleep, staring at the ceiling, watching her movements, her amblings, just enough light to make her out, a little dot with little spindly legs, letting herself down, I'll hold out my hand to catch her. She must sense the warmth of my hand. Her sensors must be exquisite. Within inches, she shoots back up. How is that accomplished? Is the thread emitted from her spinneret sucked back in? I don't understand how that works. It's like writing. A line is emitted from one's body. Sounds a bit obscene. What could be more immodest than emitting anything from one's body, including a string of words? But they can never be sucked back in. And they won't support the weight of the body. So which is it? A parallel or an asymptote? What are we dealing with here? Words. Always words. Sticky. Indiscriminate. The world described in sound. Symbols. A system of substitution. All thought. All silk. Thin silky thought. Ideas dangling in the mind. For which there's a ceiling. A dome. A home. A skull. How many cells make a brain? One hundred billion, give or take a few. And how might the brain be compared to a home? Am I ever at home in my brain? Is my brain at home in me? And where is this 'me'? Does the spider have a sense of self? What is the spider thinking when she lets out that first guideline? That she must wait a long time in the pattern that she's created. That she must wait for a vibration, a trembling in one of the radiant lines. And look forward to the meal. Ideas are wiggly. Unsettling. But food. A form of nutrition. Cognition. Fruition. Volition. Ideas will make those synapses vibrate with impulsion. With the weight and energy of their mass. Neuronal activity. It's a signature moment. That moment when the idea gets caught. And struggles for release.

Everything Is Words

Here it all is: sandwiches, textures, wheels. Bewilderment. Closets. Symbols. Everything is words. The armadillos are a minor help, but they tend to keep to themselves. That's when I started thinking about beets. Dreams of an afterlife. Christmas in Budapest. Hegel's aesthetics. The mesas of New Mexico. The sound of water roaring through the subterranean chambers of my testicles when I lie in bed at night dreaming of gluttony and how to disengage with the world. I never know how to display my emotions. Consciousness rolls around in my head like a campground full of kids, RVs and trees. Agates drop to the sandy bottom of my mind. I rub ghosts out of my mouth. I'm a whispering gun. The brighter the fire, the deeper the darkness.

What does it mean to believe in something? Beliefs are harnessed to mist. There are regions of the mind that no one explores. The feeling of powerlessness is overwhelming. This is life in late capitalism. The atmosphere is churning with our doom. I know that's an extreme thing to say, but I believe in furrows and duckbilled hats. I believe the road sews its distances on a tongue of fire and that thought can crush any emotion into a deeper feeling if the equations vomit éclairs and the differentials are orange. I believe that marriage is an adorable hypnosis and that martini olives are somnolent eyes staring at us. We live in a trance. Who wouldn't? Existence is painful.

Some of us got old. Some of us found youth in old age and some of us found old age in youth. Some of us found life in a shoestring and some of us found shoestrings in death. Some of us found welcome in the world of syntax. A few of us found words as they exist, side by side, dripping with singularity. The rich found that wealth will get your attention and everyone else found that health insurance is a whiny tyrant. We hold these truths to be self-evident: reality is mostly breath, you can put yourself in a jail of the mind, and you can make a gun out of a bar of soap and point it at yourself in the mirror and demand that you let yourself go. Sometimes that works. And sometimes all you do is get your hands clean. So welcome. Welcome to this towel.

Shall we talk of the fabric of fabrication? Is it a text, a texture, a tissue, a threadwork, a thoughtwork? What is the thread count of thought? It's blatant anarchy in my head. Thoughts turn themselves inside out and insinuate fish.

Because eating is weird. And like anything weird, it needs a ceremony to make it seem less weird. It takes time to find even a modicum of equilibrium and meaning in your life. Like delivering a breech calf in a howling blizzard in a smelly barn in Nebraska. The house is not my breath, but my breath can make a house. Why do these words keep happening to me? I'll be in the narrative next door, milking a new cow.

What is it to think? It is to fill the brain with the sticky resin of reason. Which is like sitting in an armchair having a conversation with yourself. What is going on in your head this minute? Whatever it is please, don't tell me. More importantly, how do I stop thinking? I don't like it. It isn't a car. I can't stop it and get out. I don't even know what it is. Images? Tattoos? Equations solved? Speeches given? The worst thing you can do is awaken the dead. Don't do that. I don't even know for sure that I'm in my mind when it feels like I'm in my head. Where is my mind? Attentiveness teaches the eyes the philosopher's gaze. The uncanny lurks among the known. The unknown of the known aches to unfold the map of itself. What falls away is where I have to go.

Thank You, Language

I fall into employment when I play with money. It impels oligarchy and nap-
kin rings. I'm flourishing here as an amygdala. I feel the sympathy of earth in a
loaf of everywhere. Although I do believe matter and energy power the rapids
of an eyeball. I feel you under my skin. I can hear the march of my arms in a
greenhouse while my legs carry this introspection by stepping over an um-
brella and a sewing machine on an operating table. I'm luminous to my shoes
and eager to fly a button. I boil my words to disinfect them of pragmatism.
Therefore, the pulse of Céret is in its milk and cookies. I'm committing myself
to a bag of doughnuts, because life is, you know, life.

Debt is a form of imprisonment. The banks groan under the burden of
their own astonishing unreality. That's why I'm laughing at the side of the road
while trying to sell alibis. I grab some socks and begin arguing with my feet.
Wealth can mean so many things to so many people. You'd think floating rates
and balanced equities made the world of finance twinkle like a lip with a reli-
gion on it. Motorcycles. Lights. Crumpled beer cans. This is how capitalism
works: coaxing, cajoling, rubbing, persuading, beguiling, and cycling around
on a man's tongue while he sells you property rights. Locke believed that mak-
ers have property rights. What a joke. Nobody has property rights. All we have
is the dark blistering energy of ourselves at night.

The road ahead is free and clear. Let's be like that. I'm on cruise control.
Oblivion sounds like a lonely room in the south of Arkansas. The doctors are
huddled over a body. The heart is a fist of lightning veined and red. Earth is
a long walk in a blue palace. My stethoscope is thirsty. Take this ax and split
some wood. We need fire. Is there any validity to this sense of spiritual energies
unencumbered by matter? Is the mind an essence, an energy independent of
empirical reality? Our revels now are ended. These our actors as I foretold you,
were all spirits and are melted into air, into thin air. Were you expecting Desi
Arnaz? Reality just isn't what it used to be.

I have two sets of keys. One is for the car, and one is for the Palace of West-
minster. Sleep is a key to dreams, like the Dead Sea mud in Immanuel Kant. It
is beyond a doubt that all our knowledge begins with broken promises. This
precipitates hell, which is Christmas. A skilled psychologist can help us to

see the irrationality of Paul McCartney. He glances at Oprah Winfrey to his right, and smiles. When Sartre talks about Being, I don't think this is what he means. Have you ever laid awake devising scripts for various confrontations? Aging is a very similar process. All it takes is a little jostling to make it all explode. Two days later, I'm still cleaning the walls.

But seriously, is it possible to be so well-adjusted that every day is a drop in the infinity bucket? The human brain weighs approximately three pounds. Planet Earth weighs about 1,000 trillion metric pounds. I can't squeeze a 1,000 trillion metric ton planet into a three-pound brain. I can, however, bounce through space like Sandra Bullock in a calm emerald of sound. Thank you, language. Infinity hurts the head, so it's nice to have some words around to fill it with deer and trees. It was the cities that killed us. Life became absurd. It lost all meaning. And then along came erudition. This got the ideas going. Everything else was accomplished effortlessly in sleep.

Moon Sugar

Here comes a duodenum, running away from a colonoscopy. And here I am. Here we are. Together at last. Our little secrets burn into the table, terrible and strangely indigo. What can I say? Pain is a difficult business to put down on paper. It has a lot of dimensions. You need a philosophy. A lot of philosophy. A little luck. And a bottle of whiskey. Hedge clippers, Band-Aids, Spinoza. I blow my top when solicitors come to the door. Nobody respects your privacy. Though fewer and fewer seem to require privacy. People have been hollowed out. But who am I to make these judgements? Upon what foundation? Is it my own conception of what is fundamental & essential in modern life? That should be obvious: it's waffles. Waffles every time.

I crave the power of calamity. The spin of the tornado, the fury of the hurricane, the rhetoric of the unconscious. Can you carry these words to the end of the sentence? Lift your voice and let it come out, all that feeling, like scruples on a string, like the pressure of water in a garden hose. It's what you do when you have a mouth. You let it out. You let everything out. Thought can alter the world. But so can a monkey with a ducktail and a fake tan. Reality is under siege. What's to become of this world? You can't take a single thing for granted. Last night, as I was cleaning out my brain, I stumbled over a universe. I could use a sponge. It made quite a mess.

I like music that's like a wild animal trying to get out of a cage. Will anything save us? Redeem us? Whatever control I have is illusory. When people forget how to be alone, society falls apart. A big mirror in Deadwood, South Dakota attests to the jocularity in a nook to the back, where the older men play poker and the younger men stare at their smartphones. It's irritating to have to surrender to the needs of the body. There'll be an end to that someday. Meanwhile, keep your eye out for Texas. Sunlight kisses our torment. The highway has the emotional value of a vial of nitroglycerin. It keeps the speedometer happy. The needle is stuck in infinity.

The tongue does what it wants. Whatever control I have is illusory. Try navigating in this world. Rain at the airport, a pretty comb in my back pocket. Frank O'Hara is piloting the plane. Delores O'Riordan stands in the dark holding a luminous rabbit. The lesson to be learned is simple: make sure your illusions are light. Fill them with helium. Fill them with sound. Fill them with music. You can trust music. Music is in a war with banality. Our laughter percolates the sadness evident in the ceiling, which is pressed tin, a relic from the past, the sheen of despair in moon sugar. It takes a billion molecules to make a polymer get up and sing like Etta James. A kind of glue holds it all together. Let's call that glue music. The room is full of it. Even the light is sticky.

Slumgullion

There is this to say about envy: I don't envy it. It has no palettes for our understanding. Decorations don't really help. They just lead to clutter. But what word isn't a decoration? There's a void beneath everything. I break through the skin of the cocoon and begin a journey over time and water. We're brief custodians of a life energy running through us. Our reality is something greater than the life we encapsulate in blood and bone for X number of years. Infinity hurts the head. But you calm it with a sound. Don't yell. Be quiet. The algorithms are watching. Let's ditch them in the rain. Murmuring women carrying rain babies. Pixies in their hair.

Description succeeds by infrastructure. Quick. Catch this salt shaker. I know. You don't have to tell me. I oversimplify. I see death and destruction everywhere. I want out. That's all. I'm tired of describing things. Bones. Ears. I just want to open the gate and walk up into that mansion in the sky. Did you know Brian Jones played the marimbas? He played everything. He took everything. Well, why not, as they say. Pain is an awakening. It's a hungry animal. Even stars can be gardened. We live in an age of gigantic egos. We deploy them like dirigibles. Drop the ego, and the narrative keeps rolling. Floating. That's where we're at now. Dirigibles over Hollywood.

Immanuel Kant proposed a reality beyond what we perceive which is inaccessible to us. Why inaccessible? What about using a ladder? Or a Geiger counter? Or a book of poetry? I feel the lift of a powerful emotion. I don't know what it is, but there's a dusty frontier town on my shoe, and a box of wheat thins in the cupboard. This makes everything words. All the migrations have begun. A violent wind blows over the water. I can't get California out of my head. All those fires and evacuations. We're all pulling a great weight, but here's a hit song exploring itself in another dimension. Don't be shy. Walk out of yourself, tame as a TED talk, and tell everyone that the images in the cave are just shadows. The clatter of knives, and a big tub of semantic slumgullion.

The wedge of noise that I hold like a bar of soap is words. We are all words. The problem of looking backwards causes mountains. That's when I started thinking about rags. And caves. What I haven't yet learned is how to disengage with the world. Considered as a priority, in terms of grease and blood, disconnection colors the psyche with maneuverability. If I had alcohol in me right now I'd be singing out loud. I'd turn this boat around and head out to open sea. This is what the spectrum of desire looks like from a human perspective. There is more to beauty than Caravaggio. There's also the weird energy of bugs. The drug of consciousness, & cookies & lips.

Throbbing Blobs Of Pseudopodia

What happens when words fail the intensity of one's feelings? The glitter of proverbs in a warehouse of the heart speak to the parsimony of the spleen. The universe tastes like energy. These are but the rags of passion. It's why I wear a slice of thunder around my neck. There's a great pleasure in pulling it over my head. I hear everything going on in the sky. I hear the pull of wings and the hectic winds of a coming storm. I push emotions into words, but they just sit there, throbbing blobs of pseudopodia on the outskirts of a little town in Nevada. I've got the skin of an old man. Sometimes a simple conversation succeeds when a fight only leads to more havoc.

Words go through my eyes making my thoughts fat and glittery. I think of water. I think of soap. There's so much sloshing when I do this that the whole reason gets sewn in gold thread, which leaves me feeling weighty and a trifle oligarchic. Is it a good feeling? I don't know. I don't know how to describe feelings anymore. There are so many of them. Even my intestines get confused. The architecture of liberty is convoluted. Emotions sparkle with the catastrophe of existence, wet and heavy as the Spanish spoken by a wheeze of wallpaper. Don't tease the toad. The toad is thought incarnate. It must hop where it wants, gain favors from the infinitives of consciousness.

Lately, I've become fascinated by noses, how shapely they are, what wonderful organs, basic in their utility, yet aesthetically centered on the face, two little holes for the ingress and egress of air, rimmed with the subtle curves of the nostrils, protruding unobtrusively into space with a prominence that is both eager and modestly outgoing. The nose goes before our face, announcing the loveliness of air, the rhythms of breath, which sometimes the mouth assumes, companion to the nose, inhabiting a place just below, opening to say something, or staying closed and letting the nose do its thing, that bundle of skin, that knot of membrane, sniffing & sneezing, a troika loaded with pineapples and salt, fragrances of almond in consonants like tongs.

The wind has something to teach us about materialism. And why. Why is pain necessary? It gives doctors something to do and provides vagaries for our physics. Did I hear Raymond Roussel enter the room? Early in life, heaven is everywhere. Later in life, heaven is a warm coat in a winter storm. I approve of the funny weariness I've become. Experience agrees to its journey, the steam from this morning's kettle notwithstanding. What happens when you mix the color blue with ecstasy? Sparrows bring twigs to the dead. A compilation of swords illumines the halls of Valhalla. They say the elevator at the Heartbreak Hotel is haunted. Should that be a surprise? This is life in the Wild West. An old Chevron gas pump in a Santa Monica coffeehouse.

Images Blaze In The Pickle Jar

Did the Vikings invent surrealism? No, they did not. But the parallels are significant. The Vikings may not have invented surrealism, any more than they invented the predations of neoliberal economics destroying the communities of the world, but the affinities are there. Cultural paradigms come and go, but the forces of the imagination are as universal as fire, as elemental as water, and as fabulous as the speech of birds. These are the campaign funds, not the greenhouse. I have language to do and a coconut to throw. Currents of science fiction blossom at the periphery. The only real remedy for distance is the trajectory of remorse, which goes to Borneo and back, bubbling along like a hideous sweater with Darth Vader on it.

My god the drugs people take to feel a little more comfortable, a little more adjusted. There's a power in me that drools with the meat of a thousand televisions. I cry to plaster the wall with Corot. I'm engorged with sexual memories. The seashore has no glue. It's what you do in old age. I'm hanging from my brain blooming words like a savannah. This is key to understanding the splash of words at the airport. The underlying integrity of a raspberry. Even the honey makes a claim for better transparency. The dream is to one day achieve Welsh and keep the party rocking till the break of dawn. Metal sparrows flash neon in confirmation of our powerful weakness. This vaccine, this wood, this old truck bouncing on a dirt road somewhere in Africa.

Funny thing to do in the morning: brush my hair. Sweep those bristles over my head and put everything into order. Become presentable. Less savage in my appearance. Who doesn't love a little hygiene? Perception isn't everything. Consider damp basements, the clutter of thought crawling around in my brain like a full-blown syzygy. There's a crustacean on the ceiling. It's why I carry my hair around on my head. It's never been like this before. That is to say, I feel hung up and I don't know why. Butterflies tie my shoes while the sky drags itself over a toothpick. And yes, I believe in heavy metal. I think it's important to assume a romantic position and bounce sidewalks off my tongue until a trumpet of sunlight comes gushing out of my mouth.

If you're here, present to these words, ingesting them, it means you have eyeballs, a biology. So do I. It's a fundamental fact of our existence. Hormones, glands, chromosomes. Goo. And bones. Which begins to decay almost immediately. Pretty much after the prom. It's a sad situation. Or do I mean futile? I rub ghosts out of my mouth. I feel insults in my reality. But I'm still religious. At least about pickles. Pickles are holy. Because death is a private affair and pickles make it looser. Like a club sandwich. This very minute your eyes are holding these words together. Usually this is done by hydrolysis. Where am I headed with this? Images blaze in the pickle jar.

The Flowering Of Subjectivity

You could say poetry is impertinent, futile, vain and narcissistic, a little louche and outmoded, and it would be true, it would be legitimate and veridical, perhaps a little quizzical. But so what? Who didn't know that at the beginning? Before it all turned into a dystopic, despotic empire of derelict strip malls and opioid addiction. The president is a clown and the vice president is a refrigerator. So then here comes some poetry, awkwardly handling things in the gift shop, inappropriately flirting, farting on the sly, furtively avoiding eye contact. Is someone cooking broccoli? Is there life on Mars? Will there be adequate water in the future? What is the first word to come into your mind when I say California? There are endless cups of coffee in fairyland. But few know the way. It's principally a matter of smashing all the taboos and finding a good friend.

What's to become of this world? The sun rises from behind the mountains. Our laptops converge on parsley. Our goulash, sagacious and hot, is a tub of intense semantic activity, a veritable slop of unabashed solipsism. I keep all my paraphernalia in my valise. I forgot the significance of the pig. I forget everything. The shape in the stone is calling to me. Its prophecies fold over me in waves. A violent wind blows over the water. I'm authorized to say what I want. I've got the history of Norway engraved on my belt. Consciousness rolls around in my head like a barrel of sodium. The universe tastes like energy, a sphere whose center is everywhere and whose circumference ambles by on a pseudopodium. Go, go, go. Go pseudopodium.

Our poetry is deformed because the world is deformed. It begins with extreme winds and ends with a bonfire. Words are apparitions. I can't explain their behavior. But I love the shape of propellers. I envision Karl Marx in the British Library, twirling a pencil and thinking in a vein alien to Hegel. Capitalist avarice is just a form of premature senility. Nothing I want ever adds up to a coherent picture of Memphis. It was the insistence on dialectical equilibrium in Hegel's hermeneutic which has the most immediate and controversial impact on Sun Studio. We call this The Flowering of Subjectivity. It happened when Elvis met John Keats in a dream.

I like collecting clouds. I pull them out of the sky, fold them up and slide them onto closet hangers. Everything gets soaked when the clouds burst open and the rain comes dropping down. I just pick the rain up and fold it and stick it in a drawer of rainbows. I've got a horse, a mannequin and a doughnut. I've got a Bluetooth radio, a bedroom lamp with a three-way bulb, and a compulsion to describe the ineffable. Let these words tickle your ears with thoughts of paradise. Everything here is a lie, of course, which makes it all completely true. The universe walks around in my head looking for a place to sit down. Is there a language that can describe this? I'm working on it.

Calliope Snow

Experience agrees to its journey, the pencil making marks on plywood. Steam from this morning's kettle. Grammar in a canoe, the paddles notwithstanding. These are the campaign funds, not the greenhouse. I have language to do and a coconut to throw. The general point is clear: empirical categories dissolve by themselves, and we're left with a yearning, a maze of footnotes and an elastic volume of air. There is nothing for the recognitions but larch. A scab for the theocracy of ripples, a quadrilateral mold returning in a slow idea of seals. And a moon pinned to my foot like an excerpt of dust and rock.

I turn to reach the conversation before it collapses into slate and the felons issue the usual pontoons. Apparitions seem to get everything wrong. We all need to confront reality, but where is it, where does it make the feather speed through itself? Where does it make the eyes of the peacock sparkle and the coolness under the bridge power the voyage in the violin case? It's vague to denim a naked leg, but the pleasantries are rooted in potash, which gives the sentence time to ferment a little jaywalking, a listless purification among whose many merits are poise and translucence.

I unrolled some connectedness and the drawing became a hive for lines and cells and drowsy harmonies. The vibration of a thousand tiny wings make honey and a nebula tenable as a stick of coffee. Imagine a pet, a malarkey or a praying mantis. Think of something ovoid, a basement bonfire thematic as a wind instrument, or the people next door disinfecting a vampire. Consider propulsion nearest the spine, then spill it. It can only make things bigger, more like feeling than feet. I bought a climb to the top of a mountain and flashed my kazoo to the wind.

I smear the paint I held so long in the can it became vital. I watched as it slid into oscillation, gurgling glockenspiels like a smock. I now have everything I need to confront the chrome of reality. I sparrow it over the moss, plunge an insoluble sashay into anguish, and feather a pick with cypress.

Technicolor sepals indicate we're the nimble shadow of a giant grape. I gape at the desk and marry an air of exhaustion to a strain of windchimes. This creates ramification, which is always good for a proverb, logic squashed with a heavy plant.

This is a texture that our twigs invite to candy. I express this by nerve and thumb. My exchange is mustard but my sternum curls naturally around an earphone. Spin the snow and listen to it smell. I feel life happening in the vermilion, the audacity of sprouts in a ligature of orange.

Behind The Moon

I meditate on a lake in tonic Africa. I'm painting myself toward an intestine. I wrestle raw umber. My scent is a horseradish choir. I touch my gluttonous understanding as they convulse the table. Pack it since it's a hibachi. These are my friends the trees. I've got brass peculiarities and a convocation moss that carries my salt into visibility. I crush myriad indignities. Orange is the warmth of a baseball glove. I'm the ancestry I vibrate with oars. Machine the garden. A maple is a nexus of choice. My misconceptions have a nascent blur when I spit them out below the complications. The volume by the fence bleeds structure. I fold the crab thunder. My wait for you is in the orchard penciling a wandering moon. Form is metaphorical. Growl the heavy emotions. Squeeze them into flailing pickles where the cherries shine in vestal eagerness. Let's impose ourselves beyond the galaxy. We use liniment, don't we? Then it's true. The dab truly is culminated in goop. The invocation is awakening now. Savor the mutations. We'll talk about them later. I'm my own ransom and this makes me Kansas. I feel a blaze of insight beside the battle. The daily war. The daily firs and simultaneities. The nightly darkness behind the moon.

The Realm Of Fugitives

Monday's damask is colorful and evocative of travel. When am I going to see a houseboat going down the Mississippi? Can you explain why you were not completely dressed when I broke in on you?

When I talk about habitat I try to encourage notions of comfort and courage and what those elements might mean for the further evolution of prepositions and chocolate. The rest of the sentence continues to move into furious excesses of palpable confusion, trembling in undulations like a woman who has just entered the warm water of someone's brain, a pretty little place where languages are deciphered and where meanings are allowed to increase. That's what we mean when we talk about images. The warm amniotic waters of the brain where meaning is born.

Is there a cure for history? There is never any one history. How could there be? I have to use a zoom lens to ponder the chaos. What kind of species are we? Truth and intuition advance the evolution of the T-shirt. Reality is a creative endeavor. We create it as much as it creates us. Who is the dreamer? You're the dreamer. I'm the dreamer. This is a dream. There is a swamp in my finger and a sample of daybreak emerging from a hole in a fabric of light. The smell of animal fat burning in a stone lamp.

Again: the insistence of meaning. What do those paintings mean? Why were they painted in a cave? Is the brain a cave? What is the mind doing in the cave of the brain?

Writing is the realm of fugitives. If you don't like reality, you can write a new one. All you need is a few words. You do the work of a mason: you assemble the words one by one, you slather on some mortar and voila! a freshly constructed reality. Will it be an actual reality? No. Reality isn't made of words. It's made of iron and clay. Molecules. Atoms. Subatomic particles. Chamomile and cement. The strangely unreadable expression of people's faces when they are in grocery stores. Is there a physics for this? Try to be friendly. Use your words carefully. Add some invectives. Cultivate refusal. Spit. Chew your food. Grow a library big as Belgium.

My telescope doesn't see as far as Babylon. But I can see the frontier, which is closets smelling of old clothes and leather boots, bacteria thriving in the human gut, and key chains. In a word, we should strive to attain the knowing of how little we know. It's a good place to begin. Abu Dhabi's new indoor amusement park doesn't open until July. And then there's the whole matter of mandrake. What is it, exactly? I never see it in the produce section at the grocery store. The plant has psychoactive properties and can induce a state of divine madness. It's a rare plant, and its root is said to resemble a person. That's more than an onion ever did, except make me cry.

Floating Among The Reeds

When a representation about the world makes that world a world and not just another waiting room in a dentist's office — makes Beings become Beings, words become words, & teeth become teeth — the pure gaze of the reader can be applied to its inventions without restriction to the world of an imperious grammar of Being, to a nuclei of indecomposable meanings, & can free associate more freely among the folds of an infinite weave of correspondences.

I'm implicit in these words. But I'm not entirely within their compass either. I'm at the periphery. I'm in the margin, peering in. Floating among the reeds.

Immediate certainty, the thing in itself, is complicit in the construction of our experience. Who can look at a river and not feel that river moving through your body and its thousands of miles of capillaries, arteries, & veins? The weave of the world is woven into our being. Think of the double reed & the oboe making a weave of sound in a burlesque of cymbals & drums. The oboe is key to the understanding of Being. Its pitch is more stable than gut. The reeds are thin & delicate & crucial to tone. It is why the oboe is used to tune the orchestra.

On the other hand, if you really don't like the oboe, Vivaldi can help make it more palatable. What I hear is a wave of sound crashing against a hogshead. It doesn't have to go down this way. The firth is a glossary of muck. You can find almost anything you want in this pocket, except another pocket. I don't pocket pockets. And I don't rocket dockets. I like to sprocket lockets. So to speak. The gypsies are preparing to leave. And I hear an oboe in the distance. The shine of our talk is exhausting, but I'd like to extend it into writing, where it can be seen in the shape of words, jerking forward as if to say something, then pausing, as it congeals into Iceland.

It's easy to mistake an abstraction for concrete reality, but nothing is truly static, not even vodka, still as a mirror in a shot glass. Everything is a process, a flux, a series of waves. The energy moving through these words is a surge of emotion causing values to oscillate, rise into appraisal, curl upward in steam from a cup of coffee in Reykjavik. Which I have imagined on a bed in Seattle.

Which is what language does. Splashes into being as a vagabond wave, the stratum of experience crashing down in a foam of hectic dispersal, its evocations splattered into a sheen of wetness, the cargo of a stray & distant thought.

There's a caviar of categories, a dehiscence, in the opening of the vortex, the whirl of experience & sensation in any given moment, that craves an underlying system, a pivotal delay in glass, a frame through which everything floats into representation, which I see as a throne, though others may see as a werewolf rattling the bars of his cage, or a full moon above Redding, California, in July, 1976. Words help identify our experience, while simultaneously removing it of its primal incoherence, in which it meant nothing, but moved tenderly into consciousness like a nocturne, where the notes gave it pattern, & sense.

Flick

Hit this and ruminate we say. I snake and stroll an airport into clatter where it squirts to brush a decorum. Everyone's rabbit protrudes. I remember umber as an umbilical umbrella. The fencing is timeless. But raw without meditation. I'm under you listening. This makes us liniment to one another. A parable is gray by doing pronouns and there's also a bistro to make it brown and quixotic. Colors are June on the Seine at night. I envy our time together and whisper the skirmish into the convocation where it serves the purpose of pulse. I stiffen to think of a bighorn to write. There's a structure I want to tongue into motion. The fall makes it diamonds. I'm pinned to an ego that folds into experience whenever I approve my behavior by rattling. This I do as a cut to amazement in the fabric of supposition. This is sifted for conviction and cracks like thunder as the day is murdered by eating. I'm all across the hammer, enfolded into the stew I thicken with amendments and salt. It's all for nothing, but I'm dancing anyway, and thrusting at all the walls.

Story Pole

I'm clumsy beneath the pronouns, buckled and carried by water to the sinecure maintained in structure to this cupboard, this reverie pushed into words. This subjunctive amble, this penumbra, this savor. It folds into fish by the trees. I like to extend the grammar until it permeates the books I want to write someday. This is brushes in the drawer to the languor spinning in my hand. Age is a car whose roam indulges appraisal, and I concur in bubbles.

We boil to see the garden shine. A sparkling cartwheel expands my sense of wicker. The glider is more personal. It dwarfs the moisture with its altitude and veer. Even the words shriek with the black breath of redemption, which is gold at its core.

I wander in amber along the examples provided to support the integrity of sand. Circles swallow the pi by the hairy circumference. Heft is a function of pullulation. The heart in your hand is baffling, but searched.

There's some sleep beyond the disparagement, somewhere along the coast of France. I ache around my pickle. The tongue turns it into words. The words turn it into a personality. They're what makes pink gargle its own form as a balloon, or gargoyle.

I don't know what to do about reality. The trouble is sexual. It sits in the balcony, anchoring hope in a tumble of breasts. The sky trickles down to the horizon dragging stars and cupping the smell of battle in a hawk's gizzard. Speculation bumps our fence and is exercised in singing while the sorcerers chew it into dream.

The smell of the highway supports the trajectory of the unknown. I pull a hammer behind me expecting nails at any minute. The night crawls into the shadow of a mountain. The granite is marbled with iron. Bees propose alternatives to radar. Eyes hover plains of incalculable thought at the periphery of signification. Words fall from my breath until they hit the paper and turn windmills of Leibnizian logic into idealized death-masks, shark tooth stalactites, wheelbarrows, and a dog pound in Barcelona. The tacit is often a vortex from which we derive precious oils and malapropisms. Probes are improvised in supernatural dyes. The T-shirts are completely undomesticated, unlike our shoes, which are as tame as goiters in a family of seven and make squeaky noises at the grocery store after the floor has been freshly waxed.

The ratatouille is dramatically seductive but no one knows why gravity tastes like smoked gouda. Maybe if we jump up and down an answer will arrive in a golden carriage exempt from drizzle.

This could be a sentence if it wasn't already soaked in telepathy, like the interstice over there singing with closed lips.

The cold finds itself crawling over the ground in the morning. It's followed by fog. It gets dressed in a river and attends to a forest of birch and cedar. The horses graze by a swamp. The carpenter stands on a carpet twisting his body into pretzels of butt joint and stud. Does this mean that art is capable of serving other aims in the abstract, or that an idea of reflexivity is secured by large wooden pegs at the juncture of a mode and a stepladder?

All the windows are enigmatic on Wednesday. But the door is always eerie. You open it with your eyes. Your breath. And the buzzer that creates it.

Bouquet

I say: a flower! And, out of the oblivion where my voice casts every contour, insofar as it is something other than the known bloom, there arises, musically, the very idea in its mellowness; in other words, what is absent from every bouquet. —Stephane Mallarmé

What is poetry? It's a thing of vision, tenable clean and wild. It's engaged splatter. It's the grace and mesh of infinity. It's a swollen frog and a character in my personal drama.

It's the ground in the breath around an ear, the sound of a cloud twisting in the mouth of a thermometer, an Orphic Explanation of the Earth, and is not so much the Great Work intended to summarize the universe — a microcosm where everything would hold — but the hollow of this totality, its reverse, its realized absence, that is to say the power to express everything, and consequently nothing, the presence of a power which is itself subtracted from everything and is expressed by nothing. It's a pause at the intersection of existence and nothingness, the affirmation of an enigmatic force, a parole for the slobber of the heart.

Language is steeped in contradiction. It destroys the world in order to create it. The poem becomes a thing, a body, an incarnated power. It gives real presence and material affirmation to language while simultaneously suspending and dismissing it from the world. The density of its sounds is necessary to release the silence that it encloses and which is an expression of nothingness, a void without which it couldn't be created. Presence is nothing without absence, and vice versa: the perfect crime on an island at night.

When the poet declares: "I imagine, by an ineradicable and doubtless condition of writing that nothing will remain without being uttered," one could judge this claim as being hopelessly naïve. The contradiction at the heart of this project is harsh, it tortures all poetic language, and speculation, which is the daughter of sunlight, and awakens the mouth like coffee. Tree branches spreading space as they spread into space. The stillness in a silver tray. The candle holder encased in wax drippings. The pure silence at the heart of a stone. The scraping of dishes, the lift of the fog, the breaking of sediment in the Badlands with its contrary streaks and hints of bone.

Contradiction is harsh, it tortures all poetic language, as it tormented Mallarme's speculations. Contradiction pushes the poet to seek a direct correspondence between the words and what they mean, to regret the lightness of energy in the word 'swarm' and the dark wilderness in the word Mississippi, as if the words, far from distracting us from things, cause the sensuality of language to rise into weight and color and cougars and pumice while simultaneously parodying the foolish clamor with the void at the very core of their endeavor.

So what we have is a bouquet of words. Burst body wax. A place where to moan is to smash the moonlight into stools. Raw was burning in flannel shades of light when the sapphire happened to the magnet broom and it became a motorbike. Remember Capernaum when it was abandoned? It's like that. Comb your quintessential fire, my friend. The sinking had a claw. The fact was an embalmer. And the melee of a winter moment caused my neck to erupt into ink. And thought. And blue skullcap consummating a phantom bouquet.

Meditation On A Hair Brush

Funny thing to do in the morning: brush my hair. Sweep those bristles over my head and put everything into order. Become presentable. Less savage in my appearance.

I like order. To a degree. No need to get carried away. But a little symmetry here and there, a little balance, a little harmony, a little sense of control are good things.

Most control is illusory. But I'll take whatever I can get. It's comforting to have a sense of agency. Even if it's only the agency of a hairbrush swept over one's head.

We live in a universe of such spectacular distances and mysteries that a little thing like doing the dishes can make existence feel a little more meaningful and a little less haphazard. At least I'm not an asteroid, a rock on some arbitrary trajectory. I have skin and blood and legs and arms and a pair of glasses and a mug of coffee and a trajectory that feels somewhat purposeful, a narrative of growth and disappointment, fulfillment and frustration.

Every day's pageant brings something new. Sometimes a lot of new, sometimes a shade or hue of new. Sometimes I can float through it buoyed by the right amount of insights, percipience, platitudes and drugs. And sometimes it's overwhelming. Can't eat. Can't sleep. Can't get a moment of peace. That's when a hair brush can seem like a solid piece of information, an easy way to put things in order. To put something — anything — in order. Even if it's just fucking hair.

Life is never any one thing; it's always a blend, a mingling of having and not having, reachable and unreachable. But there's always a degree of agency. There's always at least one option, one alternative available. Sometimes I'm Charles Bukowski. Sometimes I'm Marcel Proust. And surrounding it all is the daily enigma, the daily ambiguities, the churning burbling bubbling brew that is the stew of life, seasoned internally by emotional cacophony.

I never use a comb. Combs get stuck in my hair. I find hygiene in general to be a bit of a nuisance. But you can't go around looking like a mess. You can, but it doesn't produce happy results and inspire warm handshakes.

Articles of personal hygiene discovered in ancient graves are often indications of social status. Combs discovered in archeological deposits from the ancient market of York, England, were made of reindeer antlers. Combs were also essential in removing head lice. Thirty years ago, eight of the eleven first-century combs discovered in the Judean desert by the parasitologist Kostas Mumcuoglu and anthropologist Joseph Zias have revealed ten lice and twenty-seven lice eggs hidden in the fine teeth of the combs.

And then there's the whole question of laundry. But let's not get into that. I can already begin to feel the tedium permeate the day with its implacable monotony. Monotony can be a pain, but it isn't always bad. The monotony of a job requiring routine tasks can sometimes create an agreeable trance, as can a long stretch of highway more or less free of traffic.

The mind craves novelty. Sooner or later, the monotony of a job or a long drive will have a dulling, soporific effect on the mind. You'll need to stop at a greasy spoon just to hear the clatter of silverware and the sizzle of grease on a grill and the muffled intonations of a quiet conversation. God forbid there won't be kids running around, or a drunk complaining about the eschatology of toast.

What is a trance? Is it anything like a hair brush?

According to Wikipedia, a trance is "an abnormal state of wakefulness in which a person is not self-aware and is either altogether unresponsive to external stimuli (but nevertheless capable of pursuing and realizing an aim) or is selectively responsive in following the directions of the person (if any) who has induced the trance."

There's always a part of ourselves not altogether present, not altogether alert to the exigencies and peculiarities of the environment, but in accord with another dimension, another region of indeterminate phenomena. Why is that? It's a little maladaptive.

"Strange things happen in the mind of man," observed Paul Bowles in his novel *The Spider's House.* "No matter what went on outside, the mind forged ahead, manufacturing its own adventures for itself, and who was to know where reality was, inside or out?"

Clearly, something is going on. Something sublime. Something like the thunder of a waterfall, even if it's just a brush, a brush with a brush, I know beauty when I see it. Why is consciousness imbued with thoughts of an elsewhere, as if the ghostly aura surrounding all language provided a sense of presence at the far end of the bar when no one is actually there?

But let's not get lost in the clouds. I don't want to spook the cattle. Sometimes a hair brush is just a hair brush. And pulling things out of the air is as simple as speech. A white-feathered dream-catcher in a white Ford sedan. Atmospheres and maps. The solace of fire, the requiems of fog. The glimmer of the Seine in August under the Pont Neuf in Paris on my laptop screen while I wait for the blood to re-enter my leg so that I can get up and get something to drink. And brush this night out of my hair.

Enlightenment Blues

Today I saw death get out of a red sedan by the Five Corners Hardware Store. The scythe got stuck on the upholstery in the backseat. Death is clumsy. Which is why I carry a knife. The time has come to act quickly. We need a new mythology. The old ones have lost their traction. The crisis of our current predicament cries out for sandwiches, textures, and wheels. I'll go get the horses. It's time we got out of here. I smell the law at every turn. Do what I do: crawl to the door and bang on it hard. Death is at the bottom of everything. Cabbage, moss, carpentry, water polo. Vagrancy comes natural. It must. Otherwise, life is just equations of rust and stony detachment.

Whenever I feel the spirit I like to dance myself into ambiguity. It's why I read Frank O'Hara and could murder a plate of lasagna. Precision is for surgeons. What can I say? Society is collapsing all around us but nobody seems to give a shit. I remember Janis Joplin belting it out in Monterey. But now I'm much older and have eyes like damp basements. The clutter of thought crawling around in my brain is nothing else but a cascade of chemical reactions masquerading as a waste of energy. And I agree. It is. Which is why I'm here for you, twiddling my thumbs. Is there a theme to this? Yes: I can walk through a wall of granite. Provided there is a hole.

What is an emotion? Is it an osmotic interplay of flesh and feeling, or a wagon harnessed to a team of toads carrying our thoughts and perceptions into a great barn of understanding? Why toads? Why a wagon? Toads are charming. Wagons are practical. That realization defined everything there is to know about American Flag Etiquette. My tears fell like bricks. I became a man that day. I fondled my way into deeper obscurities like a supermarket. The seagulls gathered at a point in the sky and then circled one of the many islands that occurred to me just now. I became convinced that noise can be gardened, and that any emotion can be molded into small words and injected with air, then scattered over the countryside like nimble microbial villages.

I think of North Dakota and the Turtle Mountains. The universe isn't entirely in my head. Some of it's in Florida. They say the sickly odor of a dead python is what led the Greeks to name the high priestess of Apollo's Temple at Delphi Pythia. Maybe I should put a dead python under the bed. Creepy.

Like Elon Musk's neurolink. Why are these billionaire fucks always so cringe-worthy? Is it dead pythons? What happens when capitalism butts into reality? The Fed prints more money. Life shouldn't require money. But it does. And for that the oligarchy has arranged jobs education and debt peonage. Reality can go on like this all day. And it usually does: shit! I just tripped and hit my head against the door. Am I enlightened? Not sure. But my head hurts.

The Day I Turned 72

The day I turned 72 the world burned down. Fires blackened the Amazon. The Canary Islands. Alaska. France. Siberia. Greece. July was the hottest on record. Everything turned brittle and dry. Everything not already claimed by deforestation and rapine and murder has exploded into flames and licked the ash darkened sky with tongues of maniacal heat. And I had to wonder: how much time is left? Months? Weeks? How much time before the electricity and running water are gone? And we're left wondering what to do. Where to find drinkable water. Do we boil it? How do we boil it? Will there be community bonfires? Will I be an item on a neighbor's menu? Should I buy a gun? How much are they? Will I have to make visits to a firing range? Will a bullet from a 45 caliber Glock be the answer to a failed healthcare system?

The day I turned 72 my wife gave me a new copy of *The New American Poetry*. I opened it to "The Rick Of Green Wood" by Ed Dorn:

> In the woodyard were green and dry
> woods fanning out, behind
> > a valley below
> a pleasure for the eye to go.

The day I turned 72 I made scrambled eggs and toast for breakfast. I scooped a tablespoon of our cat's favorite food onto a porcelain saucer. Taste of the Wild: Canyon River Feline Formula with Trout and Salmon in Gravy. Our cat loves the gravy. She'll sometimes leave the morsels of meat and lick the gravy.

The day I turned 72 I made a request for canned fruit cocktail. Make sure it has sugar. Who eats fruit cocktail without sugar? Cotton Mather? Some puritanical WASP douche bag with libertarian values, a Vegan diet and an SUV the size of a cruise ship?

Neurotic Queen Anne mommies, answered R, slipping out of the door.

I did a French dictation exercise on Yabla, an online foreign language learning company featuring interactive videos. Serge Amoruso, a maker of exquisite leather goods: *Bonjour, je m'appelle Serge Amoruso. Je suis maroquini-*

er-designer. Et en fait, le...mon activité, euh...est de dessiner, créer et fabriquer des objets en pièces uniques en commandes spéciales et uniquement pour des particuliers. Donc mes clients viennent et sont dans le monde entier.

I scratched my ear and thought about muscle. What makes muscle grow? It's a mystery. Though there are two theories: Muscle Damage Theory and Substrate Accumulation Theory.

Muscle Damage Theory states that muscles are damaged during exercise and this damage triggers several signaling cascades that result in muscle hypertrophy and invitations to appear on the covers of romance novels.

Substrate Accumulation Theory surmises that several substances accumulate during exercise that may turn on muscle hypertrophy directly or indirectly by stimulating the release of anabolic hormones. Anabolic hormones refer to the synthesis of complex molecules. Diabolic hormones party all day and night in your blood veins while synthesizing ecstasy and singing karaoke.

I submit a third theory: muscle protein is stimulated by repetitive motion to such an extent they want to burst out of your skin and bombinate in the streets with good vibrations and ZZ Top playing in all the bloodmobiles.

I received a coupon in the mail for a free box of ökocat litter, "changing the world one litter box at a time."

I indulged in some marijuana tincture earlier than usual and thought about Superman. If I were Superman I'd blow the arctic ice back — all of it, every crystal — and make it thick as a twelve story building — suck all the carbon dioxide back to 1750 levels of 278 ppm — and have my uniform cleaned and pressed at Helena's Cleaners on Queen Anne who fixed the zipper on my favorite running jacket.

I still can't figure out how Superman managed flight. It was suggested that the force of his jump propelled him, but that doesn't explain how he was able to change trajectory, or lift things like jumbo passenger jets.

I remember seeing that first scene in the 1978 *Superman* with Christopher Reeve in which Jor-El (Marlon Brando) and Lara (Susannah York) put their baby (the future Superman) into a small spaceship programmed to travel to planet Earth as their own planet — Krypton — is destroyed by the explosion of Krypton's sun. I remember how horrifying that was. Nowhere to run to. Nowhere to escape. Where do you go when your home planet is destroyed? And then I realized that that's our current situation. Only it's happening a little less suddenly. It's happening catastrophe by catastrophe. Wildfires. Melting ice. The precipitous decline of insect populations. Giant tornadoes. Hurricanes. Monsoons. Typhoons. People in San Francisco and Seattle and New York toppling over on fecal ridden streets from opioid addiction and homelessness.

No meaning.

No future.

But who wants to be a buzz kill on your birthday?

The day I turned 72 I realized: the universe is roughly 13.772 years. Old enough to retire. But what does a retired universe do? Fish? Play golf?

And then I realized I'd been dead for 13.700 of those years before a Minneapolis obstetrician used a pair of forceps to pull me into this world. I know he used forceps because I can feel the indentations on my skull.

Would a future Hamlet one day hold my skull and say alas, Horatio, I knew this man: he wrote poetry and came to my plays and occasionally pretended to be me.

And I would smile back with the rictus of all skulls. Whose domes fill with void. And the rest is silence.

My Life Among The Crows

What a strange thing it is to have this device, this computer, this thing small enough to put on my lap, and watch the sixth mass extinction in real time. I obsessively watch YouTube videos hosted by climate scientists, physicists and environmental biologists (Paul Beckwith, Guy McPherson, Peter Wadhams, Jennifer Francis) for information on the state of things as they unfold.

Deteriorate. Disintegrate. Collapse.

The planet is out of whack. It's not working the way it's supposed to. The clouds are broken. The sky is broken. The air is broken. The plants and animals and ice are broken. We broke it. I don't think we're getting our deposit back.

Jennifer Francis: *We're seeing a new feedback develop between the Arctic being so warm and its effect on the jetstream and vice versa. The very warm Arctic in the early fall is causing the jetstream to take a wavier path and those bigger swings are transporting more heat and moisture up into the Arctic...that water vapor is important because it's a greenhouse gas so it contributes to the already warming effects of carbon dioxide and other greenhouse gases, but it also causes more clouds to form and those clouds are also very good at trapping heat down by the surface.*

End result: September Arctic sea ice is now declining at a rate of 12.8 percent per decade. We will soon have our first blue ocean event. In which case, hold on to your hat. Ginormous blizzards will bury the Midwest and eastern coast and the melt in the spring will cause more flooding, wiped out roads, flooded barns and silos, eroded fields, the inability to plant and sustain crops such as wheat and barley and corn and oats and beans, i.e. food.

I like food. I always have. Not so much broccoli or liver. But bean burritos and pancakes and macaroni and breadcrumb chicken. *Salade piémontaise* with boiled eggs and pickles.

R and I walk to Safeway to pick up a prescription for Nortriptyline, a tricyclic antidepressant. I worry about the ability to get pharmaceuticals in the future. Pharmacies rely heavily on trucking. It may be one of the first things to go. There are a lot of people who rely on medications for heart disease and a gazillion other maladies our fragile biology is prone to. What are they going to do? It's a grim prospect.

We go to the Queen Anne Farmers Market. There's a booth there that serves the best hamburgers and fries I've ever had. We sit down at a long picnic table with our hamburgers and peach lemonade and I watch as a woman in a three-wheeled motorized chair travels slowly east toward the end of the food aisles. She comes to a strip of contoured rubber for covering the cable and attempts to go over it. Her chair capsizes. Two people at the Kiss My Grits booth come to her aid and help her back into her chair. The woman's legs are completely paralyzed. She has no use of them whatever. And yet the woman has an athletic look. I wonder if she injured herself doing gymnastics or high diving. She also seems to be pretty grouchy about the situation. But so would I be. I've had a beef going with the universe my entire life and have enjoyed and continue to enjoy the full use of my limbs. I'd like to get the universe into a ring for a wrestling match but don't think I'd do well. How do you get the universe into a headlock?

It's comforting to visit the Farmer's Market, which operates every Thursday until early October. I like to think that if the food disappears from the grocery shelves people will still be growing food locally and bringing it to open air markets like this.

I notice a lot of children. This is a cause of wonder to me. What kind of future do they have? There seems to be a taboo on talking about such things. There are no taboos in poems so I get to talk about it here. Though there's nothing, really, to say. It just makes me feel sad to see all these kids.

It's a comfortable 81 degrees Fahrenheit with a mild breeze. I'm able to hold the napkins down with a bag of peanuts I brought to feed crows. I've been feeding crows for over a year now. I love crows. I love their intelligence, which shows in their acrobatics and agility in flight and the way they hide peanuts to eat later, which is a sign of strategy and planning. Yesterday I was watching three crows peck away at the peanuts I'd just tossed on a lawn when I felt something like an egg breaking on my head. There was a crow perched on a branch just above me who took a dump. I wiped the poop off with my running shirt. It smelled of peanuts and there were tiny, miniscule bits of peanut in the poop. Bird poop is the least gross poop of all possible forms of poop. It's white. White poop. That's amazing.

If you read *Le Crottin* by Francis Ponge he will tell you all about poop, the poop of the horse (*"brioche paille"*), the dog, the cat, and human beings, the poop of humans being the worse, (*"pour leur consistence de mortier pâteux et fâcheusement adhesif"*).

I talked to a woman earlier today about feeding crows. She fed crows too. I told her I got pooped on by a crow and she tells me that's good luck. I hope so.

We bought a pound of blueberries grown on Fir Island near Mount Vernon, Washington in the Skagit River Delta and headed home after I picked my medication up. The breeze was picking up and the sky was becoming overcast. The waning sunlight shone through a diaphanous filter of cloud and three crows flew down to greet me near home. I tossed some peanuts and one of them flew down, grabbed a peanut and flew high to the peek of a roof to start pecking at it.

We watch *Parks and Recreation* on Netflix after dinner and the final episode of *GLOW* and then, laptop on the bed (the datacenters that power our digital services produce 2% of global greenhouse emissions, same as the 2% produced by aviation), I watch (that is to say, I feel compelled to watch, it's a frigging addiction) another video about abrupt climate change. Paul Beckwith sits in a chair with a bunch of plants behind him, white wires dangling from his head, and discusses the fires in the Amazon and how it relates to the hydrological cycles of the rest of the world. It's not good. We lose all resiliency in the climate system once we begin losing the biomes of the planet, including rainforests. When the chain of recycled rainfall is disrupted you risk getting an amplified feedback effect: more destruction, more desert, more draughts, more hurricanes and monsoons. All hell breaks loose.

I get agitated whenever the pronoun 'we' gets bandied about. 'We' need to do such and such if 'we' are to save ourselves. But there is no 'we.' There's a megalomaniacal, oligarchic billionaire class and the rest of us. The real 'we' are people who do what they can to stay afloat, navigate the Kafkaesque bureaucracy of a collapsing healthcare system and buy unsalted peanuts to feed to crows. Blocks of suet and seed for finches, wrens and chickadees. We hang them in a little cage from the limb of a nearby tree. They go through it fast. Edward Abbey said the antidote to despair is action. I think it might also be peanuts. And suet.

Dear Nileppezdel

I'm about to complete a tour of 72 years on Planet Earth. It was in fairly decent shape when I first arrived, with a population of about 2,556,000,053, but now it's in tatters, its climate in chaos, its oceans choked with plastic, the dirt so tired and toxic the very worms have left it, much less grow anything, the entire planet's forests on fire, hurricanes and tornados ripping the cities to shreds, mass shootings a daily occurrence, and a population of 7,584,144 fucking themselves silly. These humans are strange indeed: rather than cut back when their resources appear depleted, they consume all the more passionately, as if lust and gluttony were the correct answers to an equation of impending death and catastrophe.

It's been nice having a human body and I will miss it. I'm especially fond of hands and fingers. It's amazing what you can do with these things. You can squeeze things, point to things, press things, pull things, juggle things, and hold implements such as hammers and forks.

Eating is strange. Here, one puts dead organic tissue in the orifice of what is called a face and chews it into bits with rows of hard, enameled dentin called teeth. The nutritive material is then maneuvered to a passage called a throat, which uses peristaltic motion to carry everything into a membranous cauldron called a stomach. Protein and carbohydrates are extracted and the waste material is extruded from an aperture in the rear called an anus. It's an altogether messy process, but humans seem to enjoy it.

Right now it's 10:10 p.m., Pacific Standard Time. Ssenteews is folding her clothes. She has a special way of doing it. She rolls it into little cylinders. They remind her of the sdolgiram that grows on the planet Rednilyc.

Humans wear clothes. This is fabric they use to cover their bodies, for which they feel shame and embarrassment, and to keep them warm in the winter. Some add ornamentation and doodads. A doodad is a gadget or object for which the correct name is unknown. This is a phenomenon in English, the language Ssenteews and I chose as our main communication device, by which the unidentifiable becomes minimally identifiable. Popular doodads include pockets, buttons, horns, medals, zippers, braids, cords, monograms, pompoms, sequins and tassels. A few frills and furbelows might package an otherwise monotonous personality in explosions of pink or frantic patterns of black. The effect is sad and wistful, what we on our planet call suolucidir. And yet these same people have a fascination with nudity. The males of this specie are especially fond of looking at naked females and are able to stimulate themselves sexually by watching videos on their computers. This is called masturbation and is generally done privately, as do some of the mammals on our planet, such as the eeznapmihc and allirog. The practice isn't exclusive to males, but the females are more skilled at discretion, and exercise greater refinement in achieving more enduring results.

Humans spend a great deal of time and effort making sounds with their mouths. This is a remarkable organ, equipped with a muscular protrusion called a tongue, which is capable of sculpting numerous shapes and colors out of thin air using vibrations and frequencies of sound, if I may be permitted a fanciful allusion to synesthesia, and the implementation of non-scientific terminology. The sounds burbling and bubbling out of the heads of these creatures are fissionable, like stars, and may warm and illumine a room with a torrent of cracks and hisses.

Humans have a fondness for thinking their languages are steeped in reality, when the case is quite the opposite. Their languages have so little to do with reality that they have appointed lawyers and politicians to distort them into eidolons and apparitions that have the appearance of truth while nimbly and skillfully keeping actualities hidden.

Today I had a conversation with a spider. These creatures — who resemble us in many ways—are far more intelligent than humans. Each minute of each day they achieve miracles of engineering, yet humans find their creations annoying and sweep them away whenever they encounter them. Humans have an inability to learn from other creatures. They believe themselves to be the chosen ones of a God no one actually sees. This is a God who lives in the sky and is prone to fits of jealousy. What would these humans think if they discovered that their God was a female spider and that everything in the universe is as intricately related as an orb of silken thread?

It would be a different world, and one with a future, instead of this sad, tragically collapsing sphere once teeming with life, and now turning barren as a gas station on highway 15 through the Mojave Desert.

Structure Is An Open Nerve

Structure is an open nerve. Sensations that alter pattern like the bits of glass in a kaleidoscope. Roaring creeks and cataracts of language all upsidedown and strange. My head becomes juicy whenever I read. And when I don't my head becomes a noumena floating sandwiches for work. One sandwich is composed of thin slices of corned beef or ham slathered with butter and adorned with lettuce and pickles for maximum juiciness. The other sandwich is all poetry, which is just fucking weird. Well, why not, as they say. There's a kind of providence to weirdness. It's a superpower with a soft light and sonatas of blood. The grammar of bones, silent before a storm.

Science has an answer to Riskin's thesis: the attribution of agency to the natural world is a mistake, but a useful one in an evolutionary sense. Therefore, you should allow yourself to be a vending machine. I hear someone vacuuming the hallway and I dream of Hamlet riding a motorcycle across Arizona with a monkey on his back. I banish all mass from this poem. Homelessness has been normalized and I'm sitting in a gas of nitrogen and oxygen while the glaciers melt and the seas begin to rise and flood the cities.

Hang on to your hat. I don't think we're going to ride this one out.

The slow drip of candle wax attests to the beauty of understatement.

What is grace? The spin of a wasp, a locomotive in the breath.

I want to eat a coconut and build a narrative around that. Reality just isn't what it used to be. It used to be all skin and blood and now it's a meme. Life is a mess. People are unfathomable. It's a tough world and it makes people hard. The landscape expands into buttes and canyons. I slouch through the landscape looking for God knows what. The shapes are beginning to mingle with the dark. This is what happens when a language broods in a tidepool of nouns: beautiful soup. Michael McClure's *Meat Science Essays*. The heart is a fist of lightning veined and red. I can see it in your eyes: Ferdinand Pessoa in a Lisbon bistro musing on a plate of *saudade*.

I'm religious about napkin rings. Each ring is a boiling monsoon of plasma, electrons, protons and alpha particles embracing a cotton dinner napkin folded neatly into a circumference that is everywhere and whose center is nowhere. Words have that power. This very minute your eyes are holding this language in your brain as I get off this stool and drag a bundle of magazines closer. Bezos exposes pecker, trumpets the New York Post. Wealth can mean so many things to so many people. There are regions of the mind that no one explores. I have faith in immanentism. I have faith in the mundane as well as the transmundane. Napkin rings being prime among them.

Smitten Mitten Mutton Button

Distance pulls me toward you. I search for a song I can balance in my mouth like words. Anatomies like sprocket and bungalow. Big emotions like dirt. The mosaic of the day sends me into the shade. The thick air sobs with rain. The harmonica gleams. I try to do my writing outside the parameters of time. It's subversive. And weirdly Pythagorean. I grant that mathematics is not my greatest strength, but I'm eager to give some of these equations a try. For example, fulfillment is perpendicular to both the velocity of chartreuse and the magnetic field of most mittens. This implies that mittens have a charge parallel to the magnetism of wool and fingers are agile with greeting if they're kept relatively warm. The wild knock of cognition leads me to believe that thought is waves and the waves are pumped from a well in the overall scheme of being itself. The eyes are illumined from within by a small white candle called the pineal gland. I'm doing life in pallets. The seashore flourishes in epilogues. I fondle the fog. I have a collection of incendiary escalator cubes. They spout remedies and nutmeg. The universe is harnessed in stars. Structure is an open nerve. Flying alters my perspective. I push more vapor toward Corot and cook the paint in theological chatter. I like to drift. I like the general feeling of random movement. This is why I study the laxity of wind. Walking settles my opinion in the wonderful burn of the moment. The symptoms are all shouting pellagra. The brain is wonderful with guesstimates. It's like a speedometer of poetry whose spectrum is enameled in exhilaration. I jump to ruminate. The fork is more crucial than the spoon when it comes to the thickness of the meat and the embellishments our pathos provides for the gaze of the banana mask. Yes, I'm radical, but aren't you? I mean, listen to the clank of consciousness across this table. I use a little paper to catch what I can. There's a dash of strain in the muscularity of my tie and the recklessness of my approach makes the sandwich big with sequel. And here it is, the final result: watch as it trickles down the glass of this incarnation, grasping at heaven.

Druid Fluid

Episode formed by fishing. This will be the eighth time today that a cucumber encumbered a small French village with its penetrating glow. Spit, on the other hand, shows that Being is mostly fluid. I give a good shake to a can of lather, press the button and hear the creamy lather hiss into the palm of my hand. It feels soft and wet. I never know how to display my emotions. Some of them are relatively calm and normal, others are colossal bacteria colonies that live inside humans. Everything has to be refracted through the prism of a black volcanic rock. In chemistry, it's called sublimation: it occurs when poetry unshackles the chains keeping me here.

All ideologies demand an impossible consistency. They have to be separate from the world, like eating at a picnic table in a daydream. Does the mind have reality? Not much, when you think about it. What's your favorite ideology? I've always had a special place in my heart for nihilism, paganism, and the theology of rockets. Ka-boom! Bright red flakes of fire drifting down. How can you not love a good explosion? How about the Big Bang? There's an ideology for you: Terence McKenna sitting on a giant mushroom with a Cheshire grin. The smell of old barns. Lisbon bistros. Whirlpools of light. And a quiet old road disappearing in the south of Arkansas.

The older you get the more uselessly useful you become. And purposelessly purposeful, but in a very usefully useless way, like a sentence with too many adverbs. It just wants to mean something casual and then go away and sit down and stare out of the window. Like Wittgenstein said, the sentence is a judgement on the sense data, a reading of one's own sense-data. For example, this is large and furry. It feeds on salmon leaping out of the rivers in the palm of my hand. That's it. That's all it really means. Why, then, is our gut the only organ in our body that needs its own "brain"? Better yet, forget Paris. The uncanny aches to unfold the map of itself. And what falls away is where I have to go. I like it when my body is resting. I like being still.

Every proposition must already have a sense, observed Wittgenstein. Assertion cannot give it a sense, for what it asserts is the sense itself. And the same holds true of tempo. This is what it's like to be trapped in a room with your own mind. I can't make assertions like this. Oh Lord, what am I doing here? I feel the fingers of a stellar, planetary music play in my brain like dolphins. This happens a lot. I think I know what I'm saying, and then I think oh shit, why did I say that? And that's when I realize that oppositions lead to propositions, which is cactus. Is this why I continue to have problems with jazz? I hear someone calling me for the next flight to Mars.

Here's another thing Wittgenstein said: we cannot give a sign the wrong sense. Oh yeah? How about this mister philosophy man: sentimental litmus dust. Hobnailed obstetrics seasoned with iodine. I know a geology when I see one. It proceeds by ointment. Now what? Show me your lips. Good. Now say something. Scream it into this jar. I'll add some lettuce and give it a home. Matter is often socialized by too much werewolf. Let the horn be your guide. Individuality is a fungus. Paper gives us the world it demands. Imagine swimming through God in a negligee.

The Lure Of The Obscure

I frequently find myself drawn to the obscure. Not that I don't like clarity. I like clarity. I want to be clear about clarity. I never met an ice cube I didn't like. Though I prefer my beverages without it. I like ice in the abstract. I like the idea of ice. I like the actuality of ice. The structure of ice. The stillness of ice. The medium of ice. The iciness of ice.

Ice is a hexagonal structure which resembles a beehive, composed of layers of slightly crumpled hexagons, which is not only a delightful image, but clear, and drips a little, in the heat of my imagination. Many of the physical properties of water and ice are controlled by the formation of hydrogen bonds between adjacent oxygen and hydrogen atoms. The bonds, like all bonds, are sensitive to temperature. As water cools below 4°C, the hydrogen bonds adjust to hold the negatively charged oxygen atoms apart. This produces a crystal lattice commonly known as 'ice,' which is easier to say than "crystal lattice," especially if you slip up during a figure skating competition. You wouldn't want to get to your feet and say, fuck me, I slipped on a shitload of crystal lattices.

Ice floats because it's about 9% less dense than liquid water.

Hope floats because it was a movie starring Sandra Bullock and Harry Connick, Jr. and got an audience score of 72% at Rotten Tomatoes.

Although the information surrounding ice is slippery and hard to grasp, the data bites with clarity and freezes into cubes of sound called words.

Still ponds in forests fascinate me. I like to gaze at the silt on the bottom, the branches and debris of the forest reposing in insane clarity, the tiny shadow of a Jesus bug scampering over the surface of the pond projected below through the uncannily pellucid water and over extraordinary precisions of silt.

I like haikus, accident reports and the murmur of summer rain.

But I also like mysteries and obscurity. I like looking at physics equations on blackboards. I don't understand them. They have no meaning for me. But they do have meaning. I could look into it if I wanted. And discover things. Frictional force. Uniform circular motion. Momentum. Impulse. Torque. Kinetic energy. Things that are unclear at first but then burst with clarity.

I like the idea of vast domains of knowledge and experience that not only exceed my personal comprehension, but are universally enigmatic and shrouded in mystery, like the dark matter that puzzles astrophysicists, or the water spouting out of the mouths of gargoyles.

There's a species of poetry that has enormous appeal. Poems such as those by Stephane Mallarmé or Louis Zukofsky whose word joinings suggest far more than what's on the page and do more to excite a mental energy alert to a growing multiplicity of association rather than cohere into a single meaning. I like that tantalizing obscurity, that enticing combination of clarity and shadow, like the chiaroscuro of Rembrandt, that conceals and reveals simultaneously.

Tonight, there was a big thunderstorm, claps of thunder every few seconds and heavy rain. Our cat sat in the window, riveted. Spellbound. I don't know what, exactly, was going on in her mind, but it's clear she was fascinated and trying to figure out what was happening. It's that quality of attention I find so desirable, particularly in aesthetic experience. I want to be a cat in the window during a thunderstorm every minute of the day. Enraptured. Ensorcelled. Mesmerized. Maybe a little frightened.

The sublime is supposed to be scary. Before the word 'awesome' was emptied of meaning, it meant "extremely impressive or daunting; inspiring great admiration, apprehension, or fear." Now, of course, it just means 'cool.' "I like your hat, dude. It's awesome." "You got married? Awesome."

The world needs to be re-enchanted. Whatever strange physics equations Wall Street is using to keep its financial scheming afloat when it's so obvious that real wealth — the purity of our air and water, the health of our oceans and forests — is being depleted, have, nevertheless, a strange fascination for me. I have to admire the madness and hallucinatory vigor of it. What compelling hallucinations! Money is a form of language. Paper and numbers are ascribed a certain monetary value, and that value — which is strictly numerical — reflects what is valued in the culture. Paying for something is a form of communication. I want that. Here's this, these numbers, I'm giving you in exchange for that thing I want. That hotel room in Honolulu. That doctor to look at my foot. That house. That car. That ride in the sky.

What sells easily? What hardly sells at all? Cars, computers, tickets to a basketball game or rock concert sell robustly. Even the mindfulness movement has been coopted and marketed. So much for transcendence.

Poetry is the hardest sell of all. Why is that? It takes work on the part of the reader. It can't be consumed right away like a can of soda or bag of potato chips or flashy rock stars on a stage at Coachella. It takes an investment of time and energy and a certain quality of attention. A willingness to work all day at splitting a coconut. A coconut of words. A coconut of participles and ink.

Isn't this what I've wanted language to do? Create spirits of air, à la Prospero, and inflate them with nitrous oxide and rum. Lose control. And stand back to enjoy the delirium.

Writing Is How I Feel About Paper

Language is born of absence. It creates a substitute for something not present. It's a game of substitution. I'm writing these words on a desk. The desk is present to me, but not to you, who may be sitting at a desk of your own, or sitting on a bus, or a bench in a city park. But by writing the word 'desk' I can create an image of a desk in your mind. It won't be my desk, but it will be a desk, the desk that you have imagined which will be a different desk with different drawers, different knobs, different legs, a different surface, a different color, a different history, a different weight, a different size and shape. I can bring it within a more palpable range by describing it in detail. And I can achieve this effect in writing with greater facility than in speech because writing affords me the time to think and select all the best characterizations. And this is where we might be able to defeat the negations of absence and make something feel present that isn't actually present. Its presence will be illusory. But in another sense its presence will also be essential. It will be removed from the empirical realm and raised into a more transcendent realm. The realm of writing, which is a realm of enchantment.

"Writing heightens consciousness," wrote Walter J. Ong in *Orality and Literacy*. "Alienation from a natural milieu can be good for us…

> …and indeed is in many ways essential for full human life. To live and to understand fully, we need not only proximity but also distance. This writing provides for consciousness as nothing else does… Writing is often regarded at first as an instrument of secret and magic power. Traces of this early attitude toward writing can still show etymologically: the Middle English 'grammarye' or grammar, referring to book-learning, came to mean occult or magical lore, and through one Scottish dialectical form has emerged in our present English vocabulary as 'glamor' (spell-casting power). 'Glamor girls' are grammar girls…By separating the knower from the known, writing makes possible increasingly articulate introspectivity, opening the psyche as never before not only to the external objective world quite distinct

from itself but also to the interior self against whom the objective world is set. Writing makes possible the great introspective religious traditions such as Buddhism, Judaism, Christianity, and Islam...

The highly interiorized stages of consciousness in which the individual is not so immersed unconsciously in communal structures are stages which, it appears, consciousness would never reach without writing. The interaction between the orality that all human beings are born into and the technology of writing, which no one is born into, touches the depths of the psyche. Ontogenetically and phylogenetically, it is the oral word that first illuminates consciousness with articulate language, that first divides subject and predicate and then relates them to one another, and that ties human beings to one another in society. Writing introduces division and alienation, but a higher unity as well. It intensifies the sense of self and fosters more conscious interaction between persons. Writing is consciousness-raising.

Writing is how I feel about paper. Infinity gets a tan. My neck slips through a fog of thought to my head, which rides on my shoulders, enjoying the ride through the living room, and eventually outside, where all the people endure the great adventure of being, some with smiles, some with frowns, some with the flaming gauze of sunset in their eyes, some with conversation and some in assembly making points and demonstrations.

I enjoy driving, which is also a form of writing, because it's phenomenological and metaphorical all at once and I have to look around and see what other people are doing and then make decisions based on the decisions of the other drivers while making deft maneuvers and bringing up things from the past and making hollow cylinders of thought roll around in my brain while I wait for the light to change.

Which is not at all like writing I don't know why I wrote that. Sometimes it just feels good to put one word after another and see what might happen if I add a little salt and smokestack lightning. I want to bring the roots of my reverie tree to a fat canopy of leafage and savagery by eating the sun. And then grow another way out. Another murmuring gestation. Another deformation. Another meditation. Another blow to the empire.

The claws stroke away at the moon. I swoon daily. Benevolence has a scarlet beauty, a quintessentially Friday mouth. And so I move my gelatin arm making words appear that might one day steal away into elsewhere.

And this causes sexual arousal, which is hawks circling in a sky. An unpredictable laundry. The feeling of thirst when it's first quenched. A dream explained at a kitchen table.

Orange Never Burps

How can language accurately describe the world? It can't. That's why I use a Dashcam, a sponge, and a calliope. Pornographic cows dancing on a pinhead. I pay little attention to mold. I let mold do what mold does. Revolution boils in the heart of a tiger. We'll get to that later. Right now, I just want to say that no problem can affect me if I don't give it tortillas and maidenhood. I back off and let reality do what it wants. And now a body of water goes clanking around in a sack of imaginary fish. I see your eyes sifting all the reasons as to why it's important to learn how to draw. I agree: we all need to escape ourselves. I've attached a piece of gravity to my lip. If you follow it home you may find a vacant seat. And float to the ceiling on a raft of trembling sound.

Here's some mountains overlooking a beautiful temperature. Death is a private affair. An unconditional lucidity. Frog plop in a woodland pond. Whatever diplomacy you bring to the pinnacle in Nietzsche's toolbox our life together is cerulean blue. I fell into employment when the car door opened, not before or after. But so what? Right? I can drive and play with the air simultaneously. It was my destiny to play with money but I chose musk-ox instead. Age makes us sag. But I can mime the virtue of magazines by standing next to you grinning like pickles. One day, sooner or later, people might gradually perceive the universe in a single human voice.

Lord let the obloquies give me power till some ramification gets here. I speak to wood. I love trees. A little nasty fondling here and there is good for the soul. My brain feels like an odd old bump of dusty morality. There are thoughts lying around everywhere. It's a mess. I need to blow it all up with something good. Nihilism or laughing gas. Personality is a lifetime sentence. I float in syntax. I'm all airplane. A robin listening for worms. I get ghostly near Marseille. The caboose always greets the places its leaving. I can see infinity in the curve of a spoon, the human comedy in a men's room. And this is a perception best seasoned by jingling among the guests.

Vitality is impatient. Heroin, on the other hand, is a masterpiece of weakness. Translucence consumes its weight in garbage, causing rheumatism and relaxation. Tender and pale contacts with the semantics of affection taper into light when the curtains are caramel and the tangerines are tangential. When reality intervenes, it appears masked as a drawer of underwear, then a toccata and fugue in D minor, all in one petulant athletic support. Don't worry: it's entirely braille. But don't go fussing with the curls until they discharge alternating arcs of Gaelic. Convention rarely allows boiling unless the eggs are also cosmogonal. The faucet bites the water. The sink fills with weather. The world walks into this language carrying a waterfall and a fire.

For such is the power of dirt. Imagine swimming through worms when you take to the air. The suppleness of meaning sleeps in the stones of the river. Nearby, we see a cactus. I see mind in it, and the nothingness of mind. Insects swarm over the surface of the water. There is no interior. There is no exterior. There's only the blues, twilight hues and the gradual appearance of the stars. A universe appears. You can see it sparkle at the edge of thought. You can see it accelerate into oblivion. You can see it bend, a piece of it blistering on the finger of time. Here comes some gravity to help keep us company. Here I sit laughing at a map. It's what you do when the world eludes you. I pull my dreaming through my lips to give you paregoric in a negligee. I float in syntax. I'm a roller skate. I'm iodine to meet you. I think, therefore I'm excruciating. The mood becomes elegiac. Orange never burps. But if I break my rules I can draw the sky a little closer. I feel the energy of Cezanne. Meanings awaken. Rocks enter into definition with the melting of snow. A rattlesnake coils in the middle of the road. And I know that one day I will ride a horse of oboes through a symphony of wives standing cold in the rain.

Vast Thoughts Of Nothing

Sometimes the algorithms get it right and I sigh to think how it's come to this, a minor cerebral caress during a time of rapine and global destruction. An apparition of death wades into my life pulsing with insects. I run to the moon and back. Who needs airplanes when you've got verisimilitude? Oh, to be an armchair clamp! Revolution boils in the heart of a tiger. My nose is in a state of chronic irritation. I'm going inside and make like I don't exist. Schools of tuna repeat this miracle underwater. This is why God created sleep. No society is so bad, so maladapted, so poorly guided that you can't go around naked occasionally spilling poetry on people.

I'm grotesquely shameless. And haunted by a stepladder eating blackberries. These aren't the explosives I ordered but they'll do for the moment. No edge, however sharp or dull, can escape itself. But sometimes you just have to take that leap into the unknown. Desire is a light. It will show you the way. But you have to let yourself feel it. If you don't feel it it will feel you and cause subatomic particles to cough up Karen Carpenter. The Being for whom Being is a question is a whereabouts not a will-o-the-wisp. Shall I just come out and say it? I love the smell of rain.

The Stones really got drenched in Miami. Hurricane Dorian. Keith Richards looked like he was reading a book. The security guys all looked very pensive. It's a very weighted topic. I put the emphasis on a dollop of bubbling declension & mighty flowers appeared to boil my words in a cauldron of verse. I curled up into a towering seclusion and shaved my cricket with a good conversation. Proust got entangled in all the adjectives but iron makes me happy. If it weren't for a little oblivion now and then, I'd have to build a glove and shake hands with the darkness.

It's always a little sad to go live in the woods alone. I spend most of my time itching, scratching, clearing my throat, and blowing my nose. This is how our biology speaks to us. What do you want? I want peace. I'm all hung up and I don't know why. I've got a notebook teeming with language. What good will that do me? Welcome to the Theatre of Benevolent Chairs. Why is there a giraffe on your shoulder? We all need to escape ourselves. Even my scrotum itches. I sit by the side of the road sobbing. Let's create Bob Dylan. And get up and walk back into the sky.

Thus Spake ZZ Top

Am I peremptory? Have I ever been peremptory? What does it feel like to be peremptory? It feels like dancing on the side of a bedroom window. And it reminds me of everything that is harsh and toxic and unnatural in the world, even when it's a scrutiny I'm performing. I frequently have thoughts about the volatility of our moods. But why 'our.' Maybe they're just my moods. A schoolroom is packed with children as a single teacher holds an object before them and asks what it is called in English. Mango. The world is ravenous for meaning. But we keep forgetting the world is alive, and needs our attention. Science, said Heidegger, doesn't think.

Today I woke up and I was John Keats. Which meant I had to write great poetry and find a couch to sleep on in somebody's house. A nice full tree to sit under in a laudanum glow half in love with easeful death. I feel the hunger of the elephant and bend the light so that I may stiffen into erudition and create rumors of soft alpaca in the mountains of Peru. I need to exceed all limits. I will require an airplane, a pair of thumbs and a skull packed with sunsets. I'm still waiting for a topic, but if one doesn't arrive, I'll just wedge an eyeball between a pronoun and a crab. Have you noticed? When sounds are patterned like this they crack into words and ooze God knows what.

I have expensive tastes. I like to sift metaphors for tiny samples of insight. I get excited when the answers people give me resemble abalone. I have enough incentive to squeeze camels out of a fog and call it a valid exploration for the supramundane. I keep turning and turning in the widening gyre, as Yeats would say. I'm swollen with desire and ride a horse of oboes through a symphony of wives standing cold in the rain. We're all waiting for something. Benediction. Salvation. Or the cold air on Philip Whalen's shaved head to be the first headlines of the day. Why this obsession with the undefined? The question answers itself. And this is how fugues are born.

How do you do. I'm a ghost. I was once alive and now I'm dead. I'm speaking to you from the void. This will mean nothing to anyone because we're all floating forever in the cold darkness of space. Microbes, snakes, frogs, butterflies, elk, elephants, bears, and Arthur C. Clark. Life has become absurd and has lost all meaning halleluiah. All things are permitted. But don't step on my blue suede shoes. If you do that I will take all these words & put them in a poem with huge responsibilities and tiny rabbits. Who wants that? All anyone needs is a month of amphetamine in Vermont and an open flame of consciousness throwing language at an imaginary solution.

But seriously, who am I? Am I you? I'm not you, because if was you, I wouldn't be me, and being me is a full-time job with few benefits and a headache at the end of the day. The human ego receives far too much attention. Nobody thinks about their ego when they're floating down a river in an inner tube. Especially if the river is imaginary and the inner tube is an armchair. So why not give pain a broad and open acceptance? Nietzsche saw pleasure and pain as a false and unimportant polarity. I'm not sure I see it that way myself, but I like Nietzsche's bravado and creativity. Give that man an inner tube and a six-pack of beer. Thus spake ZZ Top.

House Of Being

I'm grotesquely shameless. And haunted by a paper cow. How do I interpret this scribbling? I curl up into a towering solitude and begin stimulating forgetfulness with a pillow and a dream.

I awake and open my eyes and consciousness floods into my head. The damage done to our planet is catastrophic and irreversible. It's not an easy thing to realize. All the words glitter and I ponder their shape. But there's nothing words can do. It's like squeezing a sponge. Nothing comes out but what went in. Thinking is a strange activity. I'm the ghost that haunts myself. I carry a lavender barometer and watch mutations take place in a paragraph teeming with equations and crows.

When we returned home the other day there was a man standing on a stepladder eating blackberries. The sweet play of hemlock branches in the breeze. I felt the vibrations of a distant star and got out of the car with a song in my heart and a new temperature to feel unearthed from the treasures of the past.

Robert Plant screaming I can hear it calling me back home in Arcata, California, 1969.

These aren't the explosives I ordered but they'll do for the moment.

No edge, however sharp or dull, can escape itself. Sometimes you just have to take that leap into the unknown. And the final version of that will be dying. Which goes on all the time. And nobody comes back to talk about it. I find this strange. And more than a little frustrating.

Last week a waitress brought me a blackberry cobbler with a single candle in it. And this taught me something about gratitude.

Sometimes I say things that are the opposite of what I feel. And that leaves me feeling constricted like a shrunken head in control of nothing but soup. A renunciation of instinct can only take you so far. What matters is sincerity. The music of the spheres. Ecology and tea. And that's when it's calling me back home.

I don't understand the universe. Who brought it here? And where is here? Is here here or somewhere else?

The painters arrived without warning and stomped around in their shoes painting walls that didn't need painting. They left chewed gum on the sidewalk and buzzsaws in my brain.

Desire is a light. It will show you the way. But you have to let yourself feel it. If you don't feel it it will feel you and cause havoc to reign. Or dullness and indifference to assume alloys of silver and jade. Beauty is elusive. You can see it without seeing it and feel it without feeling it. But in the end, you'll find everything hemmed with dark matter and subatomic particles coughing up record players.

It's nice to see vinyl making a comeback.

This is the life I lead: a joker in an irrational orbit still trying to unveil chaos to see how the ratatouille might improve with a little more sage and hallucination. As Karen Carpenter used to say, the money is in the basement. The point of almond isn't ecstasy it's motocross. The Being for whom Being is a question is a whereabouts not a will-o-the-wisp.

Shall I just come out and say it? I love the smell of rain.

The Helium Of The Absurd

Pornographic cows dance on a pinhead. It's always a little sad to go live in the woods alone. I'm haunted by a thriftless multiplicity of wallpaper roses. I run to the moon and back. Who needs airplanes when you've got verisimilitude? I pay little attention to mold. What is it that flowers by your pumpkin? I spend most of my time itching, scratching, clearing my throat, and blowing my nose. This is how our biology speaks to us.

An apparition of death wades into my life pulsing with insects. I try to find a little peace within myself. The kerosene is drawn up through the wick by capillary action. Revolution boils in the heart of a tiger.

What do you want? I want peace. I'm all hung up and I don't know why. I've got a notebook teeming with imaginary solutions. But its alternatives are dysfunctional and indistinct. Sensory nerves, motor nerves, afferent nerves, efferent nerves. Oh, to be an armchair clamp! A canvas splashed with equations. Cézanne peppered with the vapor of language.

My nose is in a state of chronic irritation. There's always something. If it's not wildfire smoke it's a flat tire. What can I do with this can of automobile paint? I'm going inside and making like I don't exist. No problem can affect me if I don't give it tortillas and maidenhood.

I've tried assembling a little reality with rags and chemistry. And now a body of water clanks around in chains of imaginary fish.

I see your eyes sifting all the reasons as to why it's important to learn how to draw.

The sun is still learning to shine. Does time truly exist? Or is it more like a feather crashing on the sand? This is proof that nudity exists. No society is so bad, so maladapted, so poorly guided that you can't go around naked occasionally spilling poetry on people.

Welcome to the Theatre of Benevolent Chairs.

Why is there a giraffe on your shoulder?

There are tigers in my breath. We all need to escape ourselves. Even my scrotum itches. I sit by the side of the road sobbing. Let's create birds together. Let's create a sound around drunken Germans. Should I just come out and say it? The sawdust flower is red. It's important to share your passions with others. Farming is one possibility. I remember my father driving to Denver with a crow in the backseat. Later, when I was an adult, the smell of the garage confused me. What made it smell that way? Was it grime? Gardening tools? Sacks of fertilizer? An armadillo with a pink nose sipping coffee and belching and listening to Bob Dylan?

I was raised in a greenhouse on Titan. When I was born eight pounds of language slid out of my mouth. Schools of tuna repeated this miracle underwater. This is why God created sleep.

Thinking is a strange activity. It's like sipping a luminous beverage in somebody's basement and hearing someone cough in another room. I've attached a piece of gravity to my lip. This will make everything a little quieter when I begin to rub some words together to create a fire. I will answer all of your questions with a powdered donut and get up and walk back into the sky.

I don't suffer indignities well. But when I saw my clothes running down the street without me in them, I decided to take action and inflate myself with the helium of the absurd. And floated to the ceiling on a raft of trembling sound.

A Fence In The Fog

Life is an enigma. No one knows what it is, where it comes from, what to do with it. I find myself in revolt against nearly everything. Where does it come from? This agitation, this crazy Weltanschauung? I don't know. Maybe I need new shoes. Even if a stiffened grammar drops dead there's still a certain feeling in throwing knives. Shit. Now look. My book is bleeding. The one over there, bubbling with hydroelectricity. Dawn walks over the mountains. What do we mean when we talk of pizza deliveries? Is your reality my reality? Life is hard enough without making things more difficult. Language does this. Words. Endless games and shitty romance novels. Jesus. My head explodes. And yet, I have to say, I never met an armchair I didn't like.

Prodigies of concrete cram my brain. My head itches. I feel kicked and gynecologic. I feel expectant and louche. Life contains ingredients that cannot be said. It takes 200 harmonicas to demonstrate the square root of a delicatessen. Marie Laurencin does the dishes. Colors surge from my nipples at night & the wind chimes grow still. Could it be I'm a Hostess Cupcake? I like horses, mopeds, and introversion. Is that what identity is about? Or am I making this up? I think this is making me up. All that I know for sure is that language disintegrates when it eats itself. And then it vomits an entire universe. This sentence has 400 legs and is crawling into your eyes.

I wish I was a catfish. I could sway and sparkle in a dream of tinsel. That's the feeling I like. An existence that's partly vibrational, partly neurochemical, but mostly just indolence and dark warm water. Mass is energy. Ok, fine. But let's be clear: none of these words actually belong to me. They're packed in images because reason is a sticky resin. That's how serious I am. Water walks through itself and the capillaries in my eyes burst with fire and empire. One day sooner or later it happens to everybody. The forehead folds into a toaster and reality eats the motel stationary and spits a novel out. I pick it up and hear a madman walking around inside it laughing his head off.

Laziness is the finest of virtues. But it takes work. Discipline. Laziness doesn't happen by itself. The material is immaterial. All you really need is a couch. A pillow or two. TV. WiFi. Think of it as energy conservation in a harmonic oscillator, or alpha waves in a desynchronized pattern set. Helicopters and mollusks pursue different objectives, but these are objects and have a head start. Laziness occurs naturally in the pouring of cement. The way it oozes is conducive to trance. And anytime work is involved, the most natural reaction is to walk away quietly and hope nobody sees you. Think of a clam squirting water from its siphon. Think of the skull as a bowl. Lie back and fill it with dreams. Spoons. Metaphors. Latitude. The world desires our communion.

Out Of Control

Are you controlled? What controls you? I'm controlled by soup. I put soup in my body and the soup controls me. I have a narrative with my name on it, which is a device called an ego, that gets me through life, and controls my life, and gives me lines and directions for the great stage of existence. It's a nice firm ego upholstered in whale-penis leather. It's been with me my entire life, feeding my directions, which come from the directives of the higher social order, which is controlled by a leviathan, a huge cuddly monster sewn together by a Protestant work ethic, which is a thread, which is controlled by a needle, and that needle is in you, penetrating your skin, and is called culture. And when I'm on my own it disassembles, via immersion in language, magic language, oneiric language, the subjectivity is subverted, submarined, taken underwater and introduced to Neptune, who runs everything in Id City, and that's where it's at baby, deep in lingerie and incense, the bicameral brain, the silly sigh bin brain, minus a capacity for executive ego functions, self-awareness, adaptation to reality, whose reality, I don't know, the man, the powers that be, memory, reconciliation of conflicting impulses, mad, nuts, crazy, out of control.

The Indefinability Of Being

Dear Emergency: it's me again. Writing to you from an undisclosed location. I'll be brief: we're fucked. 90°F in Anchorage, Alaska. Thousands of dead fish on the banks of the Rhone. Gray whales starving to death in the Pacific. So yeah, I'm a bit moody these days. The rest of this paragraph will be quiet. Tiptoe past the algorithms. They'll eat you alive. The people of Earth have gone insane. They wrap everything in plastic. Water, clothing, meat. Description succeeds by slamming the door on the way out. I'm not angry. I just want out. That's all. Just open the gate, and let us all go home to that mansion in the sky. Angels mowing the lawn. Martin Luther King and Jesus playing chess. Emma Goldman doing magic tricks in Milton Freidman's skull.

Not a single object can be described. Not fully. Not completely. Not so that its essence can be entirely transmitted. Words are too clumsy. So why even try? Well, you've got to try. I mean if it's important for you to do that. Nobody's going to give a shit. Most people avoid reality. It's the sensible thing to do. Reality hurts. Illusion is its sad consolation prize. I entered life as I found it, visceral and wet and surrounded by Minneapolis. Later, I discovered nocturnal emissions and Sophia Loren. The upholstery of the troika, which creaks with infinity, and the tinkling of chandeliers.

When God sings to himself, he sings algebra, opined Leibniz. That's a relief. I'm glad it's not "My Way." Or "Can't Take My Eyes Off You." But if you're looking for the kind of poetry that coruscates up and down your spine like Queen Mab doing wheelies on a Harley Davidson, that kind of poetry is a little harder to find. It doesn't ride, smart and cosmopolitan, on a glossy page in the *New Yorker*. It hisses and seethes like pahoehoe. It says what it wants with misanthropic glee. It mutates into B movie blobs of translucent goo. It crystallizes the darkness and mails it to Denmark in a glittery skull. It's insolent in its presumptions and foolish in its claims. It's meaning itself. It's the stone of stone and the leaf of the leaf. It's a face in the lake, and a crack in the mirror.

It's mid-summer. Some of us ask, what do we really mean by the word 'Being?' And some of us answer: grits. This flipflop. This lump. This world written in scrabble and blood. The soft burning of a muted C minor. The indefinability of Being. Lights flashing. Night sweats. Insomnia. The world is burning down. It's an ugly scenario. One can surrender to the luxuries of nihilism or continue to revolt and make art. Consider Nietzsche's gnat: if we and the gnat understood one another, we would learn that the gnat swims through the air with the same pathos and feels within itself the flying center of the world. Which proves nothing, except that the gnarled branches of trees will sometimes reflect in still puddles of water, and that sensuality calls the angels to our side.

The Private Murmur Of Warts

Dear Work: I love you. I hate you. I don't know who you are. Are you hospital laundry, or a mail route? I think you're a hectic mind. You light my nerves with the breath of ovens. Pizza is involved. I think I'm supposed to tend to the pizza. If I don't I'll get fired, because that's the nature of work. Work is a bitch. If you're a spirit reading this in some waiting room in heaven, waiting to be born, choose wealthy parents. Do you see what a louse you have made of me, work? You have both crowned me king of an infinite domain of books and ideas and you've also denied me the means to be a fully realized, dignified human. Maybe you're not the one I should be writing to. Maybe I should be writing an angry letter to the real cause of my distress: money.

The artist can't ignore the economic dominance of her or his time. Those with transparent windows in their skin which allow light from photophores to shine through draw the world in and expel it again through pulsations in the mouth. They generally know what to say about romance. But they say nothing about those sensations that invert our perspectives of nudity, that cause us to try and step free of the phenomenal world to see what is truly out there. This is the reality of life in Wyoming. My arm hurts. The horse I was sitting on didn't like me there. This is what it is to love another being. I is a 300-pound bull shark discovered in my head one night. The mind is a desolate place without a sarong. The heart feels soaked in vaudeville. Words blaze with the private murmur of warts. History follows, clanking behind like a laboratory.

How wonderful that an astronomical event can provide, for the duration of several magnificent minutes, a much-needed sense of sublimity and awe. A lifeless ball of rock and dust moving in front of a gigantic ball of continual nuclear explosion and jarring our isolated selves into the open with something phenomenal and strange. I'm referring, of course, to my desk. I do all my writing here, and search for the impossible via the useless. Thinking is not an applied art. Thank God. Can there be anything more useless than thinking? Yes. But that only lasts a few seconds. I wish I could drain my head as easily.

I maneuver the proposals of the day. One of which is to visit the library. The other is to further investigate my favorite drug, which is a combination of remorse and embalming fluid. I believe that feeling can be expanded by reading and that when the rhythms of Bo Diddley meet the investigations of Ludwig Wittgenstein John Keats gets up to dance. But yeah, these are just opinions. The mosaic of life is never consummated and pain walks around looking for a nice warm brain to climb into. The more that I think about things the worse things become. That's why I recommend numbness. I believe that when art ripples into vertebrae a padlock on the mind pops open in a satori of prissy imprecision.

Distortions Mutations Limps

Benediction arrives in an exhalation of breath. My shirts aren't ruffled, but that doesn't mean I'm not dazzled by the locomotive moving through my blood, or the idiocy of hallucination, or any stimulus that leads to the exploration of clothes. I frequently have thoughts about things that don't add up to anything. Vast, vagrant thoughts of nothing. Mighty galleons of nonsense docking at Pier 86 for a load of philology. When one stops to consider a rose, the soul expands. And when the sweat of existence explodes into culture, there's always towels. Confession is good, but chocolate is better. Language is its own disaster, creating gods and philosophy.

The wind has something to ask: why is pain necessary? We need it for romance, paper cuts, and war. Gothic angels lend us the crime of desire. Hot sapphire. The warm flexibility of wax. I approve of the funny weariness I've become. Nothing is so impersonal that it doesn't require charming syncopations. Distortions. Mutations. Limps. We elect more shadows to cast on the wall. It doesn't help much. I move the oysters around in my notebook. The king rides by on a horse made of lightning. This is what writing is, what it's been along. A compensation for my lack of math, certainly, but also a fence in the fog claiming to contain what it doesn't understand.

There are things I will not do. I will not put lipstick on a pig. I will not wear the uniform of death or crown my head with parakeets. Let me show you some feelings. This one is blue and this one just spins around shooting sparks & precipitating books. This one walks around in my head chanting *nihil fit ex nihilo*. If death is simply non-existence, why does Wall Street swirl around in my neurons? What does the sublime have to do with killing things and eating them? Imagination is everything. This is a nice feeling. I can use it to invoke the spirits of breath, which are words. Hummus. Cucumber. Balm. The rest of my day is a long wide sentence leading nowhere.

What is it to be indifferent, neutral, I don't understand indifference, is it heroin, what is it? I'm fascinated by what is inside and what is outside. Where does the inside begin and where does the outside end? How do you weigh the world? Do you use a scale or an elevator? Pass the prayer kit. I have a prayer to make. I blow on my fingers and wait for the sun to rise in the east. I will plow whatever field I'm given. I'll plow it with vigor and a parakeet and a disc harrow. I will do this so that I can smell the dirt. The great heavy dirt of earth. The sweet heavy earth split by a blade. Split like a beating heart. Like a pain running its exquisite demands through a bandaged thumb.

One Big Mesh

There are knots that will never come undone and knots that are allegories of trust. Warts are clouds of interstellar gas that get bagged in skin. Words are the warts of a multicellular fairy. Irritations cause adaptive responses, one of which is poetry. The other is catapulting opinions at the unwary and uninformed. I believe that feeling can be expanded by the rhythms of Bo Diddley, letting the mind float away in a pink ribbon, finding the light in someone's eyes, and a nice warm bath. I believe that when we stand before art there is an interchange between what we have experienced and what we hear or taste in a riot of sticks and rain. The mind blossoms among its nerves and fetches the world, which is in a warehouse among the stars in a South Sea of understanding.

I dwell within the colors surrounding me. There is, I know, an allure to breaking ground with words, sentences lush with tomatoes and kilohertz. I graduated from the School of Hard Knocks in January, 1966, with a big black eye and a crush on Mary Tyler Moore. This has served me well over the years. My greatest ambition has been to dribble down motel curtains after consuming insane amounts of bourbon and its strange geometry. The external world is the work of our organs. Eyes, ears, nose, mouth. Muscles, skin, eucharists and medication. The tumult in my head will stick to the ceiling if I let it out to float up there. And sometimes it will develop a spine and walk.

The sky is pink and friendly. That's where I want to be. Up there. Shaking hands with the sun. How much does a thought weigh? It depends on the thought. This thought weighs 8 oz. and smells of cologne. This thought, on the other hand, is 11 lbs. 8 oz. and reeks of juxtaposition. I don't know what it is. Could be anything. Camels, zombies, seaweed. Agincourt, the siege of Stirling Castle, the Battle of Hastings. This is what life does when death isn't around. It seduces pain with the precision of an insect. Being, according to Heidegger, is a play of appearance and concealment. A sprig of sage in the window, a shift in the air just before it thunders.

The world is granite, the skin is soft, the balance is challenging: Philippe Petit 1,350 feet above the streets of lower Manhattan walking on a 30-foot-long cable on August 7, 1974. For some people, this is a daily exercise. This is where mathematics gets salty and brittle, like a potato chip. Poetry is more like a tight mesh of small cords than a solid fabric. This is why angels are often equipped with sewing kits. My first instinct is to grip something and hang on for dear life. The sentence shivers. A clown appears and punches a Buddhist. The recommendations are stupid and all the movies are bad. But who cares? You've come this far. Later, when we've gotten to know one another a little better, I will show you my favorite feeling, which is written in silence.

Thought Bump

Highway a trombone. The stir in this velvet is prehistoric. Phantoms in the sluice. Thought bump. As chowder whirls so whirls the world. My requirement goes until plunged into dirt, where it becomes a matter of itself to itself. We furrow it big like an indentation sympathetically floated on a desk. The drive made us greasy. I went along to stick a painted radar on the airplane. I'm a trickle of gray, a doorway slapped with russet. Art is a form of the Absolute Spirit, a phenomenological complement to a revelatory resistance to genetic spreadsheets. The equivalent to birch. A testimony enriched by horn. I'm your talk among antique thumps of tongue on a sentence made of sweat. Personality is the wandering we do in the maps around the property. Your walk is over there where your legs are going. There's a bite in the visa. A wrinkle reprises the eyes. Flowers are nature's paraphernalia. They give us a pure understanding of sensuality. A convention is aghast at this. Don't worry. Your itch is my scratch. Gauze on a seesaw. The prospect from here is yanked from pathos and pounded into habit. There's this potato to enhance. We can do it with tea. Yesterday the sky was dropped on a tent causing the pigments to increase into sags. But today the trees put everything back. Incense shakes the glass. What is heaven? Music. The cry of ooze from a peat bog. A man walking down a road to greet a woman.

Phantom Cry

Heidy heidy hi. Heidy heidy ho. Listen to the chop of delicatessen Joe. Chick chunk plunk and a bumpety bump bump. Snip. Snap. Snoop. Holy befuddlement of the cheese grater. Little slices of Choctaw stump. Sioux City bristle on a fallible yarn. Dwarf star croak. Buckthorn buffalo clambake cracker. Cavefish bicycle bloom. Word salad fricassee. Feed these words your mind. Feed it rhyme. Feed it wine. Feed it a chair and a table and a Venetian blind. Feed it philosophy and blood. Employ the graceful stride of Yul Brynner. Impressionism deathwatch lamb. Deploy a reference. Gather hay. Murder snow. Squash the languor of comprehension into lush confusion. Seed the air. Grow a pack. Hang a sound of kitchen words. Excite the crisis of silence. Construction rains ash let's crash through it. Go for a tangential stroll. I abandoned the palette and went straight to autumn. Antique smack of the moonlight reflection. I guzzle an eager beat. Exult in cardboard. Shatter the potato mirror. Glaze your denim. Enamel a configurational myth. Do it with an oat leg. Unpredictable salvation cinnamon. Caress your flutter. Euclid's sting is close to a square. Paint this swell with heft and passion. The weight of the pumpkin chops into pulp. Cartwheels control the materiality of the Fauve octagon. Oblige me to arrive flowing through your buttons. Siege bread. Subtlety's port exceeds the envy of earth. Trek glue. I steadily persuade my moccasin onto my foot. Fix this dynamic. The slide of my mouth occurs to a dish. The mirror spins listening. Let's exchange streams. Exemplify absence with pharmaceuticals. Bubbles guide my hand across the paper. This is my impersonal predicament sternum. Punchbag veins. Red eyeball inside a white skull. The zipper's reach mingles with a collar stud. My eyes grapple with a strangled coat. Vowels remedied the lost consonant. Drop and bend. Grope cod opened in jingles. Ask the escalator. Sensation's hymn thrums through the Alleghenies. Unprecedented adaptation in slouched despair. Secrete wire. Gray enhances the sting of the tongue. Let it happen. Let it all happen. Happen and happen. See it all urged into change. Every antique knife. Every abandoned affection. Hear it cry. My phantom cry.

Mr. Sticky

I'd like to say a few things regarding my personal life. First, words are clumsy. They fall out of my mouth constantly. Secondly, nobody gives a shit about your personal life. Use this to your advantage. Reality hurts. Everybody has to cope with it. I deal with it by sitting under a piano wearing a cowboy hat. I don't have a patent on kidneys or blood circulation, but I do have a pet emotion I call Mr. Sticky. The question is therefore obvious: who am I? What am I? I'm Zen mosquitos on a hairy arm, a subjectivity crammed with Motown. I believe the image that best serves the object at hand is fish. That, and cruising the Danube on a nipple of tender human skin.

My breath can make a house. You don't have to be a carpenter. You can just bullshit. You don't need a mortgage for oblivion. There's a kind of providence in the smell of a barn. Why is reality so big and architectural? It disassembles as easily as it's assembled. Pain is an awakening. And there's Wifi. Should I include a biography at this stage? Very well. I will rent a carrot and stand very still. A frontier of the heart lives in the narrative next door. Wittgenstein gives a striking example: a man who would cut the arm of his neighbor off to see if it would grow back is not an experiment, but the work of a madman. So what do you say? Let's just stay in and order pizza.

Why are ghosts always represented as bed-sheets? Death is nothing. Nothing but courtesy. Sleep forever, what could be better? The invention of sleep is the universe's greatest achievement, wouldn't you say? I'm sleeping right now. I'm dreaming of X-rays and the light behind the X-rays. Bones. Prisms. Gregorian chants. Humans invent stupid shit like jobs. Nothing dumber than a job. Although there's a certain poetry in operating a gas station, or selling pretzels. Do you like ice cream in your science? What is the source of this emotion? Buffalo on the plains in 1752.

The door gives me a feeling of percussion, if percussion were oscillations of grain in the wood, & the rhythms of entering & leaving hinged upon a knob of light. We see a wall riddled with marks: indecisive enigmatic Cy Twombly painting. A dazzling beak of divine equation brightens the protein in my DNA. I blow a tiger to power.

Lunar Module

Architecture botch indicates there's a fountain in my chisel. Piles above that I lobster into audacity like a true hallmark of juice. There's a bistro bowl which proves that my navigation is revelatory and feudal. Or do I mean futile? What do I mean? I mean dried flowers starved for rage. Strong inclinations fiddled by prayer. And so it begins. I climb into some pathos. The within looks like Colorado. The without looks like Kansas. I rub ghosts out of my mouth. They say visit the artist and be a visceral desk to your relatives. I feel insults in my prophesying, hysterics in my megaphone. I think of decorum as a unit of electrical resistance, an unpredictable voyage in relation to matter and a libido that permeates the river as it walks through itself to empty into France. Wide-eyed heat is a principle cause of blimps. My sense of plurality gets athletic near the fringe. Infrared and henna make it curve into reality where the circus finally finds its algebra in the sawdust of an enthralling energy called into being by a renegade gargoyle. And so I rest, knowing how to jiggle, how to juggle, how to nudge obscurity out of the oboe and into the public realm where the drums go lyrical, promenading in sticks, boom boom boom, fragments of rock notwithstanding, which are mesmerized into density by the breath of angels.

Kerplop

These are strange days. The world has turned apocalyptic. Blake's tiger moves stealthily forward. Time works by gear and tablespoon. Is this a dream, or a table? It's clearly a philosopher seated by a window. Is there anything more lonesome than the parking lot at what used to be Sears? Poor capitalism. It tries so hard. When was the last time you saw a frog? This will walk beside you until we get somewhere. Reverie is Cretaceous. Thinking is Cenozoic. But really. Kerplop is universal. Dip the oar, pull it, dip it again, pull it. Sooner or later you'll find yourself somewhere. It might be nowhere, but it will be somewhere. Even nowhere is somewhere.

An old man in an armchair dreams of a pretty world in which a horticulture of the imagination causes the taste of cheese to exist in a property tax like a large blue smoke in a grocery sack. There's no simpler way to say it: the gods of supply and demand are finally wondering how Phil Spector is doing in prison. The answer, sadly, is stupefaction. Art has no need to justify itself. The same snow falling on James Joyce now falls on the grave of Jackson Pollock. This ruins interpretation for everyone. There's a dangerous energy afoot. None of us owns a car. We just go from belligerency to instinct and hold the door open for the sound of the ocean.

I ignite some road flares and the blizzard pulls back into the night. A universe walks by carrying a basket of planets. The priest is late for mass. He shivers in the dark mulling parables. At least the elevator is working. The longer I exist the less I know about existence. Honesty is charming, more entertaining than mirrors, but hard to live with. This is what we do when we talk about the world. We detach the wind and put it in a jar where it blows through a little town in Texas causing people's lips to flicker with calculus. Are we entirely stuck in suffering and illusion, or is there any way to transcend these conditions of being in the world? I know that for some life is too short and for others life is too long. And that these two propositions are steeped in semantic drapery.

I like to put words together. I mean, who doesn't, right? How can anyone not enjoy putting words together? It's the closest that we can get to the infinite while still in our skin. The intent to put words together in a way that makes the words different, that makes them shiny and hard and incandescent is a very strange ambition. It will not make you money. But it will make you flibbertigibbet and borborygmus. You can get so entangled in vocabulary and syntax you'll need the jaws of life to extricate your ass. Sometimes I succeed, sometimes I lapse into habit. Sometimes I just thrash about like a madman, or brood like Hamlet on ghosts and revenge. This is me trying to be a drug. This is me riding a mustang up a steep rocky hill, chased by a military helicopter and Walter Matthau in a jeep, desperate to escape the 21st century.

Big Appetite

I want to eat a coconut and build a temperament that participates in its own creation. It seems to me that my mind is separate from the world, but I know that's wrong. Otherwise, why would I have an appetite? Nothing engages you with the world like eating. Is there any validity to this narrative? Does the mind have reality? These questions become increasingly pertinent as I age. Because the body is mortal. When it gives out, I go with it. But where? Is there a world beyond ours, a world of spirit and vision, a universe of waves and otherworldly beings?

Reality just isn't what it used to be. It used to be all skin and blood and bone and muscle, and now I feel quite different. Reality is mostly jungle.

Last night I got the munchies and learned about brining meat. I grabbed a box of Triscuits and left the cupboard door open and noticed a box of Morton salt. I read a brief paragraph on the side of the box: "Brining creates extra tender, juicy and flavorful meat. It does so by locking in meat's natural juices, which prevents meat from drying out while cooking. To brine, you simply soak the meat in a solution of salt and water prior to cooking." This is how I spent the last few minutes of 2018. I heard a motorcycle go by at a tremendous speed. I could hear the scream of the engine. This was followed by the excited voices of men and women. This guy was in a hurry to die. Would he even live to see 2019?

At 11:50 p.m. we went out to watch the fireworks on the Space Needle. I noticed a huge crowd of people just a few feet below, on Fifth Avenue North. Where had they all come from? It was as if a number of charter buses had brought them up here. Was the crowd below so huge that this was now a good vantage point? One of them sent a giant bottle-rocket high into the air. It squiggled its way into the sky and then exploded loudly. Ka-boom! Bright red flakes of fire came drifting down.

The more I think about getting high the less I think I know about what getting high means. I think I need to get to the bottom of getting high.

Terence McKenna is the guy you want to go to for information on psychedelic experience. Another is Rupert Sheldrake. I would also highly recommend the essays in Michael McClure's *Meat Science Essays*. These are brilliant, poetic, highly imaginative and intensely descriptive reactions to substances such as peyote, heroin, and cocaine.

Drugs aren't the only way to get high, achieve euphoria, or gain insights into one's consciousness and the mysteries of the cosmos. There's also long distance running and the sweat lodge ceremony.

There's always an appetite for travel, for getting out of Dodge, as they say, for the open road, the road as Kerouac imagined it, the road as a morsel turning red over the coals of a glowing rumination. When, exactly, did we lose the world? Did we lose the world when science separated our minds from our bodies, or when topiary emerged in the gardens of Versailles? Were Exxon-Mobil and Coca Cola the ultimate seals of our division from all that was holy and sublime?

The road ahead is free and clear. Let's be like that. Let's stand on the rocks and look at oblivion. It's the same oblivion as the old oblivion. A quiet old road disappearing in the south of Arkansas. The doctors are huddled over a body. The heart is a fist of lightning veined and red. Planet Earth is a long walk in a blue palace. My stethoscope is pressed against the night. I'm driving all night. If you go deep enough you don't notice the impossibilities. But if you go a day and don't open your mouth the universe will walk into your head and sit down and write a book about duckbilled hats. I can see it in your eyes: perspective. That's why I'm laughing at the road. It's adorably hypnotic.

Curaçao is blue in the red house of logarithms. Eyeliner plus lipstick equals myriad kisses. Cosmetic is a Greek word. So is cosmos. If you look closely, there's a universe in your soup. Chunks of rock and metal in a whirlpool of light. The ego is propped up by a floor, but the floor is nothing but a torrent of tears. Do snowmen have organs? What do snowmen eat? Ice cubes? Snowballs? I see Ferdinand Pessoa sitting in the play of light and shadow in a Lisbon bistro musing on a plate of *saudade*. Something like a habitable planet. Round, sweet, marbled and wet.

Synoptic Nostrils

Sometimes I see a prose poem and ask myself why anyone would write such a thing. There are so many words. We must not rush things. We must take our time and linger among the assumptions. Ruptures will occur, and moons. Mongolian yurts drift through a sleepy sister hanging below my waist. Bedsprings creak me to Paris. My arms meet their own correspondence when I roar.

The sun bubbles in its bullion and overflows. Intentions are cut into oarlocks. I rummage the heat for a thump of metal. I want rivets for my bridges and Norway for my shoes. Harmonica bombs converse with the mustard. Handles are powerfully tried by men who wear somnolent expressions of trudge.

The stew crackles on hiatus. The jug swerves to miss a stepladder. I carry a thought of titbits to a sheet of paper and put them down in bombast. The effect is fossils. The past is in the future and the future is in the past. The clouds are packed in a box and the accordion wheezes jelly.

For almost twenty years, I have been a journalist in the digital environment, a land of mirages and runaways, of enormous excesses. It was a mirror to larks and, for me as for many others, the place of a mad hope. That I attribute a colossal power of transformation to a trifle, that I am blinded by the very symptom I both laud and despise, I fully admit. But this hybrid technology is coupled with a reverse phenomenon. What brings the meaning of technology now to its fullest expression is its erasure. It tends to hide itself. One could say that that is its ambition, the meaning of its story: to blend in with the landscape. And by disappearing, it invades everything.

Thus, in theory, there is a species of absurdity to want to know things otherwise than by intelligence; but, if we accept the risk frankly, the action will slice right through the knot that reasoning has tied so firmly it will not come undone. The metaphysics or deep thinking that philosophy reserves to do in a quiet nook at the library, will receive their evidence ready-made as positive science, already contained in the descriptions and analyses from which they gave the philosopher buckets of slippery worry. For not having wanted to intervene, from the beginning, in the questions of fact, philosophy is reduced, in questions of principle, to formulate purely and simply in more precise terms the metaphysics and arcanum unconsciously, hence inconsistently, that draws the very attitude of science vis-à-vis reality. The form is no longer quite isolable from matter, and he who began by reserving philosophical questions of principle, and who wanted, by this, to put philosophy above science as a Court of Last Resort, will be led, step by step, not to make it a mere kangaroo court, charged at most to spell out in more precise terms the sentences that arrive irrevocably rendered.

Everything in life is ephemeral, permeable, and cork. Duration protects the shell of dissonance, which in turn serves the distribution of deviled eggs.

I'm not even sure what a horsefly is. I think they're bigger than your average flies, the ones you find in poorly tended kitchens, or banging against the window glass in a stuffy living room. This is why the symbolic flirts with innuendo, glimmering with manuscripts in a paregoric motel. All one has to do is think of Wyoming and then compare it to a submarine. Clearly, the road ahead is more than a little prepossessing, it might also be a little long in locoweed.

Roll the window down and smell it: sage. Hank Williams is on the radio. Whatever one may think of thunder, it's uncanny how it rolls across the distances seconds after the lightning has flashed, providing what appears to be a second opinion, a mumbling over the realities we've just witnessed.

Dot

I is a dot. The more you struggle the tighter the cylinder becomes. Kineticism is exhilarating. You should try it. Eat a pickle. Punish your sweater. You can do anything. Go anywhere. We're surrounded on all sides by other dimensions.

The wedge of noise that I rattle makes everything sidereal. We strain to milk the ceremony of words smeared on the reverse side of a church. Meanwhile, the brain moves sideways like a crab all the way to the side of the head and sits in a puddle of thought.

What is time? It's time we got out of here. I'll go get the horses. I smell the law. Do what I do: bathe in the flow of events. It won't get you rich, but it will get you wet.

What a funny universe this is. I think of all these fins and noodles, pebbles in wireframe glasses, the expansibility of flesh and a heart pumping out blood, how emboldening it is to hold a chair in the air and sing songs of the basement during an era of birds.

Yesterday, as I was descending the little switchback trail in the park, surrounded on all sides by azaleas and rhododendrons, a hummingbird hovered in front of my face for a full minute. I just stood there, curious, as she hovered inches from my face. Did she think I was some kind of hairy flower? I've been eating a lot of sugary food lately. Do I smell like nectar? Maybe it was because I go through the park every day and have been feeding the local crows daily for almost a full year. Maybe that got her curious. Who is this weirdo feeding crows every day? What's he got for me? They're amazing little birds. You don't see wings, just blurs on either side of the body.

Blurs are words. I'm words. We are all words. Everything is words. Pizza, ambivalence, mistletoe. Words.

Dreams of an after-life. Christmas in Budapest. Hegel's aesthetics. The mesas of New Mexico. Words. Words. Words.

The sound of water roaring through subterranean chambers. Membranes and amber, those really good breakfast deals you get in Vegas and Reno.

Of course, there's a slight metaphysical mystery here: who is in charge? Is it the body, the mind, or a rhododendron named Lucy? The famous duality between the mind and body is flawed by plasticity. There's the body, which is thought to be inert, and the mind, imagined as an immaterial essence. In which portion exists the "I" or "us" that rides around inside? If we reduce the mind to a neural substance, albeit a malleable one that can be molded and controlled, then where is the "I" doing the molding and the controlling? Is it in the brain? The palm of the hand? My index finger? And how do you control an immaterial essence?

How simple it is to exist. Existence is a woman braiding her hair in front of a mirror. Trees. Pigeons in a parking lot. Trash bins. A drunk cursing the traffic. Ambition is 30 gallons of gas and a red Silverado. Existence is wistful and pensive and doesn't hurt anybody. Ambition pleases the stockholders and puts 5,000 people out of work. When desire doesn't take itself seriously we call it a wish. When desire takes itself very seriously we call it Richard III. Existence is often like that. Standing, staring daggers at a couple dining on Hudson Valley Moulard Duck Foie Gras at Per Se on Columbus Circle in midtown Manhattan. And wishing you could write like Chekhov.

It is not the world but being in the world that pulls ourselves into ourselves. I'm not going to say that life is hard. That's too easy. So what's a good adjective? Unpredictable. Like poetry.

In the fourth dimension, space and time are unified in a Minkowski continuum. If masses are sufficiently large, time may fold back on itself, and the poem becomes a dragon eating its own tail. We've all seen this before. A door swings open and a piano floats in its music. Someone whispers Spain. And the hunt begins, the search for that elusive thing called understanding. I'll take your hand, you take my hand. Together we'll get away. I understand water. I don't understand dinghies.

The sentence forms and shivers. A clown appears and punches a Buddhist. Who cares? The prophecies are still boiling. Now I'm ready to close my eyes. My mind is shattered. No problem.

I'll reassemble it at the airport. The sky is pink and friendly today. That's a good sign. One day poetry will be great again and enter the cave of the blue dragon and spin around spurting words.

I see no division between the mind and the body. None of my thoughts weigh anything. This is what life does when death isn't around. It experiments with metal detectors, ultrasound, psilocybin, peyote, and Percy Bysshe Shelley. The romantic spirit isn't dead. It's just in a different time zone.

Poetry Is A Cruel Public Drug

I hear the development singing. The oats are red and taste of nudity. The flavor of the lobster is gleefully complete in its fuselage. The guides collide in the dark of the cave and find themselves bewildered by the square root of a stray cat. Can anything be truly savored in sleep? The brocade root has never sponsored a juxtaposition like this. I'm polished, towered, and propelled by a language whose gravity smells of opium. I garden cartwheels and leave the handsprings to the administrators. It takes a good break to stir a rub into earth. I consider the hotel and hold it in my hand like a moral. I heave into words this grease that I need to fill a thought with alcoholism. I usurp everything I see that isn't already detonated by morning. The supposition that something like wisdom exists is a door to our garments. I sit and sputter on the ground hanging bubbles from an emotional velvet. If tuna is my pepper than what is my pepper but a tuna disguised as a saltwater grammar? The gardenias increase my sighs. I have an attitude like a thermostat. I compose some water and play a mean flute. I agree to the fickleness of vowels and hem my phantom cuticles with a ghostly luster. Poetry is a cruel public drug. It needs to be constantly entertained by piles of laundry and beatnik vibrations. Let these waves flow over you. I'm laughing at the paint in my bag. The gravy is anchored in iambic dots like a beautiful fire escape on 14th street. It's time that time trumpeted its minutes with a horn of golden thunder. Nature is prominent in my reflections and when I walk I can hear the clatter of a million plates. I thrive on the sidewalks of Montmartre. The moonlight is smeared in the silent ovation of stars. I give this stab at meaning a little time to get unmuzzled and find its lips. The tongue is a monstrous organ. Think of what it can do when the lights go out and things turn green in the mind. I urge you to consider entomology as a profession. Let me unpack this thought in the quiet of my room, which is just now turning milky with mohair. This is what I like to do when I can't afford to do anything else. Which is climbing into me like rubber. I'm engorged. I'm pointing at something in the distance. I see planets. And triangles. And twinkle in my scruples like an instinct.

A Basket Of Reverie

I heave into words this grease that I need to anoint a thought with orchestration. Do we want a living reflection of the world or do we want foreignness & dragons? Are those binoculars? As you can see, I've created a birdhouse of words. Water can be random, & so can a house of words. This is why the lobster has a weird body. It was invented by water. Imagine being immersed in an activity with no commercial potential. This is a fluid situation. Everything floats. This is why absent-mindedness is the true wilderness of cognition. Abstraction feeds on reverie. As much as I ingest the world, I exhibit the world. Take the hammer. The hammer is immersed in its purpose. All it needs are nails. Once it gets the nails, we can build something. We can build a lobster. And call it a primrose. We can call it what we want. For this is the house of words.

The lessons of life are relatively easy. Pay attention. Notice things. Care for things. I hate giving advice. I'm not really cut out for it. But let me just say this: snow transforms the world. And so I blow soap bubbles for our cat. Because it's magic. She likes to sit and watch as the glistening little spheres come drifting down to the floor where they repose for a few seconds before popping. Which is what words do. They float through the mind causing coat hangers and boots. Closets are weird. Diseases are powerful tools. You can use them to get codeine. Fiddles are actually violins. The doors of perception may be opened by psilocybin, but don't wake the dog.

This is a messy place. The houses are full of eggs and syntax. Well-being is an altogether different matter. I have no idea what Nietzsche means when he says that morality is instinctual. If I were you I'd just get a hot dog and worry about it later. Wealth can mean so many things to so many people. The flair of seaweed remedies the carpet with a regatta of tattered memories. The fog bends itself into Omaha. Water is the central fact of our planet. All these years I've tried avoiding pain when I should've been watering it a little. Give it a mouth. Give it a pot and a calliope and a big fur hat. Give it a bed of topsoil and compost and see what grows out of that.

Did I hear Raymond Roussel enter the room? Arizona walks by carrying its canyons in a basket of reverie. Why does the universe exist? It sits blinking confusedly in a mailbox. Meanwhile, the herd goes by gazing at smartphones. A shaman stumbles out of a strip club. Heat moves the ebony wheels of a fierce consonant and a texture is born. It feels like stucco. Even the sidewalk holds still. Nothing is so impersonal that it doesn't require elephants. The landscape expands into erudition. The concertina lies in the street abandoned to its timelessness. My elbow is in control of its own reality. But sometimes I wonder. When life first emerged, was Proust in bed?

Bubbling

Everything manipulates a color today. The urge to make a shape is tilted. I feel my flight it mirrors the entire sky. Oars for a mindful calliope. The greeting is my vitamin of vocal rivers. I warp into nouns. Jingle them with a highway. The limousine within. I extrude a bewildered air. Abandon roots. I go after my plywood elephant. Pharmaceutical jar that the space milks. What this is is rain. . . The infinite teeming with opium parables. Blow into thumbs each claw and open door. This exists if it can exist and will exist and existence is incidental and beams are provided for the soap. My embarkation has been remedied by removing its destination. This is a dry public place. I've painted your beats on the drums. The address I used was fiddled by twelve elves and a bone. Elbows happen. It's athletic to appreciate mustard. The artist's ooze is a valentine to Braque. I'm over the resistance to my intestines. I believe we can endure our expressions if we use a little butter. I feel iron. A gyroscope furnishes my caboose with a spinning ripple of eyes. I grease the goldfish. I'll never abandon the life of the vineyard. The grapes bring us perceptions of another world. The operations are ordered according to eagerness. If I'm plump when I'm old does it matter if the turpentine is beaten with red sticks or blue? There's an evasion on the way. I wash my face with the tears of the moon. I feel a mental companionship with dirt. I can hear the gallop of horses and arrange my speech according to the luminous emotions I feel below. The garden is enthralling. The technology rattles and burns and stirs into life. This is by now apparent. The hammer is defined by its utility. But the nails are awakened by a piano. And this generates the words behind the grasp of the current.

Blister

A tiny blister has appeared on the index finger of my left hand. It's not on the bottom but on top, just behind the base of my fingernail. It wasn't caused by work or playing "Helter-Skelter" on an electric guitar. Nor do I see or sense a sliver. It just appeared. If I press on it, it hurts. I try not to press on it, but it's irresistible. Wounds are like that. We feel compelled to touch them. The blister is tiny, but very pronounced. And remarkably translucid. If I hold it just right in the light, I can see inside. I wish I had a magnifying lens. I wouldn't be surprised to see a fish swim by.

It's all just part of the aging process. Each day there's a new problem. The trick is to avoid seeing a doctor. My doctor is good. He's skilled and caring. The problem is the system. The medical system has become a criminal enterprise of extortion and overbilling. Sometimes our insurance will cover something and sometimes they won't. But even that isn't clear-cut. There's always confusion. Headaches and stress. It's easier to avoid the doctor altogether and hope that the malady resolves itself on its own or doesn't get more serious. It's better to live like a mountain man. Be self-reliant. If Hugh Glass was able to survive a mauling by grizzly bear in the wilderness, I should be able to live with a tiny blister on my finger.

Today is the summer solstice. And yet, at eleven in the morning our apartment is as dark as it is in the winter. The temperature is 58°F. It should be at least 70°F, our apartment ablaze with summer heat and light. I feel strangely detached and cosmic. Not so much detached as resigned, not so much cosmic as reflective. I'd like to be cosmic. Let's make that our goal. I want to be circular. It's better to be round than square. Round people roll. Square people get stuck. I don't want to be geometric at all. I want to be dazzling and romantic, like Lord Buttercup.

Lord Buttercup is an imaginary man I inhabit from time to time. He's dressed in Regency era clothes and dawdles around like a melancholy aristocrat.

Opposites mingle. It's that type of day. I want the truth, but I need my illusions. People squirm whenever you bring up the truth. It's always assumed that the truth is painful. Why is that? Maybe it's preferable to depend on those who quibble over the truth, who endlessly argue whether the truth is a reality or just an abstract concept trumpeted by narrow-minded grumps. Whoever has spent time walking on the shoulder of a busy highway knows what it feels like to be outside the matrix, to be exposed and vulnerable, but also a little wild and crazy.

One's habiliments are critical to the writing process, although I recommend nudity for the most stunning results. Words like it when I'm nude. Are words nude? Good question. I believe words light up whenever there's a mind around.

Can language get any thicker than mahogany? Mahogany is just a word, and yet the feeling it produces is breezy and theoretical, like Brazil in the evening, the phenomenology in a moment of luscious opacity. It's all signals and codes. Opacity is like that. Opacity is a few minutes of black genius making records in an electrifying wig, a pink sexuality maniacal as science. It's the specter of our future selves banging away on a piano, hidden fires looking over our shoulders.

There's a feeling that muscles its way into expression like a cement truck and just sits there, idling, the big barrel turning. This is why I like the idea of a hole. I can sprint toward it and then jump. And there I go. Into the hole. A feeling greets me on the other side. It's the same feeling that I had before, only shinier. Now it's a globule of pronouns. Clearly, this is a time for reflection. The mosquitos are hollow. Give them sugar. Give them shoes. But give them something. Give them substance. Give them experience. Give them a place to do their jobs. The sparkle of camaraderie. How about a garage. This is where we all crash into ourselves, expecting a kiss and getting a pair of work gloves instead. That's pretty much the story right there.

I'm telling you, Aerosmith is June. Turntable diamonds. The suitcase on my hip is full of bees, a whirling, sullen sea of eyes. Sit down, I think I love you. Pessimism is my reciprocal sponge, but my grammar is fat.

I walk down to the Pot Shop on Dexter to get a blister pack of Deeper Sleep gel caps. More blisters, but the good kind. This product helps me sleep better than a diazepam. It contains Indica terpenes such as Myrcene and Linalool, THC, CBD and Peony root extract.

On the way back I notice a few small shards of pottery and some broken glass in the driveway. I get a whisk broom and a dustpan and sweep it up. I return the whisk broom and dustpan to its hook in the laundry room and grab a pair of hedge clippers and go into the switchback trail in Bhy Kracke park to trim some of the thorny vines sticking out over the walkway. It gets in my way when I go for my run and I don't want to wait for the park department to get around to doing it. They appear to have cut back on their services. It figures. Property tax keeps escalating while city services keep declining.

Desire is the best way to come to know reality. Illusion is its sad consolation prize. Utopias generally lead to disaster. Avoid isms. Isms are prisons.

The way to what is most near to us is the longest and the most difficult.

Said Heidegger.

The margin constrains the circle.

Said Anne-Marie Albiach.

Our heads are round so our thoughts can change direction.

Said Francis Picabia.

Life is that which, undertaken, oscillates between wakefulness and dream. The kiwis come later, with fecundation and sunglasses. That's why I often feel the urge to introduce you to a coconut. I feel luminous, like a peach. And there's a door in my head. I'll open it and let you in if you meet me here at the end of the sentence. Can you hear it? It's the tinkling of chandeliers. The buttermilk is wearing alpine. The king rides by on a horse made of lightning. This is what writing is, what it's been along. A crustacean on the ceiling, a squid swimming out of my head.

Paper Revolt

I want to jingle when I walk. Experience shattering visions of alpine bears. I want to talk about the endless road of existence in a forlorn attic. New adjectives will have to be coined. I want to sit cross-legged in Rimbaud's grinning bones. I'm strongly attracted to everything and feel it exploding in my head. Nothing needs decipherment. Daylight ate my shadow. I'm capable of great distention. I understand a chair by sitting in it. I feel the great chain of being in my right thumb, and drop to the sandy bottom of Lake Eerie leaving behind a residue of words, syntax crashing around the soft breast of infinity.

I feel the lift of a powerful emotion, I don't know what it is, but the walls are burning down. Start your engines. Metamorphism swarms with energy. I see soap in a brown soap dish and think of digging a deep hole for a convocation of listeners. Sawdust trees. The walk will do us good. Genres can be mingled.

There's a dusty frontier town in my show. I've rigged it for salvation. I've polished the binoculars. Constancy falls into a trance. The candles are burning aloud. I hear the flames screaming like spots on the sun. I see an angel dribbling from a Christmas tree, the shadow of a vagabond merge with traffic, people scattering on the other side of the river, though a few are wading into shallow and rough water. Shout your lungs out. Tell them to stop. The implications are curiously dexterous, like the shapes in a Chicago nightclub, or a paper revolt.

I wear adversity like a garment. Gravity with a henna collar. I gaze at the wall. If we can extend the life of the grass, we will feel the ascension of angels in our hiccups. Do you believe in ghosts? Ghosts are a good idea. Please appoint me head of some confusion, any confusion, doesn't matter which, doesn't matter where, I'm just confused.

It's always tempting to accommodate one's illusions. They're all we have. Sometimes it's cruel not to say yes.

Let's explode the matrix to smithereens. My chaos is contagious. Let's pump some feeling to the surface and see what it does.

Seattle is a damp place. Everywhere I see concrete walls covered in moss and lichen, like walls of opium in a dream where I feel myself converging with the sparkle of ultramarine, and everything is taken in with gratitude and humbleness. We see birds on the ground, heads cocked to hear worms. Nothingness is underrated.

I've carved my reticence out of a bullet. But it's not working. It looks more like brocade for a thyroid gland than an infringement on my self-esteem, or a proverb with a reed mouthpiece.

I've detonated my regalia. What good is it now? Your presence here is much appreciated. Please know that.

Here I am galloping through another sentence. I like to bang around in a bong, a tube of air containing a totem of vowels, all the vibrations you'll ever need to see the fog in my blister. It comes to us by revelation, a narrative tornado tearing our conceptual greenhouse apart, yet strangely leaving all the orchids intact. I guzzle some whiskey and write a letter to the city council. We're all pulling a great weight, but here's a water pie to make your day go better. It gleams like a chisel on the wall. A hit song thrashing around in a jukebox. It holds my sweat in a stone. Exploration is a must. You can't go through life without exploring anything. That's why we're here. We're the universe exploring itself.

On Exhibit

Welcome to my museum. If this is a real day with real people in it we should give insouciance a another shove because we'll need it. I'm a mad little trumpet today, a feeling disguised as a sharp bright noise. I didn't think the neurosis would've gotten this big and walked all over my nervous system in such heavy boots. Here's an interesting exhibit it's a string of domestic animals filling the space between my furloughs. Glass case with a perpendicular speech act and the face of Samuel Beckett at age 78. Lustrous horse and a gun made of goose bumps. It shoots real nibbles. This makes everything inglenook and perpetual, the way paper trembles under a load of words.

Words do everything. Including thrust into ridicule feeling discontented and logged. Prayer is a bright multicolored beetle connecting interrelated elements for food and posterity. Or it could be. It can be anything. This is a word and it can be anything. It depends on how you read it. The boat's rudder will not be affected by your uniform. But the journey could use some old-fashioned navigation techniques, malleability and rubber.

If you ask me mysticism is celestial softball poker is a waste of television and matter is a form of energy periodically manifested as a tape measure.

Wicker fiction touchy fish that establish protocol for the behavior of water. Comical replication in a suitcase headed toward kettledrum olives. Is it literary to have more than one metaphor in your pants? Myriad virilities jiggled on a python patrol. You could say heat is a forearm frequented by shampoo. That would be masturbation's model as it scrambles for soap. Or that caring is a landscape within the reach of novelty.

I'm particularly wiggled by ninety protoplasmic mops. One of the things I think we need to take seriously is musk-ox. There's something very powerful going on. Why is it easier to imagine the end of the planet rather than the end of capitalism?

Avarice, in a nutshell. It explains everything. It explains heaven and fog horns. It explains patchwork and rain and the 9th letter of the alphabet which is just now inventing ice.

Merriment ensues. There will be licorice in our social conduct and root beer in our conversation. References in the act of determining fruit will be baked in semantic shellac.

How merry to marry a skirt. How merry to needle a toga. Together we will thread the air with rattlesnakes. Paleontological stars are perched on a backpack. An occasional nudge rewards my prison. Nearsighted recognition of a tadpole on a prescription for cough medicine the way I see porridge is large leaves and a renegade desire. I could leave now walk right out the door but instead I'm going to offer you a strong current of water and a ticket to our large stemmed glass parade. It begins at eight and soothes all substance by emitting little waves of sound and nomenclature.

Möbius Dick

Here's some thermometer thunder. You can muzzle the muzzy but you can't gratify everyone so why even try. Here's a calliope cocoon and here's a dusty daub of speed. I can feel it in this body I'm walking around in. I'm religious about mountain climbing. I'm also afraid of heights and have never climbed a mountain. But I'm still religious. Let's say I'm religious about mountains and leave it at that. Glue me to a prospect overlooking a beautiful temperature.

Death is a private affair. An unconditional lucidity. Frog plop in a woodland pond.

We all love a good fantasy. Here comes one now subversive and gray. Your age is not your actual age. Whatever diplomacy you bring to the pinnacle in Nietzsche's toolbox our life together is walnut. Push the drum kit closer. We all want to hear that rhythm, that splash of cymbals in the ovum of time. We endure the world best by opening to it. The painter's chin has paint on it.

Cerulean blue.

I fall into employment when the car door opens. I drive. I gnaw at a garden vegetable. I play with the air. It impels reflection. I play with money. It impels oligarchy and musk-ox.

Ages makes us sag. But I can mime the virtue of patience by standing in line minding my own business. I have a load of napkin rings, potato chips and pretzels. I have a door carved by a Viking sculptor and the sound of a saw screaming through a plank of wood is the bone black dissonance of a cognition modeled on the asymmetry of the hippocampus and amygdala. I'm flourishing here as a painter. I feel the sympathy of earth in a loaf of bread, how the universe is flourishing and expanding and how each star is a kneaded gob of plasma baked at temperatures above 104 degrees Kelvin and shining out of the void in a glaze of luminosity with nothing else to do but wait and see what God is going to do next.

Meanwhile the universe shines monotonous as a circumference that is everywhere and whose center is nowhere. Although I do believe matter and energy are one and the same cartwheel. You know? Something like the smell of snow, or an X-ray revealing the bones of a prophet. Words have that power. This very minute your eyes are holding my language as I get off this stool and drag a bundle of magazines closer.

I'm writing a play about a man and a woman on a raft negotiating the rapids of an eyeball. It has neither ending nor beginning. I call it Möbius Dick.

Lord let the obloquies give me power till the realism gets here. I feel you under my skin. I can hear the estuary stroll into a melody and moo like a sparrow at high tide. Wood speaks to wood. I flex both my arms in a greenhouse and power this introspection with the steel gonorrhea of a rubbed astronomer. An infinite jest enriches our confusion. A little nasty fondling here and there is good for the soul. My brain feels gray as the fur of an old cat walking over a banana and a pineapple on an operating table. The ethicist mumbles something half asleep in an armchair, a statement bewildering as a tumor, leg with an odd bump. Dusty old book cluttered with hymns. A jar of pickles.

Rattlesnakes aren't cruel they're just rattlesnakes. Morality doesn't exist in nature. Grace and energy belong to the realm of the highway. This is where words and people collide creating sparks. And where, sooner or later, people might gradually perceive the universe in a single human voice.

Word Salad Slingshot Lacquer

Sentimental litmus dust. I think, therefore I'm excruciating. This must be hokey. Hobnailed obstetrics. Vascular outlet for an inscrutable rhythm. Mustard is more than a taste it's also a transition to something disheveled. Palette on a road. Paregoric snivel dressed in a negligee. Tom-tom touchdown seasoned with iodine. I know a geology when I see one. It proceeds by Jell-O locomotive. Ok, I'm ointment. Now what?

Lissome refreshments produce a type of introversion known as oyster through the lips. Royalty in a can Yosemite mullet the rhetoric of a mineral. Tolerable tombstone I have plenty of meditation to give you please come closer and I will dissolve in your crucible of rules. Woolgathering is my favorite form of pragmatism. Trowel sentry modest as an oboe.

Here comes some gravity to help keep us massive. Matter is often drowned by too much werewolf. Socialize and return to your ivory vista. The horn is your guide. Grow patient and get a lake. Individuality is a crisp thin fungus. It takes a lot of hard work and dedication to become a crackpot.

I'm sometimes intimate with a sentence that comes to me in the night and occupies the quiet mathematics of willow. The air is electric with death. Paper gives us the world it demands. We create one by scrounging. I'm spending a lot of time in the closet. Do I want a Being that is partial and above it all, or a Being so immersed in Portugal that I can see the cork oak forests of the Alentejo plains from the olive grove at the end of this sentence? The world appears different when the traffic lights sing. The signs are in turmoil. Our language has been abused by a man with an orange face & a trumpet of hair. Capitalism doesn't love you. Would it be simpler if it did? Imagine swimming through God when you take to the air. For such is the power of art.

Grog

I meet my sweet notebook wearing an almond scarf log. One's habiliments are critical to the writing process, although I recommend nudity for the most stunning results. Words like it when I'm nude. Are words nude? Good question.

I'm the king whose singular claw has a compelling stab at grasping the sky and making dimes of water fall out of it. I understand it enough to begin combing a wild stratosphere of hair. Thursday's hibiscus is a ripple of resonance, a flambé of hip butter. I move to develop more fees.

The ocean is a stew of groaning passage. The golden law of speed is an ice clock bursting out of time. The canary recounts his gobble.

Wait: do canaries gobble?

This one does. I can use it to calculate the sweating alpine of my lungs as I climb into beauty.

This is the kite's side of the region, the aurora under a fir tree. If I say that I can bend the truth the truth will make a gun out of a bar of soap and point it at H.G. Wells. Think of this paragraph as a time machine. Or a mug of beautiful rocks. We call this poetical because it snaps into a place like a rubber band. It thickens like chowder. It summons a prophesy.

Night glitters in its empire. The horses jingle in their bells. You can masturbate almost anywhere. But try to be discreet.

All it takes is a puff or two to blow the little hairs off of the computer screen.

Nothing is really empty. Not even nothingness is empty. This is what makes Mallarmé so unpredictable. Splendor, glory, magnificence and softball.

There's a loud whack and the ball bounces to left field where it is caught by a pterodactyl and carried to the end of this sentence and dropped. I pick it up and hear a giant monotony walking around inside of it. There's a cure for that as well. But it must be smeared into the air with drums. Kettledrums. Talking drums. Bougarabou. Jazz brushes with red rubber handles.

Rubber bands didn't exist during the time of the Roman Empire. Rubber was discovered by the Olmecs who used it in their ballgames. The Mesoamerican ballgame was similar to racquetball. Me, I'm not much into sports. I prefer sitting in armchairs having conversations with myself. Wondering what thought is. And how to get rid of it.

Coffee sits in my brain knitting a rhinoceros. I go up drinking and come down netting thought. I say hi to the dagger tree and taste the Renaissance in parcels of air.

Paper head pool swarming with tar chickens. Root shirt with bonfire buttons. Bees reflected in the wheelhouse of my grommet viola. I'm telling you, Aerosmith is June.

This time what I want is completely mail. Letters from the gentry. Turntable diamonds.

Sparrows surround the ceiling injury. The elevator is distant that lifts my smile into tennis. The cynical redness of my reasons is all I have to greet the oleomargarine in your monkeyshines. But I can always moor my words in dirt. The monastery of chaos is surrounded by it. Here comes the buttermilk to this capharnaüm of a raspberry. It will open your biology to all sorts of lettuce.

The suitcase on my hip is full of bees, a hollow, archaic material that feels palpable as a tonsil in a loose robe of mucous. A sullen sea flies through my brain dropping heavy arena stars. I toss another jewel into the quantum soup I made yesterday while studying the amphibians in your eyes. It explodes into grog.

A Gorilla In The Mirror

I'm a young tour toughened by shrines, a peremptory vicar personifying bingo. My gooseberries look posy. I have lions in my mulch. Pessimism is my reciprocal sponge. I'm nonchalant about shoulders but totally creamy when I'm bouncing around in a knuckle. My duty is to elves. I'm decisive about the nervous system but a little vague when it comes to donkeys. When I see a gorilla in the mirror I know it's time for coffee. The blemish perched on my fury multiplies the springs in my mattress. I'm all about offices. I like chairs that swivel and paper that lights up when I strengthen it with words. Please feel free to explore a parliament. There are more junkyards where that came from. Yes I'm deformed, but who isn't? Coffee walks around on my canvas looking for a sport. My altitude is caustic, but my flutter is fat.

How The Fish Feel

Coffee permeates my bones. The sound of an oboe soothes my development. I feel like iron. I find the rustic everywhere. For example, my forehead describes agriculture the same way as my forebears, which is to say furrows and duck-billed hats.

A mutation goads what we graze into protein and speech. The hills groan with the burden of their own astonishing reality. I can see it in your eyes: perspective. It steams like a moose. That's why I'm laughing at the road.

I shake a rattle over the abyss of my seclusion. Seclusion is an illusory state, as are wealth and religion, but I need it for thermodynamics and alibis. The migrations remain magnetic, apostrophes of artless opacity, odd little people with astronomical interiors. The road sews its distances in the shade of an oak tree, where they leaven into a fever, a mania for wheels.

I sense the trembling of water under the bridge of what is assumed to be knowledge. The throat collects a sentence with a clarinet in it, then lets it loose on a tongue of fire. I climb into a prophecy oozing the honor of a thousand distant moons. I grab some socks and begin arguing with my feet. If thought is a buffalo painted on rock, expectation is a torch.

I like the vibrations of airplanes. I like the way wax melts on candles. I am fascinated by the trails that disappear in the forest. The colors of Illumination scream inside my anguish while the echoes of parliament elude the subtlety of steam. I perceive the glow of congeniality in the straw of a newborn cynosure.

How is the world perceived? Algebra crushes an emotion into deeper feeling. The equations are sugar, but the differentials are orange. I sift my opinions through a vermilion rain. Hallucinations elevate prospects of chalk. The story of my life is embroidered on a bedsheet, which is how the world is perceived, at least from my viewpoint, which is wedded to other viewpoints, which create a totem of adorable hypnosis.

We live in a trance. Who wouldn't? I mean, give me a break. Our instincts are embedded in grease. Our being is peppered throughout by pain.

We feel special when we bring our performance into the public sphere, and this helps to push our enthusiasm toward the kind of metamorphism that provides testimony for such events. The wings develop naturally, and the streets of

Prague fill with memory. If I fold it a sufficient amount of times, this emotion will fly through the air and land on a decorative representation of Lao Tzu, who knew just how the fish feel.

Opinion

Everything drips opinion. I like my opinions the best. They are, of course, the very best opinions that an idle mind can produce. I work hard at forming my opinions. I know it looks like I'm doing nothing, but in reality, I'm training my telescope on the universe and taking notes and forming opinions. I'm forming opinions about reality. Good opinions. Opinions that you can take to the bank. Opinions tough as shoe soles.

People get irritated and walk away. Which goes to show. You can't trust people.

What is the interaction between the body and the mind? I'm not sure. Go ask a drug. The doors of perception may be opened by psilocybin, but don't wake the dog.

If you feel, for example, that someone has injured you unfairly with a comment or brush off or cold shoulder the emotion can be quite real. But is it real? Or is it a misinterpretation? And even if it's an accurate reading of a presumed friend treating you like an asshole what does it matter? It might feel like they stabbed you in the gut but they didn't and if you look down you'll see that none of your intestines are falling out and there's no blood just an untucked shirt and a gravy stain.

Is this why life was created? The spirit crackles with hypothesis. Planet earth is a sensation of calm, until it isn't, and then it's all about volcanoes and war.

Idaho walks by carrying mushrooms and pans. Go ahead, shout at the appliances until something wet makes you beautiful. You do what you're good at. Until you're completely dirt.

Why is reality so big and mysterious? Is it an energy, or a social construction? And what about consciousness? Does anyone know what consciousness is? This much we know: ambiguity is a rolling mass of forest.

Should I include a biography at this point? Think of me as a bee dangling from a stem of corollaries. I never stop questioning the reality of carrots. They're roots, which is understandable, considering their shape, but why does the moon stand still on a hill emanating the silken underwear of a rogue tattoo? You can see it in the bear and the dream inside the bear. The mind is ravenous for honey.

You can swim in a metaphor, but will it duplicate the candor of Dakota topsoil? Dirt is the ultimate metaphor. It's where seeds take root. Sunflowers. Beans. Vincent Van Gogh.

We hop over a penumbra on the ground as it goes pulsing and undulating over a row of motorcycles. What is Being? I can see it in my sweat. But I don't know what it is. I indulge the bananas and walk toward a coincidence.

I fold myself into a ukulele and flap the air with my socks. Because I'm explosive. And little by little the doll inflates. I need to be elsewhere. And where is elsewhere? Elsewhere is elsewhere. It's not a place. It has no longitude or latitude. It has no velocity, no trajectory or position in time. It's outside of time. It's outside of science. It's beyond the reach of rational investigation. There's no way to explain it logically or judiciously. It's a mindset. A feeling. An understanding. An aura.

A dragon walks out of my mouth and falls asleep in a sentence. Everyone is invited. Each face contains a story. Another sentence comes along and crashes through the table. Space can be flat even if it isn't. It isn't mass that causes gravity. It's grief. The lessons of life are relatively easy. Avoid paper cuts and war.

Outer Space

Is being a feeling? Being is a feeling. Thinking about being is mongrel and atmospheric. Can there be anything more useless than thinking? Yes: rumination. Rumination leads to rumination, which leads to pleats in motel curtains.

Thinking isn't fun. Sometimes it's fun, but mostly it's not much fun. Thinking takes my mind to places I would prefer to avoid.

"There can be no other human activity more extravagant," observed George Steiner on the matter of thinking, "very nearly the incessant aggregate and totality of thinking flits by unnoticed, formless and without use. It saturates consciousness and presumably the sub-conscious, but drains off like a thin sheet of water on baked earth."

Consider me baked.

Life is a sadness that can be hard to maintain by hitting a tambourine all day by the side of the road. Sometimes a melody will give rise to a foundry of infinite pewter. The ribs are boleros of welcome fire. Let's choose a song and then sing it while dancing in circles around the piano. There is much to be sung about chalk. Most of the songs are about our sagas. Millions of molecules convening in skin. Because opacity is like that. Opacity is a few minutes of black genius making records in an electrifying wig, a pink sexuality maniacal as science. It's the specter of our future selves banging away on a piano, hidden fires looking over our shoulders.

Where am I? I'm hiding in my brain. The brain is an organ, a large wooden box in which wind is kept under pressure. When a key is pressed, a valve is opened in the cerebellum, and thus the pipes speak. Giant thoughts wander around like mazurkas. Heaven resides there, but that's not saying much, since heaven is everywhere. Heaven is in full view but no one sees it, except for an old woman swaying from side to side, entranced by the shine of ointment jars at the drugstore. In Heidegger's words, "To be a particular being means to be immersed in nothingness." This primordial, annihilating chaos is ever-present; wherever there is darkness, wherever there is silence, wherever any wish or belief is negated, there is Ginnungagap. This delightful item comes with a careless attitude and an adjustable waist band. Helmets and swords are not included.

Become a barefoot writer. And live the life of a famous writer without having to write a block-buster movie script or a chart-topping book. Pour yourself another coffee. Sit down. Stare out the window. Feel the immediate squeeze of circumstance. This is where we begin to drift into writing, believing in nothing, open to everything, capturing the flow of ideas and walking around in an ecstasy of convulsive postulation. Ideas tumble around in the brain like a load of wash in a Maytag dryer. My Salvador Dali underwear crashes into my Isaac Newton sweater.

I think I see a feeling. What's it doing? I don't know. But write it down.

Life on planet Earth is getting weird. The people of Earth have gone insane. They wrap everything in plastic. Everything. Eggs, electronics, sanitizers, deodorants, pliers.

And what's this? This is what outer space looks like when it's stuck to a bunch of words.

Destiny

Destiny is what happens in old age. For example, I can picture Wyoming, but I cannot picture the horror of eternity. Which is why, on any given day, I can't get Vincent van Gogh out of my head. Is there anything to say about art that hasn't been said already? The corollaries are violent enough. How do you know when something is music or just plain noise? All I know is that if we gaze behind the curtains iguanas push softly against our legs. And that's how language works. The sky cracks open holding an old guitar and furnishes us with different ways of feeling Ohio.

My brain weighs approximately three pounds. Planet Earth weighs about 1,000 trillion metric pounds. I can't squeeze a 1,000 trillion metric ton planet into a three-pound brain. I can, however, make a pot of coffee that feels like wildlife.

Why are artists always stuck with defending art? This is not a happy planet.

A careless hue expresses rain. A dragon in my head has a being that is nebulous and soft. I have a craving for indiscriminate beginnings.

Life is an enigma. Consider the lilies. They don't need jobs. They don't need dishwashers or clocks. It's a good life, being a lily. Do that. Be a lily.

Time collapses on itself and the wind is itself again. How can anyone not enjoy putting words together? The greatest realities are usually the most obvious, which makes them hard to find. For example, are we our thoughts, or braided and abstract like conversation?

We need to be more fully, more insanely, maniacally actual. I apologize for these generalities. Most of life is a huge chaotic mess. I can't explain eyebrows. We are but the sad opacity of our future specters, said Mallarmé. Can language get any thicker? It's all signals and codes, frogs in platform shoes flying helicopters around La Sagrada Familia in Barcelona.

The accordion eludes me. But true innocence deforms the sink. Nothing in mathematics is ever friendly. There are ecstasies in the rocking trees. This is where flirtatious 35-year old Charlotte Shufflebottom stumbles into the poem, explaining that she has a thing for older men, along with the poetry of Edna St. Vincent Millay. I tell her she has the wrong poem and open the door to let her out.

This is destiny in action. Death is nothing. Let your eyes carry this sentence to the end of itself. When you arrive at the end, you will find an abyss. You will see ice and snow. Pain floating in the eyes of a stranger. And that stranger is you. Or not. Maybe it's Micky Rourke. Or Meryl Streep. Did you forget to fall in love today? I didn't. I just now fell in love with a Dutch apple pie. It fills me with joy and gladness, and I am no longer a stranger to the kitchen.

Why are ghosts always represented as bedsheets?

Describe a fork. There's opium in poetry. A wedge of it is enough to light Spain. Or you can just squirt diamonds until the knots come undone. Language is an hallucination and when there's nothing left of it but shadows we still have Karen Carpenter singing "Superstar." At this very moment my favorite noun is getting naked in somebody's house and bleeding thrift stores all over the rug. Even the birds in my hair correspond roughly to the words with which I declare myself to be a coat hanger. Ok this is weird. I get it. But hey, if it ain't broke don't fix it. Just shout at the appliances until something wet and peculiar happens. I swear it will fix your dog.

Alpine

Alpine enters mechanically and velvet crusts the glass. We should report the foundry to the calliope operators. Why? Because varnish is sparrows. Because camaraderie extrudes from our metamorphic hands. Because fingers are duly employed in bone and the windows are haunted by syllables. Because the song of all the bees needs a Renaissance and all the thrilling vermilion in the world can't satisfy the hunger of our dreams.

Which are nebular as hamburgers in a landslide.

And garnished with thorn.

I feel tilted on Tuesday, incalculable on Wednesday, and kleptomaniacal on Thursday. I'm sorry I stole your stigmas. They were just sitting on the shelf looking derelict and weird. That's no way to treat a stigma. Stigmas need scars and opprobrium. Otherwise what's the point?

Kite the drinking hum. Fill the plum with swirls. Scold the lavender theatre. The birth of a Danish diving board is langoustine. It needs our full attention. This is no audiobook talking to you in your car. This is the bliss of the attic. This is the feeling of climbing an expensive tree and thinking to cure the sea with the aromatic whispers of the swimming pool. The one bubbling in the unconscious.

The unconscious is a heat at the base of the brain. The swell of an honest handkerchief. The wind ploughing the lake into itself. Plumage forged in a dazzling necessity. Scarlet raising an annoyance of lavish perception, the kind one finds in drugstores, swaying in the aisle.

But this says nothing of trinkets and the awakening awake of Sunday. Ok, you can open your brain now and find some coupons. Take a deep breath. Can you smell it? Can you feel it?

That's right. It's a coupon for ballast. You'll need some if you feel like saying something openly radical to the knives. The ground screams cloth. It's waving its levers at our clothes.

Fingers make a snowball. Muscles rock the drapery. The queen is blatantly entangling her letters in a statement about the transitory nature of everything. To die sullenly of laziness is one option. Another is to die into life as life lives itself through death. It feels singularly quantum at the edge. This is where all the dark energy of the cosmos comes together to form a cup of hot chocolate.

And yes, I agree, I can feel redemption slip through us in the department store. Maybe we should go outside. The quintessence of the needle is in its unthinking acuity. The lobster wanders the bottom of the ocean smoking a big cigar. The unbalanced forest tattoo finds a panacea in an asymmetrical car.

Let's not forget butter. If the coinage is good and the heart is willing, the fiesta will be honored at all the local haunts. Just take a deep breath and cross the threshold. The cure to pain is in the pain itself, said Rumi. That said, one wonders what it's like to actually see a language crawl around on its syllables creating hindsight and wakes. Why do I always expect to see things appear in language when language itself is everywhere doing and undoing its knots?

The answer to this is a rapid vibration, but I can't quite make it out.

Is language truly an instrument of thought, or something entirely different, junk in the garage, old albums and rakes? In the end it is alpine that matters, alpine that simmers and quakes, that shouts back the sky in the purity of its lakes.

By Implication

Implication is better than teargas. Implication can be used in multiple ways, whereas teargas has essentially but one application, which is making people scatter. Implication can be used in mining, philosophy, and ice skating events. Teargas is just good for crowd dispersal. Implication fails in this respect. I've attempted implying that people clear a room so that I may be alone, but it generally misfires. No one seems to know what I'm talking about. That's when I like to bring out a canister or two of teargas. It's pure magic. Everyone runs away screaming.

Implication can be injected into a conversation almost at any point. Results may vary, but depending on whatever it is you're attempting to imply, implication works better than teargas in virtually every instance. Teargas is not conducive to conversation, but if it's solitude you want, you can't beat it.

Once, at a UN conference, I was in a bad mood. I wanted to be alone, but was too sedentary to rise from my seat and find a private room. I just lobbed a couple of tear gas canisters and cleared the room instantly.

The ensuing wars were not my fault. But if any dignitaries were unduly inconvenienced, I apologize.

Implication can, by undertone and innuendo, have a lot of imputation in it. Implication is folding. It's reciprocal, sporadic, and casual. Implication may contain bromides, boll weevils, or venison, but it will always love you in return, especially when it waddles into a conversation like an artery and deepens someone's gabardine.

What I'm attempting to suggest here is simply this: syllogisms are clunky. It's almost always better to use syllogisms late at night or first thing in the morning. Off-peak hours are generally 8 pm to 7 am. Thus, when Aristotle begins in Book 7 of the Metaphysics to ask what makes a thing a thing, he narrows the question to apply only to living things. He doesn't infer it. He moves it into the totalities of signification and intelligibility where it can be reached by spiritual insight, and then hammered into a piece of old gray wood, just like the revival guitar players. This isn't explicit. But it's implied.

Consider The Banana

You know that cycle you get into, that Möbius loop, whenever you have an accident, to keep going over it again and again, if I'd only done that, if I'd just checked that, If I'd only looked that way instead of the other way, believing, somehow, that eventually a door will open into the past and give you another chance? I hate that. Is there anything you can order from Amazon that allows you to edit your life?

This is how thinking begins. There is an energy in the head demanding guns and knives. And then I shave and think differently.

Consider the banana. It has an amiable smell and taste, peels with ease and helps nourish our understanding of the world. A philosophy may be found there but you will need a hammer to smash it. You will need planning and concrete. Language is slippery when it enters the world. The essential thing is skin. A vowel without a consonant is nothing. But a vowel enclosed within a sack of consonants will develop a spine and walk.

What exactly does it mean to activate the organs of speech, to move the tongue and the lips, to cause a vibration in the larynx, to fill an utterance with breath and set it sailing into the world? When we say something about something, we make it lie before us, we make it appear.

For example: Wyoming. Wyoming is rocky and smells like Zen. You'll like it.

If I say I see a lotus in a birdbath and a lotus in a birdbath appears, I feel both satisfied and a little nervous. Saying a thing is seeing a thing. And if a thing appears you should talk to it and see what it wants.

But this has little to do with Wyoming. Wyoming gets up and walks away. Goodbye, Wyoming, it was good to see you.

I'm going to take a leap and say we are caught between two worlds. The world of the spirit and Costco. Costco has refrigerators, but the spirit has Netflix, scented candles, and Nina Simone. We propose methods to detect relational similarities between the slot screw and Philips head screw by using the ontological structure of semantic representation. For example, the hot dog rotator at 7-11. If that doesn't work, life itself will give us lessons in sweat equity. Doors slamming. People yelling. Buddhists carrying the banner of dharma over the dead. What does it even mean to lead a normal life? We should step away quietly and stand on the porch and listen to the rain.

Isn't Donald Trump final, incontrovertible proof that there is no correlation whatever between how much money one possesses and the quality of one's character? Yes? No? Maybe?

If I say the opposite of what I mean the result is clumsily arabesque. This is a wisdom that comes from the eye of a needle. If I sew what I see the mind considers it seen. Or sewn. Seen and sewn. Sewn and seen. The needle penetrates the fabric of thought and goes up and down, in and out, creating patterns that contradict the ontology of popcorn. Art that drags itself across the floor like hot red blood gleams with breath and sand. The buckets are carried by Buddhists. A patch of cloud walks past the moon. Isn't that what we've wanted all along, to travel in a rocket ship to Mars?

Democracy failed us. But maybe art will bring us back to our senses. Or at least Greece.

Bombast

They call it bombast. I call it kerosene. They call it inflation. I call it watermelon. Sometimes I screw things in the heat and nobody says anything. If everything and nothing happen simultaneously, I call it art. I follow fat wherever it goes. Our dramas are clumsy but our creameries are tranquil. If I have nothing to say I say it anyway. I have no secrets. I have tendencies. I have airplanes and butter. I've got movies and marijuana balloons. Coincidences and twigs. I've seen eyeballs squirt clouds into an empty sky and an empty sky walk into watercolor. I sigh anytime I see henna. No art is going to show you reality any clearer. I'm not trying to do that. It would be a waste of time. I'm simply trying to chip harder at the walls until a vein of gold appears. We're in darkness. We're in darkness all the time. On the brightest of days we're in darkness. You can feel it. It's palpable. But there are moments when a little diffuses throughout like the sfumato in Italian painting. The air turns turquoise and orange. I believe art has that power. But it's a mistake to believe it has anything to do with reality. It's about perception. It's about fullness. It's about the richness of experience. Intensity. It's about intensity. It's about unicorns and Donald Duck. Milkshakes and bean burritos. The ordinary made extraordinary. There are more than five senses. Let's get that straight at least. There are probably more like thirty. But who's counting? I want more. I always want more. And yet they say a god made us. Think of Ophelia dashed to the floor by the madman she loves. She loved. Has anyone fully fathomed this confusion and come up smiling to talk about it? They say nuclear burning of helium can plausibly give the amount of titanium-44 that can explain antimatter. I'm not going to get in the way of that. I'm not here to argue. But I like the idea of antimatter floating in my martini like an olive of tart cognition. Touching a napkin of antimatter to see it explode. Blow the whole city into oblivion. That would be one hell of a martini. I see a man performing on an open-air stage at twilight in Hyde Park London England in 2009. He sings about shooting his lover down by a river. He plays an electric guitar, sounding notes, stretching notes, banging notes, hammering notes, stroking notes, caressing notes, bending notes. Does this answer Aristotle's question regarding the ultimate purpose of human existence? No. But it describes our situation pretty well. It sounds like huge beasts clashing, howling, sparks flying, pretty trills suddenly appearing. It perfectly demonstrates Aristotle's position that the particularity of a substance cannot rest on an underlying characterless substratum. It must rest on an e minor 7. A C major 7, then G, D, DA, G, then DA, then back into the verse. Being doesn't act alone. It requires engagement with the world. You'll need a harpsichord, at least, and a nice warm bath.

Conversation

Conversation will often reveal the most amazing things. First there is an intention to shave. You want to pay attention to that. Shave. Brush your teeth. Comb your hair. Then join a conversation. That's how it's done. Primal, primitive, and fast. Consider the banana. Talk to it. Put it against your ear. What is it saying? The Rolling Stones have 36 platinum albums. Yet the impulse to make art continues. It can't be stopped. It's bigger than TV, or what is on TV, tits and dragons. Get something going in your brain then talk about it. The barter of suet, the murmur of silks.

This is why angels are often equipped with sewing kits. Reality is torn. The recommendations are unfettered and all the movies are bad. But who cares? The prophecies are still boiling.

I'm not sure what to think of it. Driving, insomnia, germs, time, death. You name it. You can worry about the government leaders so consumed with greed and power that they go mad and blow up the world or declare martial law and shut everything down. But who wants to feed that monster? And then there's the guy I saw today holding a device over the street, moving it along, it had a pointed rod and a meter at the other end, I think it was some form of sonar, radar, it made pretty sounds, melodic little bleeps, I assume he was trying to find a pipe. Devices like that are so wonderful. They help us make connections between appearances. We can know how things appear to us, but very little about the things themselves since we must rely on our limited faculties to arrive at even a superficial understanding of what they are. By device, I mean of course, metal detectors, ultrasound, psilocybin, peyote, and Percy Bysshe Shelley.

The romantic spirit isn't dead. Maybe it's not a spirit at all. Maybe it's a truck. Or a stepladder. My chief preoccupation is cultivating exotic anxieties. I realize, of course, that worrying does little to express the self-consciousness of zoos. Or outer space. Sandra Bullock lost, quietly resigned, gazing at a panel of buttons rendered in Mandarin. Outer space is freaky. If I let a thing like eternity bounce around in my brain too long a charge builds. My head will explode. I will splatter the walls and ceiling with eternity. Here's what I do: I think of the phosphorescence of foam at the stern of a ship. Which exists in eternity with all the other haunted ships of this world.

Official Anthem Of The
Ping Pong Litmus Association

Puff my unit. The crack I whisper. This zipper glaze honesty. Slither plunge configurational motion door. The crab lights up. This banana gurgles. This meditates my hirsute.

A thought flutters through a talk. I get behind a hint. It ushers a fuse to you. An ultramarine blaze.

We wear stepladder masks and crumple into frogs. A sloppy movement hefts a blue stigma. Necessitates it. We call the gnome. I scratch myself into henna.

The door gets its space over a batch of weather. My pasting for instance. The painter is innocent from swans. Smooth lake arguing increase. Opium is the pressed medication that opens diversion. If you have a spoon try the granite.

Burst dish. Atmospheric gargoyle chain. Acceptance romance. The hair has presence. The red bursts into robbery. Slouch world pulls its trickles to titbits. The snow steams on my glockenspiel.

Hold these brushes. A fiber dangles an academy. Initiates a Technicolor tomahawk. Hollywood here I come!

I collect myriad indicatives. We thicken enfoldments to marble it all.

I feel a certain wrench. A winch beneath the sun.

This will fill the scratch. The slow hold of pasting. The opened burst my impart. And then I subpoenaed a door. There rattled a crack. It burst its hinges and flew. There is a reason for radar. You know?

What gargantuan space brought meditation to hair?

The zipper puffed in heartwood and remembered the dishes.

Electric Yellow Hamlet

The rags of fever are thirsty for Niccolò Paganini's Caprice No. 3. It deserves some mention. The haphazard communion of spheres is a resistance to the rigidity inherent in order. The spheres, in this instance, are tidepools dressed in rags called human beings. The lack of necessity makes art a rag, a fabric soaked in turpentine. It gets your attention, but it won't stop the woman upstairs from doing the dishes eight hours a day, or serving dinner to a family of hallucinations. That's a private drama. It's within the purview of art, but not in an easily identifiable way. My thinking about this is an eye on the other side of this paragraph, looking at something completely different: the hot dog rotator at 7-11.

I will be the meaning I want, lavender buttons and beans. This is my electric yellow Hamlet, the sweet beginnings of a soliloquy. What's solipsism? What's a syllogism? What's a spermatid? Is it something the sperm did? Is death a journey? Is Being a thing like lilies or whippets? Or is it just a product of our thought? Does anyone really know? What about jaws, and brightness, and indigestion? I believe there's gold in the soft monotony of the brain and that dark matter is the cause of all this extra whipped cream and gravity. Should one surrender to the luxuries of nihilism or continue to revolt and make art? I don't know. Why make it a choice? The sky speaks to us through the bright red stems of a Pacific Fire vine maple. It gives us words that we don't understand. The indefinability of Being is a ball of muscle beating in a surgeon's hand.

Imagine all mental activity as a nice white knob on a door. Big decisions can be paralyzing. Should I open it? The rain walks around in my brain getting all my thoughts wet. Society is collapsing all around us but nobody seems to give a shit. What can I say? Intense people can find it hard to maintain friendships. I spend most of my time moving around in poems like Janis Joplin belting it out in Monterey. Except I'm not Janis Joplin. And I'm nowhere near Monterey. I'm in my pajamas taking in the sunset on Mars. Look at all those dinosaurs. How did NASA get everything so wrong? We live in a trance. Who wouldn't? The rest of this emotion is air.

Atoms Contemplating Atoms

It's a Thursday in late January, cold and rainy. I go for a run. I'm fascinated by a house under construction at the end of Bigelow. It's been going up so fast. Within a week, I've seen walls and a roof appear on what is a two-story house. It's fun seeing something evolve like this on a day to day basis.

The puddle on the other side of the McGraw Street Bridge crossing the astonishingly deep Wolf Creek Ravine has become so large due to the heavy rains of the past several days that it should have a name, Lake McGraw or Lake Liliuokalani, after Lydia Kamakaeha, the first and only reining Hawaiian queen. Why name a puddle after a Hawaiian queen? No reason whatever. I like the name, and will stick by it, although it is unofficial, and no one knows about it but me.

I smell food cooking when I pass the Five Corners Hardware Store. It must be coming from the Bite Box next door, a new restaurant of sorts. I can't quite tell what it is. That little business section there has always been a bit of a puzzle. There's an Edward Jones financial advisor office next to the Bite Box. You can buy a screwdriver, enjoy a snack, and plan your retirement all on the same block.

I pass Malena's Taco Shop and notice that there are still cracks in the large glass panel of the entry door. I wonder how that happened. Did someone try to break in? Did someone leave in high dudgeon over a soggy taco and slam the door?

I pass an abandoned armchair getting soaked in the rain at the corner of Garfield and Sixth Avenue West. There's a birdhouse nailed to the telephone pole.

I did not see any birds at all during my run, other than a few crows. This is very strange. I'm guessing it has to do with the wildfires of last summer, heavy air pollution and habitat loss.

I drop off a DVD at the library, *Flamenco, Flamenco* by Carlos Saura. R and I love watching dance, particularly flamenco. The dance in this movie was phenomenal. The grace, the foot-stomping defiance and life-affirming bravado are fantastic to behold.

January 19th, Friday evening at about 5:30 I lie on the bed, my feet and legs angled so as not to disturb Athena who is napping nearby, and read *Earth and Reveries of Repose: An Essay on Images of Interiority* by Gaston Bachelard. It's all about our imaginative engagements with the material world and supplemented by many instances gathered from literature. Bachelard believes that our intimacies with the material world inspire happiness and reverie.

Reverie is an important word in Bachelard's lexicon. It refers to a dilation of being, an expansion of soul and a highly nuanced multiplicity of perspective, a deep immersion in our experience of the world and how our sensations and feelings are converted to dream and poetry, how they reveal, through our unconscious, the deeper secrets of existence.

I'm currently immersed in the chapter on labyrinths. These aren't the multicursal puzzles we see on coins and rocks and sidewalks, such as the terrazzo outdoor labyrinth on the north side of Grace Cathedral of San Francisco, which is there for pedestrians to do a walking meditation, an opportunity to enjoy some reflection and calm the mind.

Or the maze in the Laurel and Hardy movie *A Chump at Oxford*, in which the two men get lost in a maze of hedges at Oxford and sit down on a bench to sleep and a hand reaches through the hedge and removes Oliver's white handkerchief form his breast-pocket and puts it in Stan's breast-pocket and tickles Oliver's mustache and makes him sneeze.

Bachelard's labyrinths are subterranean, chambers of serpentine geology, some real, some gleaned from dream. All caverns are inherently oneiric. We—like Laurel and Hardy—frequently get lost in them. Being lost is a state of mind. One can be lost in one's mind. I can attest to that: it happens all the time. I get tagged by a worry which lures me into a maze of my own making, a cognitive maze of ramifying anxieties, which may lead to a bright light of revelation, a Platonic opening that leads out of the subterranean realm into the blinding rays of the sun and ultimate reality, or just get me more deeply entangled in my cerebral convolutions. Sometimes the best way out is to discover, à la Neo in *The Matrix*, that none of it is real.

Bachelard references a work by Adolphe Badin titled *Grottes et Cavernes*, in which is described a narrow ladder for descending into the darkness of a cave. At the bottom of the ladder is a very narrow hole. One must lie on the floor and move forward by gripping what Badin describes as cakes made of honey. Bachelard seizes this detail to make an allusion to Trophonius, a hero of Greek mythology who may have been either a demon (a daemon in the Greek sense which was a spirit guide or tutelary deity) or a Chthonic hero ('chthonic,' from *Chthonios* [Χθόνιος] meaning "Zeus-beneath-the-earth").

There was a cult surrounding Trophonius, who was consulted for oracles. Whoever desired to obtain an oracle from Trophonius had to descend into a cave that was so full of horrors that when they re-ascended to the surface they were so frightened out of their wits that they forgot the whole experience. It was possible to seat the devotee upon a "chair of Mnemosyne" (the goddess of memory) which was conveniently located near the entrance to the cave, and priests of the shrine would jot down all the ravings from the oracular spelunker.

As a metaphor, this sounds quite familiar to me. Anyone who has descended into the depths of their psyche, or, propelled by psilocybin or some other hallucinogenic aid, journeyed into inner space and gleaned information from the unconscious and its various archetypes and chthonic monstrosities, is going to have problems relating these phenomena in a language corralled by reason and grammar.

Soon after, writes Pausanias, a Roman writer and geographer of the 2nd century who wrote extensively about ancient Greece, the visitor to Trophonius's dark realm recovers their sense and laughter. Everything out of their mouth suddenly seems funny, all those subterranean abnormalities spooks in a carnival haunted house.

We went to bed and listened to some podcasts. I particularly liked one called Movie Crush in which *Groundhog Day* was enthusiastically discussed.

I couldn't get to sleep. I was worried about a number of things, the melting of the polar ice cap, an erratic jet stream creating havoc everywhere, frostquakes in Ottawa, a wildfire in Greenland, the rise of fascism, the government shut down, millions of people divested of health care due to the Republican tax reform, many of whom may die, orderlies in a Baltimore hospital depositing a patient dressed only in a hospital gown at a bus stop in thirty degree weather, the privatization of education for the rich, ignorance and incivility on the increase, a decaying infrastructure, floods and famine and habitat loss. I shut off my tablet and the Bluetooth device on the radio and began listening to classical music on King FM. I started drifting off and was abruptly awakened by a hypnic jerk. It shook the bed. I closed my eyes and tried to lose consciousness again. And then there was a power outage. Fuck it. I put on my flashlight headband and went out in the living room to lie on the couch and read *The Making of Americans* by Gertrude Stein.

I heard the constant din of sirens. I put on some clothes and went outside to see what was going on. The air was mild and still. Only a section of the neighborhood was without power. The rest of the city was fine. The sirens appeared to be coming from the bottom of the hill on the south side, Roy Street or Mercer. When the power returned, I discovered that approximately 12,900 customers had lost power due to four circuit breakers going haywire and creating a cascading effect and a small substation fire. That must've been what the sirens were for. Power was back on by 6:15 a.m.

It's hard to think of a future at this juncture in time. There just doesn't seem to be much of a one. Not for humans. Or thousands of other species we're taking down with us.

Has the human experiment been a failure? Is experiment the right word? If so, whose experiment are we? I seriously doubt that human beings are the result of experimentation, unless one adopts the very broad view that everything in the cosmos is an experiment. My guess is we're just an evolutionary quirk, "atoms contemplating atoms" as the cherubic-faced British physicist Brian Cox puts it. Somehow geochemistry became biochemistry, the inorganic became organic, phosphorous and nitrogen became conversation and polypeptide chains. Mud and sand and rock became quivering blobs of synthesizing protein which became corals and worms which became vertebrates which became able to walk erect on two feet which led to the evolution of a tongue capable of speech which quickly escalated into consciousness, whatever that is, self-awareness and books and dignity and meaning.

Valentines and sonnets and airplanes.

Dance and flavor and religion and guns.

At the end of the day, who are we? No one knows. No one may ever know. We were here. For a time. And then we were gone, cooked by an overheated atmosphere.

82 Buttons Unbuttoned In Bliss

A proposition is a statement or an assertion that expresses a judgment or an opinion. It's a tentative and conjectural relationship with the world. With phenomena. With experience. With cookies and ants and pharmacology.

A proposition can only say how a thing is, not what it is. I can say, this is a spoon. The handle is bent because it's been used to scoop out some ice cream from a container that's been in the freezer for a long time and has consequently hardened into a statement such as the one I'm currently making in which a spoon is cornered into a spectacular reality, the reality of a word, which is made of sound, which is a conveyance of feeling, which is a music of raw sensation. The metal feels cold. That's reality. The sensation of coldness is a reality. But the word 'reality' and the reality of reality are sprouts of stereophonic clank. They have a moment of colorful perfume and then a distant galaxy of stars crawls through my right arm and I can feel the generosity of the thermostat twist into greater and greater quiddity.

The name represents the object. Spoon represents spoon. That is to say, a name assumes the place of an object, the alibi of the object, not the actuality of the object, which is obscured by dishwater, sudsy bubbles in a kitchen sink, and awkwardly presented to you as a word: spoon.

I do a lot of this during the course of a typical day. I make proposals. Propositions. Prepositions. I make propositions about prepositions. I use prepositions to make propositions about expositions of compositions that may be sniffed by any dog and arouse the curiosity.

This is why I like propositions. I feel the arrival of a warm darkness, the ecstasy of a fence scratched by the wind. I see the influenza tree drop tears of nebulous milk. I'm proposing a situation. Think of this as a swollen subconscious, a rolling mass of garrulity. A tree. A root. A branch of leaves. An incident of words. A sharply defined dachshund. An occurrence of vertebrae and dots. Eyes. Fur. Paws. Ears. Tongue.

Can I be your friend? Thank you.

Africa has the right idea. It has 54 countries, seven major rivers and a very high linguistic diversity. I think I could lead a good life there. I could get up in the morning and shake the stars out of the sky. I've got 206 bones and a war to fight. The war against the imagination. All other wars are subsumed in it. "The ultimate famine is the starvation of the imagination." Thank you. Thank you Diane di Prima. Thank you for fighting the good fight. And bringing such a delicious rant to the table.

The big crime of the hip is full of words for the unfurling of a drowsy quadruped. I eat the heel of a dragon and ride a finger joint to the taste of a big music caused by a chorus of chameleons. I'm a thin diver of shoals. I'm an empty thought. I'm an insider and an outsider and consider the cider to be pleasantly insidious. No sitar is completely ugly if it's also a little medical. I must go now and go to Innisfree. I smell something incendiary, something exciting and wonderful in the air. Light. Clouds. Awakening. 82 buttons unbuttoned in bliss.

A Chiaroscuro Of The Mind

Ripples in my life, ripples in anyone's life, little concentric rings across the pond of the mind, the cold still water of mind in repose, silt on the bottom, tree branches in stunning lucidity. It happens occasionally.

Or the little clanks and thuds of the woman upstairs.

Mexicans tossing chunks of concrete into the bed of a pickup truck.

This is life on earth in the year 2018.

It's 6:14 a.m., Monday, January 1st, 2018 in Australia. I've never been to Australia, but I find it interesting that it can be December 31st here and January 1st on two separate parts of the planet.

I hear the dryer going in the building laundry room. I did laundry two days ago and don't need to do it today thank goodness because I don't like doing laundry. I once did laundry for a living, throwing huge loads of hospital sheets and surgery gowns into a giant washing machine that looked like the instrumentation of a submarine. I worked with two other guys on wooden slats that were slippery all the time and one of the guys, Chico, who favored see-through tank tops and platform shoes (this was the 70s) and priding himself on being a pimp, why a pimp I have no idea, liked to play at boxing. We never actually hit one another, it was more like the Afro-Brazilian martial art known as capoeira, but without any of the grace or fancy maneuvers. Just slapping around at one another in a goofy kind of way.

We were also stoned. The other guy, Kurt, would bring in some killer weed. The washing machines were huge. You could get behind the machine and there'd be a joint lying on a ledge, lit and ready to go. You'd take a quick toke or two and go back around to load or unload the washer. Kurt brought in some especially strong Columbian weed one day and didn't say anything. I took my usual two tokes and went back around and a few minutes later I barely had a sense of what I was doing. I was just standing there holding bits of laundry and staring off into space. Kurt and Chico were in stitches.

I'm also reminded of a painting by Vincent Van Gogh of a group of women doing laundry in a canal under the Pont de Langlois, a drawbridge constructed of stone and wood, near Arles in the south of France. A print of this painting hangs in our bedroom. The women are clustered together on the shore near a small boat as a covered wagon pulled by a single horse goes over the bridge.

The water ripples gently outward in concentric circles from where the women are stooped to do their work. The colors are chiefly blue (blue sky, blue water) and lots of warm earth tones. It's a highly balanced composition and emanates a feeling of serenity, despite the hard work being done by the women, who are huddled close together in almost a knot. The colors are strong, but not explosively so, insinuating a mood of calm immersion in the task at hand.

And today in France where it is 8:33 p.m. animated films are going to be projected onto the Arc de Triumph as millions gather in the Champs-Elysées to celebrate the coming of the new year.

I find it both silly and fascinating that people celebrate a new year, which, after all, is just a functioning of time. I can see celebrating time. Time is weird. The weird, the strange, the aberrant, the phenomenological, the eccentric and inexplicable should always be celebrated.

Why does time always go forward? Why does it never go backward? Why does it move forward in such a manner that anyone's life becomes a narrative beginning with infancy then childhood then adolescence then adulthood and its thousand miseries and then old age and its sad but mellowing resignations?

Why does it never go backward? Why does it move forward in such a manner that anyone's life becomes a narrative beginning with infancy then childhood then adolescence then adulthood and its thousand miseries and then old age and its sad but mellowing resignations?

I'm in the twilight of my life. What's on the other side of this life I don't know. I'd like to think there may be some form of continuance but how that would occur without a body I have no idea. Do people become amorphous spheres of rapturous energy? What color are they? What would consciousness be like as a ball of energy without actual eyes to see anything with or ears to hear things or a mouth to say things and eat things? Without legs to walk? Is everything afloat? How to you get around? Why hasn't a single dead person come back to tell all about it?

2:47 p.m. I'm hungry. R is making bratwurst. Hurrah for bratwurst. And mashed potatoes. Is there anything in the world better than mashed potatoes?

R informs me that the man who makes deliveries for the grocery store has also noticed a drop in the population of birds and insects. I find this deeply worrisome. It's a sign of habitat loss. I worry about what we'll do when food stops appearing on the shelves at the grocery store.

There is a great deal to be said for living in the present when the future looks so grim.

We watch *The Last of the Mohicans* with Daniel-Day Lewis, Wes Studi, Russell Means and Madeleine Stowe. This must be the eight or ninth time we've seen the movie. I really like the scene in which Hawkeye, Chingachgook and his son Uncas, Major Heywood and the two women, Cora and Alice, escape after the ambush by Magua and his Huron warriors and row a gigantic canoe down a raging river and get out just before the canoe goes over a thunderous falls with a 200-foot drop and hide under the falls. The roar of the water provides a backdrop for an impassioned speech Hawkeye delivers to

Cora minutes before they're inevitably discovered by Magua and the Huron warriors who are carrying torches, adding more luster to the drama, in which Hawkeye urges Cora to stay alive, no matter what, he will come and find her, and then falls back, takes a fast run and goes leaping into the thunderous mass of the waterfall. We see him drop through the water holding his long rifle, his long black hair streaming behind him. It's quite spectacular.

I pop a cherry cordial in my mouth and go read "Reflections on African Art" by Leo Frobenius.

The first cherry bomb goes off. The cretins are out.

I watch an episode of *La Grande Librairie* from last November with guests Michel Serres, François Heritier, Eric Vuillard, Géraldine Schwartz, Colson Whitehead and Douglas Kennedy. It amazes me I can watch a television show on my lap, much less a French television show. And one about books. People still talking about books as if books mattered. It's comforting, even though it's another country.

I'm especially interested in Eric Vuillard's *L'Ordre du Jour* (The Order of the Day) because it highlights the collusion between the economic and industrial world with the rise of Nazism in 1930s Germany. There are clear parallels between what happened in Nazi Germany and what is happening in the United States today. The corporations have completely taken over the government. Neither political party responds to the population; they respond to their corporate donors.

11:55 p.m. We went out to look at the fireworks on the Space Needle. I could see Mars. The Space Needle is under construction. They're putting a glass floor into the restaurant. You can sit and eat dinner while looking down 500 feet to the ground.

The fireworks display was spectacular and went on for quite a while. We were joined by Z, our neighbor across the hall, holding a glass of brandy. He said he didn't think there would be fireworks because of the construction. I said I was also surprised since there would be open cans of paint and thinner and whatnot up there and it seemed a bit risky. But maybe that's why the fireworks are going on so long. It's all the construction supplies going up.

Time goes so fast. Fifty years ago the five hit songs were "Hello Good-bye" by the Beatles, "Judy in Disguise (With Glasses) by John Fred and his Playboy Band, "I Heard It Through The Grapevine" by Gladys Knight and the Pips, "Woman, Woman" by The Union Gap featuring Gary Puckett, and "Daydream Believer" by the Monkees. I don't have a clue as to what the pop songs are today. Or what they will be. Or what they mean anymore. Is there still such a thing as a pop song? Music is so fragmented now. There are so many mediums and channels by which it can be accessed.

"Time is an illusion," said Albert Einstein. I agree. But the illusion has left me with a lot of wrinkles, thinning hair, and memories whose vividness and shadows have become a chiaroscuro of the mind.

Weave Of The Dream King

The lung exhibits foam. I want to break the terrine's blowing mist. The shawl has a huge chalk fever. A memory of wind flows through the dream king. The tears of the bee desire sleep.

Postcards are detached and electric and funny. Supported hope is a pillow for a shoulder buckle. There is a sewing wheel for the stamp of a vintage elf and this climate ignition makes a scarf rise. I want to get a little irritated. The music pants are an agate rap. The fingers grab a roasting stool. Twisted plastic writing butter. White cosmetic chicken car.

Effulgent sapphire frozen in flexibility. Loop flicker of bold pleasures elaborated by robins. Marie Antoinette on a swing. Scab shaped like an engine on a small pink arm. Memory bee prettily coated in borders to palpate. The mushroom is failing the need of the thunderstorm. The toad that drags its own plumbing has a point to correspondence.

Damask is rising a yellow benevolence. Perplexity beak of morose swirls of fulmination. Limestone Polynesia hummingbird whose wings are knives of fog. Search to undertake a filigree loop that will oblige your blot. Oxygen denies the wall of the refrigerator. And for that and that reason only the oasis is described by vowels. The consonants are embedded with a strange invisible power that shoots valentines at anything wiry. They can only be used as feathers. They cannot be used as words, unless they explode from the mouth as yolk.

The storm says chew gum. It helps the rain find its way to your mouth. I need a gerund for my expensive sieve. The air makes a high shadow. The shadow jumps out of a fuchsia and says hi. I'm impressed with the energy. It's not always so cut and dried. Sometimes the tap water is better than the bottled water. You know? The flu affects both the neck and stomach thus propelling stories forward into the places where they get written and talked about.

Some of these stories are profligate examples of chalk. Others get tangled in their own closets.

The plumber chocolate is chapped. I mean, come on now. There is a kernel of granulated fat in the thought about granulated fat, but that doesn't mean that the laundry is done. I have feelings of privacy. Take the swan, for instance.

Now there's a bird who appreciates the value of wings. It should be obvious. The gallop of the horse and the clang of the trolley are two separate things, and yet they have been brought together in this sentence, and shine intermittently, causing the novices to scatter in all directions, including East Finchley. The Hour of the Tibia has arrived at the haberdashery. It's an ash flash rhapsody. The cruel stool starts an allegory and the kitchen is galvanized.

Fragments demonstrate the barge. A marble statue drags an oyster knife because unbalance is a delicious drink served by the courtyard. Embolden buttermilk. Perfume a burning weight. Roll a mass of tools kiss a hawk and go.

I am the one who places the embassy of shovels in a garage. It's splendid to be at the border of your lips. The shelf is full of woodwork. Even books buckle their stomachs when the theater opens. The lightning squirting out of a book is a form of reverie that I do at night when the mind grazes on words.

And here we have an exhibit of Gothic yard waste, the wood of a cat whose excavation weakens the landscape but strengthens the presence of gallantry. Conceit will only take you so far. Sooner or later there will be clouds on the horizon and pennies in your sputter. Walnuts bellow their generalities at a weeping astronaut. The pretty wires of thought hold the dashboards of memory over the mouth of a swollen description. And then we practice our fencing.

You say the extraterrestrials brought us trinkets and bus transfers, but how did the initial contact occur, and who was most bewildered, the extraterrestrials or the TV crew?

Yes. I agree. The spit of the philodendron is fascinating under a microscope. Is it warm enough in here for you? I can turn the heat up. Form is, after all, emptiness. And emptiness is form. How do I know when it's time to milk the cows? When the metaphors rise from their bondage and begin a conversation with the city.

A crowd of nouns is just now beginning to disperse leaving behind an open door in the wallpaper of the sentence. Hello in there, someone shouts. And the echo is amethyst.

I'll be the first to admit that much of life doesn't make sense. We do know something is missing but no one can identify what that thing is. Is it a thing? Does it have thingness? Or is it more like light, a thing without thingness? Steam is like that, too. And clouds. And ocean mist.

We stole the vapor of the sidewalk during the door handle experiments and used it for the opera, which was red and soapy.

Next time we get together, let's paint the perfume of time's ragged sofa. It would mean the world to me if you demonstrated the mongrel emotions of an asterisk. But not quite yet. Let's listen to the ringing of jewelry in a garden of tears while the exit signs of our childhood create an otherworldly blue. While snowflakes sing songs of wood and canvas during a sinking of the heart. And our tendencies collapse into algebra.

Poetry As A Form Of
Energy Distribution

What can be learned from watching a YouTube video about how to replace the fill valve in a toilet tank? I don't know. I will have to let that information soak in my brain for a while. I'll worry about my ancestry and sense of camaraderie later, albeit ancestry isn't really a problem so much as a bump in the fog. The words just sag under the imagery of a carrack in Portsmouth, England called the Mary Rose. The cement is something I feel when I'm walking.

Let's talk about something else. It's been years since I've gone fishing, how about you? Hölderlin advises inhabiting the world poetically, and I fully endorse that. I'm ready to start anytime you are. Should we use stilts? Or just grow our eyebrows into effervescent examples of Wednesday?

This is why I often smell of abstraction. It's a combination of cotton and meat. Sometimes the moon will appear during the afternoon and I will make the sound of it come loose in my throat. Think of the BBC. A cloud will sometimes percolate what is in the sky and let it drop to the ground as rain. It's then that I dream of one day charming a harmonica into lightning. There are some metals that are so explicit it takes time for the blood to reach the brain in a fist of amusement and impel a wandering consciousness of gas station pumps to confirm the existence of hawks.

Yes, nature is everywhere. You can't avoid it.

Mathematical equations can, however, be quite beautiful. For example, if momentum equals mass times velocity, then rabbits must fornicate in open-faced hypostasis, as would be expected by Klee's whimsy, derived in part from children's art, which are what a Paris painter's taste and skill are supposed, in some way, to awaken.

Hypostasis does not in and of itself stand in opposition to social domination (it is, after all a style of playing on the Hawaiian guitar, as well as an underlying reality, or eyecup) but it does serve to underscore the idea of flouncing, which can enhance the inner décor of the home, or the Saigon Central Post Office.

The Maxwell and Boltzmann formula of 1870 is particularly lovely. It describes the speeds of particles in idealized gases where the particles (I just love that word) move freely inside a container without interacting with one another, except for very brief collisions in which they exchange energy and momentum with each other, or their thermal environment. Not unlike words in a paragraph, eh? That is, if we're willing to risk the idea of a paragraph as being a cloud of gas, neon or (heaven forfend!) methane.

Yuk. I agree. Let's not think about methane.

I like evergreens, don't you? I can read ice but I have to think about emotion. It isn't difficult to find pleasure in quitting a job or paddling a canoe on a still lake on a still day, but try to find a postcard that depicts the boiling minerals of a serious romance. This is how emotion bares itself on impact. Little cinnamon men hang upside down from the rear-view mirror, and infinity shakes loose of its adjectives and goes on automatic. This isn't to say it's entirely circular. It's more like insects. The mayflies scatter and touch is genial rather than annoying. Being feels more penetrating. People unfold. I'm riding on a comet here I come.

Desire is French. I think that can be assumed. But English, what's that? I know it has heft. But what is it doing here? I mean, other than lying around like an ocean. We choose a wave and paddle like hell to catch a sentence as it grows into something large and passionate, something we can use to warm our lives and give meaning to the pharmaceuticals.

The glass describes itself. It doesn't need words. It fulfills its own transparency and so I resent it. But I also cherish it. Contradictions are exhilarating. Concentration comes from dirt. If you don't believe me, just ask the dirt. Use both hands. Sink them in up to your elbows. You'll get your answer. That sparkle of resistance is only natural. Use that. Use it to catch a golden pain. Use it to rip the literal into architecture. The banishment will hurt at first, but then it sweetens a little, it turns sublime.

A dream of earth will come to you in your sleep and pocket you in its napkin and run away into the night. And the following day gold will shine out of your bones.

Please Somebody Help Me

I have to wait for the feeling of nausea to diminish to begin writing. Anything. Much less poetry.

Poetry? Was Adorno ultimately right? No poetry after Auschwitz? Have I been kidding myself all this time? Have I not been taking life seriously enough? Am I one of those elitist postmodern ironists dismissing everything with my cool aesthetic and Technicolor Tom and Jerry heart? Is this my punishment? Is Trump my albatross?

Jesus. What an ego. Do you see what has happened? It's contagious. Trump has already caused my ego to swell.

No worry. It will inflate and pop. It always does. Swirl around the room in fart sounds.

Seriously. I must write something. Something huge. Something monstrous. Something to make time go backwards and undo it all. The whole election. The whole last 36 years.

1980. That's when it all began to happen. John Lennon murdered in the Dakota. Ronald Reagan elected president.

Mt. Saint Helens erupted.

Pac-Man came out.

Atari released Space Invaders.

The world, pretty much, turned to shit.

Can't help but compare this world (crabalocker fishwife pornographic priestess corporation T-shirt, to paraphrase Lennon) to that other world, the world in which I'd attained manhood, the world renowned for its drugs and soul-searching, the world of 1965 to 1967, a world in which it was still possible for an eccentric writer like Richard Brautigan to make a living (*Trout Fishing in America* sold more than two million copies) by writing droll, imaginative prose. Unimaginable, now. That world (Allen Ginsberg, Robbie Robertson, Michael McClure and Bob Dylan standing, smiling, in front of the City Lights bookstore) is emphatically, categorically gone. It's as dead and gone as the Pony Express, horse-drawn ploughs, floppy-hatted outlaws in the sepia tints of old photographs. And I, in my elder years, have washed ashore on a new continent. A continent of shameless incontinence. Of SUVs and shopping malls.

Selfie sticks and nail salons.

Which is why, on any given day, I can't get Rip Van Winkle out of my head. I have become Rip Van Winkle. I live in a time I cannot make sense of. I cannot digest. I cannot process. This means I have to invent my reality most of the time. That's dangerous. I don't recommend it.

Actually, reality — real reality — actual reality — is pretty cool. I won't call it awesome because everybody uses that word. But it is. It's awesome. Reality is awesome.

Here's why: steam kettles whistle, cats sleep with their paws in the air, my shoes go squich squich squich on the sticky floor of the men's room at Pacific Place where we've just watched Amy Adams learn the language of extraterrestrials in *Arrival* which was followed minutes later by the sound of helicopters as we entered downtown traffic in Seattle and headed home and discovered there had been another march protesting Trump's presidency 5,000 students leaving their classes, 5,000 students marching in the streets, 5,000 students under the muffled racket of TV news helicopters.

We arrived home. Checked the recycling bin. We'll take it down early in the morning, we decided. I turned on the heat, our apartment became warm, electricity is amazing, never ceases to amaze me, how much longer will we have electricity, how much longer running water and decency, how much longer people to care for us when we're sick, how much longer before the oceans rise engulfing New Orleans and Long Beach, how much longer before money vaporizes and we regret not having a plot of soil and packets of seeds. Shovels, hoes, and the knowledge to grow things.

Reality can be tricky. Right when we think you've got a bead on it it slips away quick as a quark in a particle accelerator.

Poetry works better than particle accelerators because (to quote Charles Olson, no relation) poetry is a high energy construct. Which amounts to the same thing as a particle accelerator except that the particles accelerated in poetry are churning inside my descriptions of fog, which are plump with radar, and caress the air into which they're born, and bears them, making everything paradoxical and topsy-turvy, the way reality was meant to be, before it became linear and one-dimensional. We need to break that system up and make sure it never darkens our poetry again. Are you with me? Of course you are.

There is no such thing as a literal oar. All oars are ores of the ouroboroi of consciousness, each in our own birch canoe, slapping the waves, slipping through time, slicing through space, naked in rupture, sympathetic to soap, impelled by vision, pulsing with experience.

And this is how we paddle out of our bodies and into the mulling air of giants. These words want to caress the treasure in your eyes called seeing. These words are alive with thirst and these words contain the turnstiles of abstraction. Colors walk in the bones of thought.

Do you see what I'm attempting to do with logic?

Destroy it? No. But make it correspondent, yes. Correspondent to our incantations. Correspondent to our candles and wax and walks by the river. Correspondent to the anguish we share. Correspondent to the worry dragging itself through our afternoons. To the chatter of crows. To the alchemy we use for changing lead into gold. To the folding of ourselves into one another at night. To the invention and re-creation of ourselves during the day.

Life is a delicate noise.

Please somebody help me find a conclusion here that we can all agree upon. Because seriously. I'm hesitant to turn the knob and open the next door.

Rub Me Do

We sometimes have to distinguish between a feeling and a large red barn. What is required is not entirely what you may think you need. I probe the surrounding obscurity with a delicate antenna. It's how I get around, you know? I feel my way, as they say. As soon as we enter a language a spectral agitation dances around the bone. A thing is literal when it's crumpled. But until then it's a large red barn. A door swings open. A piano floats in its music. Someone whispers Spain.

We are, essentially, sacks of blood supported by a framework of bone. You want to pay attention to that. Avoid war. Avoid guns and knives. Look at me now, an old man approaching 72. If you rub me I will stick to the ceiling. This is a direct result of playing the harmonica. Writing, however, requires planning and concrete. Begin with an embryo and end with a spine and a little hair. In fact, here comes an example now. There is nothing I can do to stop it. Can you smell it? Precisely. It is the smell of existence. Therefore be glad. Reality is mostly gas stations.

I know this feeling. It's called turmoil. It attracts thieves and rebels. Here come the woodwinds. No need to tell anyone. They'll figure it out. Spinoza saw God as nature itself. And why not? Just look at what I'm wearing. A tiara, a tutu, and a pair of dark leather gloves with a rabbit fur cuff. Don't even mention cork. I'm up to my ears in cork. Would you like anything? A glass of water? You've come this far. Later, when we've gotten to know one another a little better, I will show you my favorite feeling, which is weightlessness in the hallway where voices echo.

The very alphabet is an amalgam. A woman surfaces, gasping for air. Is this the birth of a new feeling? Who made the first sound that meant sunlight, or pea soup? Examples are jars of ruckus. I think I may have used a little too much butter this morning. This is how plywood happens: it begins as chaos and percolates from the ground. A universe walks by carrying a basket of planets. The sky becomes a question as soon as the sun appears. Linen, however, is totally horizontal. Was Freud right? Is civilization a fraud? We see a woman mount a ladder and dive. Her arms spread against the sun. Her body glides into the depths after penetrating the water.

Perhaps there's a way out after all. A magic door in our consciousness. Psilocybin might open that door. Poetry most certainly will. That's what it's been designed to do: open doors.

The Forgotten Greatness Of Poetry

I feel myself increasingly chilled by the frosts of the zeitgeist. Mounting hostilities toward contrariety, defiance, dereliction, wonder. What is desired, what is most strongly needed right now, is an art that generates itself out of the yolk of the moment. Out of the nucleus of sensations and thoughts that surround an arch of sandstone, a Mongolian yak, the smell of soup in a yurt, a knowledge dropped on the mind like moonlight. Like the integrity of a rag. A shirt once worn and now soaked in paint and turpentine. The rag is stiff and frozen. But it smells of sacrifice.

I like to bend reflections around my hands. I can handle a boiling pot if I'm the only one in the kitchen. But go ahead and moo if you think oars are involved. Or pretzels. Candy impels the pronouns for a body part I ripped apart. It's why I've called you here to come and look at it. Go ahead. Press it. Hold it against your ear. All of it. Romania. In the rain. Romania in the rain.

I grab some electricity from the clouds and throw it into a book. This produces a trance of socialism. I'm doing my best to understand the pornography of power. Seaweed is just a gimmick. It was never intended to be a substitute for thought. It was all those sails that let the sky in on our plans and the winds that knocked some virtue into them that gave our crew something to do at last. Why didn't we think of that before? Sometimes the best answers come in the form of soap.

I can smell fascism from a mile off. It smells like mediocrity. Whenever mediocrity becomes increasingly popular, you know fascism isn't far behind.

Jelly blooms in my hand like a sweatshirt. I can pay my bills now. Have you had contact with the supernatural lately? The days of my life grow into semiquavers of quivering honesty. The nerves do not like it. The nerves prefer hot chocolate and thick blankets. I don't know what I want. Do you know what you want? Is my discontent the same as your discontent? Shit. Here comes more fascism. Examples are cooperation and a woman in a chokehold gasping for air. Writing suddenly seems silly. And vital. And focused on the birth of a new feeling.

Signs you may be experiencing fascism: you think twice before saying or writing anything. You constantly feel powerlessness and dread. Futility becomes a way of life. Pensions are gone. Rents are astronomical. Health care is extortionate. Prisons are overflowing. The borders are closing. Protest is criminalized. Free speech is criminalized. WTF??!! What happened? Milton Friedman happened. NAFTA happened. Wall Street and Citizens United happened. Endless war and subprime loans happened. Illiteracy and Selfies happened. A TV hemorrhoid happened.

Poetry doesn't provide food or shelter but it does build empires. And so it begins: carnivals, friendly dogs, and whipped body butter. Just now I saw a woman pass the library with the skinniest two legs I've ever seen. This proves my theory about ecstasy. Restraints are social. There are no restraints. Please forgive me. My tongue is an afternoon.

I feel an exaltation of words emerge. They become wine. They become intimate and Wittgenstein. They become art in the United States and crusty white and colored threads and an almost abstract kind of literalness. Every fresh and unfulfilled preoccupation proves more immediately fruitful than all the things I had in my brain yesterday, which are now busy reaffirming something else, an embodiment of light, of poverty and war, for no other reason than the smashing of fragments, in order to keep turning them over to find something new, a wholly irrelevant weather of hotels and whirlpools and the forgotten greatness of poetry.

How Plywood Happens

In the fourth dimension, space and time are unified in a Minkowski continuum. If masses are sufficiently large, time may fold back on itself. This is where mathematics gets salty and brittle, like a potato chip. My first instinct in all things is to grip something and hang on for dear life. There are thousands of variables, all quite random and lovely, lovely in their own way, like maracas and drums, a little scent of hops in the air, *humulus lupulus*, the drone of an airplane passing overhead, and the hunt begins, the search for that elusive thing called an identity, a name, a coherence, a character. This is where doors become important. Open a door, close a door, walk through a door, this is how dimensions are turned into pulp and conversation.

The sky is a noun. Turn it over and look underneath. What do you see? Unzip this carefully. The next image may be your childhood walking slowly on the sea floor. Geometry is cruel. But it is also beautiful and abstract, like adolescence. Spasms of pink convulse in the muck. But which is the real ocean? The one in your mind, or the one stapled together by elves in the middle of the night? If thoughts are shadows, what is the light of the mind? Is it a wick, or a constellation? Is it God, or a homunculus holding a kerosene lantern? This is how plywood happens. It begins with nails and screws and ends with a homunculus driving your brain to Monte Carlo.

A Dragon Walks Out Of My Mouth

A dragon walks out of my mouth and falls asleep in a sentence. And why not? The sentence is a wildly savage warehouse. Anything can happen. Anything does happen. Anything happens a lot. But there are places where a dragon can curl up into an idea and fall asleep in a reader's head.

I write in a notebook ephemeral and fast yet primal like rain. Everyone is invited.

I can hear the plumage of night stir in the rhythms of day. I'm pricked to congratulate my annoyances. Irritations that freeze into ice. Each cube contains a face. Each face contains a story. I wander the room and apologize. The night wanders the streets in search of meaning, a peacock of fire.

A chunk of coal catalogues black. We're done with buttons. We trudge across the lawn to make our demands. It occurs to a few of us that we can grab a few things from the table before the wedding begins. I squirm among the folds of my hesitation creating a drug out of gravity.

Another sentence comes along and I grab it and hold on for dear life. I don't know where it's going. I think it's becoming a job. I feel myself age in interesting ways. I feel the chatter of estuaries in my bones. The shine of rivers before they enter the ocean. The diffusion of currents. Waves shifting against one another. The ever elusive equations of the divine dreaming in sweet interaction.

I don't hunt. I don't fish. I don't know the basics of survival. But I can do some things. I can write a sentence. I can put sentences together. I can make sentences croak like frogs and welcome the sheer eloquence of knives.

Will this save the planet? No. No one can save the planet. It's not the planet that needs saving. It's us.

I feel things spin out of control. Isn't this the desired effect? The codes are simple but the calculus is infinitely flexible. This means that the closest a sentence is to us the faster it's moving away from us. This is because meaning can never be resolved by thinking but must be stretched into eyes if you're going to wear it underwater.

I blow wheels of air into existence. It makes me powerful, like a kiss.

I study a puzzle in the hospital waiting room. It percolates into being. I see the face of time crowd into translucence. It translates into weight and crashes through the table.

Space can be flat even if it isn't. This is what is meant by expansion of the universe. All the contradictions must be seen as temporary and apparent. It isn't mass that causes gravity. It's grief.

And so we make sentences to fill the space with hindsight. The shattering impulse of nerves in a ball of pronouns dilate into living dragons of prodigal energy. It's not long before we begin exploring one another. Sanctuary is just a step away. See that bowl? It's empty. And yet it's not. It's filled with space. It's only the headlights that seem to farm the night with their radiant energy and piercing incoherence.

The Way Things Are Supposed To Be

Imagine a situation in which wealth had absolutely nothing to do with money or property and had everything to do with the capacity to experience life. But how could that be measured? It would, by its very nature, be a quality and therefore non-quantifiable. And what if it were discovered that wealth based on money and property was an obstacle to self-actualization and joy? People would devise ways to be redefine wealth. Which would be 1966.

I remember going to San José City College in the winter of 1968 and coming home to Seattle for Christmas. The city was up to its britches in snow. I took a taxi from Sea-Tac to my parent's house. It must've been early, they weren't up yet. I went to the basement and turned a radio on and heard "Sympathy for the Devil" for the first time & thinking holy shit, The Rolling Stones are back, big time. I don't remember anything else about that Christmas except the return to San José and walking to my gate down a long concourse, troops from Fort Lewis shipping out to Vietnam at a series of gates, me in my full hippy regalia, getting catcalls and mockery.

I remember the great fogs blowing in from the Pacific in Arcata, California smelling of redwood forests and the estuary and smoke from the sawmill tee-pee-burners, and one night in the winter of '69 going through a bin of albums at the bookstore where (a few weeks earlier) I'd bought the Perkins anthology of the English Romantic Writers & coming across the Hindenburg in flames, that famous old photo, rendered in black and white mezzotint, a group called Led Zeppelin and flipped it over for the liner notes and noticed one of the band members was Jimmy Page, who I'd seen perform with The Yardbirds in 1966, and I liked his playing so I bought the record wondering what it was going to sound like and got it back to my friend's studio apartment where I was temporarily crashing and put it on and BOOM! BOOM!, BOOM! BOOM!, "in the days of my youth..."

Those recurring dreams in which I'm locked out of my hotel room, naked. At some point I give in to the fact of my nakedness, realize that nobody will be harmed by it, and go to the desk in the lobby to ask them to let me back in.

I know it's not good for depression, but most of the phenomena around my legs are due to gravity and shoes, and the news is terrible, as always, and the oligarchs don't give a shit.

Birds are more of an international feeling. Shit happens, and then you think blah blah blah blah. It's like trying to swim in your clothes. Oh, that this too, too sullied flesh would melt, thaw, and resolve itself into a drug. Blood dribbles down the motel curtain. Today, your honor, I saw a robin tilt its head and enjoy a correspondence with the dead. Sometimes the world is a feeling in the gut. And sometimes a man picks up a guitar and sings something about ships, and war, and the way things are supposed to be.

The Music Hall Of The Mollusk

I dare to believe that ink is capable of becoming a roasted chicken. But this isn't about roasted chicken. This is about the music-hall of the mollusk. Think of a shell then think of the meat in the shell. This is the way the mind chews things. An individual carries words from one end of a sentence to another until they become golf balls, hawks, and thyroid glands. And then we liberate them. They become books and art. Life continues, though it's never fully understood. A vowel without a consonant is just a vowel, but a vowel encased in a sack will get up and walk around. Bump into things. Go grocery shopping. Roast chicken.

I sometimes imagine the dead are trying to pull us into their realm. I can feel something hopping around in my heart. Is it a dead person, or a shiny train in Texas? There are adjectives for this. They occur naturally in cheerful museums. One day, I hope to explore space as a NASA astronaut. Although a thought may be nothing, it may be used to bring back the dead. I call this necromancy. But it doesn't work. No dead people appear. Just Bob Dylan on a horse.

Top five movies about writers: 1. *Orpheus,* by Jean Cocteau. 2. *The Diving Bell and the Butterfly.* 3. *Sideways.* 4. *Starting Out in the Evening.* 5. *Midnight in Paris.*

How does late capitalism feel? Picture an art gallery. It's a slow day. Five or so employees in various states of repose. Checking tweets, gazing at laptops. In walks Donald Trump. He takes out a marking pen and scribbles over Monets and Cézannes, draws a big dick on Mary Cassatt's *Young Woman in a Black and Green Bonnet.* Takes out a jackknife. Rips out the canvas from Georgia O'Keefe's *Oriental Poppies.* Pulls his pants down. Squats. Defecates. Wipes himself with O'Keefe's *Poppies.* Pulls his pants up. Walks out. Nobody says anything. Nobody does anything. That's how it feels. Every day.

Once upon a time the dragonfly had a wingspan of 2 ½ feet. The Mesozoic atmosphere had more oxygen and so the larger bodies of the dragonfly were able to diffuse oxygen efficiently through its tracheal breathing system. The same fate of Europe found its way into words. This led to a small rotating ball held in place by a socket. A good viscous ink was developed by Lásló Biro and voila! the aching heart had open highways, lactating bloodhounds and unemployment forms.

Somebody might think my vocabulary is arbitrary as a water buffalo standing on the tip of a goose bump and they would be right. They might also be wrong. We really ought to free ourselves from the seductions of words. But what the hell. What's in a word? King Kong eating a pterodactyl. Syllables trembling with aluminum.

Clunk

I like food. I like eating. I like it when food and eating come together. I like to shop for food, and look at food, and select and prepare food, and do not buy in the grocery store things unrelated to food, unless they be items of hygiene, or lozenges of calcium to quell the acids in my stomach. Much of life is learning to quell agitations. I shall do so in the night with me in the bed, and learning of Proust, who writes of food as if it were music, and where women do sometimes sing in the ways of food, and in Paris where it is served. For food and fuel are made by the vibrations of the air to be musical sounds that are caused by plates and clanking metal pots.

We came home and acted bad. We had too much coffee. Near the end of this is my answer. To others it is not to be silent, because there is nothing else to say. For I was hungry, and hath not eaten her.

What makes the automatic transmission make that clunk? You know what I say to clunk? I say to clunk, clunk. But what, I ask you, is to come of this?

Clunk. Naught but clunk. For clunk is clunk and the moon is stone. And dust. The moon is dust and stone.

I tend to worry. Anxiety creates its own path. Every engine is fearful and just too large, I have added, if the engine is fueled by fears.

With me around the earth in orbit, and the testimony of its top events, I see a little of Hawaii, but it's too weak. London is a large bright oblivion. Venice: the skin of Venice is no longer a dream, but a lingerie. France is circumference, Mauritania a swirl, and what I see, I saw, and what I saw, I see. The place of the seriousness of which is me, for it is of me, as I am of it, and I talk about the weight, it is in my heart, if not my voice, and spins in weightless confusion.

If a man of flight asks me, as I do ask myself the big questions about life, the answer is not simply to administer exertion, but answer in good faith, and mirror the many subtleties of space. And after this, if this man may ask of me questions of the big bang and black holes, I must answer as well as I can. For the universe is large and its mysteries burn like absinthe, penetrate one's being with a surfeit of absence, that exquisite silver of the mind, that artful switch by which the absent is present & the present is absinthe, and by which one can hold and let it breathe, sip its ineffable charms, and let it soak through you like a sponge, diffusing the euphoria of all that is null. The question: "What is in our universe?" is linked to another question: "Who are we?"

We are creatures of skin and bone who walk in wonder beneath the stars. This I say in kisses and sweetness. In a moment I will come to see the occurrence of words in a row, and how they create depots of camaraderie. Life on Earth is — so far — the only known life in the universe, but that is not a compelling reason to persuade us that we are alone. In fact, to live here is to speak naturally of the probability of lives lived elsewhere in the universe.

What worries me is the transmission clunk.

A wise man of habit were up to that time of life as they say, a Copernican principle, and not on earth simply as a rock, but a thing of life and beauty in orbit around a yurt, or dwelling of metaphors and expressions, a hamlet or thorax. Something irrepressible, like astronomy. And so we see how to provide clues as to how life and culture might intersect in order to live in the universe or the earth. For clunk or no clunk, it is protozoan, and blazing with prose.

The Woman Who Loved Water

I hear the woman upstairs running water. But that's incorrect. I should say the woman upstairs is running *from* water. She loves water. And water loves her. She loves cooking and doing dishes but especially running water. She runs water all day doing dishes, doing laundry and taking showers. This has been the pattern for years. Running water. Loving water. And now the water is in love with her and chases her all over the apartment. She barely gets any sleep. Water doesn't sleep. Water occasionally sleeps in ponds in the forest, but mostly water is busy doing other things, like running onto sand when it becomes an ocean and grows deep and restless or tumbling over rocks in the mountains when it comes bounding down from the regions where men dig into the earth seeking gold and silver. And now when water takes the form of a current coming out of a kitchen tap or a bathtub faucet and helps with cooking and getting clean it has been so loved by this woman that it awakened and turned ferocious as it sometimes does and chases the woman around her apartment. And sometimes she laughs and sometimes she cries and the water comes out of her eyes and moves slowly down her cheeks humbly and accepting as it is when soaked into mops or boiling in a pot and rising out of this world as steam.

Rhapsodies Struck With Steel

Indecisive thermostat terrine. Slices of beat hormone. Squat that arrives by abstraction. Grumble canvas of hot usurping rain. Action gripped by nouns.

Testimony ablaze with forceps. This could be it. This could be a deliverance. Cabbage babies marching in a museum of exotic punctuation. I live in a willingness built by zealots, leprechauns, and lavish conjecture.

Cool house whose aims fall into the logic of interiority, closets operable by nerve, angles hypnotized into string. Cream is pondered with a delicate sky, clouds in a spoon-induced swirl of liquid reverie. There is sometimes a TV in the corner knitting necromantic mittens and a club chair squirming in conceit like an ontological argument for the sanctity of ticking. Dirt stirs with the strange innocence of worms.

I want to change. I want to paint an apprehension. I want to paint it red with a blue centipede and a black lap. Indignation supplies the monotone of grievance with a mezzo-soprano kiwi. But everything else requires muffins.

To weigh a chestnut is an embalming of one's absorption. It is to spurt out a confession of feeling, the many whirlpools in your neck which result in rosary sweeteners. My pillows are washed in a wooden mailbox. I receive letters that ask for my attention. I savor a gay science in a wild root of translation. I find a cantata to sing, a ball to punt. I answer what I can with a squeamish pontification. A voice like bees. The carpentry of association.

Feeling clean is done by thorn. Cash is muscle and contrariety. An eccentric lung canopy makes the planet foxy. I row a chain of clothes and wear them like snowballs. An open shirt of Morse code and hilly tickets that never stop craving the company of elves.

Perplexity's shadow rests on the hard edge of my palm. Blow on the radiation paint as it is chapped and hangs in space pleading for sugar and understanding. Provoke the lavender to bite a cloud. Quintessence is an undecided alpine well-being. The tincture of the ground is still hooked to its ecstasy, the pleasure of seaweed.

What we need is effervescence, not another hypotenuse.

In other words, an intervertebral stabilization assembly for arthrodesis including an inflatable intra-discal member and corresponding ancillary equipment: conjunctions, tropes, isotopes, exotic particles, alloys, block and tackle, glass and rubber tubing, buoyancy, sincerity, vaginal speculums, dipole magnets, proton synchrotron boosters, advanced tongue roots, bound morphemes, clause chains, glottal stops, hortatory discourse and a 4-stroke outboard motor.

I will come and make sense to you as a lump of earth, form considered as a prerevolutionary momentum. Literature is a problem. It always has been. And so the language is lanolin. Heed my contusion. The mechanism outstrips its own intentions. It becomes a moon. A combustible hobby. Thinking is really an insatiable project, you know? Of course you do.

Let's say it's the transmutation of a humor. Nozzles enhanced by vascular owls. Fragments of a reality alien to language, which is what? Archaic ratatouille made with ripe tomorrows and overlapping zithers. The kind of clothes that express toads and buckle with secret handshakes. Timeless slop. Road flares. Footprints in the mud. Slopes on all sides and rhapsodies struck with steel.

Spannungsbogen

I wish. I wish for this, I wish for that. I wish death and war and diseases didn't exist. I wish I had a silver buckle and a golden sleigh and a slingshot hat. How simple it is. How simple it is to wish. I wish I was rich and young and a highly regarded numismatist.

What is it to wish? It's desire. It's a form of desire. A shade. A nuance. Not the full deal. Not a lust. Not a craving. Not an ardor or longing. Those are strong. Those have power. Intensity. Wishing is softer. Wistful. A fantasy while gazing out of a window. A woman braiding her hair in front of a mirror.

Why is it even worth mentioning? It's always a boost to the spirit to at least appear interested in life. Wishing is a confirmation that life sometimes lacks the right spice, a satisfying response to an elusive flavor. A debt paid in full. Wishing isn't like that. It's just a confession that this is what might make things better, but it's not within the realm of the possible. Or it's possible but is it worth doing? Not currently. Perhaps never. This is why people gaze abstractedly at the ground. Or the sky. Or the view out of the window. Which is quite often shrubs. Trees. Pigeons in a parking lot. Trash bins. A drunk cursing the traffic.

Wishing is a glass of wine. Ambition is thirty gallons of gas and a red Silverado.

Wishing is wistful and pensive and doesn't hurt anybody. Ambition pleases the stockholders and puts 5,000 people out of work.

When desire doesn't take itself seriously we call it a wish. When desire takes itself very seriously we call it Richard III.

Writing is feeling increasingly like wishing because we live in a postliterate world in which millions are captivated by a social networking service called Twitter in which statements are limited to 280 characters, which is death to literacy. Death to thinking. But a boon to wishing. Wishing is quick and evanescent and walks around with a glass of chardonnay admiring all the artwork on the gallery wall without being able to afford anything. Wishing is tweeting and tweeting is fleeting.

Let's look at more granite kitchen counter samples when we leave the party. That's wishing. Nimble and carefree. You can be starving and wish you had a slice of bread to eat but that's not really wishing. That would be the wrong word for that situation. If you're starving you're not going to wish you had a slice of bread you're going to be murderous and desperate to get something into your stomach. You're going to be haggard and dangerous.

That's not wishing. That's staring daggers at a couple dining on Hudson Valley Moulard Duck Foie Gras at Per Se on Columbus Circle in midtown Manhattan.

And wishing you could write like Chekhov.

You could be in jail and wish you could be invisible and had the ability to walk through walls. You could be in jail and so desperate to get out you carve a handgun out of soap. This is what the spectrum of desire looks like from a human perspective. On the one hand soap. And on the other a gun.

Corona Hum

Trek an anonymous testimony and shout. Float electricity. Aim at incandescent change.

Necessity spout. Bandaged snow.

Recognition and disavowal are thus inseparable from one another and basically mean the same thing: a look at the "structure" of the unique. Analyzing the illusion that some subjects are bouncing through their perceptions and have the impression of living somehow twice is pure paleontology.

Do the fleece in the net basement. Knowledge is a wire of diamonds.

Once in the mode of the present and once in the mode of memory, Bergson does not fail to find the theme of destiny: "What is said and done, what one says and what one does oneself, seems inevitable." This is similar to the tamarind of craft.

Wallowing planets stir the universe.

At any moment, we will have to deal with that, and with nothing else: that the circumstance is gay or sad, whether it triumphs or dies, it is in any case cornered by beauty.

Flex the shaking wind. Purpose shoves the snow into meandering streams of butter. Swim through the steam. Drop an organic thought on the piano keys. Collect paraphernalia. Echo dollars of eyeball tumble.

The metaphysical dialectic is fundamentally a dialectic of the here and the elsewhere, of a place of which we doubt the geography or taste the bittersweet overtones of chaos until something like a hill or a canyon makes us wonder at the vitality of it all, at the oleander and rhubarb.

One recuses oneself from pumice and brings a fire from elsewhere whose salvation is discounted. Immediacy is thus dilated by reflection, by a restless need to mutate, metamorphose. Would it not rather be an orchestra? Or a mushroom?

Smoke the flake disaster.

Leaning muscles shine during the robbery. Build a choke and pull. Glaze the pungent skidoodle.

Rumble on a tour of plants. Pepper the area with pulse and cries of personal liberation.

Swallow the day. Sip the night. Hack at reality with a large recognition.

Wear a goldfish coat. Box the spoons until they fork into knives. Perception makes the artists want to draw the delicacies of the forest. Most feelings are elemental, but some are more like fights.

Gallant pin cough. Subtlety pitch. Empty expansive mirth.

Hit think. The cardboard messenger stands among his own gender groaning like an idea.

The medium is the baby. Squeeze the elbow until a visible detonation tingles with subtleties of afternoon. The conspicuous flourishing of a stray light. The implications of prayer.

A slice of lamp black harmonics.

An unrivalled prodigality propelled by the power to ponder a speed bump. The crowd grows restless.

Daylight bumps into a conspicuous species. They're called libraries.

Gooey Evolution

Examining and consolidating his affinities with nineteenth century French painting, Matisse painted with a new subtlety with which the nineteenth century painting received new illumination. Ocher walked in a stratosphere of grace. Yellow grew an orchestra of jingling bells. Black became a zone of placental navigation. Green plugged into a surge of telepathy. Blue agreed to disagree. And then parachuted upward into a realm of clashing cymbals.

Red hands held a universe of clay.

The human form had become unmanageable. The human form could no longer be controlled pictorially. He had to let it travel. Male or female, clothed or naked, the human form stomped into glory.

Tickets were purchased. Suitcases packed. The human form sneezed the dust of centuries and dove into fresh new energies of rampant ventilation.

Feelings sailed through pineapple syncopation. Fairies gamboled about in the garden.

This explanation finds its source in the nineteenth century's preoccupation with the medium of paint. Even pre-modernist painters such as Géricault and Daumier were more acutely aware of how the edges of a shape cut into the space around it. This was the problem that haunted Cézanne. His art arrived like a new dispensation.

Now we can begin to talk about painting.

Painting, what's painting, painting is bristles and daubs and gooey evolution. Colors dwell in tubes. They're squeezed onto palettes. They're applied to a canvas. Schools of tuna glide through gradations of blue. A man eats alone at a solid oak table. A storm of red liberates fingers of black. A galaxy of suns emerges from a cloud of pink. A woman ponders a new pair of glasses. Spanish orange breaks out of a structured jungle green into armadillo brown.

Painting is images and forms. Painting is consideration and cylinders and searching. Milieus of tin attached to a salvo of gunmetal gray. Milk in a bucket. Books on a shelf. A door hinge pondered in dark Rembrandt rust.

Matisse leans forward and makes a black line flow down. Two lines, three lines, four lines. An arm appears, breasts, a white cap, tufts of black hair, a leg moves forward slightly, a solid black line forms a gracefully alluring buttocks, a hand holding a towel lightly, so that it might drop at any instant, so relaxed, so informally poised is this woman, the carpet is red, she gazes at a vase of white flowers on a table, the light in the room is a mellow tint of yellow, two pillows — one green, one chartreuse and speckled with red — rest at the head of a red bed. The bed is a deeper red than the carpet. The difference in shades is subtle. But the sense of calm is not. It's voluptuous as a woman after a bath.

Naked. Holding a towel. Gazing at flowers.

In a hotel in the south of France. In paint. In color and space. In imagination. In the warmth of an afternoon. The fullness in the way the towel flows from the woman's hand to the floor. That's called form, and is a manner by which something presents itself, manifests itself, as a man with a brush brings it into being, into light and vision, into the flowering of the mind.

Open 24 Hours

Immediate certainty, the thing in itself, is complicit in the construction of our experience. Who can look at a river and not feel that river moving through one's body? It makes Beings become Beings, words become words, and teeth become teeth. Sometimes it just feels good to have a pen in the hand and put pressure on it and make it move over a sheet of paper causing words to come out of it by pushing thought and sensation into linguistic phenomena syllables and images that crystalize in the air of the mind where experience stumbles around looking for light and wisdom words riding through space amid tall sparkly buildings shouting themselves into existence.

The external world is the work of our organs. Which means that the body is its own continuous drugstore. I know this feeling. It's called ointment. Let's not get into that. Spinoza saw God as nature itself. And why not? I'm up to my ears in syntax. Would you like anything? A glass of water? This is another feeling I've learned to accept over the years. It lasts for a minute or two and is followed by dizziness, mermaids and outer space. I'm not an astronaut but I know how to swim. I just get supple and grope.

I do most of my writing at an old oak desk in the bedroom. My grandmother kept a diary at this desk, making brief daily entries about the weather and people visiting and the health of the cows they continued to milk in the barn that stood in a shallow gully protected from the wind until they were in their eighties. The last time I visited my grandmother and grand uncle was in the summer of 1968. I remember they still had a few cows but I can't remember them being milked. I do, however, vividly remember my grandmother's knobby, arthritic hands. It hurt to look at them. I see my grandmother's hands in Keith Richards' hands. How odd that of all people it would be Keith Richards who would most remind me of my grandmother.

Mania defines the moment. It shines like the stubborn metal of personality, which is in continual motion, and makes a sound like swordfish breaching the surface of the ocean waves.

Ok, I get it, you probably want your armchair to make sense. Well pass me the gin. I'll do something. I'll squirt blood at the ceiling. I'll steep myself in reading. Here comes some death. That said, the rest is somebody to love you. Doodled pupils of quadrupled noodle.

It used to be fun to think about death but now it's a little less fun and a little more serious since I'm pushing 72. Shit. It hurts to even say that. 72. Wow. So that's happening. Time is happening. Age is happening. Heartburn is happening. My eyes are stumbling around in books, reading sentences, wrestling ideas, lifting things in the mind, ideas, the shapes of sounds when they become words and flap their wings and leave the ground. The moody muddled puddled ground. Of the written page. Where the voice is mute and the words wink at you from the hijab.

There is a mind moving through these words. Not my mind. Your mind. I just put the words here. Never mind. It doesn't matter. I'm not sure what to think of it. Whatever eternity is, I feel better knowing it's around. The romantic spirit isn't dead. You can worry about tyrants so consumed with greed and power that they go mad and blow up the world or declare martial law and shut everything down. But who wants to feed that monster? A brain walks by dressed as a human being. I wave. The brain waves back. We have power in powerlessness, we tell ourselves. It's a brainy thing to say. But is it true? I don't know. I'm open to anything at this point.

Éclair

I like it very much that Whitman broke down the division between the body and the soul. He put divinity here, right here on the ground, in this space, a living breathing entity in what is a domain of the sublime, which is a notion foreign to capitalism, anathema to capitalism, because if this realm is sacred it is much more difficult to exploit it for money. That's why people that follow that thread can be so darned troublesome: they go around trying to convince people that this planet is our only home and fragile and sacred and once we realize that no more trees are chopped down, no more rivers poisoned, no more smoke and toxic chemicals in the air, no more slavery, no more prostitution, no more Walmart greeters, no more bored clerks at 7-11, no more gas to pump, no more wars to fight, no more corporate buildings full of young men and women playing ping pong and paying for apartments no one but them can afford.

Subjective bias is a happy illusion. It convinces us that selfhood is mostly confusion and that a small wheel in the hollow of an understanding might reward our efforts with the translucency of a masseuse or the opening of a Playboy Club in Shanghai. But poetry is a different animal. It may thrust its biology at a revolving door or crawl into a corner and nibble on the possible. The field of art is so much more than rigorous tweaking. Photographs in the water prove it has outlines that suggest that the ego might also be a beautiful breast letting go of a norm.

Consider a stone being whirled round on a string: does a daguerreotype of Emily Dickinson matter to you as much as stepping out of a spacecraft into the zero gravity of space? If so, then I recommend jewelry by Victoire de Castellane, and in particular her Baudelairian extravaganza Fleurs d'Excès, which consists of ten floral jewels, each representing a woman in the ecstatic embrace of a different drug.

Most of the time I don't know what to think. Is it better to suffer the slings and arrows of outrageous fortune, or take Xanax against a sea of troubles and by numbing oneself forget them for a while? What would Emily Dickinson do? Go to Starbucks and stand in line like a loaded gun.

My emotions are wet and powerful. Traffic, meanwhile, was good today. It was surprising. The sun was out, although the humidity was high, 79%. It's that time of year (late March) when you don't know whether to leave the window up for warmth, or down because it's too warm. I did have to turn the heater on briefly, but mostly because the windows were fogged up. It didn't take long. I turned the heater off. And suddenly I realized: the trees are loaded with blossom and the air feels benign. Proof of spring. As for my emotions, they will remain intuitive, spinning outward, radial and panoramic.

Feeling is always perspectival, a continuum of potentialities. And then a cake appears and the mind takes it in, by way of the nose, takes the smell of it into the skull, the cranium, the constellation of nerves surrounded by skin and bone, hair for a few, at my age, continue to have hair, and does something with it. Bakes it into food for the intellect. I believe that would be the primary difference between a poet and a pastry chef. But the definitions here get really fuzzy. Things overlap. They always do. Every scrap and tack and chunk of wood in the doorway is interrelated. And that's a huge poem in itself, right there, waiting to be written by someone.

The Great Mind Of The Ocean

Free will is a charming concept. Thought enhances the experience. The rest of life is learning how to endure it.

The world is a tapestry of energy concentrations. Much of it enters through the nose, which is a domain of nerves, receptors within the mucosa of the nasal cavity. The odor registers on the brain and becomes a search for understanding, a yearning, a pair of arms, and embraces immanence, the grand nature of the universe itself. And the universe loves this sort of thing. Don't agree? Fine. Go ask the universe. The universe says yes, I will marry you. But you must be willing to kiss my stars, and crawl on the ground with your sisters and brothers the crocodile, and howl like a wolf in the middle of the night, and alarm the neighbors with the sudden reality of themselves, which Artaud called The Theatre of Cruelty.

I feel curiously explored by my own heart. Here, there, and everywhere in a Cupertino garage. Fuck, I'm tired of this imagery. Roughly speaking: objects are chopsticks. I don't want innocence. Innocence is circular and sterile. I want to pull a silence from the other side of night and fill it with words. I will wait for you at the end of this sentence and show you some soap and towels I have that prove the existence of Norway. If that doesn't work, just focus on the sublime. Avoid doing work that doesn't suit you. Jobs are largely stupid. Wherever you go always have a book and a bookmark handy. Aquariums are fun but a little creepy. Zoos are horrible.

A 300-pound bull shark was discovered on a road in Queensland, Australia following the blasts and flooding of cyclone Debbie twelve miles inland. Even dead, I watched nervously as a teen age girl touched its head with her bare foot. This got me thinking about feet, and how wonderful they are, how such small surface in square inches can hold a being upright, balanced and poised, or allow a full range of movement while simultaneously dodging bodies and dribbling a basketball to the end of a court, and a great jump is made, and the ball goes through. And what was the shark thinking as it swam over the Commonwealth of Australia? The summit of Mount Everest was once at the bottom of the Tethys Sea.

Back in the day writing was largely a matter of style. Then it became content. Style no longer mattered. Celebrities dominate the book market. People with a story. Self-help shit. Life coaching, which is the stupidest thing I've ever heard of. We need a Jackson Pollock to come along and destroy content again. Splatter it drip it lunge at it throw it smash it bludgeon it into being. Raw, uncensored energy. Dangerous energy, the energy of art, which climbs down from the wall and gives us convulsion and beauty, mental categories masticated into a soft moist pulp.

We need songs. There's nothing more wonderful than a new song. A really good song. We all have our favorite songs. It's partly what defines us. There are songs that make you want to buy a horse. Songs that make you want to fall in love and songs that seek redemption and go in their own directions. Songs that make you want to cry. Songs that make you want to disappear in the forest and eat trout and truffles at sundown. Songs that touch heaven at four in the afternoon and songs that crawl out of the heart and become an afterlife of blackberries.

That lump of matter in which thought resides is the brain which is the source of C minor. The ego is something different. It's more like a dinghy.

This room is a mess. I apologize. Let me finish the rest of this paragraph by removing all the words and leave a nice large empty space. This is that space. But words keep wanting to enter it. It's a problem. This is how messes begin. It's not that I'm lazy. It's more like I keep exploding. Afterwards, I go through the debris and see if there's anything worth keeping.

I like sifting things, sifting through things, sifting. The sensation is soft, like buttoning a shirt. Because really, who can take it all in at once? Imagine everything out there on the other side of your skin, your eyes and ears, your glands and agitations, all of it the whole universe flooding into you raw and unpasteurized. You could produce some pretty hot rock with that situation. You could flood your head with the Flathead National Forest and go medical and backward into the uproar of yourself. Wander alleys of Goth Pop spidery swagger spewing blaring melisma.

One of the great romances of surgery has been to remove a wealthy man terrified of women from a can of whipped cream. The gist being that if you keep trying to get at the bottom of things the substance of the world will wait for you at the end of this sentence and show you that the ocean is really just a sink with some dishes in it. And that's ok, because the dharma can fill you like a glass of water. Whipped cream is just another way to describe yourself in a job interview. Buddhists refer to our inner life as a bitter ocean of life and death. Echoes under a bridge, a woman shouting, a door slammed, a new sentence started, one with a hook, for pulling a shark out of the heart.

The great mind of the ocean lifts itself in thought and smashes itself against the rocks.

Gomek

Grammar is a phenomenon that the heart affirms with its rhythms. It comes ashore as foam and whispers cypress and palm. It retreats. It advances. There is systole and diastole. There is dreaming and wakefulness. I become a notebook filled with descriptions of the local park. My birth happens every minute. I feel the membrane of the universe connecting me to the stars that stir in my sleep. I see the flesh of giants in the melting of candle wax. I join a caravan and explore the world of silk and paleontology. Every theory needs repeating and arguing because there are so many different realities. It can be exhausting. But we all pack a lunch of peanut butter sandwiches and Oreo cookies and go to work merrily as the winds buffet our clothes and the cliffs defy our embrace.

Give me some sauerkraut and a tap and I'll be happy. Marinate some crocodile meat in a mood of inconsolable weariness and I'll be happier. Why? I don't know. I like the word 'crocodile.' It rhymes with turnstile. Which rhymes with argyle. Which rhymes with reconcile. Which rhymes with tactile. I like anything tactile. A tactile turnstile reconciles argyle to versatile. And I like that. It's symphonic and silhouetted and cud.

Gomek, a saltwater crocodile captured in Papua New Guinea in the 1950's, grew to be 17.8 feet long and weighed 1,896 pounds. He was quite tame and people could approach him within one meter at the St. Augustine Alligator Farm in Anastasia, Florida. He died of a heart disease on March 6th, 1997, and was believed to have been 80 years old.

I like crocodiles. Though, to be frank, I've never been close to one. We have a lot of developers in our neighborhood, but that's a different kind of reptile. Much more destructive. They've become bloated with greed and corruption and vomit up luxurious apartment suites for the androids who work at Amazon.

The vigorous periphery of your embalming goes to the heart of things. But I have my lassitude to protect me from the tremors of ambition. The stems by the water provide theories of life that the vagueness of the fog welcomes with the chimerical hardware of commas and cashmere. These are simple things, but they're the script I was given when I showed up for the audition. I was told to play a king, and so the words I uttered helped me to walk in the gold of redemption. I forgave when I could forgive and was forgiven when I forgave. Yet nothing felt as good as slapping the air with my sleep.

And I awoke feeling quadrilateral. A little disheveled, but fit for service. It's true, there was a little meringue on my chin, but I could still play my role in the sensible world, and say sensible things, and do sensible things, while feeling nonsensical as birds.

So yes. There is a teleology, however undernourished it is at the moment. We can make improvements. I can walk on all fours and eat things. Shoes, furniture, people. Don't come too close. Prose poems can be dangerous. They have large membranous wings and manifold ideals of steel. I can suit your temperament or pour you some wine. Your call. I just want to surface occasionally and eyeball the surroundings until some words appear and the entire mechanism rumbles about like egg whites on a journey of glossy superfluity. I can't promise taffeta, but it's a direction.

Egyptian Blue

Tendency finds my fingers and I use them to impose on drumsticks. The very dollar winces at its own reciprocity. Admonitions blossom in the rescue of banks, but plunge into pathos when the libraries step forward. Thundering cartwheels crackle in the ooze surrounding our lake. I'm enthralled by the abandonment of form. What did Hegel mean, exactly, by the death of art? He meant the stars climb into our respect when we do something loudly heterogeneous. When we unite the engines in metamorphic landscape knobs. When I carve the words out of air they seem to smolder like the ash of prophesy. Rub your fingers, comb your peculiarities. We're going out to skulk in a stream of consciousness. Float letters. Slip into shapes of skin and faucet. The solace of the museum is in its buckles. The Fauves sew opinion into wood. Elevations dig into the troubling sky. The incursion of oil has consequences of chrome. Cézanne's snake secretes devotion. The vague cough of an adjective. The office garlic engaged in nature. Bump the taste of candy. The odors wear our blundering orchids. I work to flare the robin. I stir in my pepper shielding you from hymns of uncontrollable passion. The joy in the light of a moose. The piano's hungry work. We will expand our endurance to include ourselves in the long inspiration of falling. The bounce of lightning on a coin of light. Buy a whistle and shout by the stream. Defend the probe of the bulb in its patch of eyebrows. It's rough getting the rattan to express itself. And now it's just a chair. It's been a chair all along. And then I sit down and discovered the gluttony of enamel. The clatter of algebra has finally run its course and become a burlesque to explore, a quantity, a brush dipped in Egyptian blue. This is what Hegel meant. Generations of laundry adrift in the canvas sky.

Whirled World

We're riding on a planet. All of us. The whole biomass. Biota. Whatever you want to call this teeming mass, these creatures, some of them in shells, some of them in jails, some of them in hell, and not a few of them minding their own business on a bus headed downtown.

The world is swimming in its own narration. It's all I can do to lather myself in the shower and remember to pay my hair for the nice job it's doing.

The world is a nonlinear tablespoon. Sooner or later the trees will multiply the sky and the goldfish will compute their bowl in erratic circles, implying a sphere of glass in a one-bedroom apartment in Poughkeepsie, New York, and this will turn out to be another equivalent of parsley, which is photogenic and coincident with thought. This is proof that there are infinite sets which cannot be put into one-to-one correspondence with Limoges porcelain, but must be preserved in the cupboard, until they are needed to serve Leibnitz's pi.

The world is a mess. It's chaos out there. Nobody can even get the news straight. What's real and what's fake, what's made up and what's actual, what's solid and what's treacherous. I need time to digest things. Figure things out. Try to find answers. Unravel enigmas. It's navigation, is what it is. Making a map of your life. Identifying coasts and rivers, swamps and mountains, the whole geography of emotion, which is an ocean of its own, a deep full of strange luminosities, mouths and goggly eyes and long spindly antennae. Because there are worlds within worlds and the pinnacle of night is midnight, which is the crossing of an equator, traveling from one sphere to another, from the clarities of day to the soft obscurities of night. From the blunt morning telephone to the pillow where the head lies drifting into infinity.

The human head is a world. It's round, it's got regions and natural features, not the least of which is a nose. The nose is protuberant, like the bow of a ship.

There's a lot going on in a head. There is the soft filtration of the exterior into the interior, the confusions of the brain sloshed back and forth until something sparkles and rises to the surface like a bubble of description, the slop of representation, a homunculus painting the world in the brain, God and Adam on the ceiling of your skull, experience murmured with ripples and waves, the clay of rumination, which is a process, an intention similar to the drift of jellyfish, the play of resurrection, ambitions fondled amid the candles of Stuttgart. Because really, isn't the nose after all gnostic?

Were it not for extraversion I would feel stuffed with myself. Yuk! Until then I just stood around counting the number of tiles on the floor. It's as though I suddenly realized that identity is a semantic abnormality, a grope in the dark, and that makes everything pebbles. Why else believe in cause and effect? Thinking dribbles into Manhattan eating various forms of experience. The end result is a little too utopian for a guy my age. Nietzsche was right, don't catch the abyss looking back into you. That's a hard feeling to shake. If you stumble across one, don't freak out. Just start throwing words at it. Hopefully that'll scare if off.

Why We Have Drills

I hold the world in my mouth. My tongue makes it warm with plausibility. Anything I say can, and will, be held against me, like a T-bone, or a sheet of cellophane. Afterwards, my life combs itself with a sea cruise. The distance undresses and whispers opinions of form.

In this house (the House of Language) we believe bulbs are eggs of light. That reality is a letter for the loud eye of the universe. That predicates must be romanced with funny hats.

Writing has an ideological aspect. In this respect, it is similar to money. Much of the inherent chaos and brutality of life has been rationalized by monetary exchange. The conversion of wealth into securities gives it a giddy insensitivity to the vagaries and sorrows of life. Meaning money isn't wealth. Money is a medium of exchange. Securities are fungible, a cruel hoax. Real wealth is the loyalty of a friend, a good stand-up comic, and a shelter — however crude — to protect you from assholes and blasts of lightning. King Lear learned this lesson the hard way. Art embodies what is wild and unmanageable. It reduces nominal wealth to the noxious and grotesque. Regan and Gonorrhea.

Phenomena, for all their complexity, turn quickly to memory in the same way fine particles of earth turn to silt in the bottom of a river. Much of it is lost. Sensations are felt and usually dismissed, if they enter into our consciousness at all. It's hard to catch a phenomenon in the act of being a phenomenon and getting it written down, described with the fumbling implements of language.

Phenomena are always in flux. They come in a cluster of subtleties so exquisitely singular they seem impenetrable, impervious to our attempts to bring them ashore to our understanding.

The motivation behind most objects is clear. They all want our attention. Especially shovels. There is something tragic about shovels.

Existence precedes essence, or is it the other way around?

I just like the nothingness of everything. The divine undercurrent. The mystical unknowable. It comes in waves. The reflections in the sand are memories. You can write in the sand with a stick. When phenomenological events are small and compacted into an aggregate we call them a thing, or entity. When events are big and worrisome we call them news.

Today in the news tempers at a town hall meeting in North Dakota boiled over when a man confronted Representative Kevin Cramer demanding to know whether the rich would benefit from the repeal of Obamacare. He tried shoving a wad of cash into Cramer's shirt collar and was restrained and escorted out of the room by police.

The human body is gentle as adjectives.

I'm a muscle for the puddle of night. I was told it would be a solution.

This sentence is only slightly cod. The rest is a runway on which words are taking off.

Does Godot have my telephone number? I don't own a telephone. I just pick up rocks and listen to what they have to say. My prolongation pleads a stunned hibiscus. Oh no. But yes. My rattling peas must furnish your trigger to ooze. And that, my friend, is why we have drills.

Undefeated Despair

Our main injunction in life is to reproduce. I failed at that. Or should I say succeeded? I chose not to reproduce. In the same way I got out of the draft, I got out of reproducing. I didn't want to kill people and I didn't want to bring people into this world. I knew very early in life that what I wanted to do is write books and that writers, generally, do not make much money. In any case, I did not reproduce. I made books. I will leave books behind. The good thing about books is that you do not need to save money to send them to college, or invite them to your house on Thanksgiving and Christmas. Is there a bad thing about books? They cry at night. I hear them on their shelves whimpering with ideas.

I arrived in this world because of World War II. My father met my mother when he was stationed in Denver during the Second World War. He was a flight instructor for B-24s. My mother was a WASP. This is a how I came to be here, but it is not how I came to be who I am. I don't know how much identity matters in the long run, but without Chuck Berry, Miles Davis, Bo Diddley, Buddy Guy, Jimi Hendrix, James Brown, James Baldwin, Billie Holiday, Etta James, Tina Turner and Lisa Fischer, I would not be me. I would be Pat Boone. I would be Colonel Kentucky Fried Chicken. I would be bland as a golf course and blind as a statistic.

Losing consciousness is a delight. It always is. Don't ask why. I don't know why. The reverse is less pleasant. Entering into consciousness is a complex process, conflicted, ambiguous, huge. It is a shock to my system each day I get out of bed.

It is, in many ways, a beautiful planet. It offers lots of water and blue skies and ocean surf and strawberry jam. But I don't feel that I belong here. Is that not strange? I'm at home in oblivion. I'm at my best when I don't exist. Not existing feels better than existing. But how can I feel myself not exist? It's tricky. First, there is you. Then you get a big rubber eraser and erase yourself. It's easy. I do it all the....

We are sacks of blood supported by a framework of bone. You want to pay attention to that. Avoid war. Avoid guns and knives. And when you shave, be careful. Begin with an embryo and end with a sack of consonants. Use something soft to describe your inner parenthesis. For example, on Friday the world weighs 5.9 sextillion tons. But on Saturday it weighs less than a DVD. This is because my arm hurts. Art can be a stupefaction or a shy astronaut floating in a valentine of dirt. Which reminds me. Yesterday at our favorite Mexican restaurant there was a fly in the window. I couldn't hear a word it said. Or even if it said anything. It just seemed focused on the glass. On getting out. On finding release. Welcome. Welcome my friend to Planet Earth.

Life is a thematic snowball, a night of beautiful tar. It propagates by banjo. I use my fingers for opening the mail, closing and opening doors, and creating a sausage that propels itself across the sentence. People often ask if own a comb. I answer no, but I do have a brush. Then why don't you use it, they ask. And I shoot them. Afterwards, I clang like a bell, and shout at the books to get off of their shelves and do something about breasts. This, too, becomes a lip.

Life drags itself through its own distress seeking resolution in a melody of sand and bone. The maneuver hurls forward producing utterances of shiny cuticle. The park invades Holland. The grass sways guessing at what death is about and offers a place for food and outdoor fun.

Tungsten is different. It requires semiformal evening clothes.

Buttermilk is all about weight. It is the hay of the forest that echoes my emotion. The only thing missing from this sentence is a hummingbird splashed gently with adjectives.

In a recent interview, writer China Miéville referred to our current apocalyptic state as being pretty much insurmountable, and offered, as an antidote to feelings of hopelessness, the phrase "undefeated despair." What a marvelous phrase! Hope makes things worse. It leads to denial. So you let despair happen. You make art, you persist, you keep going. It works. Despair is a lousy feeling, but it's real, it's more affordable than health care, and it's not that bad. It doesn't kill you. It's not strychnine. It's just despair. It's the stuff of great novels by Cormac McCarthy and Fyodor Dostoevsky. Optimism is Norman Vincent Peale's frozen, idiotic grin on West 29th Street. Pessimism is a femme fatale in a sexy black gown offering you a shot of heroin.

Power to the ideology of socks, which is soft with sequestration. Power to the tenderness of cork, which is porous, and to coffee, which has blends. Power to the theatre, which tends toward action. Power to humming, which accompanies strumming, and the ring of syllables, which are assimilable, and the blossoming of speech, which circulates in words. Power to the symmetries of structure and the enchantment of floating. Power to the oval, which is almost round, and to the ellipse, which is a generalization of the circle, and resembles a circle, but isn't a circle, and has eccentricity. Power to the jackknife, which folds and can go in a pocket, and to the shoebox, which is full of tissue.

The towels are clean now and not as hirsute as the hobbits around here, partying late into the night, drinking Old Peculiar and smoking Tolkiens. We can drift. We can let our hands hang in the water. We can continue our sewing later. There's no hurry, only a few burning sensations and longings to play in a rock band. Other than that, I feel that my escape must come from within. Running is a personal favorite, but desperate times call for desperate measures. It is why I began slouching and hanging out at the drugstore. It bites to think a tree is authoritative. But yes, a twig exhibits feathers, and this, too, is a collaboration.

Before You Dig

We all speak our language with ease, but learning to speak another language is best achieved by talking in tongues.

Do I sound bossy? I apologize. I feel pungent with airplanes.

Everything in life is mutable. The moon is the moon. If the moon hits your eye like a big pizza pie, that's amore. If it doesn't, the moon is just science, and you should let it go.

The world is about anything, really, including itself. I have enough clothes until Thursday. If I'm arrested for anything, I have memorized a Philip Lamantia poem that can cut through steel. As long as that poem is in me, I can fly a helicopter through the eye of a reliquary. And see San Francisco.

I'm warm in the legs in a bed where sleep happens. When I get up I shout at the books to get off of their shelves and do something about vegetables. I like extreme, indeterminate values, but I don't like war. Who does? Daytime is not a brain.

I have a thin piece of deity in my hand. It has the scent of lavender soap. But where's the rest? We feel the absence of the divine most acutely when we're at the shopping mall. But what happened to the shopping mall? Even Sears is struggling. Macy's and Nordstrom's are closing at Northgate. I will miss the smell of caramelized popcorn and the faces of shoppers lost in reflection. All those shirts and pants and bathrobes, all those wedding gowns and mattresses.

Do you like doors that pull open or swing out? The best things happen in garages. That's pretty much the story right there. We all crash into ourselves.

And so I arrived in the 21st century bearing with me the values of the 60s, which all had to do with raising consciousness, and joy, and seeing things you've never seen before, things that were there all the time but you just didn't see them, and now this, a bloated billionaire as president of a country that offers nothing but war to its citizens, extortion in the place of health care, debt in the place of education, poison in the place of water, stinking methane in the place of beauty. Clearly, a mistake has been made. Where can I buy a can of 1966?

Sleep is the other side of life. This is that door. It opens by snoring. It understands eternity. Shovels are like that, too. They understand holes. They understand burial. They know how to dig. But first you have to dig the shovel. If you dig the shovel the shovel will take care of shoveling. All you have to do is stand there, put your foot on the back of the shovel and press down with all your might. When the door opens, go ahead in. You will be greeted by the smells of outer space. You will burn brighter. You will smell like a door.

What's Up, Dock

Dropped by Five Corners Hardware to pick up some Gorilla Glue. I mention to the young woman working at the counter how nicely cool it is in the store. It's a hot Seattle day. A rare phenomenon. She tells me it's 124 degrees in Las Vegas. The asphalt is bubbling.

Nicolas Cage lives in Vegas. I wonder why. What has attracted him to Las Vegas? Why has he chosen to live in Las Vegas rather than Los Angeles, or New York, or Chicago? It occurs to me that not only do I not know Nicolas Cage, I know absolutely nothing about Nicolas Cage, other than the roles he has filled in the movies, such as Ben Sanderson, the suicidal alcoholic in *Leaving Las Vegas*, or Cameron Poe, the ex-Army Ranger finishing a ten-year sentence for killing a man and being flown to Alabama where he is to be released aboard a C-123K transport prison aircraft in the movie *Con Air*, which came out in the summer of 1997.

Nicolas Cage is good at playing troubled, passionate men, whose triggered intensities lead them into desperate situations. I wonder if that has anything to do with Nicolas Cage's decision to live in Las Vegas, where he is friends with Carrot Top.

I come home with the glue and fix the white trim on the upper shelf of the refrigerator, which cracked.

Roberta swabs some glue into the crack with a Q-tip and I squeeze the shelf. The glue dries quickly. I lean the shelf against the coffee table.

I mention the Beatles at an informal meeting of neighbors. I do not recall the precise context in which I rather awkwardly extended this information, but I think it had something to do with my age and arthritis and that, more than fifty years later, the Beatle's music was still fresh and engaging, a fact I found to be relevant of something, I'm not sure what, perhaps that time and aging are illusory on some level, that despite one's wrinkles and arthritic joints the spirit can remain vital and young, full of élan and spontaneity. Unfortunately, the awkwardness of the situation did not permit that kind of elaboration.

But it's true. The computer allows an access to the past that seems quite within our reach, almost palpable.

How strange, for instance, to watch a Beatles video. I listen to "A Day in the Life" and the accompanying video in which the Beatles appear to be at a recording session with a symphonic orchestra, the Beatles all full of smiles and laughs and eccentric clothes, the members of the orchestra in formal wear, Keith Richards and Donovan visiting, a young woman leaping about. The time is drenched in nostalgia for me. Compared to the current dystopic plutocratic police state in which we now live the time seems strangely carefree, as insouciant and charmed as the Beatle's music. Of course, if you listen closely, you can also hear an undercurrent of menace, such as the man who blew his mind out in a car. That doesn't sound at all good.

I find great irony in our access to the past via computer and smartphone, a time when there was much more community. It's very easy to communicate with people now, at least electronically, and yet everyone is so isolated. Why? What happened? Why does so much information seem to separate people rather than bring them together? Why is everything so fragmented and steeped in insult and conflict?

There is also less privacy. The loss of privacy makes people feel more isolated. Fearful. Afraid to freely express themselves.

These are the judgments of a private man. A private man in a public medium.

One frequently overhears the phrase "don't judge me" these days. No one wants to be accountable. No one wants to make a statement. Except for tattoos. One's skin appears to be the parchment for one's history and declarations. What do the symbols mean? You could keep a conversation going for quite a while with someone and their tattoos.

Yesterday I saw a man in a wheelchair, his shirt off, covered in tattoos head to feet, getting a new tattoo just outside the new KEXP building at the Seattle Center Fairgrounds.

I watch the French news. The lead story is Emmanuel Macron's invitation to Donald Trump to visit Paris during Bastille Day, to which Jean-Luc Mélenchon, former president of the Left Party and founder of the progressive movement La France Insoumise, for which he was elected a Member of Parliament recently representing the Bouches-du-Rhône, a highly populated and diverse department which includes Marseille and Aix-en-Provence, strongly objects, saying that Monsieur Trump is violent and has no business being there.

The world has become a very strange place. Or should I say humanity has become a very weird species. My brain is inundated with enigmas. Little enigmas. Big fat enigmas. Beefy enigmas. Galactic enigmas. Cloudy enigmas. Enigmas running on love gasoline. Enigmas growing like vines around an aqueduct. Enigmas in embryonic underwear. Enigmas riding bicycles wrapped in Eiffel Towers.

How many molecules does it take to make a mollusk moral and a proverb elegant?

I never met a molecule I didn't like.

I don't understand the sadism of billionaire politicians. I don't understand the mechanisms of denial. I don't understand the persistence of delusional thinking.

"The only way to be in agreement with life is to disagree with ourselves," observed Fernando Pessoa. "Absurdity is divine."

Do you prefer pulling a door open or pushing a door open? I prefer pulling. If you push the door there is a greater chance of hitting someone. Revolving doors confuse me. I get a little anxious when I approach a revolving door. I feel that it is something you have to plunge into. Like knowing when to begin singing a song after the band has started. I cannot do that. That is how I know I am not a musician.

But I am absurd. Who isn't?

Here is my diagnosis: the lake is absurd. The waves are absurd. The water is absurd. The shores are absurd. The canoes are absurd. The reflections are absurd. But the dock? The dock is not absurd. The dock is totally ridockulous.

We Are This Sensation That Keeps Happening

How many people live in your heart? I have a population of two million. My back hurts. I'm stuck in this position until my mind spreads its wings and I leave the earth and remember the power of my grandfather's coffee.

Most of my narratives include at least one accordion but this time I'm going to insert a slice of cherry pie and the dream of a silver moon.

We are this sensation that keeps happening, you and I, because we're alive and that's what happens when you're alive, you grow a periscope or you don't, and I mean that in its most metaphorical sense. I like to explain how things work. Words work fine by themselves, but if you give them some advantage, like talking, or writing them down, they tend to reflect this attention back to you in the form of boardwalks and sand.

The infinite horizon. Folds of motel drapery. A sock on the floor.

The world works best when you step back and let it all happen on its own. Think of this as water running through a hose. The house of language is spinning through space. I'm immersed in language and pushing these words toward you. Why? Because I visited Great Falls, Montana, once. I mean, what exactly goes on the life of an oyster anyway?

These are my experiments in dirt. No, the locomotive isn't an oval, but it is symbolic. I put it here for the details, which are combustible, and brassy as a T-shirt. The river is full of counsel. We should listen to the water. It seems to know what it's doing. Water is like that. So transparent, so full of currents and fish. Even the ocean is a dead giveaway. The groupers are choirs and the angelfish hum. Life is a journey. Or so they say. The ghost of a pig, for example. Or boats. There is a sky at the bottom of the ocean. It is made of churchyards and clouds. One day it will rise to the surface and I will feed it my wounds. How do you weigh the world? I blow on my fingers and wait for the sun to rise in my thumb.

I'm concerned with the camels. Arthur Rimbaud keeps piling goods on their backs. It's a long way across the Danakil Desert. The horizon resembles a rugged knife. The salt has the weight of an archaic stamp.

But that was another lifetime ago, before the Beatles or Allen Ginsberg. Today the goats are helping the carpenter of the sky build a beautiful waterfall. This will achieve the humidity of a cardiovascular tomahawk as fleshy folds of indignity boil in the vigilante's violin.

The air gets cool and dimples the intervals like vespers in a Yorkshire gym. I see no chicken whose shape in chocolate would circumscribe my guests. Ergo, I forego the lanolin, and prepare for transit.

Independent portholes chronicle the passage of Greenland. Glaciers calve. The ship rises and falls. Our nerves are alert with the ocean's unpredictability. The thrill of ice and its groans.

Did I mention cranberry? Colors burst out of me. Some of them are charming and some of them are bitter as wormwood, or the chancellors of Germany. These colors drift quietly to the floor and become fairy tales in which the marsh tells tales of thorny sprawl. Colors are just the humors of an icy whippoorwill. There will be more when the kneecaps arrive with their lambent taxis and vegetable hats. Nothing is insentient, not even TV evangelists. Everything grins on the subatomic level. The recitals are sluttish but the diseases are memorable.

The world itself is a fabrication, so why not the crunch of gravel beneath your feet? There are circumstances in which a panacea of light strikes the lake with its ribbons of gold and I can hear the smell of the ceiling and it's a balm to the axle of my nerves. This is called reflection, and is welcome to the portfolio of life.

Are you aware right now of what's happening? The mailbox antenna speeds into the sponge of the future spinning strands of the past.

This search isn't over. There is a bubbly autonomy to these words as they percolate through consciousness.

Where did the goats go?

They're still here. They're standing on my head, grazing on tufts of Ethiopian coffee.

What would I do without poetry? I'd still have the creak of the door and the laundry to fold.

Spaceship Coffee And A Dog Named Hoax

Why is there no income for making words glitter? I will look into it.

The murders may have been a mistake.

Where is this going? Is it empowered by a telos? No. It is not empowered by a telos. It is empowered by a 20-volt rhubarb. I am an embassy for a Danish rhinoceros. I love gelatin and clutter. A thorny Gothicism speaks to my need for seasons and felts.

How do I feel? Like a 20-volt rhubarb.

Thought is the other side of life. It happens in the head. The head is an ideal place for thought. It's round, it's hairy, and everything in it has a feeling of charming detachment. Nothing I think seems to matter. That means I can think anything that I want to think. As long as I don't write it down or open my mouth and let it come out. As long as I keep it in my head we're all safe. But if I feed it words and let it out we're in trouble.

Or not. Who knows. Getting a bunch of words out there can have unintended consequences. I didn't invent this language. I didn't invent any language. Truth is, language invented me.

What is it to think? It is to fill the brain with images and questions. Worries, apprehensions, judgments, anxieties, regrets are the byproduct of thought. The sticky resin of reason.

Here it comes again. The English language. This time it's got a girl in its claws.

People who think mathematically have mathematical thoughts. If X is an integer then what is Y? If Y equals zero then X is an alias. This is because you can only add or subtract variables that alternate between eternity and a rodeo. A penis cannot be expressed by a coconut.

I continue to think about life on Mars. It's probably microbial, not a creature with arms and legs or tentacles, big head with bulging veins and huge cat's eyes of outer space mysteries, but I don't care, life is life, even when it's invisible, or in my case, fucking up my gums. And so it begins. The suppositions are ripped into radar.

Whatever happened to Melanie Safka? Girl about my own age. Old lady now. Sang "Lay Down (Candles in the Rain)" at Woodstock. Does it matter? Probably not. It's about this time of day that my pants fall down. It's my way of saying hello. We are, as a matter of course, conscious of ourselves, but we do not, as a matter of course, know ourselves. For example, the bacteria are holding me hostage. And I'm beginning to like them.

People gather in the square as Julius Caesar passes. Somebody shoots him with a rubber band. He doesn't notice. For he is Julius Caesar and he is preoccupied with things of state and empire. Also, rubber bands did not exist during the time of the Roman Empire. Rubber was discovered by the Olmecs who used it in their ballgames. The Mesoamerican ballgame was similar to racquetball. Me, I'm not much into sports. I prefer sitting in armchairs having conversations with myself. Wondering what thought is. And how to get rid of it.

I am the language that you worry about. I have a dog. His name is Hoax. You'll find a gun in the glovebox. It's loaded with truth.

A cup of coffee is a moody excess, but what the hell. I don't care for tea. Tea is a bicycle. Coffee is a spaceship. Forget bourbon. That won't take you anywhere. At least that's my version of the story. It began with a voyage through the treetops and ended somewhere on Park Avenue. Jackson Pollock pissing in Peggy Guggenheim's fireplace.

Agitation is a feeling but not a very good one. It's unreliable. Religion pretends to be an answer and then crawls through the sentence searching for an unseen power. The words say consciousness is an amusement park in Florida called The Holy Land Experience and ends with a slave rebellion on Mount Noam Chomsky.

Everything else just seems to sleep unwritten or drift around my index finger. Come here baby, sit down on my knee. The high raw honey of your eyes heats the words of the Bible.

Where do songs come from? Where in the world did Willie Dixon's "Insane Asylum" come from? That's one mysterious song. The emotion is so intense. It's a song of tragic import, but he takes it so far into the realm of melodrama it almost seems to have a comedic sense underlying it. It would be laughable if it weren't so compelling. When Koko Taylor begins singing, "when your love has ceased to be," I get shivers. Her voice cuts through me and nearly brings me to tears. The emotion is so real, so gripping. It would open the cruelest heart to tenderness.

I hear an identity chattering under my skin. It's exciting to see our minds come together in a sentence. Is this that sentence? I am standing here dressed in words. It's a little embarrassing. This all takes place in a moccasin. The pamphlet said so.

Listen To The Water

Everybody wonders, what am I doing here?

Dishwashing does this.

The sponge is squeezed and is a cause of conversation. But the me, or the sense of me that is within me, that seems to be in my head, viewing the events of my life like an air traffic controller at Charles de Gaulle Airport, the me that is squeezing the sponge of me, that's listening to Joe Cocker, taking in his voice, the song, "I Shall Be Released," digesting and reflecting and swirling it around in my consciousness, the drama of a man imprisoned in his skin, a cell, cells doing what cells do in a cell, silly cell, cell of cellular knowing, the brain like a cabbage, a head of cauliflower, all those convolutions taking in the world and letting it back out in words, altered, renewed, muted and mutilated. The exchange is constant. There are fluids everywhere becoming solids. Solids turning liquid. Liquids becoming vapor. Clouds hung over a distant horizon. Any day now. Any day now I shall be released.

The important part of living is to wonder about why one is living. Just hold on. Grab something if it helps. Write something down. Yell at your hair. A genie will appear and murder the mirror.

Clothing becomes bizarre in the summer. Call me Captain Fuchsia. Would you like anything? A glass of water? You've come this far. Let's grab that stupid zeitgeist and yank it right out. Who needs it, right? Later, when we've gotten to know one another a little better, I will show you my favorite feeling, which is prodigal and squishy. I struggle with scruples all the time. For example, if you cut a word in half, does a meaning spill out? Salvation doesn't come in a box. It sits down in a sentence like George Harrison surrounded by dwarfs.

It is not the world but being in the world that pulls ourselves into ourselves. My neck squirts out of me like a Roman Catholic. I agree: space calls for water. If you're feeling transcendental, I suggest William Blake, Hieronymus Bosch, Salvador Dalí and Max Ernst as a good place to begin.

Listen to water. The river is full of counsel. It seems to know what it's doing. Water is like that. So transparent, so full of currents and fish. Even the ocean is a dead giveaway. The groupers are choirs and the angelfish hum. Life is a journey. Or so they say. Who really knows? All the prophecies are boiling.

There's a sky at the bottom of the ocean. It is made of churchyards and clouds. One day it will rise to the surface and I will feed it my wounds. How do you weigh the world? I blow on my fingers and wait for the sun to rise in my thumb.

It was believed in ancient Greece that if a snake licked your ears you would have the gift of prophecy. I rub fat on the glow of a sound. The sound crawls into a sentence and coils around an irritability. Here comes the prophecy: hiss. flicker flicker. hiss. Consider your ears licked.

Hills Like White Elixirs

I love my desk. Nothing is insentient, not even TV evangelists. Everything grins on the subatomic level. This morning, as I ate a banana, I thought about the quiet life of the refrigerator. It's exhausting to be around other people. Any fine-grained rock will tell you that. But you must chip at the edge with a geologist's hammer. I have to go now and patrol the maples in their underclothes. Together we will respond generously to the face of Tutankhamun staring out of eternity.

If you want my opinion, poetry is mostly autumn. Then winter comes and turns the world into prose.

I'm breaking free of my chains. I'm no longer in this world I'm looking at tourists. I'm adrift in rivers of reverie. I feel the wet of the universe like two sweaty wrestlers locked in a fierce embrace. Whatever you may feel right now don't go hungry. Eat this sentence. It will make you strong and beautiful. Trust the pain in your life. This is the André Breton room. Portugal materializes across the desert in the middle of a cuticle while Peter Green plays "Albatross" and a lobster tap-dances on a picnic table. The bird is a summons. The body is a witness. Blood runs down the motel curtains. Everything else will walk beside you until we get somewhere.

I'm out to prove the worth of writing in a postliterate culture. I do that by drifting, like clouds. Sobbing does the rest. Hills like white elixirs.

Subatomic particles bum around from bikini to bikini until I'm nothing but adjectives and hairspray. I use my fingers for ceremonies and vandalism. This is called reflection, and is suitable for public performance. All I need is a garage, a mattress, and an inflatable doll.

Dear pencil: are you sugar? It must be love, a viscous mass of mischief riding around my thumb. Poetry dares to boil in a Hawaiian shirt, which is sticky, and collides with reality, but smells of employment. The sky bangs around like a pizzeria. The sunset dwarf has a long barbiturate in his hand. This is how we do it, baby. Kansas says "welcome." And the Rockies say goodbye.

I have been around the sun seventy times. This means that I am entitled to the use of the showers and special events that help me stay motivated. I dip my pen in the ink of sleep and write my name in water. I have the etiquette of a carnival. I walk through Thursday, a nebula of stars and hammers soaked with yo-yos, and I clank. The abyss caresses a road. There is honey in the wind. A mollusk has a round purpose and a nacreous soul. It all makes sense as a Ferris wheel, a large sparkly rash oozing amusement. What does Mammon mean in the Bible? How many babies do you have? The umbrella doesn't need you. The umbrella is its own door.

I have no theories of life. Logic suggests that at one point there was an intersection of the organic and the inorganic. A mixture of molecules became animated. Metal catalysts formed proteins and lipids and ribonucleic acid. This is one theory. Another suggests that acetylene and formaldehyde underwent a sequence of reactions that resulted in a chain of nucleotides. Still another suggests it's all about spontaneity and outer space. Me, I think it's mostly jeans and gas stations. Random acts of kindness. The mind likes these things. It's exciting to see our minds come together like this, isn't it? The door opens and here we are, packed with straw and crinkled like a scrotum.

Monster Eyeball Brandy Snifter Blues

Here's a smear of poetry on a glass slide: little microbial words create sugar. A sweetness for the mind. Hormones propel us into trouble. It's amazing, all the ways the world might enter your head and assume a presence there. The leathery smells of a shoe repair shop. The smell of the sea. The feel of the sky. The labyrinth of halls in an insect. Ever stick your hand in a bucket full of minnows? Anywhere you go nature goes. U2 in Las Vegas, the brushwork of Vincent Van Gogh. The roar of the sun in a turbulence of gold.

Saxophones moan with apparitions of surf. Is this a dream, or a table? There is this to say about envy: I don't envy it. It will come to you as a yacht and require navigation. Who wants that?

Almost anything in language or done by words is an invention. I smell the filet of a dead chimera. The power of Picasso is most evident in the nude. So please: don't touch my desk. My head is an arena of scars. Afterthought can be helpful but don't get lost in rumination. Rumination will ruin you. Ruin you with rumination. Eyeballs circling your head.

I travel the flame of an old woman. The wick is a sentence. I insist on chairs. There is this to say about skin: expect secretions. They will come to you with sentences of their own. They will decorate the void beneath everything. Our journey ends in Bellagio. And then there is swimming. That's a whole new sensation. It has to do with aging and synesthesia. Hear the odor of the hippopotamus in my desk drawer. It sounds like a tongue falling through buttermilk.

It's hard to tell a joke when you're drowning. Don't drown. And keep joking.

Logic suggests that at one point there was a chain of words seeking to become a city in Pennsylvania. The door opens and here we are, watching a movie. William Hurt hurries with a hurt back to a Paris taxi. They stop a few blocks later to pick up Geena Davis.

This is a typical afternoon for me. The mind likes these things. Creosote and ice cream, the ocean rolling in and out. Everyone needs a sense of the sublime. Otherwise life gets awkward and ugly. It's like holding a brandy snifter with a pair of boxing gloves on your hands.

Winter expands my sense of black, especially that bone black of Rembrandt's paintings, which he got from the charring of animal bones or waste ivory in a closed crucible, and used it to clothe his subjects with the somber facts of life. And what, pray tell, are the somber facts of life?

Mortality. Hard-to-get-at elbow joints. The rumble of the stomach during group meditation. Sticky fingers, seborrheic dermatitis, the taste of grass when you're grazing on a mohair dish of monster eyeball. The weight and movement of the world, which is constantly in rotation, constantly changing, constantly demanding that you change with it.

Can a pain be ugly or beautiful? I once saw an oyster in a low-cut gown. It made me get in a car and drive. I was mad with energy. I had to tell people. I had things to share. Sensations and feelings, oysters and gowns. Neurons glimmer, exchanging impulses like sailors in a topless bar. Nothing is profane. It would take a Paganini to get even close to describing the scent of olives in southern Greece in late November, or the flight of a barn swallow just after the sun rises in Shoshoni, Wyoming. Form is emptiness. And emptiness is form. How can you not be in love with guitars? Imagine what you could do with hooves.

Gray Morning

I gorge on wheat thins while gazing at the remaining liquid in the bottle of dishwashing soap. It's a pretty color. I'm engrossed. Dreamy. High on marijuana. I wonder about things. Warblers. Disk harrows. Ponds. Is Schrödinger's frog the same as Basho's frog? Is one both leaping and about to leap? Can a person simultaneously be alive and dead? The Buddha once said: "Every morning I drink from my favorite teacup. I hold it in my hands and feel the warmth of the cup from the hot liquid it contains. I breathe in the aroma of my tea and enjoy my mornings in this way. But in my mind the teacup is already broken."

The basis for reality is the circle. Context. Intertextuality. Conservation of the circle is the core dynamic in nature.

New day. I hear the crows cawing. It's a still gray morning. Winter is retreating, leaving behind a patchwork of snow and ice. The streets are bare. The sidewalks are almost bare. There are still patches of snow and ice here and there.

Pyrotechnics are the rhetoric of donkeys.

There. I said it. And now we have a road on which to impose our impossible thoughts. Pull them like wagons. Push them like wool.

The lid on the Smucker's strawberry jam jar is plaid like a tablecloth. I maneuver the remaining jelly at the bottom with a butterknife. It comes easily, goopily to the edge, and I maneuver it onto a slice of toast.

It's as if the universe were under my skin, and everything I did and saw and smelled and heard and lifted and touched were a continuous satori of enormous translucence. That said, where does this anguish come from? Is it sequential, like a TV series, or the neurotic intrigue of a woodcut? Is it idle worthless worrying, or something bubbling up from the unconscious, a muskrat or diphthong? Oil. Rain. A little brown cloud.

These things happen. It's a big planet. Any distress can serve as the lungs of an equation that can't be solved by self-indulgence or joviality. One can coax the mystery of yellow into fuller expression by affirming the fragrances of spring with an ancient melody. Animals swimming toward the shore. Miles Davis in Montreux.

Who we are might be predetermined, but there is nothing perfunctory about a paper towel. Great lengths have been taken to make it absorbent but tough. We defy time, but time doesn't give a shit. Time is time. It slices space into nice little manageable bits. Act One, Scene One. Old friends are reunited. New triumphs are celebrated. Courage is found to face the dishes. A little circumlocution can go a long way. Remnants of mousse wash away into the dark. A rationale is found to ease the remorse for everything percolating in the italics of a whirlwind impetuosity. But who is the man in the black coat, and who is that woman with him? She looks like Maria Casares. And yes. The big plates go on the lower shelf.

Now you shall see everything will go very slowly. Time is flexible. You can bend it. You can make pretzels out of it. Time is what gives space its special character. This is a meditative business. This is why things go slow. The snow takes a long time to melt. Each day there's a little less. Each day there's a little more traction, a little more purchase on the surface. And the crows come swooping down in elegant resolution, sure of one thing: get that peanut. The ground has been covered in snow for a full week and there's been little to eat.

When I think of suede, I think of violins. I have the greed of the novelist whose lecture is unseasonably bulky. Nevertheless, the story moves forward, modulating itself as the detonations thunder in the distance and the sights of Moscow begin to shape our philosophy of empire.

There's a dragon knocking at the border. Three hundred miles to the south, a woman combs her hair in the basement of a book about tug boats. I'm trying hard not to harm her propeller by using too many words to describe it, but the cat has a shadow and the bureau has a silence that only an egg could offend. Trust me. I'm not here to oblige any algorithms. This is about lucidity, how it writes its own meat into existence and then wiggles around with a genetic irritation. I enjoy creating personalities for boxes. Their lids are always so unfettered. How can you not study molasses? I work every day to enhance the feeling of elephants. The river is slippery because it's wet not because it's indecipherable. Although, there's that as well. I aim to bring about a state of verbal tourism. I'm a little weary, but I think I can make it work if you're willing to pay some attention to the confusion. Ginger and rubies sleep in the plaster. The mushrooms approve of damask. The shawl is aromatic, but the digressions are shocking. It's what we want. What we all want. The cold hard stare of the moon. A man playing a trumpet. Reality granted its final wish: the ghost of a pain gurgling the heart of a mockingbird.

Customs

It's splendid to be at the border of your eyes. When the metaphors rise from their bondage and begin a conversation with our minds we will create an otherworldly blue. I apologize for these generalities. Am I on the wrong planet? Is that it? The short answer is yes. The long answer is art and books. Apes. The crackle of twigs.

The universe opens its mouth and goes askew in the warm sugar of a paragraph. I groan like a woman tilting to the side. This could be the end of pinball. I say: be a beautiful applause to yourself. The truth is not always slender. Sometimes it is reptiles. Language is a puppet. It is simpler than all the other pulleys strung together making the scenery come closer. Egypt steps into the Nile and shines. I'm the only one here. But I do feel carnal and wet.

The writing of the mollusk finishes its fingers in the sink. And so it is written: there is nothing sadder than a forehead.

Reality just isn't what it used to be. The mind craves meaning. Watch as it tilts into cohesion. The skin of a balloon produces sparks when it's rubbed. It will stick to the ceiling. You can leave nothingness in the dryer for as long as you want. It has an amiable smell and helps our understanding of the world. Therefore be glad. We hold these truths to be self-evident: bath towels are magnificent and jelly is a friend of daylight.

Existence may be a linguistic predicate, but it is not a "real predicate," or property. It's mostly a middle-aged woman standing in the rain in a leopard-skin bathrobe waiting for her dog to take a shit. The rest is tits and dragons. No, the romantic spirit isn't dead. Maybe it's a truck. Whatever eternity is, this poor old planet has been trashed beyond repair. But don't worry. The whole idea of death is prevented by iPods.

Life on planet Earth is getting weird. Everything is getting dry and dead and archaeological. Holes play openly on my chin. One of them is a mouth. This would be clumsy if it weren't rich brown gravy on my mashed potatoes at night. That's how strong my love is. The people of Earth have gone insane. They wrap everything in plastic. Not me. I'm wrapped in skin. My body goes walking down the street like Charlie Musselwhite's harmonica trickling giant pieces of music.

I know this feeling. Just look at what I'm wearing: a tiara, a tutu, and a pair of dark leather gloves. Now do you believe me? My proprioception flirts with magnetism. This is a feeling I've learned to enhance with drugs and incantation. And that's the strangest feeling of all, the one that smells like a smudge pot in a cherry orchard, and walks around like Baruch Spinoza feeling the planets in his arm.

There is sometimes a good clean feeling of being alive and wet in the rain. Not to put to morbid a spin on it, but that's what's real at my age. Arthritis, bursitis, appendicitis, conjunctivitis, and Columbus Day. The world is largely a matter of perception. But there are problems with that. My brain weighs approximately three pounds. Planet Earth weighs about 1,000 trillion metric pounds. I can't squeeze a 1,000 trillion metric ton planet into a three-pound brain. I can, however, make a pot of coffee that feels like wildlife. Why are artists always stuck with defending art? This is not a happy planet. Nothing adds up. I just like it when frogs grip something and hang on for dear life. I leave hope to the angels. I'm better with a hammer.

Thus Begins The Tarpaulin Day

Faith engineers clouds. Splash hears an onion. The western climate is a god. The tamarind tends to its tendrils and thus begins the tarpaulin day.

Monday's raw glass clinks against the evidence. It's dramatic shaving a hook, but also a little soapy. The coupon edges toward the jump and finds a pocket of rope. The polar rake is talking to a funeral pyre. Twist this into a gulf of Sunday and I will mint a new spatula.

The new pan is already a big hit. Plastic ravishes the bicycle, which rattles with prayer. Phenomena engulf the expansibility of the notebook. Saturday's bones are Sunday's lungs. It's another King Moiré Thursday on Mars and the floats are passing by. Princess Di waves to the dead.

I wash my face in buttons. Time is a molecular caress. The planetarium is our jump room. We find ourselves by creating facsimiles of California. The point has a radius fork, diamond teeth in a plaster wall. All of us flickered when the magic became eager. It was shaken by revelation and crackled like moon shadows as it was folded and put in the suitcase. Magic isn't always what you believe it to be. There are steps involved, and chewing and tilting to the side. Euclid secluded in books. Nothing denies the daughters of the staircase. This is where the butter finds its full force.

I know. You thought it was jam, right? Memory keeps its needles in the recesses between the spectra of our everyday lives. Prickly guts cause division to imitate the curls of evolution. I belong to the fence. The mat kicks keenly, but the welcome never grows thin. Its mirrors urge reflection. Its charter promotes elk.

My career in poetry appears to me as a fever dream. My bones are still a memory of that time I drifted down the Danube. The tibia's scarlet temperament rises into touch where it assumes a greeting in the intimacy of skin. Asian designs walk around in metal. The emulsion is a fugitive corollary. It's apricot roast material, a science bullet tiger, a watermark's buckled harness. I climb through the thorny season of your eyes. I don't build bonfires only to deny them. I build bonfires to warm the crustaceans and all the contagions possible in a sphere of words.

When we talk of engineering, we attempt to design a better world. Clothes like wasps, huge nerves folded into walking, each step a potential rattlesnake, flying walruses, polar coronations. Bears stirred into personhood.

The eccentric weight of the bandage on my toe is bulbs to my cartilage. The thin distress of twirling an imaginary baton results in unlocking its inner appeal. Glue loops for a pink candle. The foggy corners of a coconut spring. The fragrance of lavender cut into slivers of wisdom. It makes me want to mourn the death of my shoe.

I begin every day in the same blood and mucous and begin looking immediately for metaphors to adorn the tumult of stimulation.

Stimulation assumes a form of lyrical abstraction until it reaches the image sensors at the edge of our breath and becomes a space for private reflection. It's just a little like being on the shoulder of the highway instead of behind the wheel of a jaguar when little else makes sense except glitter.

The tender caliber of the hummingbird starts the knives of the puddle. Chestnuts and snowballs make a mosaic out of the accordion afternoon. The cathedral rests in its stone. We prop the ocean up with desks. The sensuality of reverie is apparent in its agility. The textures dispel the mysteries of the elevator. Cubes with kinetic holes crash through the bingo game causing a stampede to the door. This leaves a space for the poem to sit down and mean something. What, I don't know. It just steams and crackles. Balloons pop. French ochre profits mightily from black, and there's nothing obscure about energy. It's all rails and gravel and the gospel of iron. Flux, horses, and the flap of tarpaulin.

Intramural Outlaw Cookies

I'm guessing a dashboard cohesion. Let me introduce you to a nuclear peacock. Unlucky fecund checkers played by portico toys. The masseuse jumps through a geometry book. Fireside figurines obviating typewriter darts. Purple jets for a portable marathon wink. It takes three days to collect a sequence. Lonesome road on which an elf finds a radio whacking a furry garage in a song about macaroons. This is naturally phrased as a form of flimflam, which is always hasty to swing on an insinuation.

Horny smut infusing a delirium of wardrobe refrigeration. Titanic life of a bohemian vaudeville. It could happen to rawhide. Please muster a conduit and tell me what the introspection can confiscate. The brain moved sideways like a crab all the way to the side of the head and sat in a puddle of words throwing dishes at a thesaurus. A porthole sucrose invented itself in butter. The photography had a fierce climate in its knobby linen. We used it to care about a diagonal. Hornets of the underworld wielding gumdrop vaginas.

The moisture of an alibi stumbles into evaporation revealing wainscot and caricature. I taste the flame of a vision. The sweater swoons in its knitting blinking like a taillight on the back of a vicissitude. The weight of a door hides from the street. The moon is old and extracurricular. I feel leavened, as if about to clamber aboard a mountain and ride it into hysterics, places where the rock kisses the sky and the sky reclines in its sessions of sweet silent thought, dropping rain on the robots and making the mulct succeed at spring.

Paregoric garden for a misanthropic afternoon. The python is thick with punctuation. Semicolons hiss with courtly neuralgia. The montage reciprocates with a cacophony of luxurious wax. All the mirrors come together in a rebellion and vomit reflections on the floor of a greasy spoon. Today's special is a halibut garnished with cowboys. History is a nightmare from which we're all trying to awaken. The seismograph sponsors an inquisitive tentacle. It wraps itself around a coatrack, impregnating the day with a lisping vulnerability. I like the seats by the window. I can hear myself think. It sounds like the rustle of taffeta in a Texas brothel.

Intramural outlaw cookies overrule the mantel vortex. Pleasantries are always genealogical. I don't know why. Recognition is squalid. I prefer to be crinkled. There is wisdom in soup. We must sometimes look elsewhere to find the proper retort. It's not the weight of the insult that counts, it's the radioactivity of the zeal. Witchcraft is for babies.

The peanut is a perfect star. But the star is not a peanut. The star is a zip code. Aristotle states that happiness is the most desirable of all things. I can't argue with that. The peanut is a perfect zip code.

A female movie star stumbles around backstage at a TV quiz show wearing nothing but a search warrant. Pencils subsist on graphite, thereby proving the existence of palmistry. Fingers are tabloids teetering on bobsleds. I see no reason not to clean the senses with a Hollywood premier. The longitude of an irritation is ransomed by a ginger snap, while a latitude requires chocolate. I also have a theory about sagebrush, but I'm saving that for a Beatles concert. I live in the past. The rent is cheaper and the landlord is dead.

Crackling Out

A proposal is our squeezed footnote, our ticket to snow. Pungent rawhide to cool your hurl. Sensation horses running into enamel. Wave there like a bend deformed on clatter. Proximity if we crawl to a diagnosis. I henna the painter's ascension to beatitude. It makes for better rags. This aerodrome beneath shakes a gulp to dilation. I swell adherence to a crimson lake. Orchid catalogue at candy. A vertebrae of fire beaming a boa to this moment to make it lengthen into thought. Haunt cactus below alkali where my fidgeting happens. Invisible cylinder your enfoldment subverts to fish because none of this is slender.

I'm beginning to get that feeling that words are about to interact with mushrooms. Inches believe it to a gluttonous throng. Bulb by it focused orange. Ruminate secrets as pain. The garments I unravel cloud the coffee. My asphalt compass is just a shape.

Wander consciousness knowing soap into wedlock. Afternoons we skulk through technicolor. If a blaze is propelled by dimes then the light alights on foam. Energy brings the horizon to this car. Sky bulb my climb into your heart. Plant snow if they want the walnut. Eye am my own Fauve clutter. A fight edges my construction. Stilts Ear erects your eyebrow below your intestine because a handstand requires folklore. It's not the heat it's the experiments that reach through time. Seashore sidewalk I move by cog and whistle. The emotion about life has been expressed as a thistle, not because it's unemployed, but because it's yucca.

I drag the cat bicycle to the other side of the universe and ride it around a drawing. I think it's a tug. It's a long fiddle we mirror you and I. My twig painting has since been rubbed. Murmur with a prominence then pummel it and add a soupçon of urine. Explode beyond perturbance dig my parable. My ramble riddle is haunted above its secrets. The groan happens if it's pinned to your throat follow it to the words hunched together in venison. There's a version of this in Russian that evolves into torpor. Umpteenth sweet bug I feel on my thigh. Indispensable secretion we have unofficially designated to conclude in thumbs. I fall through joy in a little boat of my own making called a hodgepodge.

I feel the power of an African road. Clatter your counsel to a life of canoes. The lightning I see behind the Pythagorean birch impels our development. The athletic wind flexes the fence. I turn infrared if I murder a recruitment. It's as if I yearned to supervise breakfast with a tentacle and a Celtic harp. Ask the spirits what I can soothe and if I can soothe it I will soothe it with backrubs and fungus. My opinions about biography glide through this sentence malleable hot and cloth. We mint Cézanne images with our brains and our ironing. Quicken the trigger and I'll build a sleigh and crackle on out of here.

So, you see, words are important after all. They float here from England and walk through me like Mother Goose. If this infringes on the truth of mousse, I will seek other symptoms with which to diagnose Florida and its semantic predicament as a drawer of silverware. Taproot is immaterial. It's the loops that stir the lips to aluminum.

A Frog Crashing Through Silverware

I open a jar of ointment and say "cure the knee." And the knee is cured. Or not. I see a package hover the table and then the table issues a pink melody to put in the air. I feel the elephants heating the interior of the helicopter. And then I visit certain regions of a chicken. Echoes move the oil. The clouds mingle with meringue. Sorbet exceeds the build of electrons and issues a direct stump for the combustion of understanding.

And to think it's only Wednesday.

Snow fingers chrome the keepsake. My memory of your outskirts. Which is a small organ at the front of the vulva. The fuchsia lung law courses through my realism. And what is realism? The stubbornly held gym franchise, that's what. The ingots of honey I find at the summit of the mountain. The underworld misunderstood as a mackerel.

I smell turpentine. The sequelae of my theatre clothes is preoccupying. But I like it. I like it. Yes I do. The gerundive shoulder of time strengthens with isometrics. The hum of muslin, the scratch of blackberry vines. I roam to figure a fiend of lust and luster, rattling throughout.

I want to furnish a thoughtful black with a universe of pearls. Sugar is a key to snow. The phenomenal bang of the coconut tree, the soft hand of darkness. The chief cause of maps is tables and chairs. Rivers are more mercurial. They shine like prophesies. They roll over rocks brimming with picnics and whirls. Old wood. Candy in a birch canoe.

I have thorny hummingbird fingers. My favorite beverage is a pendulum foundry. Is pasta a form of exultation? Yes, it is. If spring meets its own abstraction, the result is citrus. A frog crashing through silverware. Moonlight on a suit.

I'll take your hand, you take my hand. Together we'll get away.

Sings Neil Young.

A conflagration of waves glories in the sound of clouds scraping over a caribou. The rush of the greenery capsule blossoms in my index finger. I burst, twisting to buy a sad honey bee. I climb onto a black awning and become a minute of mirth.

I need a marshy button to live. The fulminating phenomenon of a note-book. I want to pin a climate to this paragraph so I don't have to dream alone. My shoulder twinkles with understanding. I understand water. I don't understand neoclassical economics. I offer it a fat kick to the groin.

You can't walk away from an experience. They get inside you and become you. Good ones, bad ones, monsoons, moratoriums, dinghies. Wind, sunlight, horticulture.

I paint a cuddly knot. The darkness of my gym toes is strangely vertical. The fox rids himself of aggression and becomes a better fox. I maneuver the detached crust to the side of the plate and muse on the zigzag of ancestry. It all leads to welts and lingerie. I suck the iron teat of contrast. And return home to a rising tide of unrest and skeins of worry. This will be answered by the wasp. Agreement between nations. Legs distressed by their own similarity. Get out. Get out now and stir yourself into circumstance. A red crack aglow in the crawl of the sun will lead you to the other side where the molecules are sewn into musk and the dead are clawed into light.

Fantasy With A John Deere Tractor

The sun at my back, I watch my silhouette slide over the sidewalk, head and shoulders and two swinging arms and think that's it, that's ultimately what life is, what being is, the ephemerality of it all, we're only shadows after all. I'll leave some books behind that I authored, no kids, just the books, so hopefully a few bookstores and libraries will continue into the future.

What's real is the sky. That lush blue summer sky. Air and air and air thinning and thinning all the way into space.

Sometimes it gives me a sense of peace to think of myself ploughing a broad field in North Dakota, way up north by the Manitoba border, I'm riding a tractor with a sound system, listening to a Brahms symphony or Shakespeare, Hamlet brooding in his Danish castle, wondering whether to continue living, wanting out of it, oh, that this too, too sullied flesh would melt, thaw, and resolve itself into a dew, or that the Everlasting had not fixed his canon 'gainst self-slaughter! O God, God! How weary, stale, flat, and unprofitable seem to me all the uses of this world! And how strange to be hearing and mulling that in a tractor grumbling over Dakota topsoil. Because some of those tractors have fantastic sound systems, one can make furrows for wheat in a John Deere pulling a disk harrow comfy in a cab with Bluetooth, CD player, MP3 and Weatherband. Heidy ho heidy heidy ho.

Every time I sit down in a chair I feel the weight of my body find immediate relief, bones and muscles all going thank you, thank you for sitting down. Hard to imagine all this biology gone. And me with it. Whatever me turns out to be. What is me? What is I? What is subjectivity?

Scientists say subjectivity may have begun with insects. Brain scans of insects indicate that they have the capacity to be conscious, that they have something like subjective experience. It's there in the midbrain, the ancient core of the brain, where memory and perception are mingled, stewed, digested, mulled and woven into a sense of the external world, flowers and dirt and hills and sky, neural simulations of being in space, moving through space, representations of reality from a subjective point of view, subjective being Latin for "brought under," thrown out into the world under a dome of thought, perception, navigating the problems of the world, predators and prey, hurricanes and dinosaurs.

This all strikes me as odd and marvelous but missing a key feature, which is idiosyncrasy. Some of us are odd. I identify with the odd. Like old William Blake. I love that guy's defiance. He was true to his imagination. Like in his letter to Reverend John Trusler in August, 1799, "Mirth is better than Fun & Happiness is better than Mirth — I feel that a Man may be happy in This World. And I know that This World is a World of Imagination & Vision I see Everything I paint in This World, but Everybody does not see alike. To the Eyes of a Miser a Guinea is more beautiful than the Sun & a bag worn with the use of Money has more beautiful proportions than a Vine filled with Grapes."

There are boots in the closet that I hardly ever wear. But they're there.

An actress off to the right of the screen on Facebook catches my attention: Mischa Barton poses topless on a balcony in Mykonas, Greece. Her breasts are mostly in shadow. But it's not her tits causing all the fuss, it's that she's smoking a cigarette. Well, it's gross, I agree, but it's her life, her lungs.

Virtue for me has always meant living to the fullest, exceeding limits. Being absurd. Because being is absurd. Tell me it isn't. Tell me a few brief years on this planet with all these hungry, battling, sobbing people isn't just a little strange.

There are drugs to help with this. But be careful. Drugs can fuck you up.

There's also cherry pie and dollops of whipped cream to make you smile a little occasionally.

I mean, some things are obtainable. Water, fruit, shelter, fire, tall kitchen bags, dragons, infinitives, one-night stands and onions.

As Eckhart Tolle says you've got to trust the pain in your life. Because there will be a lot of that.

I see *Intérieur en jaune et bleue* by Henri Matisse reflected in our bedroom mirror and dangle a language over an abyss.

Grammaire française.

Tortiller comme un ver. Squirm like a worm.

I study George Harrison sitting in a chair in a huge English lawn surrounded by dwarfs. I've long been captivated by this image from the cover of his first solo album, the one with "My Sweet Lord." He looks so utterly at peace with himself. He seems to be really happy in those big rubber boots. He took gardening very seriously, says his son Dhani, and would stare and stare at the surrounding trees and garden making changes in his mind.

I think he and William Blake would have gotten along just fine.

Trigger

I recently watched a YouTube video about Willie Nelson's guitar, the one he plays at every concert, every studio recording, and probably when he's just hanging loose at home. The guitar is a Martin N20 nylon-string classical acoustic guitar. Nelson named it Trigger, after Roy Roger's horse. He bought it in 1969 from Shot Jackson, a Nashville guitarist who repaired and sold guitars from a store near the Grand Ole Opry. The instrument is battered beyond belief. The surface, which consists of Sitka spruce, has been gouged with autographs and chafed and smudged and scratched after having been played solidly for forty-seven years. The frets — ebony from Gabon or Madagascar inset on a mahogany neck — are so worn down they seem more like suggestions than frets. Beside the soundhole under the bridge is another splintery hole, shaped like a crescent moon, or mouth, which the constant flick of Nelson's pick has created as it brushed past the strings. The instrument looks as fragile as the web some errant spider constructed not long ago on the rear view mirror of our car, as if the tap of a finger would turn the ancient Martin to a pile of dust. What holds this guitar together is a mystery, and yet it produces a very pure and mellow sound, a strong sound.

Can an object have a soul? Sometimes, the difference between the organic and the non-organic seems negligible. Nelson has played this guitar so often, and with such loving devotion to the music, that the guitar seems to be endowed with its own soul.

I find a parallel in heat. If I turn the heat up in the room on a cold winter day I luxuriate in it. I feel enveloped by a benevolent energy. I 'm guessing that has a lot more to do with imagination than actuality, but who, when it comes down to it, can speak with final authority on what is living and sentient energy and what is merely an excitation of molecules? What is dead matter and what is a breathing substance? If matter is ultimately and essentially solidified energy, isn't it possible that the qualities of that energy are not always those opposite to life?

There's a frontier which art and poetry and music reveal. We enter a zone where the edges of things blur in distinction and presences make themselves evident in sensation, not as dead matter but living phenomena.

Is that crazy? "I'm crazy for trying and crazy for crying / And I'm crazy for loving you."

I don't have conversations with the furniture. Matter is static. Life is full of animation. Life *is* animation. The furniture doesn't mate and reproduce. Not that I know of anyway. I've never seen a couch copulate with a table, a chair eat a carpet or a carpet that needed mowing. The ceiling never changes its mind and decides to become a floor. I know the difference between a living organism and a block of concrete. And yet, it's difficult not to believe that the music that brings an instrument to life doesn't, over time, invest it with a certain talismanic energy, or like a splintery mouth in a soundboard of Sitka spruce, enrich out of loss what time has vainly claimed.

Breakfast

This morning I removed the screw holding the handle to the sauce pan I use for making scrambled eggs. The handle has a tendency to come loose. You don't want a handle coming off in your hand when you're cooking something. For a long time now it's been my favorite pan for cooking scrambled eggs. I think that's all I've ever cooked in it. I thought if I bought a new Philip's head machine screw to replace it I could do a better job tightening it. But once I got the screw out and wiped it off with a paper towel it looked fine. The problem wasn't with the screw. Something else had worn away. We'd simply have to get a new pan. That was the prudent course of action anyway since the Teflon was beginning to flake and come off. You don't want Teflon in your stomach. I have enough problems with too much butter and keeping my cholesterol down. I don't need a bunch of polymerized tetrafluoroethylene added to the mix of toxins already scrambled in my belly.

Breakfast is otherwise fulfilled. A piece of toast slathered with peanut butter and strawberry jam, scrambled eggs and a glass of grape juice to wash it down. I love food. I've grown to appreciate food more as I've grown older. I remember in my 20s breakfast consisted of a cigarette and a cup of coffee. I didn't begin eating an actual breakfast of food until my early 40s, after I'd quit drinking and smoking. That was the general pattern — a sip of coffee followed by an introsepective inhalation and exhalation of smoke — but there were mornings in my 30s when I was grievously hungover yet weirdly hungry when a helping of bacon and pancakes and fried eggs sunny side up was heaven on a plate. So I've had a good couple of decades now of enjoying food, including breakfast. I've gone through a number of phases and appetites: scrambled eggs and toast, bananas and toast, bagels and toast, oatmeal and toast, doughnuts and grape juice, cinnamon rolls and coffee, always coffee, coffee has been a staple since late adolescence.

I worry about Nebraska. The flooding there this spring has been catastrophic. Roads, bridges, buildings, homes, farms and levees have been destroyed. It's the worst flooding in anyone's memory. The most terrible thing in my mind is the loss of livestock, pigs, chickens, cattle and calves being carried away in cold, muddy, turbulent water. The extreme cold of the winter, blizzards, subzero temperatures, strong, relentless, biting winds was bad enough. But the flooding was its own form of holocaust. I can see the panic in their eyes. I can't imagine the horror of that.

And the early harvests were destroyed. Food prices will be astronomical this spring and summer. And then will come the wildfire smoke from the north in Canada and east in the Cascades. The planet is quickly becoming uninhabitable.

It all makes writing or painting or building look ridiculous. There's simply no reason for it. Though I'm not sure there ever was. There are lot of things you do in life that don't make any sense, but you do them anyway, as if you're being carried off by an invisible, supernatural current of some sort. It's an energy. A very goofy energy. It drives you. You could call it libidinal, there's elements of that, it's always generally there in one form or another getting people into trouble, but it doesn't have an erotic vibe. It is something moving through you even in moods of despair and gloom, it expands you, dilates you, makes you feel a little lighter, a little less dead, a little more worried about dying, but not overconcerned about dying either.

I go for an annual physical. I'm early. I fill it out a short form asking questions about the state of my health (hell, I could've filled this thing out and mailed it in and skipped the damn physical) and sit and read *Le parti pris des choses* by Francis Ponge, which I stuck in my jacket before I left. I wonder if Ponge ever wrote about pans? He must have a prose poem somewhere about pans. They're a natural. Such beautiful objects. I start fantasizing about sauce pans and butter and scrambled eggs. That first pat of butter that begins to melt and diffuse over the surface of the pan and then the eggs plopped in, the shells cracked expertly and evenly, the two halves tossed into the compost.

I read "Conception of Love in 1928," "I doubt that true love involves desire, fervor, passion. I don't doubt that it can: born of a disposition to approve anything, then from a friendly abandonment to chance, or to the usages of the world...," as a young man and woman walk by. The man is pushing a pram with a newborn and the woman is walking awkwardly, her legs spaced apart as she hobbles along. Funny how Ponge's quiet and rather opaque reflection on love is echoed by this ongoing reproductive drama of our species, even as the climate warms and the animals die off.

The physical goes fine and I get dressed and go back into early April sunlight and drive home. I fasted for my blood draw and have for the last few days been avoiding all my favorite foods like eggs and butter so my cholesterol levels aren't too shocking. I hate statins. All I've had so far today is coffee. I'm starving. I can't wait to get some food into my body.

No new pan yet. I get the old pan out, slice a pat of butter and drop it in and watch it diffuse into transparency. Eggs always feel wonderful in the hand. What a wonderful shape. What incredible smoothness. They crack so easily. The insides glisten, goopily, into the pan, the yolks still whole, shiny, bright yellow, like something out of fairyland. I get a wooden salad fork and when the heat of the electric burner begins to make the fluidity congeal I being stirring it up into a chaos of lumpy yellow. I add two pieces of toast slathered with peanut butter and jam and pour a glass of grape juice. Breakfast.

Crows

I take a handful of unsalted peanuts and give them a hurl onto the grass and try in my hurl to scatter them as much as possible. The crows are all waiting, perched on telephone wires and roofs and trees. As soon as the peanuts hit the ground they come swooping down from different directions. Their flight is smooth and agile, their movements quick and acrobatic. These are highly intelligent birds. If they get too close to one another they caw loudly and go on the attack. I love the way their feathers fan out and catch the air. The comical hop they do to cross a patch of ground. Their phenomenal alertness and sensitivity.

I add a two-pound bag of unsalted peanuts to our groceries while visiting the produce section at the grocery store. More peanuts for the crows. The man at the cash register is familiar. He's worked at the store a long time. He always sings. He sings everything, whatever the exchange may be at the checkout stand. He'll sing "how are you" and "is that all" and "are those cookies your cookies" in a baritone operatic voice. I frequently want to join him in song but I'm afraid he'd think I was making fun of him. I mean to ask if he sings in a choir but I'm often so taken by his singing and wanting to sing along that I forget to ask him if he sings in a group or ensemble.

Crows are associated with death. It's their black feathers. And their knowing demeanor. Crows always seem to know something. I find it uncanny how they can hear me leave the apartment building within seconds and come flying from a respectable distance.

I guess that's why they're called — in groups — a murder of crows. But I don't find death in crows. Death is everywhere. Everywhere there's life, there's also death. I don't associate death with crows. I find them lively in the extreme. Their energy is contagious. They feed greedily and bicker but when in the air they're the very model of grace.

In world mythology, the crow is often represented as an irritant, or a favorite of the gods, or Norse giants. In a Sioux legend, the people are starving because the crows — which are white — keep warning the buffalo of the approach of hunters. The leader of the crows is captured by stealth and tied to a rock with a rawhide string. An angry hunter lunges at the crow and throws him into a fire. The crow escapes, but is singed black, and ever since all crows are black.

English poet and children's writer Ted Hughes devoted an entire collection of poems to the crow, published in 1971 and titled (aptly) Crow. He describes the crow variously as a being of prophecy and mischief, a hierophant, "humped, impenetrable," a creature of "delirious joy, with nimble balance," refrigerating an emptiness, and "with the faintest breath," "melts cephalopods and sorts raw numbers out of their dregs." Hughes's crows are conduits of weird spiritual forces; ageless, inscrutable, unfathomable. "And he realized that God spoke crow — Just existing was His revelation."

God speaks crow. That's good.

Crows occasionally make a rattling sound, or clicks. I have no idea what their meaning is, what is intended, what is being remarked. And I like that. The mystery of it, the nonsense of it, the uniqueness and peculiarity of it. It's primordial. But also a little silly. A goofy sound. Wacky, yet also a little mindful. Savvy, alert, fascinated.

Nocturne

The hand is evidence of fingers. The forehead plays havoc with the local syntax committee. It's time now for a little abstraction. The world doesn't get to be empirical all the time. How else can you appreciate someone like Neil Young? Transcendence makes me feel bouncy, like Fred Astaire. Clouds and powwows float in my head like mushrooms or baptism. Until then I'm just energy. Only if we created a piano made of soap could we pursue the smoother crescendos of a woman's leg. All it requires is an attentive disposition, a little cooperation, and a velvety nocturne.

There comes a time when the news is too much. Too awful. Too demoralizing. Even the propaganda stinks. The duopoly is corrupt, income inequality is cruel & pharaonic, & the algorithms won't leave you alone. Energy impels us to run. And so we run.

Reality can go on like this all day. Structure is just the howl of ooze. Imagine a polymer. A compelling blob of elegance. Sew a face. Sputter into rock. Then invade Norway.

Existence is largely presumption. My hands smell like an emergency room. Penitent, and intent. I don't want to force a discussion. But everything just dangles in the air like a burst of gunfire. And all the surgeons are drunk.

I like things that support my body: chairs, floors, beds. Imagine a mood of pure receptivity, a zone between yes and no, a region which is all layers, stratum, lamina, folds. All words are palimpsests, but existence grumbles in the corner like 16th century Holland.

Existence, for Heidegger, is the ground of presence. It is a mode of being in the world. It is being true to life rather than self, which is really just an epiphenomenon of life, a goofy but welcoming disposition.

I don't even know for sure that I'm in my mind when it feels like I'm in my head. There are nerves throughout the body, including the intestines, so thinking involves the whole body. Anxiety is the sign that the world of familiarity has slipped away and what we find in its place is the uncanny. Mystery, enigma, inscrutability.

Without releasement, without meditative thinking, without this capacity for incongruity and transcendence, we become infatuated with calculative thinking, we get mired in the quantitative, we lose the qualitative, and nature "becomes a gigantic gasoline station, an energy source for modern technology and industry." (Heidegger, page 50, *Discourse on Thinking*).

The unknown of the known aches to unfold the map of itself. What falls away is where I have to go.

Analysis Baby

Analysis baby. Rhetorical rattlesnake with a hoe in the background. Calexico in Poland. Tour around your voice. The fence enkindles respect for knobs. Society is a construction whose umbilicus is attached to a giant goldfish named Bruce. Let my solvents touch your injury. Let my proverbs affect a kind of robin. There's electricity in your hum. My feelings are among you. They puddle into faucets. Facets. Faucets with facets. Faces. Walt Whitman sitting in a chair old as religion. It hugs my eyes like a sweet dream of nineteenth century nerves. There it is. What I've been wanting to say all along. Wheels of fire for breakfast. The way we powder our wigs. It's all so beautiful. Even the warts come out and mingle. It's not the way you smiled that touched my heart. It's not the way you kiss that tears apart my heart. It's my doggone movie collection. You can eat almost anything these days. I feel a moral coming. Here it is: walls. Embryonic personalities in the kiss factory making cans for shaving lather.

Words As Cubes In A Tray Of Abstraction

Ice implies preservation. Freezing things inactivates microbes. Bacteria, yeasts, molds. It also means preserving the polar ice cap, which stabilizes the jet stream, which stabilizes the climate, which insures the growth of food crops. We're losing the ice at the north pole. I write during a period of immense crisis. Not that words preserve anything. Words aren't ice. Words refer to ice. Stand in for ice. They are not ice. But they could be. If imagined as such, these words could be hard translucent cubes that clink in your glass. But they won't save the world. Nothing can save the world now but Superman. And a colossal quantity of ice.

Yesterday I discovered a city of elves beneath the bed. It's nothing unusual. I find strange things under our bed all the time. I find everything except what I'm looking for.

Does fragility awaken a sense of beauty? Yes, I believe it does. Beauty is often fragile. But to what extent does frailty create beauty? It's generally hue and nuance that dazzle the eyes with beauty. But aren't mountains beautiful? Are mountains frail? There's often frailty in the mountains, but the mountains aren't frail. Mountains are enduring. Mountains are sublime.

A lot of experience eludes words. There just aren't words for certain perceptions and feelings. There may be whole dimensions of experience and physical laws that puzzle our grammar and sounds. Our own biology may have limits to what we can and cannot experience. And yet I keep putting words down, putting words out there, pushing words forward, trying to sound what's out there, what new thing, what new perception, what new insight might save us from imminent peril, might save us from ourselves.

If ice didn't exist, but a cube of words, a paragraph described ice so perfectly that it created an idea of it, we could say that ice had a potential for existence. Can we say the same of gods and angels?

I like writing paragraphs that cohere around a thought, a motif thematic as mushroom. Paragraphs full of anger and sunlight. Methane embedded in permafrost.

I like the idea of words lifting things. Lions, lips, solutions. Lift your lips and say distend. Timber. Vivacious.

What would you do if a foreign language followed you home? Would you give it a bowl of milk and a pat on the back? Would you try to speak and understand it and ride it around the room?

You could knit a gallant canary.

Here's a whisper of something knocking on your brain. What is it? Georges Braque rattling a shape at a palette of paint.

I keep seeing a pair of socks at the end of the bed. A colony of meaning floating in the room. Music on my earphones. "No Stars," sung by Rebekah Del Rio.

Music soothes the lonely. Though it also helps to be palpated occasionally. Massaged by someone.

The signals of night are naked and strange. I consider living in Senegal. It's a nice fantasy involving warm, friendly people and walking down streets of lively activity and the scents of a thousand different flowers and foods. The fragrance of tea, the pungency of garlic.

My body likes to float. Whose body doesn't feel good floating? Making and drinking coffee in weightless conditions is quite difficult, but it can be done.

Biology has a face of papyrus. It's ancient and holy. Yet no one is satisfied. I hear the constant sound of construction.

You know that feeling you get when you shove a shovel into the ground? It's a rich sensation. Sometimes it's a matter of planting something and sometimes it's a matter of burying something. The context can be a broad range of things. But the actual sensation of sinking steel into the dirt is a divination of subterranean forces. Worms and roots. This is the world in its rawest form. Not even the chronology of a bottle or the sound of thunder has the force of a worm seeking direction in a sudden exposure to cold and light.

The great, wonderful physicality of the sun. Those constant explosions. Day after day.

My neighbor pounds the dirt. He's putting in a patio.

I choose my words carefully. Amphetamines are pretty. I have an antique disposition. The habit of doing dishes. I can be shrewdly obtuse or obtusely shrewd. Each life is a novel. The narration might change from day to day. It's an ongoing project.

I think of the thousands of juices and liquids that compose the functioning of my biology and wonder how it is that the amalgam of all these cells and membranes has found a story to pursue, a shore to explore.

What place is this? It's a place of dislocation, a grave unreality. Yet some of it remains real. Pain in my right arm from a dislocated shoulder. Pain in my heart from a dislocated country. That country for old men in the Yeats poem. The young in one another's arms, birds in the trees.

Beckett 88

I'm looking for a good exoplanet. Earth is finished. It's been trashed by humans. I need to get out while the going is good. We may get our first blue ocean event this summer. If you think the weather is crazy now, you haven't seen anything yet. Goodbye food security, hello famine.

Unfortunately, I haven't found any listings at Red Fin, Trulia or Zillow. The best source I have right now is Wackypedia. Wackypedia is the wackier version of Wikipedia. The information is roughly the same, it's just wackier. Wacky is good when you're looking for an exoplanet. The margin is wider, the ceiling is higher, and there's less resistance to the restraints of logic. Logic isn't going to get me where I need to go. I need to travel long distances. For that, I'll need lots of logorrhea. A Winnebago RV capable of space travel and a ton or so of pepperoni sticks.

A recent review ascertained that the exoplanets Kepler-62f, Kepler-186f and Kepler-442b were currently the best candidates for being potentially habitable. But habitable by whom? Habitable by me. My wife and cat. A murder of crows and a washing machine. There are few restaurants or laundromats in space.

By space, I mean outer space. The cold black void on the other side of our atmosphere. Once you get out of Earth's gravity, hold on to your hat. There's not much out there except neutrinos, asteroids and comets. I'm hoping we might discover a Motel 6 on Pluto, but once we get past the Kuiper Belt, it's doubtful we'll stumble upon a Denny's or Applebee's. And the likelihood of a Best Western or Four Seasons is abysmal. Outer space is long on distance and short on amenities. We'll need plenty of fortitude, ingenuity, and towels.

Kepler-62f is 1,200 light-years distant from planet Earth. I'm guessing I can do it in about 1,500 light-years if I can get the Winnebago near to the speed of light. I won't have to worry about detours or traffic.

Kepler-62f has a radius and mass bigger than Earth, so we'll weigh a lot more. That's important to consider when building a house. A rambler with no upper floors might work. The equilibrium temperature on Kepler-62f is a chilly minus 85°F. I'm definitely bringing a coat. The good news is that it most likely has a rocky surface. It receives roughly the same amount of sunlight as Mars, which isn't a lot, but if we stay indoors watching whatever reruns are drifting around in outer space, who cares.

Kepler-186f is a little closer at 582 light-years from Earth. It has a radius similar to Earth's and orbits a red dwarf. I'm not sure how I'd feel about orbiting a red dwarf, but it's got an orbital period of 129.9 days, which means more birthdays.

Proxima Centauri b is the closest, at 4.24 light years away. It, too, orbits a red dwarf. As yet, its radius and mass have not been calculated. This is discouraging. It also gets 2000 times the stellar wind pressures of Earth, which is enough to blow any atmosphere away. I'm guessing Proxima Centauri b is just not what we're looking for in a potentially habitable exoplanet. We'd have better luck in Arkansas.

Kepler-442b is more promising. It's 1,206 light years distant in the constellation Lyra. It's got a radius and mass bigger than Earth, meaning surface gravity would be about 30% stronger. It receives about 70% of the sunlight on Earth. These statistics are not filling me with excitement. I'm beginning to get that feeling when I go on virtual tours of homes for sale and cheesy rock posters are still on the walls and toys and socks litter the floor. It's as if the realtor was too demoralized to stage it properly.

I think we can do better than Kepler-442b.

Steppenwolf is a planet in the Triangulum Galaxy. It has an unscrupulously rocky surface and a fat shiny atmosphere of whisky and Benzedrine. The climates are nuts, but the oceans are lush harmonies of jelly and hallucination. It orbits a red giant reeking of garlic and motor oil. It is among the closest of exoplanets, only a magic carpet ride away from all that is holy and vivid and born to be wild.

Wishful Thinking is an opulent ball of congenial rock and clay in the forearm of the Dumbbell Nebula. This is a fixer up planet. The drywall is crumbling and the orbit is decaying.

Planet 9 is actually my index finger in an astronomy textbook. I'm trying to understand celestial mechanics. I thought it had something to do with belly dancing. I was wrong. It's all about prairie, convenience, and fondue. Community is so important. Unless you hate people. That's the beauty of space travel: the isolation. The long hours of navigation punctuated by quiet interludes of masturbation.

I like Beckett 88. Beckett 88 is a planet in the Molloy constellation. It glows like a candle in the pineal gland of a chipmunk, alluring and gloriously unscientific. It has the mass of a black opal and a radius similar to the hormone of a beautiful green wind. The surface varies from the bald round head of a granite Sibelius to the soft white sand of an unnamable soap. Water is abundant and forests of fluorescent beauty wink and glimmer in the light of a giant red moon. It orbits a white dwarf named Smutty every 400 days and each day is 400 hours long and four days wide. Temperatures vary from 65°F in the far north near the pole and 82°F near the equator. I think this may be the place. As soon as I get there I'll plant the flag of indolence and claim it in the name of all that is good and lazy.

The Answer to Yellow

Too much coherence squeezes the bloom of solitude. Coherence can lead to stagnation. A swamp. Decay and fertility in balance. But where's the tempo? Where's the stir of anticipation? Something must be left out for fulfillment to occur. If I could forge the unpredictability of wind I could sell a wilderness of moods to a strand of dreams and retire in Stockholm.

Despair is circular. If despair had a direction it would cease being despair.

Pure despair answers the call of vacancy. Vacancy has a kind of beauty. I say kind of beauty. It's not a blunt, indisputable beauty. It's a subtle beauty. It's a sign on the prairie at night. It's a soft light in a blue room.

Pages of a book flap in the breeze as the Burlington Northern Santa Fe freight crashes and bangs under the Magnolia Bridge.

Democracy meanders through a banana. But why does the bank shatter into seismic parquet?

Luxury drools from a myopic sentence. I salute the garage with a rag and turn to wax a fresh generality.

I like to bring things to a boil and then discover undercurrents interacting with a whistle. The railroad quietly sips a distance and spits its ruminations in coal.

This is why I take care of my fingernails. My blood glows. Butterflies flip the thesis into a landscape. Everyone unites in humor. Meanwhile, the man who lives upstairs worries about a small hole in the parking lot, which was asphalted only a year ago. And now there's a small hole at the base of the building. It becomes the subject of a robust correspondence. Was the hole caused by a small burrowing animal, or erosion or fate?

I believe it was caused by a urinating calliope.

The calliope flutters in the leaves each time the wind passes through.

Sometimes it's better to suggest something than to declare something firmly and unequivocally. But frankly, I find that declaration gets things said quicker. It's clean and Etruscan.

A lot depends on the quality of the charcoal. That trembling and burning you see up there at night is a sure sign of anguish among the stars.

There are agitations at the heart of everything. Life assumes way more forms than I ever imagined. Look at the birds. Write something. Follow your instincts.

Take the color yellow. What does yellow signify?

The totems speak among themselves. The trees bend. Elegance folds itself into mohair. Everyone understands mohair. Do you understand mohair? I don't understand mohair. I'm just not like everyone. I go for wool. Wool gets me every time. It's thick and slides easily over my head.

You'll find, however, that fire rarely requires a zipper. It's all about heat and nakedness.

The answer to yellow is obvious: five guitar strings equal the fondue of paradise.

Tie a balloon to a potato. Fill it with helium. Watch the pronouns dance.

I crash my mimicry into an imitation life and watch its history unfold in cormorants and afterthoughts. The mind is sometimes a strain to bend into ivory. I'd like a sandwich now. Adaptation lacks coherence when you get to the edge.

It's always our machinery that we choose to celebrate, never our lust for form and potential. There's a heart beating beneath this sentence. It yearns for the flair of tusks. Consider this free of charge. Just think of it as a spoon. You know? The kind that tokens honey.

Big European Butterfly

We look for fulfillment in different ways, different places, different people, different scales. Me, I find fulfillment in the clarity of silence, the structure of the lens, the experience of silk. I try to escape the burdens of the ego whenever I can, not by assuming another identity so much as letting the idea of identity go, or expand into enthrallment. It's harder than you think to attain a state of enchantment. This is not a situation where drugs are of much help. I recommend art, goldfish, and string.

The following sentence has gone in quest of fulfillment, folded itself into a parabolic dish, and disappeared. This would be that sentence had it not vanished into thin air. Why is it always thin air? Why does nobody ever refer to thick air? Or disheveled air?

Is gravity truly a force or an acceleration? Is mass a scalar quantity or a soft pillow on a hard mattress in a town without pity?

Where is Ibiza?

How is meaning possible?

And most importantly, where do all the vanished sentences go? The ones that never get written. The ones that go into the dryer but never come out. The ones that are imagined, that float in the mind like roller skates and shaving cream but are forgotten before an utterance gives them structure and poise. Are these the stillborn? Are these the apparitions of a rampant phenomenology? Are these the fragments of popped cartoon balloons or the confused gestation of predicates and nouns in quest of being in groups of other predicates and nouns?

More subtle problems of grouping are presented by what is called scope. Thus take "big European butterfly": is it to be true of just the European butterflies that are big for butterflies, or is it to be true of all the European butterflies that are big for European butterflies?

Let's start there. If a sentence disappears, is it possible that the sentence developed a cocoon and became a butterfly? Is anything in the world truly static? Isn't metamorphosis involved in all aspects of existence?

Nobody can say that a disappearing sentence is not unlike the magnificence of a setting sun. It's just that every time NASA spots a UFO they cut their feed.

I did spot a few words lying around sparkling, but they belonged to a different idea, a different theme altogether, and were calamities of poorly conceived meaning. This made them all the more interesting, but hard to maneuver into something declarative and bombastic. Some things refuse to cohere. They crack apart revealing gristle and loopholes.

It's rare to see a sentence disappear, especially before it's been written, and is still a nebular cluster of words and ill formed grammar. Webs, membranes, tactile associations.

The ocean groans with infinite nuance. Let's take our cue from that. From surf. From sand. From waves pounding against rocks.

I poured a cup of vinegar down the bathtub drain, then boiled some water in the coffeepot and poured that down the drain. It helps unclog the drain. Steam rose scented with vinegar. It seems to work. Day by day the water drains more quickly. It's a satisfying feeling. Not that I have anything against plumbers. But the last time we hired a roter rooter operation we got taken for $400 dollars.

Goals are fulfilling in their own peculiar way. Even if you never achieve the goal, just having the goal keeps the blues at bay.

Today I want to forge a new objective and distill a moral of helpful orientation in a post-literate world. It's strange being a writer in a post-literate world. You find yourself making things that will not garner much of an audience. It feels self-indulgent. What is it, you ask yourself, that I'm contributing? And how important is it to make a societal contribution? Is all art selfish?

Yesterday, after watching a French game show called *Question pour un Champion,* four separate people in four separate locations each recited a line from "*L'homme et la mer*" by Charles Baudelaire.

> *Homme libre, toujours tu chériras la mer!*
> *La mer est ton miroir; tu contemples ton âme*
> *Dans la déroulement infini do sa lame,*
> *Et ton esprit n'est pas un gouffre moins amer.*

> Liberated man, you will always cherish the sea!
> The sea is your mirror; you contemplate your soul
> In the infinite rolling of its waves,
> And your mind is no less a bitter abyss

Which reminds me. The wash needs doing.

There's a spectrum of mermaids and chimeras in the privilege of insinuating imaginary folds of time in the process of writing or achieving just a few of the impulses lying hidden in any given language.

I know this feeling: it's mud. The memory of a boardwalk crashes through me. I feel the energy of healing in a metaphor reaching for heaven. It's a symptom of yearning that turns into candy.

Yesterday's epiphany is today's driftwood.

I feel the daily sexuality of a gaudy intentionality. I shake and scratch with unfettered glee. The trembling of consciousness is awkwardly transmitted. Acceptance, however, is enlarged by a rumination of penthouse vermilion. It grows into phrases, phases, blazes. The feeling of a body, or a conglomeration of bodily sensations, becomes a benchmark of phenomenality. What I want is often confused with concepts that will never quite provide the banquet of my dreams. But what it does do is provide a sanctum for my sunbursts and woodbine.

The sentence sparkles. The placenta circulates a stream of blood. It won't be long now. Another sentence takes form in the bathymetric valley of insoluble fish.

Balloon Dog

My diatribe for the day: if you go to poetry for little epiphanies to brighten your day, sweet little nougats of lyrical candy for your mind to suck on, you won't be disappointed, there's lots of that kind of poetry around, a lot of it getting published all the time. But if you're looking for the kind of poetry that coruscates up and down your spine like Queen Mab doing wheelies on a Harley Davidson, that kind of poetry is a little harder to find. It doesn't ride, smart and cosmopolitan, on a glossy page in the New Yorker. It hisses and seethes like pahoehoe. It says what it wants with misanthropic glee. It mutates into B movie blobs of translucent goo. It is insolent in its presumptions and foolish in its claims. No good can come of it but ramification and ice.

The locals say the skin of the Colorado River Toad makes a good hallucinogen, but my irritations assume a life of their own and continue as words, pulling images and thoughts behind them, forging new injuries, new resentments, new guilt trips, new brooding ruminations, new fitting rooms for the mall, which is deserted, thanks to Amazon, and a dreadful economy. Hence, words, which have an exchange value of their own, I don't know what, bitcoins, recommendations, comments on Facebook, seesaws, patents, descriptions of pain, the strange behaviors of cats.

Metaphors set up camp in Romania. The door opens and here we are. A calm green moment bubbles out of the floorboard. They say the lake is garish and extroverted, but I found it hanging from a branch of words, braided and abstract. I'm taking it home and hanging it on the wall where I can sit and watch the water lapping at it. The breath of the poem is not the panacea I thought it was but just another busy conception of dirt. The sky offers us its sloth. We can use it to build our conversation. Or just let it sit there, hippopotami popping out of it.

How many things that we consider ours are external to us, come from elsewhere? And then there's coincidence. Today, while waiting in a doctor's office, I read a prose poem by Francis Ponge about clay pitchers, how easily they break, how careful you need to be when walking with one, and how — if it drops and breaks — the shards look like flower petals. I finish the poem and pick up an issue of *Architectural Digest* lying on the table to my immediate left.

It's a thick magazine with glossy pages. I open it to an article about a Chicago ceramicist named Theaster Gates, who stands "inside his sprawling studio....a ceramics atelier littered with pots." Weird.

Bob Kaufman crouches in my heart, a forgotten corner I didn't know I had until he stumbled into it, a brilliant maniac waiting to be loved. I know how privacy happens. The sky leans over the horizon and pours eternity on the world. Maybe golf is a bad example. Thousands of jellyfish wash ashore, and sigh. Then we walk around. It feels anonymous, like sand. Which reminds me. We are caught between two worlds. The world of the spirit and the world of the fashion industry. In between is kitsch, Jeff Koon's monster balloon dog mocking the sublime.

I Don't Know What To Say About Nose Hairs So I'll Talk About Despair Instead

Today I will be the meaning I want. If space is within space, then spatiality must have something to do with the negligence of rocks. I will be that, too. I will be gneiss and negligent.

What is causation? Giants lifting the ocean into rain.

Hype is a cause of hope, which is appalling in its nothingness, which is an insect bicycling around an apple.

My head itches. Marie Laurencin does the dishes. Cubism clanks by with a nougat as I approach the Palace of Tears.

I miss my youth. It was a colorful time. Charles Laughton laughed maniacally as he swung back and forth on those giant bells in Notre Dame because jaywalking hadn't been invented yet.

I wish I was a catfish. I tremble with words in a Mississippi of the mind. Words are packed in images because science is mohair. Mortgage your confusion. This sentence has 400 legs and is crawling into your eyes. That's how serious I am. Pink with the ambiguity of it all.

I enjoy the sensations of things, doorknobs, laundry warm from the dryer, spider legs scampering over my palm, water when I'm thirsty, symphony strings, the weight of a book in my hands. Cold meat seethed in savory oil. Daydreaming. The grain of an old oak table. Apple strudel and cinnamon rolls.

I often dream of the prairie. It must mean something. I've seen water walk through itself and distribute itself evenly to all the fish, especially the ones on the bottom.

Sometimes I just sit and think. And sometimes I drip. Welcome to the north. Welcome to the stepladders and engravings. To the doors opening and closing. The cat on the hearth. Which is calico. And whose eyes shine like the eyes of Baudelaire.

Maybe this doesn't happen to everybody. But if I see something weird, it makes me want to rush out and get a bean burrito.

For example, an old woman hobbles out of the drugstore holding a broom and digs into her pocket for her car keys she's wearing a Seahawks jersey and is seriously overweight but that's not what this is about this concerns mass extinction. Humanity cannot survive in this current paradigm.

Speaking of which, do you feel it? Do you sense it? This is a sentence that wandered out of a poem by Percy Bysshe Shelley and appears to be lost. Can you give it a home? Thank you. It's 3:44 p.m. I wave to a poodle, who looks up at me with warm liquid eyes, and waits pensively to get on with the business of defecation, so that she can go back in, and resume whatever life occupies her world.

Despair is pretty. I see it as a voyage across the River Styx. But if that doesn't work, try picturing your reflection on a downtown window. One must adapt to the world in the best way possible. Romance is mostly a wet feeling. Meanwhile, let's just sit in the park and watch the evening sky grow dark. I like to go swimming in sentences where everything flutters like the ghost of a clarinet. And that makes the world beautiful. Turn it around. Testify. It feels good to be vague and greasy. Especially when the gypsies arrive and rattle their castanets.

Drugs Taste Like Adjectives

This is a haiku. It's a bad haiku. It tastes like zucchini. I'm dragging an eye through a hospital. All the surgeons are absorbed in thought as they bend over the patient whose heart beats back the night and the sunlight at the mouth of the cave gets brighter and brighter.

We look for fulfillment in different ways. I find it in goldfish and butterflies. Let's start there. Tie a balloon to a potato. Fill it with helium. Watch the pronouns dance.

Can an object have a soul? I don't know but, every time NASA spots a UFO they cut their feed. Sometimes, the difference between the organic and the non-organic is like a splintery mouth in a soundboard of Sitka spruce. This will explain Roy Roger's horse.

What's real is the sky. Because being is absurd. There are drugs to help with this. But be careful. Drugs can be adjectives.

At my age, the body begins feeling like a rental I have to take back.

I think it's wonderful that things exist. The nose is naturally Zen. One's chains are imaginary. Break them. Drop them. Success can mean so many different things to so many different people. This hour will dissolve within the limits of another hour and various sensations will hatch out of that and become words in a sentence. Drop everything and run into the sky.

It takes courage to foster a delegation from a future that doesn't exist. Hölderlin advises inhabiting the world poetically, and I fully endorse that. I'm ready to start anytime you are.

Emily Dickinson will come to you in your sleep and draw the noise of your skin.

Hello, world.

Everyone knows how life happens. It's over in a flash. Meanwhile, there's soup and mythology. You can't stop extinction. But you can focus on the present. The slippery, elusive present. Now it's here, and now it's gone. Here again, gone again.

I'm the Rembrandt of butter. I spread by intuition. Think of chiaroscuro as a diplomacy in the dark. Negotiations between worlds. Mickey Rourke gazing into a tank of rumble fish.

Money comes with complications. Some of them have ears. And some just sparkle.

Perception is a process. Thus my being supports a mode of being of which it is not the source. The source is elsewhere.

I admire your willingness to read this far, and attract a crowd of astronauts and prostitutes.

What is thinking, we ask ourselves, and hope it doesn't happen to us. But if and when it does, you can always hope it occurs somewhere on a sandy beach. This is why I believe I was born to be a comma. I like swimming in your voice. Look what happens when you stay alive this long. You learn. For example, if you don't like the view, you can always close the curtains.

70 MPH Of Enhanced Screaming

Why don't I have fur? If I had fur I wouldn't need clothes. Why not scales and fins? I need to be more oceanic. But who am I kidding? I'm already oceanic, an amalgam of earth and water. Mitochondria, centrioles, endoplasmic reticulum.

I left the oars in the boathouse. We'll just have to spend the rest of this sentence making the world beautiful.

The welder lifts his helmet and nods to the apparitions dancing on the walls. Is life a simulacrum of somewhere full of sad, enigmatic objects with stories to be told?

You can masturbate almost anywhere. But try to be discreet. Words command a powerful reality of their own. For example, I would never tell anyone "you should sit down and write a novel it's easy anyone can do it." It's not, but here's a clue: the word pineapple is its own abstraction. The rest of the groceries have been carried into the mind on paper. The saga fits the distortions. It is there that we find glass and morals. Things like desks. Consciousness. Bed springs.

The hammer realizes itself by hammering. Hammering is a trance of hammerness, which is not the same as becoming a T-shirt.

The shape inside a rock is noisy. And here in Florida the candy tastes like syntax.

Does law even matter anymore? The triumph of agriculture has been an unmitigated disaster. The entire galaxy drove into a garage and shut off its lights. I don't know what to say about the guitar in the corner. When I hold it close to my body I can feel its pulse. Then I pull on a sweater and wonder how to coax an atmosphere out of the G chord.

What is a thought exactly? Does anybody know? Heidegger had his ideas. They involved the meaning of Being, the fundamental ontology of existence, and to what extent the structure of language is involved with possible ways of being in the world.

If you look closely at a Viking ship you will immediately notice the magnitude of grace in the sweep of its lines. This might be used as an example of thought. Abstraction doesn't always wear a hull of wood and nails. Viking nails, which were iron. Although, in Norse mythology, Naglfar is a boat made entirely from the fingernails and toenails of the dead.

I can walk through a wall of granite. Provided there is a hole.

Or not. It's the icicles that capture my attention. The way they drip.

And drip.

Existence is fullest when it eats itself and all the words disappear. But the words come back. The universe never stops vomiting itself. I get it. It's easy to get sick on too much infinity.

I feel immediate and pink. The grapefruit is proof. Coroners, too, are sometimes vast and soft. Picture a mime robbing a bank. The precision of his movements eventually results in an understanding among the tellers. It's all imaginary. His gun is imaginary. The bullets imagined. The blood imagined. But the money is real. As real as money can be. Which isn't very real.

This is a mean old ugly world. But where else can you find peppermint layer cake?

If you rub enough words together they make a sound like time and water. But it's not quite enough to bring the U.S. constitution back. It's got some pretty big holes in it. What happened to habeas corpus? What happened to journalism? Julian Assange rots in a British jail cell. There's your democracy, crawling into the skull of an oil baron.

Philosophy On The Freeway

I'm the ugly wars of my own perspective. Consider the chowder of insinuation that exists in the magic belt of my description. I'm the rocks that hop into paper. I happen in my wrinkles. Indolence is a gift. The weather sits beside me and I listen to the day as it slops through the door. This is how thumbs were invented. When we're alone the sounds have a conversation with our fingers. Time collapses on us and rides a beard to Scotland. The war ends. The castle climbs into itself and offers a sanctuary for the sloppiness of life.

Dishwashing did this to me.

Life is subversive. I find myself in revolt against nearly everything.

The circus taught me how to throw knives. At least I know how to do that. Conversation taught me how to exaggerate. Which reminds me. I'd like to tour Protestantism one day. Meanwhile I'll just go ahead and inhabit poetry like a shoplifter. The idea that anything can happen on the other side of my skin is exhilarating. The staircase hugs its shape and Massachusetts flies out of my mouth. What can I say? I see the potential of water just by moving the oars.

I like the way elevators adjust to the level of the floor so naturally. You don't really feel all those gears and pulleys. I sometimes imagine what's going on in the elevator shaft, they're such mysterious places, if an elevator shaft can be called a place, with those cables and blank, merciless walls. It amazes me how smoothly elevators operate. I've never been trapped in one. Though I've had those awkward moments of waiting for one when I'm late for an appointment and I want to keep punching buttons as if that would make them go faster but don't if there are other people around. And most of the time I myself am around myself keeping myself within a compass of rational behavior, or least what might pass for rational behavior, to the rest of the world. Even when no one else is around I like to keep up appearances.

Sexuality comes easily to some people, whereas it is a constant problem for others. This is why I prefer the music of the early Beatles. They sweetened the pangs of adolescence until adulthood happened and jobs and responsibility. Ugh. When you get to be my age, it all looks silly in retrospect. Nowadays I just want to sit and percolate in an armchair. Here's a salute to nothingness. Sometimes the quickest way out of something is to get into it.

Driving the freeway at night can sharpen your perspective. Particularly if there is suddenly a number of lanes closed for repaving and there are lights flashing and a row of orange barrels forcing the flow of traffic into one of several lanes and the perceptions formerly lulled into quiescent attentiveness while sitting in a dimly lit restaurant among friends are now fully awakened and frantic and consciousness is a radical cloud of unknowing. Do I want a Being that is impartial and above it all, or a Being so immersed in the fiber of the universe that it continually begins beginning itself? Do I have any choice? Isn't there a general all-encompassing energy of Being in which I'm a part, a partial expression, a fleeting concentration? Should I speed up and pass this truck or fall behind and move to the right lane?

Gnu Glue

Language is an event, not a potato chip. For example, I open my mouth and a huge bright light walks out of my mouth. Who are you, I ask. I am the ghost of Christmas dryers. You forgot your socks. Is it true that the limit of my language is the limit of my world? Yes, but this doesn't always include warmth and communion. It's mostly underwear. Sometimes a small grammar walks around looking for resolution. And then something intuitive feels warm. And that's how language works. Together we are able to lift the sentence and push it into the air. Who am I talking to? I don't even know anymore.

Today, I would like to build a mysterious ocean of space and time. The buckets will be carried by Buddhists. Most of the gas stations will remain open. Christmas will be tuned by quantum vibrations, requiring presents and generosity, a little hypocrisy, some fakery, a lot of diplomacy, and spices from the netherworld. Sometimes there are symbols and ikons to help with the process. For example, murky, igneous colors with fragments of Dante. This is where sensations refine themselves and step away quietly to stand on the porch and listen to the rain.

All works of art are founded on the groan of heavy equipment, the crash of detritus into the maw of a garbage truck. Some skinny little limbs in the kitchen introduce themselves to me as Samuel Beckett. I'm trying as hard as I can to believe that life is something separate from NPR and is a place of spirits. Meaning we are caught between two worlds. The world of the spirit and wait wait don't tell me.

Recipe for Fascism: exalt aggression, greed, and bullying; discourage reading, thinking, and compassion; stir in racism, xenophobia, and bigotry; encourage rape, sexual domination and the disparagement of women; insist on patriotism, nationalism, and religious piety; control the media; aggrandize militarism and hypermasculinity; cover, and cook on low setting for 10 to 12 years; when water comes to a boil, sit back and tweet your head off.

Every day we see our lives play out in miniature what the universe does at large.

I apologize for these descriptions. They're all I have. The good thing about descriptions is that you can get up and walk around like a slinky on a surgical table. Zaum, Zoom, Zipper. I support anything that builds a horse out of vowels and a tube of gnu glue.

These are the judgments of a private man. The mind likes these things. It's a form of power. Perception is easy. All it takes is a puff or two to blow the little hairs off of the computer screen.

When somebody does you a wrong, do you stay out all night long getting drunk, or do you fold yourself into Brazil? My nerves belong to another world. I'm sure of it. I feel like I'm on cruise control. I don't grow my hair, my hair does that on its own. I'm tired of looking for myself. I don't have a self. I have a pet monkey. My mind comes out at night and keeps me awake. Will I ever understand this shit? It's like having a courtroom in your head. And sometimes a Russian novel with some really beautiful passages in it.

The Smell Of Heat On Marble

A shy hip provides an almanac. Candle language. Drama driven by feeling open. The wind elf satisfies the monastery. Go summer lift the puddle to sparkle.

Begin a walrus muscle plaster. Bear kite memory that hovering is a body of mist. A neglecting season of notebook encounters. Radical swell for a cave of noble pedestrians. Thoughtful need for a planet that forges magnets of Nevada sage.

Fill up the redeeming career time with basement toys. I hope that a sad poplar will be born on the border. Hollow are the words of algebra. Run to the agate bandage and think of a design for the beauty of indecision. My arms swing the world in muslin it's lush and swirling and hitting our prayers with black shadows.

Wire for a map of pain. Palm underneath the weight of its own existence. Slip it where the mat is chained to propagation. The bear implies an embassy of onions, a turpentine Sunday opposite the reach of radar. The plumage of writing flows vague and verdant above the sleep of Big Sur where cypresses whisper philosophies of dirt to the sailing heavens and ants swarm the hills like famished opticians.

Climate caresses the wrinkles of the sea's evident wish to create sensation, which is presumed to be assuagement, a solace for the traction of time. Wellness logs hover over the mucus of feudalism. Shadow plumage is drama, the narrative equivalent of starting a circus. Asia's dream of an antenna tangle. Dagger spade needle soak.

And then he kissed me. He kissed me in a way I'd never been kissed before. The house, meanwhile, drinks its coherence from a cup of visibility. Visibility has a strong taste, a bit like Madagascar at twilight, or a banana split in Laramie, Wyoming, at about 7:00 p.m. on a Wednesday evening in late July or early August. Opinions stroll through the glaze of a distilled squint resulting in hawks.

This means that roots offer religious truths and paper. Anarchy seduces the Prince of Eggnog and gets naked in reincarnation. Incense hugs the distinction. The story proceeds by writing itself into tarantulas and performing a tarantella on the kitchen stove, which is distracted by an overhead fan. Infinity pauses to bark.

Bee rock browsed in a fever no one would tear up in a million years. Saucy astronomy. Cricket attic cantata muscle. Emotional vibrations rippling in an irrigation ditch. Thermometer during novels written in food budget randomness.

Meaning is sometimes a pillow in which I hear time splashing its hands on a sandstone nose. Sadness sloth. Conflagration twirling. Gun kitten gentle geometry. Prickly prose available for ebullient mustache hunts.

The tongue stirs streams of words which go into the air and do things. The little king lowers himself on a knee below the awning and anoints a knuckle. I worry about the blatant kit of hoping to go fast in a field today. The hot melt to flex a drinking noise. The border has trees and yet a lazy pin is overflowing the image of itself.

When somebody does you a wrong, do you stay out all night long getting drunk, or do you fold yourself into a prayer and roll into the soft oblivion of sleep? Don't be mean. Don't lose your balance. Stay home. Squeeze something.

Is it getting better? Gray reason echoes a background of stars and hangs from yesterday, a hum of sonic jewelry. Time is a tenable crust, a shoulder of sun, a street for walking around in pants. Dramatic ripple of well-being that pops into drapery and lets the light come in and destroy the obscurity of fear. Meanwhile I'm sitting here waiting for you to enter my dream.

Flooding metal will want to solder socialism together with symptoms of resurrection. Avoid the north and be a mouth to the table. Habitat stool of milky history, abrupt and wet as a jellyfish. Undertake a beautiful ash, a wagging chameleon handwriting, and multiply. The mohair clarifies the ribbons by an aberrant speculation based on coffee.

Choose a muscle, choose a bone. Take a soldier, take a king. I will be waiting in the hallway. My shoes want to go somewhere. The pronouns are at it again, bending the world to their purpose.

Well, it happens. One must compose oneself. Combine hopping with hoping, imminence with immanence, thyme with time. And there is always sand, always some form of motion to be performed, thumbs raised, gardens tilled, wonders to behold. The sad beautiful clock of the backbone, the embroidery of winds on sandstone.

I undressed my beard bow and threaded the breast of morning with the gospel of nothingness. The cathedral puddle will help us find the consonants we need to soothe our nerves. The swell in the paper is a benevolent face. It appears when sunlight enhances the hardware the elves have so craftily arranged on the table and the face of the sky begins talking about France, each lip a tumble into charm. The weight of the sand will indicate that the weight of the oysters has been splashed by too much ocean, which is what the fingers expand as soon as we enter the waves, and so must be entered into our records, numbers full of wool, creosote falsettos.

It is the force of the wind to be smashed up to the mound. Accidental pedestrian kettles make it feel like a diving board. The process is also a form of sigh, an admission that words occur like sounds in a forest not of my own making. Sauerkraut and radar are enigmatic forms of fez. Carry the planet to the barn where we can get a better look at it.

My nerves belong to sapphire. I'm lazy that's true it's a theory of hope. Feeling is for making noise. The garden's distress is dazzling at the top of the pool. The smell of heat on marble is soft as the memory of well-being, and so becomes an occupation, a sport like baseball, but with more pauses, more mustard, more hanging around the dugout.

Weightless

Drink the onion candle. There is aggression glue for the membrane shade. This works best in complete quiet. This is oats for the jellyfish, but insoluble for the rain. Below the spout there is nothing but stars. Be a beautiful polish to them. Allow yourself to butter the truth with applause.

The truth is not always slender. Sometimes it is reptiles. I recollect remaining in the tinted grooves of *Blonde on Blonde* until the dimes began to shine in exemplification of the scrapbooks up in the attic and the world seemed easy and green. That's when the streetlights were nearly everything we needed, and the sidewalks had intent. The lightning continued to burn on its open side. It's as if we were somehow enthralled with Cubism and yet continued to enjoy winter.

The plunge into powder is my way of saying that the knife delineates a dimension hanging over the evocation of fingers. At least, I like to look at it that way. What else can I say? The towels are clean now and not as hirsute as the hobbits around here, partying late into the night, drinking Old Peculiar and smoking Tolkiens.

Late afternoon is stirring and the growls coming from the shrubbery convince me of chickadees. Summer is so simple. It is simpler than all the other pulleys strung together making the scenery come closer.

As for oars, who cares? We can drift. We can let our hands hang in the water. We can continue our sewing later. There's no hurry, only a few burning sensations and longings to play in a rock band. Other than that, I feel that my escape must come from within. Running is a personal favorite, but desperate times call for desperate measures. It is why I began slouching and hanging out at the drugstore. It bites to think a tree is authoritative. But yes, a twig exhibits feathers, and this, too, is a collaboration.

Our monthly intake of water does its melodies by making the ink of its descriptions do things in a grimace that, once it's written down on paper, appears more like the luxurious juggling of tambourines. You can also do this with your suppositions and theories. It's easy as twine. Space is forgiving. But gravity is hilarious. I mean, come on. Can it be more obvious? I think I'm falling in love with the weight of a movie ticket.

The greenery of the wind relocates the darkness. The Alps defend Sunday from the pretty clouds of Monday. Nature is mostly scorpions and wasps. Maybe poultry. I'm not sure about poultry. Are chickens natural? If you rub something obscure long enough it begins to shine like varnish and do the hully gully. Every faucet has a mouth, every sentence has a purpose. The purpose of this sentence is frequented by a group of words that want to reflect on the suppleness of the human tongue. They urge conference. Listen to the bees grow into the sensual drool of calculus. Listen to the predicates click their lyrics into the scenery of gills.

This is a moment for pearls. The king thought his bones were expanding and wrote a sullen letter to Egypt. Egypt responded by saying that the encounter with the terrine was languishing in seaweed. This directed the king to seek beatitude in the peripheries, out of the direct sunlight and in the shadows by the window. Egypt stepped into the Nile and shined.

The lighting here is busy. The bulbs sweat sauerkraut. The eyes groan on the bookshelves. The hives come to us in our dreams, bearing the softness of moonlight and the raw fleece of autumn. Our carpentry is jubilant in its rudiments and demands the glory of fact. Scraps among the harpsichords prove that the effacement of music is paint, not noise as we suspected. Noise is just a sound spinning in the face. Not everyone can twinkle. Some of us have stories that seethe with trapezoids. I like generating peculiarities of failure. Escalators, unicorns, tidepools.

The eyes are lounges for the judgments of the brain, which are suspended in microscopes.

There is a movie in which a naked woman welcomes you at the door and a movie in which a fish clarifies hints of clay.

Welcome away blatant woman. Start your stomach logs. We have toes for the snow and organs for experience.

Theory blurs the rough terrain. Jelly drags the chair across the room and Marie Laurencin waits for it in her sleep. The pure way of the monastery is to go hiking and pick blackberries. We seduce one another with a little driftwood and a lot of cupcakes. There is an apricot that feels sad for the pill of regret which is a bear whose veins make a case for the imaginary money of a canary. But it's hard to swallow. This level of anthropomorphism is alarmingly literal.

Eating exhibits parables. We find a path toward the butter and the imagery of this requires a pineapple. You must envision playground slides for the potatoes to happen. They've been mashed and put in a bowl. A drool bends the surface so that it feels kinetic. Postage stamps speak of a floating office. This means that the derivative takes all the cake and leaves us with the cost of shipping. And that, too, calls for the use of infrared filters.

We cut the lawn with a kind of knife. You're probably wondering why we skipped the backyard. I think it has something to do with Italy. Florence is beautiful. My sense of the outdoors is a little scratched but zips together nicely in order to tell you that the lions are roaring. Please continue drawing.

Congratulate the mass of the street during an era of clouds. This makes eating saws. This makes saws walk. This makes walking saw through making. Making is incarnation. I've seen it happen before. It helps make your bones stronger. This is especially important in space. Weight loss diminishes bone mass and raises the amount of calcium in your blood. But now we're getting technical at a time when we need to be instantaneous.

I'm not interested in blue laws. I want to burn the calories of night and rid the morning of tar. I want to be weightless. I want to sit in an armchair dreaming of apricots in the Tuscany sun.

The west is an agate of darkness. Faith can be complicated. I aim for grace. Blurred wings of a hummingbird hovering in front of my face.

A Little Storm Of Amino Acids

Irritations are my favorite drug. But don't tell me that. I prefer to think they're just irritating. I shout at the books to get off of their shelves and do something. Invade Belgium. Deliver babies.

The Burlington Northern goes by at eight. That's when the coffee mugs rattle and the mirror swings back and forth.

My relation with space is more than conceptual, it's downright intimate, at times a little erotic, especially when the clouds billow over the horizon and the walls begin to sweat.

I've always liked the term 'primordial soup.' But who, or what, stirred the soup? Who or what sequence of events caused an amalgam of inanimate substances to cohere into a body with a goal? Was that when eating was invented? Was eating the first motivating force? Or was it reproduction? Was the first internal directive one of procreation? I wish I could've been there 3.9 billion years ago to see that occur. That little storm of amino acids stir into action. 3.9 billion years later I sit here typing words, bubbles of air in pandemonium, wallowing in nihilism, nothing to do but drift around the room like a noctilucent jellyfish, dangling tentacles and socks.

I don't understand worry. I don't understand the point of it. It accomplishes nothing. And yet I keep doing it. Weighing this, weighing that. This is a big risk, this is a smaller risk, but I don't really want to do that, I'd prefer doing the other thing, which is a bigger risk, but do I want to take that risk, really, what's going on, why is my mind flailing around in my skull like this, I wish it would stop, I wish my brain would turn into a Caribbean island, Curaçao or Martinique, either will do, I just want sand on my beaches, a place to stretch my body, and leave all this thuggery and robbery behind, the gangster zeitgeist of the United States, its Andrew Wyeths and Norman Rockwells, fascist kitsch and simulated places of fake fun like Disneyland.

Last night reading *Leo Frobenius On African History, Art and Culture an Anthology*, with a foreword by Léopold Sédar Senghor, I was greatly amused by the story of a disobedient son who — against the orders of his father — sets a trap for animals on the road to the village. He ends up catching various family members and then the road itself. He rolls the road up and puts it in a bag.

He and his father get lost. Finally, admitting defeat, he puts the sack down. The road leaps out and father and son are able to return to the village. But the son catches the road again and decides to keep it. No one can use the road. It grows so sad that it dies.

The inimitable sound of an old oak drawer full of freshly laundered and folded socks and underwear shutting. Indescribable. But palpable. Quietly, calmly, subtly thudded into a convoluted ear.

I can't believe I've traveled this far into the future: 2020. Holy cow. I can't wait to get back to 1968 and tell everybody what I saw: the United States is now a fascist plutocracy in which a handful of people are wealthy beyond measure while 80% of the country struggles with poverty; millions, including children, are homeless; civil liberties are under attack; the U.S. has the largest prison population in the world and seven wars going simultaneously; a college education costs a fortune and is utterly worthless; healthcare is a racketeer's wet dream; the highways and bridges are all dangerously dilapidated but Bill Gates's mansion has 24 bathrooms because he's a philanthropist and philanthropists must have to go to the bathroom a lot; there are zombies everywhere staring at a little handheld device that is a combination telephone and TV; marijuana is legal in seven states; Kentucky Fried Chicken and Taco Bell fused together halleluiah.

I believe there are invisible realities moving through us all the time. We're porous. Division isn't vision. Division is derision. I feel the nickel of the chisel in the ring of your spittle. The entire spectrum of experience implicated in the word reality is ripples in the ocean of consciousness. It's there that we float and contemplate our immersion. Our excursions. Our diversions. Our perversions. Our paradiddles. Our grooves. Our beats. Our chops. Our hi hats.

Ripples in my life, ripples in anyone's life, little concentric rings across the pond of the mind, the cold still water of mind in repose, silt on the bottom, tree branches in stunning lucidity. It happens occasionally. Clarity. I'm in the twilight of my life. What's on the other side of this life I don't know. Drops of white light on a spider web. Weeping women. Stones cold to the feet. Fish in green waters. Is there anything in the world better than mashed potatoes? Yes: cherry cordials. I pop a cherry cordial in my mouth and go read *The Waves,* by Virginia Woolf.

Nature Is Everywhere

There are hundreds of ways to learn the guitar, but writing poetry isn't one of them. This is unfortunate. I like guitars. But I feel at home on paper. This is the André Breton room. Anarchic chairs chatter to the shelves about the fizz of lacrosse. My allegorical knee is nebulous and soft. The other knee is a hill of dormant tinsel. I welcome all forms of butter. What can explain the strange serendipity of our universe? I don't know. But this will walk beside you until we get somewhere.

Has the human experiment been a failure? Is experiment the right word? If so, whose experiment are we? I seriously doubt that human beings are the result of experimentation, unless one adopts the very broad view that everything in the cosmos is an experiment. My guess is we're just an evolutionary quirk, "atoms contemplating atoms" as the cherubic-faced British physicist Brian Cox puts it. Somehow geochemistry became biochemistry, the inorganic became organic, phosphorous and nitrogen became conversation and polypeptide chains. Mud and sand and rock became quivering blobs of synthesizing protein which became corals and worms which became vertebrates which became able to walk erect on two feet which led to the evolution of a tongue capable of speech which quickly escalated into consciousness, whatever that is, self-awareness and books and dignity and meaning. Valentines and sonnets and airplanes. Dance and flavor and religion and guns. At the end of the day, who are we? No one knows. No one may ever know. We were here. For a time. And then we were gone, cooked by an overheated atmosphere.

What if this whole moment was a piece of candy awakened from its slumbers to remind the blood of an explicit understanding of being and then left you wondering what to do with the wrapper, which is so true of all traditional ontology?

Support groups I wish existed: Facing the Sixth Mass Extinction; Living under Trump; Keeping Your Cool in a Sociopathic Militaristic Corporate Fascist Empire; My Nightmares Are Real and Trigger Isn't Just A Stuffed Horse; Safe Haven for Social Media Refugees; Loving Books in a Postliterate Culture; When Everything You Love Is Being Systematically Destroyed and Everything You Hate Proliferates; Whatever Happened To The Sixties and

Where Am I Now and Why Do I not Recognize Anyone; Understanding Mediocrity; Why Is Andrew Wyeth Being Featured At The Seattle Art Museum; Understanding the Relationship Between Kitsch and Fascism; When Douche Bags Become Billionaires and Nice People Live in Tent Cities; When The World Is Totally Fucked Up and You Have Nowhere Else To Go.

Can't sleep. Too many worries. The melting of the polar ice cap, an erratic jet stream creating havoc everywhere, frost-quakes in Ottawa, a wildfire in Greenland, the rise of fascism, the government shut down, a decaying infrastructure. I listen to several podcasts (Movie Crush, Stuff to Blow Your Mind) then classical music on King FM. I started drifting off and was abruptly awakened by a hypnic jerk. Shit. Almost had it. I closed my eyes and tried to lose consciousness again. And then there was a power outage. Fuck it. I put on my flashlight headband and went out in the living room to lie on the couch and read *The Making of Americans* by Gertrude Stein.

Can there exist a romantic nihilism? An objection to dogma and institution based on popcorn, cinematography, and ginseng? What if the only reality turns out to be the Saigon Central Post Office? The Maxwell and Boltzmann formula of 1870 is particularly lovely. It describes the speeds of particles in idealized gases as tawny. This is why I smell of abstraction. Nature is everywhere. You can't avoid it. I'm not even going to mention methane. But if you'd like, you can give meaning to the pharmaceuticals by swallowing some words. A dream of earth will come to you in your sleep and the following day shine out of your bones like gold.

Fat Hot Moons Of Transcendent Possibility

Language is a puppet. You can make it dance. Crustaceans, night crawlers, fondue. But mostly birds.

We have a stuffed Viking in our kitchen. He hangs from a hook on the wall. I don't know where he came from, or what he does. History says little about stuffed Vikings on refrigerators, although there is sometimes mention of migraines and dizzy spells.

Here comes some death. I see it through a peephole. I'm pretending I'm not at home. I'm good at deception. I like illusions. I like cultivating them and believing in them. One illusion is that life has meaning. Another is that meat grows on trees already wrapped in cellophane.

I can see it in your eyes: perspective. It steams like a moose. That's why I'm laughing at the road. I shake a rattle over the abyss of my religion, which is what I need for an alibi. The migrations remain magnetic, apostrophes of artless opacity, odd little people with astronomical interiors. The throat collects a sentence with a clarinet in it, then oozes a thousand distant moons. I grab my socks and begin arguing with my feet.

I tell my feet we have to move. I hate moving. My feet aren't a worry. They follow me wherever I go. But go we must. The world is broken. We broke it. We broke the weather. We broke the oceans. We broke the lakes and forests. We broke the animals. We broke the insects. We broke the dirt. We broke Greenland. We broke privacy and solitude. We broke silence and fog. So where are we going to go? Good question. I'm working on it. Keep it simple, I say. Stab gravity with an umbrella. Everything drips with reverie. Reality is a rattle in the elbow of the wind. These words are teeming with wormholes. I'm going to walk through one now, and when I come out the other side, I will drape a cape over the back of James Brown.

Errors of judgment are inevitable in a medium of extended cognition that relies on a system of speech sounds and alphabetical symbols. Remember "The Sorcerer's Apprentice"? As soon as words are put together, they assume a life of their own. The next thing you know Arnold Schwarzenegger is breaking down your door and a magic black swan is carrying you away to Mars. Why Mars? There are no vacancies on Venus, and Titan won't accept pets.

Poets spit fat hot moons of transcendent possibility at the zeitgeist eating its own progeny. It is not the words themselves that form poetry but the smell of New Mexico in turquoise or the appearance of angels on the brim of a sombrero. It is the trembling in the atmosphere of the most distant stars, the digestive organs of worms, or the shawl of a single bacillus hunched over on its way to an important disease. The disease of living, which is a terrible disease, as it leads to more and living, and spontaneity, and loons.

Everyone swarms with opinion. It's anarchic to do otherwise. Even the crows approve. The shovel clanks against the concrete floor of the garage and the glockenspiel collects dust in the corner where the shadows stumble through the afternoon. I can hear Istanbul in the distance. It sounds like a café in twinkle mode. I infringe on nothing but my own emissions. I can't control my opinions. I just let them wander around on paper until they become reptilian.

Studies have shown that birds have syntax and grammar, even dialects. Since birds are the direct descendants of the dinosaurs, is it possible there might have been an Emily Dickinson dinosaur? A "thing with feathers" chasing butterflies through the Cretaceous jungle?

The words will never be what I want them to be: horned lizards everywhere. I've never seen anything quite like it. Words squirting themselves into combs. I think I know what thinking is but I don't know what it is I'm thinking. For example, think of a sleeveless one-piece jumpsuit extended into a sideboob tattoo of atomic theory. Thanks to the invention of extraversion the individual can become a stiffened mass of personality and think whatever it thinks about tattoos and scrap metal. There's still a teepee, still a tattoo or two to occupy. We've all seen it before: the eyes of the mailbox watching your every move as it discharges letters from all the Romantic poets. And then a kangaroo hops by wearing a velvet fedora.

I get a bang out of cashmere. This makes my grammar pink. It's the B side of the aforementioned membrane, the one rolling in and out of my mind. If this sentence is missing, it's because I didn't write it down. I thought about something else instead. But I don't know what it was. I didn't write it down. I sat down on a bench and helped the suffering of the piano. I became a man that day.

A Portrait Of Time

I get asked at my annual physical exam what does 11:10 look like? The nurse wants me to draw it. It's on account of my age; they're trying to determine where my cognition is at because I'm old. I draw a circle and my mind goes blank. I don't know what 11:10 looks like. A monkey? An elephant? Is it a prairie? Is it a picnic in the future? Is it a fetus? Should I write a haiku? I decide 11:10 is William S. Burroughs mowing his lawn in Lawrence, Kansas. Morning. The grass smells sweet. I have trouble capturing the full essence of Burroughs's expression. I give up. I don't know what 11:10 looks like. Next time 11:10 rolls around I'll try to pay better attention.

Time hops around like a kangaroo. There's no way to remedy existence except by accepting it on its own terms. Successes are few, failures are many. Failure is the form life assumes when it concentrates too zealously on achieving the impossible. And then it squeaks like a rack in a gift shop.

Joni Mitchell was right: don't it always seem to go that you don't know what you've got till it's gone.

I remember on a visit to the men's prison in Monroe a few years back seeing a cluster of inmates in the yard grouped around something that held their attention in what seemed like a trance, or very deep focus. I got close enough to get a glimpse of what they were looking at: a dragonfly. It must've flown in over a wall. One of the men held it in his hand, its wings glinting in June sunlight, as the others gazed in wonderment.

I spend a lot of time these days sifting through my thoughts looking for oblivion. It's pretty easy. Cognition is largely gray, sometimes violet. I don't understand any of it. One thing I do know: perception is a creative act. Is there a universe in which this makes sense? Yes. The universe of baking soda. In the universe of baking soda all one needs is a little conviction, a little butter, and enough energy to power a small frog. There is no such thing as the absolute truth. Today, for example, I poured some salt and baking soda into the drain of the bathtub and washed it down with a cup of vinegar and watched as it frothed and bubbled up out of the drain. And there is truth in this. And frogs.

It's ten a.m., June, 2019. As soon as I ascribe a date, the day feels reduced. Labeled and put on a shelf. Ten a.m. looks like a plate of scrambled eggs and toast slathered with strawberry jam.

Eleven a.m. looks like little rocks offshore. The rustle of feet in the grass. The vague cough of an adjective. Generations of laundry adrift in the canvas sky.

Midnight is a frog hopping across my mind.

Later, around a fire, a feeling greets me on the other side of my life. I can sprint toward it and jump. And there I go. Into the hole.

Consciousness is essentially Gothic. The brighter the fire, the deeper the darkness.

Saudade

The Portuguese call it *saudade*, the sadness of an unappeasable longing. Venus is gone for a week. The sky walks around dressed in a flagrant romanticism. The dead play croquet, laughing at life. We should give the junkyards a chance. Who's going to mine this data? Is this even data?

Feelings are big mushy things to carry around. Anger is odd. It feels more like energy than mass. Dark energy, to be sure, but accelerant, gasoline, diesel, kerosene, butane. Anger can get you into trouble really quick. It's a mad brahma bull kicking at the chute. Despair is even weirder. It's a black ugly hole. Your best way out is to go all the way in. Lean into it. Later, I will come and make sense to you as a lump of earth.

Thinking is really an insatiable project, you know? Timeless slop. Road flares. Footprints in the mud.

The world is ravenous for meaning. It makes one wonder. What does the dark side of psychedelia look like? I see fancy bags of water walking around sucking acetylene popsicles. Phosphorous camels glowing out of a gray fog. Newspaper taxis. Tangerine trees and marmalade skies. Utah, basically. Only with methane lakes and pressurized clocks telling time as a form of mental construction involving TV dinners and exasperated housewives.

Cognition is largely heuristic, Arthur Rimbaud doing photography in Ethiopia. It just goes to show there's an application for everything. For example, mops and solipsism. It's not what you think, it's what I think that matters. I was a once a cowboy on TV. I know what I'm doing. What if solitude could be bottled like alcohol? This is why we need prepositions. They help us understand water.

I believe words are mostly abstract but sometimes they clank with the chained suspension of theocratic concerns. The bones sag in grief. The sublime is stitched together like the rhapsody of an Icelandic fumarole. Consciousness springs into language and runs around creating crickets and crocodiles and cypress. Creosote smells of opinion. The train tracks shine. The scene is lucid and peremptory, lustrous and nickel like a poem by Arthur Rimbaud.

I'm hooked on the pragmatism of mustard. The age of the manifesto. The time of rebels. The time of tingling and cheap thrills and Brian Jones's silly grin.

It's a complicated package, this life, this enormous pink lung, this lousy HMO. Dirt stirs with the strange innocence of worms. Feeling is mostly hydrogen with traces of fudge. Timelessness is crushed into clocks, but the elbow is in control of its own reality. Be an emperor to yourself for the sake of naiveté, for the enthusiasm of dogs.

Write a letter to Iggy Pop. Do it with letters. Float animals. Do you like your shoes? Bend your being to their eloquence. The novel is constrained to break in half anyway. Later, the plot will be rescued by a convalescing pessimism. You can cure it with talking, or go to the library. In any case, it's the literary life for me. I like the stunned embrace of nails. Being marginalized and ignored is a treasure as well. Who doesn't like to play with string? The goldfish just keep dancing on my lips.

How To Write A Novel

Take your head off and put it somewhere safe. You won't need it. It will just get in the way. What is needed are tropes, isotopes, proctoscopes, telescopes, block and tackle, glass and rubber tubing, vaginal speculums, penile pumps, dipole magnets, advanced tongue roots, bound morphemes, clause chains, glottal stops, hortatory discourse and a 4-stroke outboard motor. Eventually, the novel will come and make sense to you as a lump of earth. This is how feelings experience the world. At the end of the day, who are we? Metaphors and soap.

Death is at the bottom of everything. Cabbage, moss, carpentry, water polo. How about you? What are you up to? Nostalgia seems to annoy some people, but me, I like to reminisce. I close my eyes and see 1968, molecular blizzards, long roads and itinerant misfits. You can approach this world from different angles, but one way or another, you must find a direction, a goal, however illusory, and let it guide you through the murk of feeling, the hum of neurons. Those were the days my friend, we thought they'd never end. And then Brian was found floating face down in his swimming pool and the world shimmered with the refracted light of a setting sun.

Writing is the ghost of a dead sensation. I was once a blob of protoplasm. And now I'm this. A puddle of words. Call it a fugue. Call it a hammer eating a bowl of goldfish. How will I be able to explain any of this to the parole board? I see an adjective dragging itself into another sentence and shoot it. There. It's done. Now I understand what is meant by brooding. Brooding breeds more brooding. And then it falls asleep in a bingo parlor.

There is more to beauty than sausage. One example might be everything in Japan. Another might be cake. Lately, a lot of people have been asking about the Caravaggio in the lobby. What can I say? That I met the Beatles? I frequently have vast, vagrant thoughts about nothing. It's what I'm good at. Mighty galleons of nonsense adrift in an ocean of beautiful pink vapor. Each morning, the cold air on Philip Whalen's shaved head woke him before the alarm clock. Skin is the first response to the headlines of heaven. The second is the tremble of a cobweb.

Paragraphs are glockenspiels. The play of bells. Incidents, like someone ploughing the sand with their foot while looking dreamily at a crab. That's why I like them. They're small, like woodcuts. You can put them in books where they become romantic, someone young leaning against the walls of a ruin, or someone (say me) curing diseases in a small village. I knock on a door and someone lets me in. A man sits in a chair, storming in his teeth. I tell him that it may be a good time to sell the vineyard and he immediately feels better. This is the paragraph I've dreamed of all my life.

The birth of a Danish diving board is langoustine. It needs our full attention. This is no audiobook talking to you in your car. This is the bliss of the attic. This is the feeling of climbing an expensive emotion and finding a mud pot in your cerebellum. The one bubbling in the unconscious. The unconscious is a heat at the base of the brain. It's the kind of place where your fantasies come true. The kind one finds in drugstores, swaying in the aisle.

Amalgams of sound find their meringue in sound. I slouch forward spilling adjectives on a slavish emotion. I set it free by murdering reality with a rancorous idealism. Reality comes back for more. I give it everything I can. Eventually, we agree on the chintz, and the potassium creates a patch of maidenhair. This is what is meant by the abandonment of subjectivity. The brain flares open and bounces into Norway. Hallucinations do the rest.

I've discovered a planet named Cindy. She's in the Andromeda Galaxy. It will take a while to get there. I can begin showing property next Monday. Meanwhile, I'm packing my ship full of pepperoni sticks and root beer. Atmospheric pressure on Cindy is approximately that of Earth. Bring a bathing suit.

What did I learn in life? Eat well, keep warm, get plenty of sleep. Thoughts are waves. They bring us food and silverware. Honesty hurts. It's difficult to be honest, particularly with ones-self. Try to get along with people. It's easier to avoid people, so if you can do that, that would be the ideal thing, but if you've got to be around people, it's hard, I know, but try not to kill anyone. Above all, pay attention. Snow transforms the world. War wrecks the world. It helps to be numb. Empty inside. Shiny outside. A bubble. Drifting down. Reposing. Thinly. Delicately. Pop.

I like to put my fingers on the warm pages of a book and feel the world that way. Thank goodness there are people that still write books, that will spend a lifetime pursuing poetry in a society that cares only about money, that judges everything against the gauge of money, that sees everything as commodity, which is material that is bought and sold, which is amazing as paint, as millions for a painting, a Pollock for $140 million, bought by a Hollywood mogul. I find that baffling. And weirdly encouraging.

These are the judgments of a private man. The world has become a very strange place. I don't understand the sadism of billionaire politicians. I don't understand the mechanisms of denial. I don't understand the persistence of delusional thinking. Revolving doors are especially confusing. The truth of anything pivots on multiple factors, including cognition and funding. Things can get silly in the lab. A shadow jumps out of a fuchsia and says hi. The pretty wires of thought hold the mouth together. And then we practice the wallpaper of our childhood.

Most people avoid reality. It's the sensible thing to do. Reality hurts. A person is not just the sum of the chemicals in their brain. There's more to it than that. Some believe that the sole object of perception is the thing-in-itself. Others find nourishment among worms and darkness. Leibniz found the universality of his binary system in the solid and broken lines of the I-Ching. Whatever you choose as a next step is entirely up to you. There's a door of ice hinged with silver that creaks open to infinity. And then Cher appears, dressed in a full glitter pantsuit, smiling hugely.

When somebody does you a wrong, do you stay out all night long getting drunk, or do you fold yourself into a fist and go to bed? The pronouns are at it again, hopping around like bugs. I'm soaked in New Orleans. Otherworldly concerns. Is there a world beyond the grave? I hope so. Last night I watched six men stab a man to death. The man was Julius Caesar. The six men were friends and colleagues in the Roman senate. Caesar appears later as a ghost. There are lots of pissed off ghosts in Shakespeare. I don't think that surprises anybody. Least of all Julius Caesar.

The future doesn't look good. But we'll see what we can do about bringing the saddles and bedrolls to Iceland. If the hedonism is a success, and the tarts careen through our digestive tracts the way they're supposed to, we can move on from there. My nerves fondle the idiosyncrasies of Reykjavik, which is paroxysmal and warm. The expedition stumbles along until it arrives at the capitol of an ominous feeling. Everyone stands still and listens to the peculiar noises a garage door makes when it opens and you see Lou Reed sitting in a lawn chair sipping coffee.

We slither through a world that is partly the invention of our perceptions and partly the harp of a towheaded python named Trinket the Mighty. And then I ask myself: why do I do this? Why do I constantly search for outer space? Why do I search for a semantic portal to another dimension? I'm guess I'm just not satisfied with the usual paradigms. It is what Alfred North Whitehead called the Fallacy of Misplaced Concreteness, though I prefer to call it a sandwich.

I feel elemental at times like this, the vibration of electromagnetic forces creating a hotel for my mind. Your mind, my mind, makes no difference. Maybe there is no mind. Maybe there is only *mu*, non-existence, non-being, the original non-being from which being is produced, which is sometimes overly gruff, sometimes strangely swollen. But thank you for sending the parrots.

Chrome is out of date. I keep getting this message. Chrome is out of date. I'm out of date. The date is out of date. I haven't been on a date in many years. I once ate a date with a date and later had a box of dots. Today is a date but I won't tell you what it is until you do something about your millennium. It's my millennium, too, you know. According to the colander on the wall today is Macaroni Monday. I have to go now. I can feel a zeitgeist crawling up my aeon.

I frequently have thoughts about things that don't add up to anything. These thoughts are sometimes interrupted by the clatter of activity in the kitchen. That would be the washcloth telling its story of magic and shame. Henri Bergson had an interesting notion of time and identity as pearls on a string. Moments are pearls. The string is the continuity of time connecting the click and volatility of our moods. And yet Bergson has nothing to say about doing the dishes. For that you have to consult George Orwell, who did a lot of dishes. And we know where that leads.

Existence Gets Me Wet

Sometimes I see a prose poem and ask myself why anyone would write such a thing. There are so many words. It's exhausting. But really, all one has to do is think of Wyoming and then compare it to a submarine. The poem will crawl across a sheet of paper and reach the border before sunrise. Sometimes you can think you're fooling the language but the language is urging you to keep your mouth shut. The poem will drag you out of yourself until you hear the cry of a nipple. Nipples are simple. They express tenderness. Do that. Express tenderness and Montgomery glands. Muscle contractions. Areola. The stride of emperors, the fireflies of queens.

Nothing feels quite so good as clean sheets right out of the dryer. Or the first hot shower after having a cast on your leg removed. It will become a reverie. Iowa is larger than you can imagine. Illusion is its sad consolation prize. So is squeezing and dirt. I've developed a taste for Barbizon cows. Rancorous idealism and planetarium popcorn. The road flare compliments the landscape. Whatever you do in life, experience penmanship. Find a trombone and hop into a dream. Enjoy breakfast. Life is all noise and bondage and the poetry of Frank O'Hara.

The meaning of life crawls around in spices. It expects words to grow it into food. And why not? The shapes expect description. This is where art murders reality. Meanwhile, the mirrors enhance our elbows. Is life truly this unjust or just fascinating? Everywhere I look I find drugged snakes and Cézanne. I slouch forward spilling adjectives on a twinkling uvula. I will expand it into alligators. Shoes are important. The brain opens revealing Madrid. And finally, in the bistro, we discover that life is alchemical. This isn't a big surprise. But it chose us to make the diagnosis.

What divides the organic from the inorganic? Is it a mysterious Vital Force? Is it a chemical process? Is it Philadelphia?

Lately I've been incubating resentments like a physician's assistant. I do this by implication, which is also a miracle. Nothing soothes anxiety like food. Or a tincture of Indica. That works pretty good, too. Opium breaks Chicago in half. Do you ever have feelings so powerful you can't share them with anyone? I think it's ok to climb into yourself and pepper your heart with the debris of heartache.

Can I be personal for a moment? If existence is wet, existence gets me wet. If existence is existential, existence makes me existential. But what happened, exactly, in 1967? The world got weird and weirder and then it got cooked in tasty morsels of narrative. The world is largely imaginary. Our past undresses in our emotions. Or is it the other way around? What worries me is losing an entire planet. What kind of species destroys an entire planet? If existence is a synonym for being there, I'm here, trying to solve life with a lubricant and a film projector. The act of painting holds the disease of elaboration. Sometimes it's really objective. I take notes. Inspissate in goop, separate from reality. Time doesn't matter anymore. Beauty pants for a woman. My character creaks into view. I become a pterodactyl and circle the sky higher and higher on rising currents of hot air. Here is where painting becomes a little beard of foliage. The dishwasher contributes a little intelligence to the sexual detergents of struggle, and the painting hangs there, sobbing revolt.

Water Lapping At It

Camel camaraderie away like bones and get mixed in tongues. Plop cat of chaos paint. Street on the roof of my shoulder where the pavement is speed. Body pins falling from an edge of morning. The weary emissary crosses the field. A church bell rings. Religious practices are charming if they don't pinch too much or provoke guerrilla warfare.

I get a bang out of cashmere. Perception is easy. It's also bugs.

Grimace talk chair. Swarm and swirl and swirl and swarm and hold my eyes in this sentence long enough to read what is coming next which is blinding in its brightness. I am coming toward you in ashes. The beauty of ash is primordial. Support the rod of wandering. Thursday's salt. Heaven in a warehouse.

A snap plumps my heft into operation. I constrained an imponderable crack to say obstetrics to you and mean it. And I do I mean to stroll to the end and make another beginning out of moss. Innocence adapts to figures of speech. Metaphors set up camp in Romania.

I hear an identity chattering under my skin. It's exciting to see our minds come together in a sentence. Is this that sentence? Are we greenhorns in paradise?

I stand here in your café riveted to your definitions of sluice. The snow is an embodiment of heaven and I can understand its presence in the spoons, but the fugue that just went by was big as a truck and hinted at tin as a possible resource in the future of our confusion.

Pile up the food of thought on pallets of mimosa butter. The stone makes the toad go up the mountain in a chivalry of popping thunder. Queen Mab in her greenery swarms the climbing she does with touch and artery. Flashing pins of complicated speed cause the manuscript in the attic to mimic a Mustang and dive through the air on San Francisco hills. Later, after breakfast, the words convene in glass and I feel the obstinacy of the window when I photograph the turbulence of the aurora borealis as it existed three million years ago in an agate.

I'm writing an enigmatic mimosa, a mundane welcome ticket for the velvet hippopotamus of my congenial rage. I'm foggy, traveling in a misty state. Nothing is clear except wax. The wind climbs my capharnaüm. The introspection rivals the transcendence of a hinge.

The door opens and here we are.

I need the elf because the ice cracks. The caboose has a frog for rent, and a calm green moment that bubbles out of a floorboard. I'm visiting the barge right now and forcing myself to pray for the penumbral irritations I've managed to gather over a lifetime of irritations. The penumbral irritations are special because they exist in a timeless margin of funny brochures.

The locals say the skin of the Colorado River Toad makes a good hallucinogen, but my irritations assume a life of their own and continue as words, pulling images and thoughts behind them, forging new associations, new immensities of penumbral art, new irritations, new speculations, new fitting rooms for the mall, which is deserted, thanks to a dreadful economy. Hence, words, which have an exchange value of their own, I don't know what, bitcoins, recommendations, comments on Facebook, seesaws, patents, descriptions of pain, the strange behaviors of cats.

They say the lake is garish and extroverted, but I found it hanging from a branch of words, braided and abstract.

Lassitude of twisting quintessence. Sunset cloud sleeping in the orchard. The breath of the poem is a perusal of Eden floating in a red fog of absence. Frankly, the handkerchief is not the panacea I thought it was but just another busy conception of dirt. The sky offers its sloth in a crate on the shore. We can use it to build our conversation.

Or not.

Hey, here's a boat. This makes my grammar pink. It does it to cinnamon and then crumbles into upheaval. Garments are often green but the pretzels weren't and that makes everything harked or something. Crinkled like a scrotum.

Packed with straw.

Children behave. That's what they say when we're together. Watch how you play.

I don't remember much after that. There was a knife on the bottom. I didn't know quite what to do, so I just flared into talk and added myriad subtleties of tone to my voice to confuse the crowd into thinking it was a form of invocation. You can tell them back home it didn't quite work. I'm out on bail now. It's spring, and that rusty old hook is still in me. I can't quite cut loose. Not just yet. There are still some things I need to do.

I want to magnify the magnetic air until the words in my mouth catch fire. You know? I'm not superstitious but there's going to come a time when I've got to spit them all out like chrome buckles on Attic Street. William Hurt hurries with a hurt back to a Paris taxi. They stop a few blocks later to pick up Geena Davis. This is a typical afternoon for me, my dazzling teeth gliding through an almanac of hope and despair while my shoulders brace for the next burden. This is the membrane of my sparkling world. See the needle nail in the wax man? It's the B side of the aforementioned membrane. The water shouts meaning at a revelation purged of cows and the scribbles in the sand murmur of impersonal pressures. The mind likes these things. Creosote and ice cream, the ocean rolling in and out.

Giggly Tinkles

It's hard to be honest in life. I mean, all the time. With everything. How can anyone do that? Thank god for illusion. For the mercies of cognitive dissonance. I want more of that. More hopium. More Costco. Cheap shirts and three-bean salad. It's not that amusing to watch a society collapse. You can see it in the way people push their carts. You know that desultory zoned-out tiredness on everyone's faces? What brings the meaning of technology now to its fullest expression is its erasure. It tends to hide itself. One could say that *that* is its ambition, the meaning of its story: to blend in with the landscape. And by disappearing, it invades everything.

Thank you propaganda. Thank you for all you've done.

Life is complicated. There are realities we intuit, realities we suppress. Realities we deny, realities we invent. And then there are movies. Hurray for movies: Sandra Bullock goes tumbling through space. Jeff Bridges strums an acoustic guitar in a seedy motel. Keanu Reeves dodges bullets. It's a philosophy. Every philosophy discovers its capacity for sitting alone in a basement. And when we reemerge into the world, we will see it in everyone's eyes: the latest holocaust.

Call it writing. Words in herds for no particular reason, just the nudity of a moment, humming and drumming, whistling and bristling, bubbly like a pie, a dough containing cherries, a circumference of air, a radius of crust, an approximation of pi, intermediaries, libraries and wood. Beckett's flinty old face, a face of crags, the eyes of a hawk. The bristle of a thistle. The riddle of a scribble. Rumple of a shuffle. Simple dimples. Pickled ripples. Giggly tinkles.

I entered life as I found it, visceral and wet and surrounded by Minneapolis. Later, I discovered secretion and oysters. I sat under a piano and wore a cowboy hat. The kiwis came later, with fecundation and sunglasses. Everything is a process. Life is unceasing creation. Everything is in flux. Thus, I have no alternative but to drive to the drugstore. I arrive a few minutes later creaking with infinity. Most often, it's just a matter of finding the right ointment. I return home and rub myself silly. I become 171 pounds of dark energy pounding images into a laptop screen. Possibilities of action quiver with majuscules. The rest is mostly Hollywood.

A description crawls across a sheet of paper in search of something to describe, a cloud or a mood or something. This feels stupid. Is that so bad? Stupidity is annoying, but you can say anything you want because, you know, you're stupid. It's the preferred way to be in these here parts. We live on the edge of chaos, a region of bounded instability that engenders a constant dynamic interplay between order and disorder. If you don't believe me, just look under our bed. I apologize for the geometry. Nothing is perfectly round. Mostly, I drift through life like a ghost.

I know what to do.

Hold this sentence a minute while I write it. Ok? Ok. I think it's done. Life is a whisper. This is what is known in phenomenology as a temporal awareness within the stream of consciousness. The rest is doughnuts and open sea. This is when the mind awakens to the spin of the planet, you know? Like when the act of writing becomes so fantastically futile you can feel the ohms of its resistance burn into human reality. The lucidity is stunning. And you'll wonder why you didn't see it earlier. All those sentences knotted together to make libraries and wood.

Fingery Things

Here comes another puddle of words. Two hundred camels stand around being literal and Arthur Rimbaud keeps piling goods on their backs. It's a long way across the Danakil Desert. The horizon resembles a rugged knife. The world itself is a fabrication, so why not percolate goats?

Sometimes you can think you're fooling the language but the language is fooling you. You might picture it as a hat, or feathers and sweaters. The meaning is not outside words, but caged inside, waiting for a mind to come along and release them. It's the semantic equivalent of linseed. We must rattle our funerals at Little League. And while it is true that the simplest random variables can be a private matter, the surest way to find yourself is to use your anguish.

So we stop to wait for the light at the intersection of Elliott Avenue and Broad Street, hot day, the Duck Truck goes by, people yelling. A cop car comes down Broad Street, lights going, and stops. Across the street is the Neukom Vivarium, an 80-ft long greenhouse housing a 60-ft nurse log, a fallen hemlock from the Cascade forest giving life to other organisms as it decays. I wonder if the cops are there to arrest the log for loitering. I can't see what's going on. The light changes. The cops leave. We cross the street and discover an angry man in a trench coat fountaining a steady stream of expletives and curses as he moved on up to Western. We stopped for the light at Western. He was down the street, still yelling loudly, full of rage. I don't usually yell like that. But I know that magnitude of rage. It's there, in my head, 24/7.

I never know how to display my emotions. Some are relatively calm and normal, others are colossal and fierce. Enough to frighten people. Intensity is laudable in a rock star. In real life, people tend to avoid it. Incandescence doesn't go well with small talk and wheat thins. Intensity is easily mistaken for madness. And why wouldn't it be? Often, when I think of the membranes and molecules of which I'm composed, it astonishes me that a single coherent identity emerges from that. The mind is larger than what appears. The more we think, the more we become immersed in a ruminant murk. The less we think, the more the phenomena of our attention lose their names and become wondrous blossomings of amiable qualia. Guacamole and wheat thins.

The maneuvering to get the final bit of corned beef sandwich into my mouth while a wasp perches and hovers there, don't want to be too aggressive and piss him off and get stung, but I want my bite of sandwich, I'm anxious to finish this thing off and get to the potato chips. I swing my arm out far enough to confuse his strategies and get that bite into my mouth, sans wasp, sans swollen tongue.

If I had the right words, I could lift a piece of reality and show it to people. The universe isn't entirely in my head. There is no boundary that begins and ends at my skull. A skull is just a skull. The stuff inside is amazing, but has its limits, until the limits dissolve, and the universe comes flooding in. Spoons. Metaphors. Chandeliers. I don't know what else to call it. If I speak in the language of enigma, it's because I'm dressed in bells. The King of Time goes by in a carriage of gold. This is probably happening to me right now. And while it is true that the simplest random variables are mongrel carbonations of ontological paint, my expectations lie around at the bottom of this paragraph, bubbling like a branch of death in a sheet of plywood.

How did we lose our way? Did we ever know the way? Is too much consciousness too little consciousness? Is walking erect with a big head bobbing around not actually the silliest permutation to ever emerge from the goop of polymers that brought us here? Bees have learned far better ways to inhabit the world and navigate. They use dance and magnetism. We use GPS, ARPA, ECDIS, and postcard racks. We have very little in our language that actually conforms to reality, whatever reality is. We invent Gods. We devise religions. We use mobile phones to buy drugs, pesticides to grow biofuel. The disconnect is abyssal. We have nothing as expansive as echo location. Nothing as informative as odor. Nothing as illuminating as a waggle dance.

Today I'm happy to find my fingers doing fingery things. I make paragraphs until the libraries step forward and say thank you. I appreciate that, I do, but what did Hegel mean by the death of art? Was he kidding or something? This upsets me. I'm going to go skulk in a stream of consciousness. It's rough getting the torn upholstery to express itself. And now it's just a chair. It's been a chair all along. I get up, and sit down, and get up, and sit down, and discover what Hegel meant.

If you're going to spend your life shaving in men's rooms along the highway, you must also endure the insufferable chatter of elves.

Go away haberdashery fish. Let me be a leg of sugar.

Absurdity Is Divine

Does fragility awaken a sense of beauty? Yes, I believe it does. Yesterday I discovered a city of elves beneath the bed. That was nice. I like elves. I like other things, too. I like trees and furniture. I like summer and yakitori. I like writing paragraphs that cohere around a thought, a motif thematic as mushroom. Paragraphs full of anger and sunlight. Methane embedded in permafrost. Which reminds me. We're losing the planet. Or is it the other way around? Is the planet losing us? What matters is electricity and running water. The paper towels in the kitchen window. That's where we're at now. Hanging on till the next minute. As always.

I don't entirely understand Kierkegaard on despair, but I understand despair. I know how it operates, how it breeds and propagates, how it unbolts the door of monsters and lets chaos loose. But let's not dwell on that. Nothing can save the world now but Superman. And a colossal quantity of ice. Here's a whisper of something knocking on your brain. "No Stars," sung by Rebekah Del Rio. Music soothes the lonely. Though it also helps to be palpated occasionally. Biology is like that. Cells and membranes. The habit of doing dishes. Pain in my right arm from a dislocated shoulder. Pain in my heart from a dislocated country. That country for old men in the Yeats poem. The young in one another's arms, birds in the trees.

One frequently overhears the phrase "don't judge me" these days. No one wants to be accountable. No one wants to make a statement. Except for tattoos. One's skin appears to be the parchment for one's history and declarations. What do the symbols mean? You could keep a conversation going for quite a while with someone and their tattoos. "The only way to be in agreement with life is to disagree with ourselves," observed Fernando Pessoa. "Absurdity is divine." Is there a tattoo for that? Say, Sisyphus rolling a rock to the top of a hill? Put it on my forehead. That's where nothing much happens except hair and disappointment.

When beliefs collapse, thought is laid bare. A bare thought is a thing to behold. It looks like an accordion but sounds like two sweaty wrestlers in a grudge match in upstate Michigan. Imagine thinking as an unemployed poem. It will make you strong and beautiful. But it will not answer the enigma that is you. Surrealism is for airports and hats. Everything else is just clouds. Nocturnal discharge. The smell of the sea. No perception should have to walk around in dirty water. It's unwholesome. Lift this sentence with your eyes: it will help you enter another world.

Henry Miller Was Right
About Everything

Revolving doors confuse me. They make entering a building look amusing, but confusing. I'm absurd. I know that. But who isn't? Is the human condition absurd? Hell yes it's absurd. Is disease absurd? Is leukemia absurd? Cholera? Typhus? Capitalism?

Here is my diagnosis: the truth is not always absurd. Sometime it's scenic, like hope. Space is forgiving. But gravity is romantic.

I think I'm falling in love with the weight of a movie ticket. If you rub something long enough it eventually becomes your friend. Therefore, you should send me some money.

Is life in the 21st century a simulacrum of a reality that doesn't exist? Our journey begins with unicorns and ends with billionaires. I'm not one of them. I'm a non-billionaire. But I try to be discreet. I try to keep my poverty to myself. If you manage to keep your pants up, the world will treat you like another redundancy of legs and arms and leave you alone. Let us tromp through this simulacrum like God's spies looking for traces of democracy here and there.

Do you remember democracy? It was a fun but brief ride, better than the House of Totalitarianism. Walt Disney speaks to us from the dead. Any reality lying around is just too obvious, so we ignore it. Just keep following the line of least resistance. It leads to numbness and cooperation. But if you're curious about what's in there, what's under your skin, God help you.

I think it's wonderful that things exist. That the nose is naturally Zen and that one's chains are imaginary. It's wonderful that sensations can be words in a sentence. Hope is cruel. Drop everything and run into the sky. Anyone who says Chicago is ugly at night hasn't seen its cutlery. Not up close, not at The Purple Pig.

Death is nothing. Everybody does it, so it can't be too difficult. I'm old enough to remember streetcars, so obviously I haven't gotten around to it yet. I like to procrastinate. What can I say? This is how I intend to feel at home. Mad brilliant blood pumping me into words. I pull prepositions out of the air and feel the sweet friction of silk on my arm.

The older I get, the more I realize: life's overflow is the infinite, poets are a holy glass in which life's wine sloshes around releasing bouquets of smokestack lightning, the need for art is itself largely ideological, flossing your teeth is important but a pain in the ass, the medicine cabinet grows increasingly populated with prescription drugs, nothing is wholly obvious without becoming enigmatic, and if we have a good understanding of facts it follows that life's greatest luxuries are probably not the answer you were looking for.

Henry Miller was right about everything. Reality itself is too obvious to be true, and napkin folding is a true art form.

Gelassenheit, as a mode of comportment, of receptivity, is an ideal mode of human understanding.

We look for fulfillment in different ways. Me, I like to expand into goldfish and string. Is gravity truly a force or an acceleration? Gravity is an accordion caused by beer barrel polka. It is a tiny sample of snit. And yet there is meaning. How is meaning possible? The short answer is European butterflies. A longer explanation requires bombast. Today I want to forge a new objective and shake with unfettered femininity. Let's start there. Webs, membranes, tactile associations. The placenta circulates a stream of words. It won't be long now. Here it comes: Ibiza at daybreak.

Mania

Mania defines the moment. The rage of the sea. Omar Sharif and Julie Christie standing under a chandelier in a mansion in which everything is coated with the sparkle of frost.

It's possible that what needs to be said about art doesn't need to be said at all. This is why I've nailed my voice to the wall. We're in crisis, and something needs to be said by a voice hanging objectively in space like a gavel. The uptick in military helicopters is worrisome, not to mention the smoke and crazy weather. And that's how language works. Iguanas push softly against our legs. The sky cracks open with thunder. What happened, America? What happened to that big adventure of life on the Mississippi? Who am I talking to? I don't even know anymore.

Today, I would like to build a new reality. This isn't the one we were promised. It's the other one, the one with blisters and cemeteries. Expectations turn sour here. My invocations sputter meaninglessly while the stars pour eternity on the world, which orbits a finite sun.

Not that there's anything wrong with orbiting celestial bodies. What else are you going to do in space? We can sit around by the side of a pool. The ghost of Bob Hope will elevate our despair. We can do cannonballs. And drink ice tea. There's no morality to pain, though one may be provided, given sufficient time for thought and the hot dog rotator at 7-11. Everything else is just haircuts and root awakening.

Write a beverage that tastes of revelation. Garden the inscrutability of time with a hypnopompic trowel.

Age is not my friend. Because this proves nothing, which is shinier than the truth of coupons. There is something you can only find within. It's called Costa Rica and it contradicts the ontology of frost. All I ever wanted to do is probe abstractions.

Astronomers tell us that there is dark matter in the universe but they don't know what it is. I know what it is. It's Saturday night in Jackson Hole.

Today the sky is pink and friendly. It tastes of shadows and paper. This is because the human brain weighs three pounds and could use a touch of cologne. Sometimes I will feel the explosion of something huge in my brain and so I feed it to the camels. Which answers nothing. This is what life does when death isn't around.

The romantic spirit isn't dead. It's just on sabbatical.

We're stuck in a world of stepladders. Twinkling lights, gas stations, hats. Basically, a middle-aged woman standing in the rain in a leopard-skin bathrobe waiting for her dog to take a shit. Because, you know, eternity. A man sitting in the dark trying to get rid of his mind.

Blockbuster

This is how thinking begins. I trek into the wilderness after watching the spirits dance. Everything feels like a movie, images commingling on a wall like the one in Plato's cave. That's the way the mind works, which is a projector on which the film of your life is projected. I'm the star of my movies, which is nice, but like any other movie with an undercurrent of *weltschmerz*, the thinking is gray. It stars Wallace Beery as my uncle Fritz, Scarlet Johansson as my sister Burp, and Octavius Caesar as the wise old garbage man, Jimmy Bones.

This is as far as I will go. Paper is where I like to put things. The very alphabet walks among my bones. Nothingness is a noun. Turn it over and look underneath. There is nothing there. And lots of it.

Geometry is cruel. It runs around with its claws raised trying to grab your oblongs. I don't know why the harmonica is so mutant. But if you tap on the binoculars the air becomes a place. Romania in the rain.

Which is, you know, feelings. The mind is a sky. Pain opens like a suitcase, but the soliloquys remain the same. Oh, that this too, too sullied flesh would melt, thaw, and resolve itself into a dew. Space is everywhere. I feel eels swim between my legs. Blood dribbles down the motel curtain. I realize that the science here is a little awkward. But there is a general understanding that the external world is the work of our organs. Don't worry. I'll pay my bills now.

I like a man that can do drywall. Most feelings are elemental, but some are more like libraries. This is why tripods happen. The medium is the baby. It is as though life itself became a semantic abnormality. A type of look, Mesozoic insects trapped in amber. Sometimes a vocabulary can be used to hack at reality until it yields a larger reservoir of meaning. Wear a goldfish coat. Words trapped in children.

An umbrella flies through my sweater. It is as though knowledge had got hold of a total eclipse of the heart and used it to wash my mammals. And that makes everything growl. We really ought to free ourselves from the seductions of holes.

The next sentence is hungry. You can feed it your attention and it will move forward making meanings and shit. And this connects us in rhubarb.

In later years, I became obsessed with invisible things. Electricity. Homeric poems. Walmart greeters.

Nietzsche was right, if you're going to look into the abyss make sure the abyss isn't looking back into you. That's a hard feeling to shake. Go in any direction and you'll encounter yourself. There are no pedestrians in the ecstasies of the forest. Intensity is easily mistaken for madness. And why wouldn't it be? Society wants us ground down so that we're easy to deal with. Society doesn't want complicated people, testy people, it wants easy people, obedient people. Meaning awakens, then goes back to sleep. Words are clumsy, but nobody gives a shit. The lessons of life are relatively easy. Eat well, keep warm, and try not to kill anyone.

Refrigerator Light

I used to make great sandwiches for work. One sandwich was composed of thin slices of corned beef or ham slathered with butter and adorned with lettuce and pickles for maximum juiciness. The other sandwich was all peanut butter and butter and strawberry jam. They were delicious and made the work day slightly more palatable. Most food is literal, but sometimes it's sublime.

I also like getting undressed. There is a real universe beneath my clothes. Snowballs, junkyards, torrential rains. It sometimes happens that people become strangers to themselves. There are drugs for this, and conversation.

Sometimes I'm so happy that a light comes on in the refrigerator when I open the door that I think of André Breton. Who said: we gaze at the unbelievable and believe it despite ourselves.

Real wealth is spirit. The strength to endure, and the means to do it. This is beatitude. Beatitude is as much of a fact as death and liverwort and gold. Beatitude is an elephant, the bones of a paragraph trying to break free of a petrified reality. It is a subtle but not entirely clumsy refrigeration of time. And when it breaks free everything crashes out of its own being and becomes the one activity in life that doesn't require an explanation.

Human skin is phenomenally soft. Follow me. I will show you the effulgence of Walt Whitman walking down a street in Camden, New Jersey. The blood jingles with sunlight. Nothing is wholly obvious without becoming enigmatic. Our language is in prison. Open the gates and let the words loose.

I write for people who don't exist. Readers that don't exist. How exciting is that? How do you explain the subjective quality of experience? I try everything: hammers, drills, washers, dryers, shovels, algebra, calculus, festival events, incense and ribbon.

Mostly ribbon. I can't really control what an entire language wants to do when I begin to express myself using that very language. It got Hamlet into trouble and he knew how to see through people and fence and direct plays. It's true that words set free free us all. But they can't repair the damage done. This is the song of the misanthrope. This is the language of water. This is the place where the separation between the organic and inorganic ceases to exist. This is where reality comes to question itself.

Wherever you go always have a book and a bookmark handy. Aquariums are fun but a little creepy. Zoos are horrible. Be wary of ideals. Submit to nothing. Don't rub your eyes if you ride a city bus. Try not to take yourself too seriously. Avoid giving advice it's obnoxious. Jobs are largely stupid. Life is mostly brutish survival. Always have a flashlight handy. Don't break your brain on worthless shit. Wool hats are better than brimmed hats in windy cities. Success is mostly silliness. This is why I take silliness seriously. Which is silly.

The Universe In A Tablespoon

My emotions are wet and powerful. Some have bluish tints, and some are hectic with daguerreotypes of Emily Dickinson. This makes me a loaded gun.

There are indications everywhere that reality resists the kind of descriptions I'm prepared to offer. But I'll give it a shot. I give a good shake to a can of lather, press the button and hear the creamy lather hiss into the palm of my hand. It feels soft and wet, like the bibliography of a worm.

If sandpaper is a parody of Utah, then what is the value of shaving lather?

The world is a nonlinear tablespoon. Sooner or later the stars will continue the conversation without us. Reading poetry may give you some assurance that you're doing all you can to avoid insipidity and stultification, but you may also experience side effects: vomiting, indiscretion, nudity, gratuitous violence, the dizziness of freedom and developing the head of an antelope with blood squirting out of its nose.

This is the syntax of the soul. Make a sausage of words that can squirm in the hands like a toad. Dimethyltriptamine is a naturally occurring psychedelic that's also found endogenously in the human body. You know? So keep looking. Until then, keep squeezing that dough until the disease of living starts crawling around on the junk in the garage and finds an old Led Zeppelin LP. It will all begin to make sense. The creakiness of the doors. The dust. Even the black smoke vomiting into heaven.

The days of my life grow into winter. The drawer fills with medicine. A universe walks by carrying a basket of planets. The longer I exist the less I know about existence. The nerves flicker with apparitions of semantic transport. Helicopters, for example. Or prose.

Was Freud right about the winter of our discontent? Is civilization a fraud? I'm not completely on board with scientific rationality, but the diversions of dumplings house a hidden purport, and thanks to the genius of the human hand I can make words jump into a sentence and crash around in metaphors.

I was born into this world with abstract expressionism and television. My first memory (age one) is that of John Wayne wrestling a giant octopus. The movie was *Wake of the Red Witch*, a 1948 adventure film based on a novel by Garland Roark. That was my first impression of life: a struggle with tentacles in an enchanted undersea realm.

Roughly Speaking

There's a beautiful country in my head. There's a mountain that sits down so that the sun can spread its light around and a lake that does pushups so that you don't have to. I can feel it in the eyeball of a balloon. The soft moist mass of desire and drugstore awnings. Life is a journey. Or so they say. I'd call it a disposition. The ghost of a pig, for example. Or a winery on the Kitsap peninsula. The universe says yes, I will marry you. But you must be willing to kiss my stars, and bring your own potato chips to the picnic.

Roughly speaking: chopsticks are objects. I don't want innocence. I want the hard embrace of the ocean. And I promise you, it won't end there.

Until they're scrambled, facts are inert. Dull and without life. It is not the facts themselves that form cognition, but the tumult in which they ignite.

My subversive feelings are at work today. They're everywhere, undermining institutions and creating mayhem. This is, of course, a private matter, and the world has yet to be informed of my insubordination.

There's no simpler way to say it: libraries are cool. You can bring a book home and conceal your aggression in the dangerous energy of art. Thought takes the form of Hollywood and recedes from the elevator doors like a documentary on plywood.

Where is the end of this sentence? Is it here? It just wants to keep going. Can a sentence do that? I have come to understand the universe as a giant skating rink. What do you see? I see churches, gardening tools, and Tonya Harding doing a triple axel.

I, too, have great ambitions. One is to visit the library. The other is to finish this sentence, which contains twenty gallons of water and a contagious longing called life.

The mind is a desolate place without a haircut. Nothing makes sense except fish. Problems clank behind you like a string of laboratories researching the Boolean logic of snickerdoodles.

Today's poetry is brought to you by haircare. Just lean back and let the world fall over you. It will feel like alcohol. When the Greek surgeon Galen discovered the circulation of blood, he was chief physician to the gladiators in Pergamon. Think about that: a chest torn open by an opponent's blade, the heart still beating. My strategy is to not get too hung up on any idea but let the stigmas wallow in their own misperceptions and follow the flow of the river to its own conclusion. The sentence finishes its sweater and the ocean fits cognition like a hairspray.

Most Feelings Are Fights

Most of my narratives include at least one accordion, but this time I'm going to insert a shovel. There is a sky at the bottom of the ocean. We should dig it up and hose it off and examine it for foghorns and lost prime ministers.

We know so little about indignity. How do you weigh the world? You sit at a desk and write things about vegetables and hats.

Forgiveness is slowly percolated through the heart. Nothing is insentient. Everything on the subatomic level can crawl backward, like a ceiling. The world itself is a fabrication. Where did the goats go? They're standing on my head, grazing on tufts of Ethiopian coffee.

Most feelings are fights. All you need is words. Music can get you feeling pretty expensive. I recommend flumpets, a hybrid of the trumpet and flugelhorn. It will give the others in the room an idea of how pleasure is often mixed up with pain, and is often confused with sadomasochism. Everything, especially job applications, are the product of a semantic instability. Daylight bumps into the library and the readers look up to see my face in the window. Aren't we all looking for something? The truth? A clean bathroom? A freshly constructed reality? You know, onions. Multilayered stuff. Molecules. Atoms. Puppets and drugs. Providence and pizza.

They say sugar is extroverted, but I find it deeply engaging, and a little abstract at times. Drool is what happens when the lassitude of our conversation topples over into cupcakes. This makes my grammar happy. I'm not much given to optimism but there's going to be a sparkling world when the rest of the words get here. I know this feeling: it's despair. Tinged with carbohydrates. I'd like a cookie now.

Neil Young plays a few chords. The river moves gracefully into comprehension. A dead man floats out to sea. You can distance yourself from a definition, but will it duplicate the virtue of Dakota topsoil? The bath towel is soft as thought. Human nature is everywhere, including bubblegum pink. We pass one another on the freeway knowing nothing about one another. And this serves as a form of civilization. None of this requires a zipper. The mind is a sandwich now. George Harrison sitting in a chair in a huge English lawn surrounded by garden gnomes.

Infinity shakes loose of its adjectives and goes on automatic. Being feels more penetrating. People unfold. Concentration comes from dirt. Just ask dirt.

Transcendence does a backflip. This we know for sure: it's hard getting a piece of hair off of a piece of soap. And then, finally, nothing else matters.

This sentence has 400 legs and is crawling into your eyes. We can talk about that later, after some reality gets here.

Garrulous Asparagus

We keep forgetting the world is alive. It needs our attention. There is sometimes the clatter of activity in the kitchen, the smell of creamy asparagus soup, diced asparagus tips going into a sauce pan, and sometimes the house is quiet. That should be telling us something. It should be alerting us to signs and omens. Rhythms of rest and sustenance. But let's not dwell on that.

I don't always like reality, it can be overly blunt in my opinion, but it's all we've got.

For example, death. It's cruel to awaken the dead. Don't do that. Try dazzling the world with pancake syrup and megalomania.

Do you see what I mean? Writing poetry is weird.

We pass one another on the freeway knowing nothing about one another. And this serves as a form of civilization. What is Being? I don't know. Sighing, breathing heavily, shuffling papers at a desk? I know injuries largely go unnoticed and healthcare is a scandal. The body is essentially a theater of molecules convening in blood. Frogs in platform shoes flying helicopters around our ears. Sometimes words are best left alone resting quietly on paper, waiting for a pair of eyes to awaken them, bring them to life. And then what? We see an old man hitting a tambourine all day at the side of a road.

Nothing is simple. Everything is intricately interrelated. That's one explanation, although it's a shitty explanation. I'm still lost. What makes water wet? What creates a sense of personhood? Is free will real? Or an illusion? I smell the scorch of rebellion. A colossal lobster thunders down the street howling the secrets of the ocean. So go ahead. Saddle a primitive urge. Ride to Reno. Smile and wave. The mind is wild for a little free will. A good hotel and a pair of dry socks.

Wrinkles explain the history of a face. They tell a tale of unappeased ambitions, weary compromise and popped bubbles of glistening illusion. But most of the time wrinkles just sit on your face and simmer and boil. Mucus is the music of the nose. I feel the ooze of blood in my veins. It helps me relax. I like to think about not thinking. And suddenly another sentence wants your attention. The thing to do is to let things be what they want to be, including wrinkles, and leave the rest to randomness and dolls, a mouth tossing itself into words and a Russian novel stomping around in anguish and paint.

My telescope has asked for a point. Is there a point? A point to anything? I crawl through my biology seeking redemption. Broken eggs sizzle in the pan. I scratch my leg and amuse some DNA molecules with my ability to make friends with objects. Garrulity can be a good quality in life. But it's not easy to maintain. My view of humanity keeps growing increasingly Hobbesian.

Must be the season of the witch. I just saw Donovan walking down the street carrying a jug of white lightning. Sure is strange. He bent to pick up a stitch. Oh no. Must be fiberglass. I don't see a veneration. All I see is cracks in the sidewalk and a piece of aluminum foil and sunshine and pump-jack in the distance outlined against a sky of cerulean blue. Imagine lying in bed listening to gravity. I just want to see Nebraska one last time before it's all underwater. Lord have mercy. Let's exaggerate ourselves.

All the clichés about old age are true. You don't just die. You get pushed into the Parthenon at dusk. You get philosophical. You take drugs. You go to bed and let go.

Fingers Of Rain

It's wonderful to have a drawer full of freshly laundered socks and underwear. But what is it to be invisible? To be unheard? To be old and forgotten?

There. I said it. But I regret the way I said this. I intended to have bubbles come out of my mouth. And words. Things like thought and vertigo. I carry a metamorphosis pistol. You never know when you need to change something. I see a haiku poking out of a book. Zen will do this. Zen will walk you into an emergency and then drop you flat. And there you are, sitting in a chair propagating words. You and your underwear. Elastic as a religion based on upholstery. The solace of furniture is a cowbell for hope.

The awareness that human existence is both joy and woe is prerequisite to accepting medication for the effronteries to one's insignia. My inseminations will sometimes be exaggerated, but I ought to do my best to adhere to metaphors rather than to heave the bulk of my language on you before it has been refined with a little tennis and statuary. The rest is guano. A little cut on the finger and it all coagulates into structure. Dollars of grotesque lucidity and florists languishing in pandemonium. The snapdragons are in rebellion. But the roses are big as suitcases and the black-eyed Susan and Heart of Jesus come together in sweet alyssum.

The pixel cells in a plasma TV have things in common with the golden luminosity of the brain and can be more intoxicating than any drug. I think of Charles Laughton laughing maniacally as he swings back and forth on those giant bells in Notre Dame because he's discovered romance.

Romance is a big ideology. My heart throbs. A few soft vowels create an armchair. This can only happen in language, which is a romance with words. Today, for example, I will comb your hair. I will crack some syntax over a sheet of paper and listen to its sounds. Here comes some now. The sound is oily, and quiet like guile.

If you cut a word in half, does a meaning spill out? I mean, come on. If language is a hallucination, then metaphors deform the sink. The Jolly Green Giant smashes a teacup in rage. The deeper angst of meaninglessness becomes a blob of protoplasm. I would like to explore this jelly later, when there is privacy, and morning blends with the river. I've got a reason now to wear overalls.

There's no formula for experience, there's just experience. Snakes and knives. A word cut in half. The coagulation of blood. Fred Astaire sitting in a chair tapping his feet.

A fugue results from the mathematics of sound. The mathematics of sound is baked in the legs when dancing occurs. Dancing is baked in blood. Blood becomes warmer with age. Age is baked in maturity. Maturity is baked in cognition. Cognition is knowledge. Knowledge is what you know. Impenetrability is what you do not know. The drone of cognition clarifies the stutter of rain. Traditions are chiefly glass. If a tradition is upside down washing machines and talk-shows fall out of it. This creates gurus and duplication.

Examining and consolidating his affinities with nineteenth century French painting, Matisse parachuted upward into a realm of clashing cymbals. The human form could no longer be controlled pictorially. He had to let it get out of the bath and become human. Tickets were purchased. Suitcases packed. Matisse leaned forward and made a woman stand alone in her hotel room after a bath. Naked. Holding a towel. Gazing at flowers. Grab a pencil. Draw something. I feel a moment's reflection gliding through a lip.

It's true, much of life is a matter of causation. But there's nothing like a giant catfish inventing itself on the telephone with Van Morrison.

Vowels are luminous embryos of meaning that creak of embellishment. Thanks to vowels, I'm warm and safe among the Huron. We chant as we paddle. The waves slap against our bow.

If I were to frame this moment in a single image, I would call it a wave and ride it into the infinite.

The Heart Sutra says, "all phenomena in their own-being are empty." This means that vowels don't suddenly get up and look for a job. Vowels are cool. They ride around in consonants. Ease feeds eels. The wind is its own vowel. It passes over the consonants of earth with fingers of rain.

Leibnitz's Pi

Math fascinates me, although I don't understand any of it. I don't mean addition and subtraction. I mean those bizarre symbols and letters. Circles of titanic stone. An ostrich at a strip club. Extraterrestrial probes.

Buddhists refer to our inner life as a bitter ocean of life and death, a constant churn of internal clashes and contradictions. The polynomial for this is furious oratory. Therefore, if density equals squirrel the sum of my local tensions will result in Limoges porcelain. We give it a plus sign and put it in the cupboard, until it's needed to serve Leibnitz's pi.

Pi is a constant nuptial, a marriage of lips and circumference, meaning that for all circles of any size, Pi will be the sand, the sanctuary, the circus we all need to attend. Because it's infinite, irrational, and attracts philosophers and books.

When you love books and every day you see thousands of books, books that you've purchased and collected and sometimes actually read, when you see them all with their spines and titles and thicknesses and thinesses all wanting to be read, books that you want to plunge into, or taste a little like an hors d'oeuvre, it can be more than a little maddening. There are so many of them. How can this planet die when I have so many books? How can I get them on the spaceship? And where's my book on how to build a spaceship? Look at my forehead. You might see goldfish swimming back and forth. I believe in imagery. I believe in the underworld and the aroma of Texas. The rest is guano. Now we can begin to talk about painting. Painting is bristles and daubs and gooey evolution. Milk in a bucket. Books on a shelf. A door hinge pondered in dark Rembrandt rust.

I carry a sexual argument to the table and give it a good polish. Birds scatter. I sift through my memories to venerate the past. A universe appears. You can see it sparkle at the edge of thought. A piece of it blisters on the finger of time.

If the truth is bland, we verify it with salt. But is there such a thing? Does the truth exist?

I know this smacks of romance, but it's too late to harmonize with the other guitars. My problem isn't with birds. My problem concerns free will. If I move fast enough, I can extend myself into fiction. This is where free will gets its willingness to be free. I can't control the lighting, but I can replace it with mushrooms. England is another way to do push-ups. You begin with a bias and end with a bang. The circuses are gone. But I feel a new stimulus stirring in the sweaters. Let's fold our sheets together. We can send out for more autobiography when the pillows arrive.

I've been selling ink and shaking a sausage all summer. It's very hard work. But it's intellectual work. Meaning I don't use my hands. I use my nose. My spirit. My intuition. My lake of bronze, my boat of paper.

Such an odd phrase, "intellectual work," as if the head were a warehouse, an Amazon of the Bizarre, and time was spent pushing thoughts around like furniture. Big, bulky armchair thoughts, mahogany credenza thoughts, shiny varnished armoire thoughts with coats & shirts in them, thoughts within thoughts, thoughts hanging from thoughts, thoughts full of randomness & blood, thoughts floating in a pool of thoughts, thoughts pulling thoughts out of thoughts, green thoughts, fireside thoughts, imploding thoughts, exploding thoughts, recycled thoughts, ornery nihilistic Nietzsche thoughts, throbbing voluptuous deviant thoughts, this is work I tell you I'm sweating. I've got blisters on my neurons.

Is there a cure for history? You'll need lots of rags to soak the blood. It gets pretty messy. There is never any one history. Just a lot of ceremonies and massacres. Palaces and barbed wire. Screams and explosions. Medals and dead children. But thank you for the rational perspective. I get it. The map is not the cake. The map is baked in the cake. The cake is upside down. Does this mean we're still friends? Good. I don't want to rattle anyone's cage. I just want to get a few points across. Here comes one now: war is a racket. This is where history gets its E Pluribus Unum on.

Here I am, a mechanical pedestrian dressed in seaweed. And this? This is an aggression, the unknown sugar of life opening in the eye of a mountain. You can find yourself in the auction over there by the barn. Look for the red wheelbarrow. Ask for Worm. Would you like a catastrophe to go with your coffee? Here. Have a sheaf of hummingbird gum. Pearls glitter in my necktie as an igloo of ultimatums is born inside a cup of memory sauce. This is your brain on words. Can you blame me? said the postman just as he was leaving. It's essential to a thing that it can be a picture walking out of its frame and shivering until someone drapes a blanket around it.

The Adventures Of Yolanda Squatpump

The days of my life grow into winter. I ignite some road flares and the blizzard pulls back into the night. A universe walks by carrying a basket of planets. The priest is late for mass. He shivers in the dark mulling parables. At least the elevator is working.

The longer I exist the less I know about existence. Honesty is a charming proposition. But let's leave it at that. I prefer hypocrisy. I don't know what I want. Do you know what you want? I want a flapjack. I want a knick-knack. Sometimes I can feel a sense of purpose and I try to keep it going but then it's disoriented by semantic drapery. Feelings from the nineteenth century climb into my house and cause Balzac.

As we prepare for the inevitable, as we brace ourselves for trauma, for chaos, for turbulence, for famine, for loss of habitat, for existential anxiety, for meaning, for enlightenment, for extinction, for obliteration, for rain bombs and floods and fires and mayhem, there will be one indomitable force remaining, one constant, one obdurate phenomenon continuing its strange, stubborn existence: the arthritis in my right shoulder. What will it do without me? It will crawl into the shoulder of eternity and drive eternity nuts.

My lightning hammer comes down hard on the world. I was born to be a complete sun, a frantic plaster bath. I am now to be the ballast to my bumps, the filter to my perceptions, the beat to my fugue, the fug to my fuggery and fog.

I like sifting things. I like the sound sugar makes when it's poured from a sack into a bowl. It's a faint whisper. It's that sound. That whisper. Sugar. Soft, like the feeling of a spider's legs on the skin of your hand. Like a bubble of description, the slop of representation, a homunculus painting the world in the brain, God and Adam on the ceiling of your skull, devotions fondled amid the candles of Stuttgart. Because really, who can take it all in at once? Imagine everything out there on the other side of your skin, mouths and goggly eyes and long spindly antennae. Because there are worlds within worlds & the pillow where the head lies drifting into infinity.

Ladies and gentleman, may I have your attention. Please exchange your injuries for a rocket. Stop dragging my eyes around. Injuries are arbitrary but unequivocal. If you don't believe me you should try running for government. Use tattoos for running the machinery of the arm. Height is often its own width. Sit beside the empty brown animal and cry out for liberty and argyle. The feeling will whistle you. You must speculate on something. Can you hear it? The fall of neoliberalism? Here's your yellow vest. Try it on. Be a dialogue. Even the fish are out marching.

I'm tired of looking for myself. I don't think there is a self. Not in any real way. And who cares? Isn't self-hood more of a liability than an asset? It's mostly a lot of role-playing. You have to write your own script. That sucks. What if somebody delivered a script at your door every morning? X says "......", and then you say, "........" Words are heat. Afternoon reveries. A lot of dialogue goes on in my head. But I think that's called monologue. I call it complaining. I call it clashing words together so that they make a sound like Tchaikovsky. A slammed door. A bank robbery. An octopus fart. A sentence with a hook for pulling a shark out of the heart.

Ancient Egyptians believed pain other than that caused by wounds was the result of religious influences or spirits of the dead. Plato believed pain could restore order to the soul. Aristotle believed that pain could be overcome through logic. Avicenna, a famous medieval Muslim physician, classified pain into 15 types, including itching, pricking, compressing, stretching, breaking, penetrating, etc. Descartes defined pain as "fast moving particles of fire" that pass along nerve filamentation until they reach the brain. I hurt, therefore I am. Nietzsche believed pain was a source of great art. I'm reminded of some lyrics in Bob Dylan's song, "Not Dark Yet": "My sense of humanity is going down the drain / behind every beautiful thing, there's been some kind of pain." I believe we should make friends with pain. Enjoy conversations with it. Give it a name. Yolanda Squatpump. Shit Fun Chew. Doo-Doo Zopitty Bop Bop.

It's Christmas. Dinner will be good. Dinner will be rigatoni, which comes from Italian *rigatooni*, plural of *rigato*, past participle of *rigare*, "to draw a line, to make fluting," from *riga*, "line; something cut out." Consider a daguerreotype of Emily Dickinson. Is she rigatoni? She is not rigatoni. She is dark and Victorian. She is Lou Reed before Lou Reed was Lou Reed.

Here comes another sentence: it's wiggling its way across this field like a spermatozoon on its way to Ovum City. If I were to frame this moment in a single image, I would cram it with pterodactyls and shake it into money. The Heart Sutra says, "all phenomena in their own-being are empty."

Everything else is lingerie. Vowels persuasive as sugar.

Modern Agriculture

To be mindful of a tangible shape is congenial and magnets. Twinkling loco-
motive that a line can print. Cabbage tied in admonition of itself. The mean-
ing that crawls around in spices. And expects words to grow it into food.

Bulb slash that a gauze bends. Pathos is goaded into the infrared where it
turns porous and tastes of planetarium popcorn. This is where sense happens
and canvas. Drugged snakes and Cézanne. Fingers. Opulent packs of dizzy
enthusiasm. Boxing squashed by haunch. The referee sips out of a botched
throat. We plough the dirt into nomenclature and respect the bubbles. Umber
fidget bent into roots. Garish flavors we put in scales and weigh.

There's a rawhide wheel that rolls into arguments of dirt and a percep-
tion amazed into problems of growth and correspondence. Sift supposition
and find experience smoldering in alpaca. Shapes expect description. Describe
them as oats. Describe them as extracurricular. Breakfast skimmed by tiger.
Iron and velvet. Thoughts writhing within a philosophy of slaps.

Milk in my arms and the harm of form when it turns shovel and sweat.
Barns flutter. The song is soaked in fire. And finally, in the bistro, we discover
that life is alchemical. This isn't a big surprise. But it chose us to make the
diagnosis.

Meanwhile, the mirrors enhance our elbows. There's an athleticism to en-
hancement that may be further expanded into alligators. The world waddles
around in words and the trumpets approve of our disarray. Is garlic a form of
will? Or just fascinating?

The table is hungry for its form. Amalgams of sound find their meringue
in meaning. I slouch forward spilling adjectives on a slavish emotion. I set it
free by murdering reality with a rancorous idealism. Reality comes back for
more. I give it everything I can. Eventually, we agree on the chintz, and the
potassium creates a patch of maidenhair. This is what is meant by the aban-
donment of subjectivity. Joy to the world. Let us sing hymns of asphalt. Let the
words catch fire. The rivers are hungry in their movement.

The wire walks through its hammers and dilates into a sepia landscape. It
purports to be an art made of hands but I think it testifies to the light spitting
out of the ground.

Yes. Shoes are important. They dazzle the gargoyles, which are stone, and not liable to mess around with the mermaids, who float by waving at us like snapshots.

The brain flares open and bounces into Norway. Hallucinations do the rest.

The World Belongs To Cats

I am not your wax. I defy wax. Let me linger under my umbrella and ponder the ceiling. I'll steep myself in reading. Here comes some death. Hi death. Goodbye death. Death is in a hurry today. There's so much to do. The structural necessities of a sentence must be impelled by real words. Keep running after the sun fast enough and you'll find that one person's sunset is another person's morning. So happy solstice. I hope you're thawing out. I think I see a feeling. Is that your feeling or mine? Does it matter? Is being a feeling? It's the wild hour of allegory. There are no clear answers. There's only the mania of milk-secreting glands and the pantomime of excuse.

I feel a storm coming. I can see it in your eyes. Does the truth exist? Are we a dream? Let's fold our sheets together. Together we can learn to congeal. I have plans to imitate a stretch sock. Thus, I lend my lungs to the rhetoric of rubber. And then one day the prairie comes to me with a question. I don't have any answers. My tongue is a moment of butter. Norway, however, is topographic and blunt. Outside of Oslo, I don't know of a single driveway that doesn't relish its being, its ontology of necessity and convenience locked in an embrace of imagery and wheel.

I'm a proud deplorable. We are on the eve of a paradigm shift. We see the spirits of the dead ride on a roller coaster, and a monkey play a piano of coconut shells. Mermaids X-ray yaks. Being is a drunk of mad luminous contrariness. This is how to be deplorable. This is the essence of deplorability. But why does it take so long for my hair to dry? We walk around with oceans in us. Everything is incidental. Nothing is permanent. I say forgive all debt. Nothingness flows through me like a doorbell. I have no intention to chain myself to a configuration. Existence makes a thing useful. Nonexistence makes it work. Mismatched socks make it deplorable. I can feel the bacteria of life. I feel curiously explored by my own heart. A land of shadows squeezes out apparitions still lingering in the brain. Here, there, and everywhere in a Cupertino garage.

There was a strong smell of bacon on 4th Avenue West today. That must mean something. I think it means bacon. The ghost of a pig, for example. The universe says yes, I will marry you. But you must be willing to kiss my protein. One day it will rise to the surface and become a knife. You may give it the freedom it craves, and I promise you, it won't end there.

I feel the immediate squeeze of circumstance. French buttons roar their annotations into muslin. Feelings pull us in and out of history. A prodigious energy animates the sky. Some people walk poodles. Others walk postulation. Some people posit sand. Others posit seeds. A murder of crows awaits me outside.

What is consciousness? I'd say it's a sky. I will wait for you at the end of this sentence and show you some insouciance. The world belongs to cats.

Puck

Bubbles restore the punchbag. This is done privately, by making the leather sag into itself. Not all meaning is calculable. For example, the novel is mapped on a sternum, but the railroad expands its eyeballs into small eternities, new contexts, nouns and gowns and trinkets and things. The crab twitches and turns. All the monuments are ablaze with the fires of history. The marble is absorbed in horses and swords. Fall throws itself through the office in its beautiful dying light and the windows rattle with a nearby stampede. We find a sense of seclusion in umber, the rawness of life symbolically dangled in a narrative of atomic bric-a-brac. The ochre is improbable, but fits somehow, once the ripeness of the dimension finds itself pushing out of its skin, and the reference to pagination cannot hurt the moment with any death-bed perspective, but grows into a deeper understanding of being. It takes a quart of reflection to make a stew of rumination. The lament is visceral. The cabbage patch is tempting, but the tulip bulbs have reinvented themselves as locoweed. Even the logarithms seem sad. The guitar expands into hallucination. The adjective thrusts itself at a hill and unfolds its syllables until they enchant the surrounding minerals. Elephants discharge streams of urine. The world is exasperated by all the exploration. Conceits of travel step forward into perception. The spirit screams at things. The wrestlers skulk around in their bones doing radio flutter and murmuring metamorphic hymns. Shield the stars. Don't let the void hurt them. Stumble through yourself. It's spicy and green to abandon a brain. The table squirts its joy in rain. Sift the pepper for form. It's broadly French to meander through the country, but it must mean something to us in relation to our lives, imply something exciting and lime, perhaps a little translucent, like space. Goad the painter to put more blue inside the majordomo, but make the eyebrows pumice. Include a newspaper. Bounce the harmonica butter. Life isn't always this captivated by its surroundings. Sometimes it just needs a little further scrutiny. And then it explodes into hockey.

Giving Lip

What's the first thing to come into your mind in the morning? I mean, besides suicide. Me, I can't help but think of indiscriminate corollaries, the islands off the coast of Ireland, Great Blasket, Clare Island and Knockmore Mountain, Inishmore, Skellig Michael, Rathlin Island, and its colony of puffins, gannets, razorbills, guillemots, kittiwakes, fulmars, swooping, diving, swirling, plummeting vertically on shoals of fish.

I hear the radical tea of prayer, the gentle maneuvering of yesterday's food. And I throw a peach at the wall. The awareness that human existence is both joy and woe is a prerequisite to accepting medication. The rest is guano.

Does this mean we're still friends? Good. My point is this: pain is ubiquitous, but suffering is optional.

Or at least I think so. I'm a little uncertain. If you have pain, how does one not suffer? You isolate your pain in a lens of deep inner focus and so absorb it, so fully allow yourself immersion in its dark, hidden glamour that it gives you its power. It gives you its secret.

What is thinking, anyway? When we stand in awe of a hot dog, what we are truly doing is wondering whether to apply mustard or not, or paddle our canoe further up the river, away from Costco. And I can't help but feel a little glad. My favorite hat walks around my head looking for cognac.

Definition arrives in a jeep. It's another lonely day. But not for everyone. For some it's a raw reckoning and a tight grip and for others it's a yodeling competition. It's so nice to have a diversion. Consciousness isn't what it used to be. It used to be thinking but now it's all urgency and breath.

I maneuver in a pool like John Ashbery. I don't really own a pool. But I am. I'm a pool. I mean, who isn't? Isn't the body 70% water or something? This is why I recommend snow. Be a snowman. When the sun appears, melt. You will be lifted into the sky to become vapor, eventually condensing into Popeye's forearms.

The monk credited with bringing Zen Buddhism to China — Bodhidharma — is often represented as a snowman, based on the myth that Bodhidharma meditated so long in front of a wall that his arms and legs fell off.

I'm fascinated by what is inside and what is outside. Where does the inside begin and where does the outside end? I'm not into views. I prefer books. This is where the real panoramas are. I have a book about life that propagates by banjo. The book finishes its sweater and then achieves shape and shampoo. Words assume mass. Mass assumes the morning fog and sunset coloration of the hummingbird. What is outside is inside and what is inside is a mind trapped in a lip. What do you do with a truant lip? I clang like a bell. I shout at the books to get off of their shelves and do something about metamorphism. I think we should support it. But I ask you: is this how to adapt? By becoming something else? Assuming a different shape? Different attitudes? Concepts? Hairdo?

Would you look at me, shape-shifting into a Weimaraner.

I consider the latitudes of our naked existence and this, too, becomes a lip.

The Superfetation Of Itself

I still feel the heat of the king's forge, the insufferable chatter of elves. I shave in men's rooms along the highway. If you tell me what you want, I will write it down, and it will become a kingdom. Go away haberdashery fish.

And here is a falling open mimosa. A knife trimming the lake with representation, which is easy, like pushing a door open. Drink some amalgamation radius. The circumference brimming the chest of the moose. Bean the theater lift. Go somewhere that is mutable and become a romantic, someone young leaning against the walls of a ruin, or someone old curing diseases in a small village.

I know, I sound like I'm giving orders, who does that in a paragraph?

Paragraphs are just little rocks offshore. The big rocks are catechisms of surf. The ocean keeps questioning the land, the land keeps answering with sand.

An inflatable paragraph is a balloon, plain and simple, a cry floating into the heavens. Help us, please. Come down from your throne and soothe these waters with your breath.

It might also be called a prayer. Or a headland.

Buy the red musk. Slow the pleasure of wax. It's radical getting dressed in rocks. I find a universe in the fuchsia and wear a shirt of rudimentary dissociations, including the buttons, which conveniently reflect the bonfire by the sea, mirroring it in brass and causing a great lapse in the fabric of time. We call this lapse the Mademoiselle of Insight, and she reciprocates with sugar.

Attention forces the glasses to my face. The bones dream of flocks and a person nearby plows the sand with their leg. It has the quantum effect of ice and dazzles the guides.

The allegory forgives its inflammations, each one blatant as tarpaulin, and just as ubiquitous. A warm nomadic almanac finds it way to my lap. A man storms in his teeth. I come to a palm door and open it to a narwhal sitting in a throne of ivory smoking a harpoon. It's a funny notion, but I think it may be a good time to sell the vineyard and take up the life of a plumber. The cave is dyed in its own darkness. This is the color of oblivion. The singular aromatic piece of night we all carry in our hearts. Add the clatter of absence and you've got a hawk swooping by. The rustle of feet in the grass. Nature overflowing with wind.

Meringue

I feel lucid and sad, like a cold day. It's good to forget oneself. Good to remember that one doesn't exist. Not in any true sense. That is to say, if non-existence is our ultimate destiny, life is sweeter and much more tolerable when this awareness penetrates consciousness and becomes a reality. This is the condition into which we are born. The other animals don't appear to have this problem. This need to avoid feeling cheated. This need to explore one's interior complexities, one's moods and inner geography. Some people call it a journey. I like to call it meringue.

This cream needs an elevator. Will you be that elevator?

Just think of me as a surgical device. I have nothing but magnets for you baby. I hang around in the belief that catastrophes of grammar can lead to great success as a predicate. I've embarrassed myself before and I'll do it again. I drink a broom of emotion and am swept away.

The noun is a hummingbird of meringue. There's nothing sadder than a naked heart in a blur of meringue.

And so it shall be.

Ain't reality a gas? There's a lot more to it than just sparks. And then there's Peter Green's "Albatross." That lovely, incomparable, rhythmic pulsing bass, like the slow graceful moves of the bird's flight over Antarctic waters, dreamy, crepuscular. A nice way to ease into the *shōbōgenzō*. The wonderful heart-mind of Nirvana.

Let's keep things simple and enjoy a sip of universe. It's calm tonight and my needs are congenial to the employment of various prepositions. Sometimes it takes a powerful drug to walk through a wall. And sometimes all you need is a few prepositions and a warped sense of space. The heart is an armchair for feelings. So sit back, and let yourself float. The ugliness of time is remedied by Christmas tinsel. And the swans on the barn are quiet as a man assembling a light fixture.

I like to put words together. Drugs, music, chocolate éclairs, the God particle. The possibilities are endless. It's the closest that we can get to the infinite while still in our skin. Marcel Duchamp and Gertrude Stein enter my mind. I walk around in giggly liquid shoes. In other words, embryos. Embryo comes from the Greek, *embruon*, meaning fetus, which stems from Greek 'em,' meaning 'into,' and 'bruein,' meaning to 'swell, or to grow.' Now certainly, when I say a word, I don't just say it, I put my breath into it, I breathe into it, and the word assumes life, the vibrations trigger a chain of never-ending associations. Very soon you will wonder: what's happened to me? Why are my friends avoiding me? Why can't I pay my bills? That's when you know you've done it. You'll get so entangled you'll need the jaws of life to extricate your ass.

Words are sticks of meaning tap-dancing on a China plate. Water running. Two pieces of meat stuck to a spoon. What shall we do with this loaf of space? Loaf in it. What else. That's how it always is. Just listen to Gregorio Allegri. Or the murmur of doctors focusing on a bone. Breakfast explains nothing. The dreams of a halibut are different than those of a junkie. But not by much. The dreams of a halibut resemble the furniture of winter. But I must say I'm not pleased by the taste of oysters. Did you forget to fall in love today? I didn't. I just now fell in love with a Dutch apple pie.

Today's Special

I can't explain my eyebrows. They do their own thing. You've just got to accept it. Being is predicated on multiple meanings. For example: magenta.

I'm on a path to glory. I can feel that now. The facts of life are just so extreme. Each moment gets tangled in the sensory organs on my head. The doors of perception opening to a lobster tapdancing on a picnic table next to a hole in the rain.

But go ahead. Eat this sentence. It will make you strong and beautiful.

Society is mostly hallucination. Norms that make no sense. Xmas trees, jobs, plastic surgery. I prefer mushrooms. The world of mushrooms is complicated, like the prostitutes on Aurora, but with happier results. One thing I know for sure: there is sublimity in music. It releases the mind from its prison. I enjoy the sensations of things, doorknobs, laundry warm from the dryer, spider legs scampering over my palm, the taste of strawberry jam, that moment when a plane first leaves the ground.

Did you know that horses are able to identify emotion in human facial expressions?

I think of George Clooney in *Gravity,* floating in space after the space station has been decimated by debris, Sandra Bullock at the far end of a cable tethered to what remains of the space station, barely holding on, slipping, holding onto George Clooney by hand, both keep slipping, Clooney realizes — with stunning sobriety and calmness — the danger of the situation and nobly lets go, despite Sandra Bullock pleading to hold on. He knows it's untenable. He lets go. And drifts off into space to die.

The look on Clooney's face is one of quiet, sad, dignified resignation. I don't think a horse would have trouble recognizing that. It's the expression I'm most apt to see on the face of a horse. The look on Bullock's face is one of horror. She is alone in space. Alone as alone can be. This is why we need language. Language is the tether holding us together.

Here's another new feeling: the warmth in a shoe someone has just worn. This is why I adhere to the asterisks forged in a kimono. Dishrags have faces. Consequences have consequences. Not everything in a submarine is modified to limit noise. I'm often amazed at the ability of people to bring the color of thought to a boil.

Language is a carnival. It's amazing, all the ways the world might enter your head and assume a presence there. Especially food. The tyranny of hunger is enough to bring a government down. Imagine what you could do with hooves. I say this because numerical instability can occur anywhere there are bad roads and swirling mist. But things eventually settle down.

Is it possible to find some passenger pigeon DNA and resurrect that magnificent species? Once the grid goes down, I'm wondering how to keep in touch with people. Would it be possible to do social media with passenger pigeons? Facebeak?

I like the light bulbs in the bathroom. The little bulbs at the top rim of the mirror. Where it begins in the morning. My face. That person standing in the brightness wandering how it all began, where did it all go, why is there something rather than nothing?

It's been years since I've gone fishing. I try keep my fingers out of goo. I prefer quills and inkstands. But nature is everywhere. It's even in my equations. If a blue suede shoe equals whiskey, then Glasgow equals smelt, and the value of coffee is personal. Hence, the volume of any sphere can be computed by spurting luminous secretions into shiny threads of social media. This suggests hormones.

Most emotions present a picture of intense internal strain. They arrive in the night carrying a charge of 500 volts and leave behind a deposit of coarse sentiments and little pink birds. Infinity shakes loose of its adjectives and turns sublime.

Should we use stilts when we walk in wonder beneath the stars? Or drive around Vegas with Nicolas Cage? Little cinnamon men hang upside down from the rear-view mirror, and infinity gives meaning to the pharmaceuticals.

Why does so much information separate people rather than bring them together? Why is everything so fragmented and steeped in conflict? The loss of community makes people feel more isolated, afraid to express themselves.

These are the judgments of a private man in a public medium. The knife describes itself. It doesn't need words. But you will need lots of rags to soak the blood.

How do you preserve critical thinking during a time of intense propaganda and mass surveillance? Thought undermines beliefs. When beliefs collapse, thought is laid bare.

Do you see this dust? That's a thought collapsing. It was brought down by worries, apprehensions, judgments, anxieties, regrets and other mental millstones.

What is going on in your head this minute? What do you make of these words? I think they're an army of air clashing with hundreds of shaggy ideas. Ideas provide the meat. I provide the bones.

The Cold Meat Of A Daydream

Today I will be the meaning I want and hide among the camels. I think my nerves need a holiday. There will come a time when the mood of detachment dissipates and I will have to join the rocks and cry the long thin tears of indigestion. But for now, the propane will be stored in a liquid state at essentially atmospheric pressure. Boil-off vapors will be collected and returned to the umbilical squad.

Effects are oceans in the rain. The dimpling of water. The cause of the cashew is noble. The cause of the hammer is nails. The secret to having enough money is to bang around in a coconut palm shaking the soft hand of darkness. That's why I'm here. I need turpentine. I have thorny hummingbird fingers. Get out. Get out now and claw your way into the light.

Proximity is a tray upon which the antlers of the concertina at Costco are immaterial. Keep it simple, I say. Nipples are the mushrooms of the human chest. That much we've stablished. But there are landscapes I could never describe. Each word is a history, a palimpsest, a landscape in itself. How can I describe anything with the cold meat of a daydream?

The loose dirt of the Palouse is called 'loess.' It's soft and fine and nourishes the soft white wheat of the Palouse, which goes into the making of pastries, apple strudel and cinnamon rolls.

This stuff called consciousness seems to be localized within my head, and resembles the eyes of the Mississippi, and is full of catfish. This is why I'm weirdly green in color, and like listening to Sera Cahoone. She makes me feel urgent, like peace.

I dip my pen in the ink of sleep and write my name in water. I have the etiquette of a football. I've been around the sun 72 times. That means that I'm entitled to knit something. I mean, you know, words. I can make them do things. Jump through hoops. Pretend to mean something. I live in a shabby hotel. I like it this way.

Tell me, what brings you to a boil? Is it politics? Developers? Jeff Bezos? Please. Feel welcome here. We're among friends. I'm the ghost of 1966. I dissolve into rain. Reality is just another bedroom teeming with socks. I'm going to walk through a tunnel now, and when I come out the other side, I will hand you your coat. Thank you for coming.

I adhere to the profligacies of coffee. Language is a carnival. It has to be that way because space is permeable and needs a dimple. Demi Moore shaping a phallic vase.

How can you not be in love with mud? The head of a seal emerges from the water now and then, confirming my suspicion that there is life in the water, and that it is hungry, and that some of it is translucent, and jelly-like, and much of it is quick and supple, and has weirdly led to the evolution of creatures on land, creatures with hair, and limbs that enable them to walk upright, gazing at the water as if it held an answer to the riddle of their own existence. Which is Van Gogh's maniacal sunflowers. The whole idea of death, balloons in the rain, and the timeless string of the yo-yo.

Ecstasy isn't just a drug. It's also a shoreline. Five women swimming through the brain of an impressionist painter. First comes gladness, and then comes rain. This is considered by Leibniz to be too imprecise to be used as a foundation for calculus.

But ok for windows.

I'm not ready for the future. I float upstream and lie there staring at the ceiling. My intestines seem faraway, bunched in ooze and spurring a resurrection of lost saloons. The warp of a warm front twinkles over a crimson lake. It feels gold, like a moral, or a crack in the wall letting the sunlight through. A cardboard elegy is dipped in seven seas and given an anatomy of sidewalks and stilts. This makes everything words. Let's see what they do: a sexual fantasy scratches its genitalia with a tired enthusiasm, while all sorts of verbs come loose and become a paragraph of peripatetic ducks in stiletto heels.

Is this fair, meaningful, or helpful in any way?

No, probably not. Who cares?

Have an Oreo cookie.

Ha Ha Tonka

I seek the logic of the chameleon my brain walks around in my head looking
for something to do I put a little heat under a pot of rigatoni and reflect on
the failure of the suburb to solve the problem of pain
I live on a planet of waterfalls and birds, engagement rings and barns I get all
my clothes out of a nearby swamp
Of emotion
The waterfall is a continuous narration of itself the swimming pool is shy and
keeps to itself I dread the wildfire smoke this summer no one thought the
planet might die
I'm the pilot of a big personality it's basically a feeling how do you catch a
quantum butterfly words stir in my mouth and become the fat crash of
words in a book it's a simple way to live if there's a waterfall in my breath
I must remain calm
I put a hive in my dream think of these words as experiments in cognition
Strange people, strange amphibians, strange countries, strange scruples,
strange enchantments
I like to travel with abandon honey is a dream of glass the world is in constant
flux
I can't assume that a single molecule of my body belongs exclusively to me I
think I can be quiet now we all become art at nine in the morning
I discover a universe in a begonia nature is inherently unpredictable a pound
of cloud is worth an ounce of thought words are bees in the hive of a
dream the life beneath me is a parable of old dry leaves it's why the lonely
sentinel endures the winter and wears the chivalrous metaphysics of a red
sombrero
I have enough milk to bake a cake but not enough to build a cow
Anarchy and chaos are but a single loaf of bread away

Gas has a point it's why I wear a bloodstream Roberta is outside cleaning the litterbox the silhouette of a hornet trembles in the expression of a heliotrope there are reasons for that but I don't know how to explain the mechanics of a tornado without slipping on a dynasty of useless italics

What is law law is the study of rules that are created and enforced through social or governmental institutions to regulate human behavior I have confidence in eclairs even the inelegance of nothingness has a little extra fat in it to make you smile

If I was a park I'd be Ha Ha Tonka State Park in Missouri

If I was a town I'd be Humptulips, Washington

It's like something tickling your brain

Tenderness is free but the fire inside is dear

If the paradigm fits you must wear it to live among bones is to live among structure I remember how the windshield used to be covered in smashed insects I found an allegory for the potato in the cream sauce

The technological superiority of the Gothic approach is the result of three stunning breakthroughs: the pointed arch, the ribbed vault and the flying buttress

It appeals to my sense of the bizarre

I can't remember the last time I saw a frog but your face right now is quite dynamic you should see it as you look down absorbed in these words

This controls nothing but a little bit of squash I have named Elijah the Tishbite

Whether nature enjoys a very real external existence or exists only in the apocalypse of the spirit is for me equally useful and venerable I do not wish to expiate but to live

Emerson and Thoreau can make us realize that the danger of no longer thinking for oneself is still in danger even in a democracy

Understanding that from this loneliness something creative can arise is the only way to grasp my existence without missing out

Wealth is an abstraction fold the honey into the butter with a pinch of salt I praise the generous spirit of the attentive reader the energy of your smile exceeds the kiss of the air conditioner

Which is an eye of flame in the ice of Superman's palace

I push a rapture of words until they collapse into a bridge I must cross to get to the other side of a black hole a gorilla opens an umbrella mirrors embellish space the Queen of Luminosity has eyes like diamonds hands like rain I must paddle the very idea of the river upstream until it becomes a rapids of proprioception the muscles I use for this are wonderful outlines of cellular

combustion mountains and rivers percolate through our senses I see a nov-
el chained to a dogma get up and walk away I like things like that things
that favor the dissolution of the ego a family of five living in a paragraph
My nose runs all the time let me give you a congenial squeeze
The tin morning of an uncoordinated religion waddles across the page drop-
ping gearshifts and caterpillars writing comes out of a hungry unconscious
I feel fire in the blister I got from paddling and now it's a riot of sensation
traveling from one place to another what are you going to do if my words
turn to powder the rain scatters its punctuation on the river and every-
thing just keeps moving with no end in sight

Data Dump

Whenever I travel elsewhere I alter my inner kaleidoscope how do you take
a picture of a black hole welcome to Alaska a voice of scarlet awakens the
elves cooking sockeye salmon on Chilkoot Lake surrounded by behe-
moths of nothingness I need to bend this ink into bells a big vibration in
which the universe sweats with chaos

I'm worried about the ice in the Arctic the gospel choir sends shivers through
the fabric of space and time I drool meaning on a napkin of metaphors yel-
low letters on the sidewalk sometimes saying anything at all is like throw-
ing a stick of dynamite and running

To assemble time from the data dump I want to be nicer to people perhaps
it was language that brought us into being words constantly weaving
between three planes as extragalactic beasts leap about under a tempest
veined with lightning two Australian researchers hypothesized that an el-
emental form of consciousness in the form of a neuronal representation of
the universe was born in insects 500 million years ago

How do I get off this planet what led to this turning point history bends un-
der a burden of details inorganic molecules came together to form organic
molecules nights in white satin the sexual freedom claimed by feminism
and the gay movement has become a way of resexualizing female bodies
through what I call scopic capitalism the one who exploits bodies by the
look

Were we preceded by consciousness if you're never disappointed with reali-
ty it's because you've fallen into a conspiracy atmospheres relationships
self-knowledge I could use some flamboyance we can't know entirely what
a body can do the feeling of living days that are more like a frenetic list of
obligations than a deep and meaningful existence the wind opens the door
to the church and walks in there are shops selling cups photos stuffed an-
imals on which are written messages tailored to all affects joy sorrow love
depression happiness

When you whispered in my ear it was like putting a fresh cold strawberry in
my mouth life and culture have a complexity that can't be reduced to the
symbolic

Bazaars of objects thrive in introspection I've got a flair for finding good pas-
try divine protein in hepatic neon appreciate the flashlight dirt it's particu-
lar and rural few things in life are as good as a jelly doughnut

There are moments when I want to be detached with the accentuation of fam-
ily life love cooked up celebrations Mother's Day Valentine's Day we ex-
press them as emojis likes hashtags on Twitter which are then sold as viral
data

I worry continually about farming communities Polynesian knee tattooed
with diamonds a flame above a bronze Buddha talking a cosmic abyss so
deep and dense that not even light can escape it love has become the indi-
cator of self-worth which is why it has never hurt us so much

Making a statement of any kind can be like forging a pattern welded Viking
sword I feel weirdly powerful when I ask myself to explode

Into matter space and time vanish like a dream an iron house beating in a rib
cage full of lightning this is the essence of my thinking there's a clear sense
that we've botched our time on Earth

Social reality is intrinsically ambivalent I try to avoid the bad breath of politics
I like to growl my emotional life into ecstasy our highways are falling apart
as hot dense gas swirls around a black hole my own approach to reality is
just as important the prodigal allowance of a pretzel means the garage is
tilted this is why capitalism gives the feeling of being unsurpassable be-
cause it has redefined subjectivity itself not by authoritatively drawing
norms but by fitting into what is most essential to it I see hummingbirds
occasionally they seem almost preternatural and this is related in some way
to the invisible forces of the universe nonlinear processes like gravity ther-
modynaics harmonic generation and electromagnetism that cause energy
to squirt from either side of the nucleus of the galaxy rolling through a
restaurant in Thessalonoki that is on the opposite side of the word for gas
(αέριο) the dazzling honey of thought green letters extruding into oblivion
the subtleties of travel are written in faces people in lines at the airport
passports in hand

So fatigued they seem more theoretical than actual the time grows centrifugal
the helicopter hovers over the flood victims farms and barns of Nebraska
and Iowa and Minnesota I'm a stevedore of the discursive and compound
I personify miscellany in the hullabaloo of the barnyard I fling manure
at the old suffocations the superficialities I can't stand them anymore I'm
done with this place I envisage horizons where the angels have their own
capricious inclinations the planet below speckled with presentiment a

brontosaurus lifts its head dripping swamp water the poem brings a wide
eye to the vagaries of international capital the curriculum at last splashed
with patois the windshield wiped clear of rain

Breakbulk

The internal constitution of a word feeds the slow hum of a blue induction
    which is empirical and positive a taste for the immediate the rapture of fish
    tangled in gossamer webs of diamond dust

Your weather is a personal matter an overall distorter of reality blue and yellow
    and green an escape from the constraints of reality what a big wig you have

That spot of piss in the cat's litterbox looks like freshly poured cement the
    speedometer of our car is spitting hardware and very humble church can-
    dles there's a medication for this novel harmonies and vigorous rhythms
    strands of turmoil dripping with violins

Reality must be an awful place although there is wisdom among the masses a
    thoroughly romantic feeling the Kotoko of Chad are descended from the
    ancient Sao civilization who are known for their intriguing statuary in clay
    and fine personal ornaments in copper and iron today Lake Chad is disap-
    pearing it has shrunk by nine-tenths due to climate change

This line is a single strand of wire that supports nothing but itself

I have a formula for communion a longing for spring I pave an entry into
    trance

This is a mosaic of words it exists for and by itself literally and ranges in color
    from bone-white to Roman gold it's robust and globular a big sound an
    epistle to the stethoscope pungent in creosote like a call to awakening the
    final flare-up of something about to die somersaulting in my breath a dra-
    ma involving bedsprings and underwear and emotional intensity or cubic
    mass gathered at an unnamed place

The healing propagation of stars finds me at home I have a bunch of ideas
    struggling for expression fossil-bearing semantic strata objects underwater
    feelings of oceanic bliss embedded in consciousness linear intricacies an-
    cient rocks we keep the universe under the bed for reasons of safety it acts
    as a connective tissue and can be detected by its openness and transparen-
    cy and weightlessness which releases energy by combining words

The elegy for elephants moves along its path swinging its trunk through a series of foreign keys I never realized what a kiss could be your kiss is like a sonata of membrane that seems to groan in a sugar paste somewhere in southwestern Greenland

An emotion is transformed into motion when it rumbles in enunciation and someone gets up from the couch to open a window space is there to be shaped vision is sounded in a fog

The cultural mechanics that manufacture religion have turned toward the embodiment of energy the earth is billions of years old and has begun to smell like a garage every little thing has just gone crazy a sense of reverence is critical to the understanding of thread

The poem has acquired a new flexibility although it has worn down by running water we can still make out certain features the world is an egg and will outgrow the problem of fate orioles hatch about 12 days later and are noteworthy for their flute-like songs

The mechanism that powers poetry has been shoved into a bouquet of stars here is an organ for nourishing an unborn horse go ahead open the welcomed doors of new imagined worlds we will fuse the words together at white heat while imitating organic substances things like oysters and cheese mental health prophylactics I hobnob with mushrooms and as you can see living forms spring out of the material itself without regard for the laws of gravity

Think of a colossal wagon drawn by animals camels elephants peacocks bears I seek salvation in art I envision a body of words imparting movement forward propulsion I can display both nerve and conviction via the physics of sentiment the slippery smell of a night fallen into the Mediterranean suffused with the spirit of dance sensuous and huge without being soft I will simulate an understanding of your legs let us embark on a raft of octaves sit at the piano and flower gently into the smell of the Italian courts the measured shuffle of shoes the first breath of air when the big oak doors open and the sunlight hits your eyes and everything rushes in at once causing privacy and cargo

Heading Out

So here's me in a Viking ship drifting out into space it's a fantasy of course the
way I envision a good death look at all the drama I put into it ridiculous of
course no death has that kind of glamour it's all ego and cheesy sci fi post-
ers the kind those heavy metal bands once favored for their vinyl record
covers

Space isn't a thing per se it's an expression of interrelations among events when
my words touch the air a skating rink explodes with Tonya Harding I like
the way red powers its way into green and Tonya lands a triple axel imag-
ine that you awaken one day to find yourself floating in a sealed elevator a
fathom is a ceremony of depth thin-boned as a bird all masses all velocities
all forces are relative

I'm hungry as a mailbox in Pittsburgh a divine presence has eaten our greed all
we have left is one another the taste of a pineapple is sharp and generous
adrift in deep space as the more furious energies in the wider universe of
galaxies make me think of the faucets of finance as absurdly illusory I'm
building space and time like Bill Frisell playing on his Yanuziello guitar
a stack of papers black with equations at my elbow morning comes and
delineates the crest of the mountains the entire world is but a grand il-
lusion spun in the loom of force fields objects approaching the speed of
light increase in mass I feel the temperature at the core of the sun in my
vituperative misrule

The interferometer floats in a pool of mercury an enormous ooze seething
with declension the clutch of the real holds a two-dimensional wafer of
infinite mass I feel like a lost explorer discarding my things on the desert
sand to lighten my load I don't like making oaths my descriptions harden
into bone and I keep walking keep following that photogenic grammar of
string as matter curves space and I see a man's head rotating in its mercury
pool weaving a web of words across the sky

Ink and butter are lions of moral progress an aroused mind present in glimpses
disperses periods of concentration with balance and precision and delights
in moving worlds hurtling past one another at staggering speeds through
the undulations of space

An old man on his way to acupuncture a ghost ship alive with Saint Elmo's fire
everything clinging everything reaching the whole shebang the modem
the piccolo the misdemeanor all make me realize my job is in the nature of
being not doing the new soap dispenser arrived yesterday it's got a sensor
you put a dish or your hand under there and soap squirts out

Like words I don't like it when the same thought circulates in my head we
refine our search for gold by walking sideways like crabs and tie molecules
together to form objects

Everything on our planet has been created by a fat massive sun which hangs in
the sky like an orange squashed between a titan's hands what if the most
exciting thing in life is to die an object increases when it absorbs energy
picture a subversive gazing at the silken surface of the sea

Poetry amplifies the air a whirling magnet will generate an electrical current
in a surrounding web of wire I knit a black noise bouncing radar waves off
Mercury

Out yonder is this huge world which exists independently of we human beings
and stands before us like a huge riddle I know my rights I know what I can
say and what I cannot say this is true not just for a spaceship gliding to-
ward the stars I have roots in Peru we look up to see a hawk every dynamo
houses a whirling mystery I wear my hunger like I wear my sleeve rolled up
and lenient nature lives in motion endless covers of "One More Cup Of
Coffee" delivered with the energy of a steam engine mass and energy are
interchangeable my transformation sparkles underwater

I rise and become a temperature squirting sperm everywhere I put my anguish
up for sale my attention is absorbed by a raisin the invisible field that con-
veys magnetic force I'm a citizen of the universe it's just that demon life
has got me in its sway I fall into morning as morning falls into afternoon
the flowers of sedition talk to one another sunlight penetrates the Black
Forest I want to paint a flame like Georges de la Tour and push it toward
the red end of the spectrum

This Is Your Brain On Words

At no point during my existence was being me my idea the world is out of my
control I'm the dazzling thermometer of a giant temperature in which get-
ting old becomes a theatre of broken bones and bad cholesterol and bald
nouns screaming for nuance

A moment of taste is a moment of truth nausea solves itself we wear mush-
rooms it's why I don't like haircuts

I have a very friendly penis I have to reinvent myself every day a synthetic elu-
cidation requires four ingredients recitation, rhetoric, grammar and dirt

But what about horses? Horses are alright horses are perpetual and bone hors-
es are responsible for chivalry and conversation horses are the epitome of
wisdom

We all make an effort to get out of our skulls I like to play with all the pos-
sibilities the engagement ring represents a ritual I remember the bells of
Saint Sulpice

Bronze overflows the dream of a frog I don't like to operate machinery when
I'm naked it's hard to hear impartial credible sources above the din of the
garden gnomes

A lot of people on the stage struggle with acne give me dumplings or give me
death I feel the need to describe something I don't know which is more
toxic capitalism or identity politics

I can describe the immaterial with a tube of air how many atoms does it take
to build a violet shadows wave in the grass I have conversations with my
right arm

My feelings are mine but I didn't invent them I enjoy the sugar of anticipation
the geometry of a personality is in its wardrobe I pedal an anorexic bicycle

To the moon and back can you create a feeling?

Yes of course you can you can reverse a verse by rehearsing a verisimilitude
of diction which is spokes around a hub the first public appearance was
discursive as a spring thaw

The hammer swims among atoms of iron stars tumble out of the sky I don't understand patriotism the severity of distance is mitigated by driving sometimes all you need is an Oreo cookie

We have a panoramic intimacy you and I don't we our virtue is in the ooze of the estuary even the flowers need manure distance is such a funny phenomenon the emissary of a dark algebra palpates the silence of a worm I understand my legs best when I'm standing on them

American society has lost its ethics and no longer functions as a real society I perceive the word 'should' as a shoulder turpentine complicates the air I would like to live in a cloud I've got nothing but sunshine and garlic in my suitcase I didn't become a poet for that, no, but I can squeeze an accordion and make sounds come out of it I want to build a novel out of wax and fishing tackle

What planet is this? I'm guessing these echinoderms are homalozoans the haunted house could use mechanical arms to grab rocks and throw them at the children when Eric Clapton began wooing Pattie Boyd she had a pet tortoise in her purse and all her kisses felt like everyday things just stopped at the edge of the atmosphere and all the angels sang it's a mean old scene when it comes to double crossin' time the photons that are emitted by interstellar dust taste a little like old apples even the world's best theme parks can be overwhelmed by what John Ruskin called the pathetic fallacy which is just old-fashioned maple syrup drooled over a stack of hotcakes at the Denny's in Tillamook

Death entered the thesis and made itself at home flannel feels good in the fog how easily a table becomes a landscape I'm the ambassador of rhubarb we've redeemed the time with succotash

I watch a cloud struggle up an orange staircase books are like mountains they have peaks and valleys I'm often seized by the lamentation of birds I cross the border into a country of sleep what is music creosote hugs the caboose

It's pretty in my brain sunlight speaks to the trees I chase a chimera down the street the binoculars have extended my vision I have gorilla glue on my fingers we keep all our shoes by the bedroom door there's a lot of work that goes into making a loaf of bread I'm worried about the flooding in the Midwest I drink from the well of poetry but the bread comes from the grain grown in North Dakota and eastern Montana and Nebraska and Iowa Kansas produced 333.6 million bushels of wheat in 2016

I raise my hand in favor of tentacles the signals have all been mutilated by our urbanity I played with the Beatles in my mind

I throw myself into action our furniture overflows with the warm logic of the human body the cat hides under the bed I respond differently to different people this is your brain on words

Auditions For Hamlet

I have an itch to travel I study the zipper on my pants it gives me something
    to do most of my emotions are incongruous they lead me to an intriguing
    seclusion and I slip into another dimension
I don't like getting old I like to sweep the ceiling with my eyes looking for
    other worlds other things that I can say about this one the fabric of this
    sense requires a structure like a tent set up in a park it needs poles and a
    framework it needs prisms and goulash it needs Hound Dog Taylor there's
    a light shining all around me this is the rascal called poetry it causes my
    balls to rattle I exhort one and all to visit a junkyard it's our new sideshow
    built entirely out of sugar
Right now I'm busy doing push-ups I need to get my shoulder in order it hurts
    all the time I don't want to see an orthopedist but I will if I deem it neces-
    sary at some point
I might do some things here that I haven't done before I might produce energy
    using words I've got a little device here it's made out of calliope hearts
    ascension is aided by an oboe I purify it with the seamlessness of a fetus
Hanging in the closet
Don't be seduced by so many worries some of them are abstractions bubbling
    with minds I twinkle like a thyroid gland among the magisterial camels of
    a caravan headed to Djibouti
Rip the stiches apart and you'll find a heart beating beneath the stars are made
    mostly of hydrogen anything technicolor is proof that a drink is aggres-
    sively red if it's a bloody Mary and the day is grand and large as Nevada the
    emotive pulse of a noble resistance visits me at night what is a mind I'm
    only sleeping but one day I shall awaken and rise and assume the form of
    Euclid's ghost
My ancestry is bacteria microbes of the Archean era stromatolites and grand-
    mother thrombolites microbial mats formed in shallow water please recall
    that mass equals energy and by doing so win a sound in China impart-
    ing words to no one in particular as a boy I was put in the outfield where

I could daydream and pretend to catch the ball when on rare occasions
  someone hit it into my air space I stood there luminous and trembling
  until one fine day I sat watching the Beatles in Hamburg John Lennon be-
  ing goofy wearing a toilet seat around his head newly minted coins of air
  opposed to empire
I like pebbles and planets because I'm a little clumsy and amber is the umber
  of lumber experiments in knife throwing tonic cement supersonic coffee
  empire is no umpire the pain in my heart won't let me speak where can my
  baby be
I step into the garments of magic I have a new ingredient for happiness it's
  awkward to say such things I feel like a caboose on a Cubist train I hold a
  world teeming with grouse and shine like a sinus I'm focused on a poem by
  Max Jacob the window sighs
Look here at these rocks collected by Apollo astronauts you'll never break this
  heart of stone darlin' you won't break this heart of stone you'd better go
  home I dream of Ireland I like to dig the earth I like to drop anchor and
  study the beach alpha particles flying through tinfoil crows on a wire
Texture is the literature of touch the eyes throw themselves at paintings the jel-
  lyfish are hungry for personalities I do what I can and boil I like to stretch
  out on the bed having taken time to cool from a molten ball this is my only
  Cézanne before we split into groups and look I can see the rain underwa-
  ter this is my chemical identity gushing with elbows that were once adrift
  in space Heidegger's hammer emitting photons before the rumor found its
  milieu and I drive a Subaru thus proving the old adage that a novel must
  be made of durable twilled cotton cloth and have words in it and exciting
  ideas thrown with a light quick action into writing where it all happens
  sand dunes and fragments of shells depressive realism and auditions for
  Hamlet

Harlequin Words

Harlequin words are the laxative the mind needs to liquefy and flow into pic-
colos and viscera. The harlequin is a figure of perpetual endorsement. Madness
in a mule. Misdemeanors of seismic inventory. Imagine a grievance with teeth
and a haircut. The quorum is open to lips.

My tendons are happy to do this miscellany. Any time I have a fig newton
in my hand I want to be a novel full of underwear. Lingerie and subtleties that
occur in italics. Sexual innuendos so large and monumental they make the pre-
requisite shoulder do things no other shoulder could which is to shoulder the
shadow of the moose on the moraine. The wilderness on the tip of my tongue
is dripping with fire. I'm principled as a knife. I have the blade of position, the
edge of perspective.

One of these days you're going to come walking through that door and
I won't know what to say. I'm always on patrol. I'm always watching for that
rhombus in utter incarnation. The jiggle of meat in salt and oleander. You
won't find any indifference here. I'm not going to coerce anyone into believing
that any of this matters. It's just a nuclear tattoo jacked up on variegation. I rec-
ommend the hash browns. But look out for the pancakes. They're dynamite.

No claim can be too inflated if the immersion is honest and the fingers
are willing and the strings on the guitar are flagstones of justice. I presuppose
nothing. But I do find that hauling anything can cost money and should be
properly secured.

The sounds are taffy to this form of salt. Oil in the dust coagulating into
little green men. Elves, I think. Are we in Ireland suddenly? Is this a word, or
a world? Every word is a world. The word is a detail waiting for a sentence to
theorize pounds of old thoughts said aloud.

Hysterics are the pyrotechnics of fate.

Although there are other ways to look at this. There always are. Other
ways. Theories. Speculations. Goulash and metronomes.

The light of a pearl is a glistening sphere of opulent beauty. I try not to worry about the puddle on my shoulder. I like it when the medium becomes a phenomenon. The camel's bushy rock confesses to a spinal cord and stands up. We pile up while praying to a cosmetic. Everything is religion. Even the horseradish has a fatuous merit to uphold among the mushrooms.

Marijuana also makes a nice handbag. You can bring it to your visa interview at the U.S. Consulate or gym or favorite restaurant and your introversion will be quenched by symbols. Much of my life has been recorded in rocks and my fedora now swims with radar. The interview was conducted by an ogre, but the view from the window was pleasantly stiff. I paint everything with saffron. It decides what I will do to pulchritude, if there is any geometry I can further advance with my urine.

The human bladder is a place of immense natural beauty. You will love the crows and frog hopper ride. I tend to favor style over content, but you can decide what is true for you and let the rest just crash and burn. Firecrackers will always lisp the patina. Music is so important today that I will spend the entire day walking around the planet in my sweatpants distilling hormones in my little corner of paradise. Forget the walls, it's the doors that you want to open with your bare hands while your insecurities rustle among your nerves like a school of herring lost in an observatory. Just smile and wave at the penguins. You'll be glad you brought a chair.

Eating Dressing Talking

I feel the immediate squeeze of circumstance. But what circumstance? There is the circumstance of weather, which is all around me, and time, which is monotonous as a bedspring. These are not the nectarines I had in mind. The sensation is more scattered, more intermittent, more like drawing or cartilage. I believe there are forces at work, few of which involve the concertina, but rub against the bulwark, creating gracefulness and the color green.

That's what happens if you watch proteins build a mussel from scratch.

French buttons roar their annotations into muslin. This is where we begin to drift into leather. The sonorities of maidenhair transmit teakettle reveries in the shadows of the opera we call life.

Feelings pull us in and out of history. A prodigious energy animates the sky. There's a form of magnet that functions like a library to capture the flow of ideas and stimulate them with a spirit of revolt and contradiction. A murder of crows awaits me outside.

Some people walk poodles. Others walk postulation.

Some people posit sand. Others posit seeds.

There's a sky stirring in my brain. Fluffy thoughts drift through dropping pirates and pioneers on the softness of a boundless equivocation. A huge flower blooms from my throat. It declares itself a cylinder of being and pounds its way into chiaroscuro. A doorknob in a powdered wig declares the door officially open. And I can't help but feel a little glad. My favorite hat confesses to counterfeiting the spontaneity of dogs.

Is it possible to think a sky? To think it into being? Why not? What is thinking, anyway? It's some kind of activity in the brain. Thoughts getting shaped, molded, assembled, greased, polished, disassembled, broken, repaired, the mechanism is uncertain, but the formations resemble rock, trees, mesas, ravines, the feeling of mental activity acquires the shape and color of a landscape, the pathos of distance, incalculable reaches of outer space, moments when the mind focuses, or tries to focus, on space, on nothingness, on the hard cold reality of existence, a million stars bubbling in a cauldron of time.

What the fuck?!?

This is the phrase that pops into my brain the most on a daily basis.

I'm really not an expert on thinking. I do very little of it. I do as little as possible. Thinking isn't fun. Sometimes it's fun, but mostly, it's not fun. Thinking takes my mind to places I would prefer to avoid.

So let's think about something else.

Let's think about judgment. What's that? It's a form of thinking, but what kind of thinking?

According to Kant, a judgment is a specific type of cognition. It's a form of structural creativity with respect to its representations. Which means what?

It means that judgments are propositional cognitions. Humans are propositional animals. A judgment is an act of logical predication whereby a concept is applied to a thing, as expressed by the copula 'is' or 'are.'

Ok, sounds simple enough. The mockingbird is a songbird. It's also a perching bird. The box is a container. The paper towel is absorbent. Most vowels are sounds produced by a vibration of the vocal cords. Vocal cords are sometimes gravelly, sometimes silky. Do you see how it works? Reality is assembled by using the formula 'is' and 'are.'

Kant believed that the human mind has two essential cognitive faculties: an understanding of concepts and thoughts and intuitions about sense perception and mental imagery. Both are served by the faculty of imagination, which is the engine of synthesis. Imagination mediates between understanding and sensibility by virtue of being a third, autonomous cognitive capacity. It doesn't weigh anything, but it can thunder, and bend, and tumble around in the brain like a load of wash in a Maytag dryer.

Imagination imposes coherence and consistency on all sorts of cognitions, helps carry out pragmatic or moral choices and recognizes categorically normative concepts. It does this by putting the world on exhibition and meditating on mediation with gymnastics and ointment.

Paradox is convulsive, as are greed and mirrors. When we stand in awe of a hot dog, what we are truly doing is wondering whether to apply mustard or not, or paddle our canoe further up the river.

Judgment is the central cognitive faculty of the human mind.

One must distinguish between an experiential state (eating, dressing, talking, smelling, listening, pressing, pushing, pulling, etc.) and our judgement or belief underlying this experience: this cookie tastes good, why is that woman talking so loudly, should I wear my red shirt or my green shirt, this new laundry detergent is extremely fragrant and lingers a long time in the wool of my gloves, is there a benign intelligence moving and imbuing everything in existence, how is it possible that something as brilliant as a hand or an eyeball could evolve without some inner force or consciousness guiding the atoms and molecules into this shape and function, I know that it takes billions of years of natural selection and adaptation to form a hand or an eyeball but who or what created the process we call natural selection?

What is consciousness, is my consciousness singularly bound to the neurotransmitters in my brain or is it larger, integrated into something far more vast than I could ever imagine?

Is it possible that what I perceive as a direct awareness of my inner thoughts and judgments is, in fact, a highly inferential process that only gives the impression of immediacy?

I leave a string of words here like a trail of gunpowder. Reading them is a form of ignition. Reading them is tantamount to giving them meaning. The words intend explosivity. We have minutes to run behind a wall. Kaboom!

The knowledge that anyone can use is the only knowledge, the only knowledge that has life and growth in it, and becomes throw rugs and shrugs. The world belongs to cats.

Legends Of The Mailbox

Think of a lung. This is where it all starts. Words. Breath. A membranous sac. Two of them. Nature does everything in twos. Two legs. Two arms. Two ears. Two eyes. Two lungs. Almost all. There's the matter of the nose. A singular organ, mounted importantly in the center of the face, protruding imperially and irrefutably into the oceanic dominion of space and time like the bow of a ship, but with two little nostrils. Two little holes. One of them — the cavities around the nasal passage, a labyrinth of thin-walled chambers (*labyrinthus ethmoidalis*) interposed between two vertical plates of bone (nasal septum) — is often clogged. If I'm in bed trying to sleep, the air begins to burn in the good one. The free passage. It helps to turn, lie on my other side and breathe through the other nostril, as soon as it opens.

Words are made of breath. Air is the central ingredient. It becomes breath as soon as it enters the lungs. It enters the aveoli (air sacs) and passes to the surrounding capillaries, which moves oxygen into the blood, and so nourishes the brain, which is always hungry for news and adventure. It becomes a string of words as soon as the mouth and tongue shape the breath into currents of meaning and the larynx gives it all a vibration and the cerebral cortex bothers itself with pertinence and meaning. The proper sounds. The proper structure. The proper weight and inflection. If you're lucky, someone might actually be listening. They may sigh with acknowledgment. They may nod vigorously in agreement. They may look quizzical, or irritated. They may concede to your desires, or slap your face. Who knows? People are weird. Their language makes them weird. Which came first? Human beings or language?

I believe that language shaped our destiny. Our physique. This whole bipedal operation. Two legs carrying us forward and backward and jumping to put a ball in a basket. It's a belief. It's a conception I have. A mindset. A position. A caboose on my train.

Who hasn't been swallowed by a belief? You find it in all kinds of correspondence, at least from the past. People articulating beliefs in letters. Ideas, declamations, unicorns. A good word: correspondence. Meaning connection, alliance, accord. Exchanging letters. One imagines an inkpot and a quill. The lone rider of a pony express. A guy like Charles Bukowski delivering the mail on a hot Los Angeles afternoon. It seems dated. Obsolete. People don't correspond anymore. Correspondence has gone the way of the dodo.

I miss correspondence. I miss getting letters typed on paper. I could feel the letters. The impact of the typebar on the ribbon indented the paper. When you held a letter in your hand you could feel the impact on the other side of the paper. I could almost read them like braille. Language was tangible.

Although letters were most often written by hand. It seems so quaint now. You could see the fetus of an idea evolve by longhand into noodles of wishful chitchat.

There are correspondences to all sorts of things. Externalized. Thoughts were materialized. They had substance and tread. Telephone cable and horse hair.

I miss corresponding to salt. To bread. To the heat of an idea. To the things of this world. Phenomena. The slosh of water in a bathtub. Waves are sequential occurrences of energy. The same way an airplane venerates the air with the shape of its wings.

Shape is essential for the reproductive success of cells, and the obscurities of the Fun House. These include distortion mirrors, snakes, aliens with laser guns, flying pigs, and the tendrils of declension: noun, pronoun, or adjective. We get entangled in them all the time but you can't assemble a semi-coherent idea without these instruments. Soliloquys make good house pets. But you've got to feed them words or they wander into darkness and are lost forever. An unkempt intolerance is sometimes better than a woeful compliance. Thinking makes the head speak. The words come out into the light of day and startle the houseguests. Does anyone want pancakes? Pancakes are the metaphysics of breakfast. But butter is the birth of meaning.

So much for the Fun House. It may not be fun for everybody. There is a sense of things that some people have, and many people do not. You know who you are.

There's an area of the garden where I can feel my senses rise to the occasion and fill me with cadence. There's a rhythm in the way the earth yields its luggage to the grip of our attention. We step back and consider the white chickens beside the wheelbarrow which is glazed with rainwater. So much depends on a curandero with a sparrow in a red sombrero. What I find in the past can sometimes be applied to crystal. We often get dappled during our ensemble. It looks pretty. Oh well. Here comes the night. I can see it striding over the mountains to the west. Its phantoms already walk among us, legends of the mailbox, the faint scent of heaven commingled among their letters.

Odor Plume

The wind takes what it wants and deposits it elsewhere. Whoever has owned a flying carpet is familiar with this effect. You don't always go where you want to go. You don't always arrive at the destination you had in mind. Movement is sometimes a joy, sometimes a great exposition. A 10,000-pound tractor in Harding County South Dakota sitting in 14-inch high crested wheat grass was hoisted straight into the air by a tornado and deposited, in pieces, a mile and a half away in Montana. This would tend to indicate a presence in the air, a movement whose predilections are as capricious as they are enigmatic.

Our interpretations of this world are often overstated and misleading. What can anyone say? Nobody understands this planet. Nobody understands this life. If they did, we wouldn't be in this predicament. Thanks to the many heat engines that comprise civilization and its emissions of methane and carbon dioxide, the atmosphere is a complete mess, jets streams meandering in tropospheric chaos creating climactic havoc all over the planet, drought in England, murderous heat waves in Japan, forest fires in Sweden, tornados of fire in northern California. Typhoons, monsoons, hurricanes and cyclones howling through our cities like merciless banshees. Crops failing, the sea rising, the ice sheets of Antarctica tumbling into the sea. Greenland will soon be green again. The Arctic Sea a deep blue where the ice once deflected the rays of the sun back into space. That heat will be added to the oven that is now our planet.

We fucked up. Royally. Has there ever been a species this misguided? This wrong-headed? This stupefyingly myopic?

How did we lose our way? Did we ever know the way? Is too much consciousness too little consciousness? Is walking erect with a big head bobbing around not actually the silliest permutation to ever emerge from the goop of polymers that brought us here?

Bees have learned far better ways to inhabit the world and navigate. They use dance and magnetism. We use needles and glass. Latitude and longitude. Bees use pheromones and ultraviolet. Cognitive maps.

We use Rand McNally atlases. Roadside museums and postcard racks.

We have very little in our language that actually conforms to reality, whatever reality is. We have nothing in our vocabulary that links directly to the phenomena oscillating through our nerves and aggregating into the appropriate words, the right syntax, the right grammatical machinery to convey the ontology of a chrysanthemum. The disconnect is abyssal. We have nothing as expansive as echo location. Nothing as informative as odor. Nothing as illuminating as a waggle dance.

We invent Gods. We devise religions. We create philosophies and customs. We use mobile phones to buy drugs, pesticides to grow biofuel.

Bees use associative learning. Bees pair stimuli together to form three-dimensional models of the world. Bees abstract orientation or symmetry and integrate it into a global representation.

Our methods are empirical, heavy on technology. Sextants, astrolabes, ring dials, chronometers. Our understanding of the world requires satellites. Global Positioning System. Automatic Radar Plotting Aid. Electronic Chart Display and Information System. Long Range Identification and Tracking.

Bees have figured things out abstractly. They've evolved the honey of cognition into cells of active memory.

Sleep will sometimes carry us to distant places and leave us there until the tides of consciousness rise and we awaken to a new life, or an old life with a new interpretation, something like Petula Clark singing "La Nuit n'en finit plus."

The pendulum, meanwhile, swings back and forth. A biography trembles with seagulls. Sandy eyelids judge the Salvation Army to be full of goodwill.

Flannel deepens our sense of tincture, how juicily the light of the chandeliers enchants the luster of music.

Wherever you go, there you are. My sentiment regarding cartilage is generally allegorical, as it should be. Allegory and bone are the fundaments of this narrative we call life. They structure narratives of illusion and truth. Plato's cave. Orwell's *Animal Farm*. The oranges are hypothetical, but we sense that their juices intend a communication of elves and algebra.

I may appear a little irrational at times, a bit unkempt, a little delirious, but I know a hawk from a handsaw when the winds are southerly.

I was thrown into this life like everyone else by a set of circumstances unique to the time in which I entered this world. War was one, the splitting of the atom another. Bombers, uniforms, raging dictators. The film footage suggested that humanity had gone insane. But we had television to comfort us. If you want to call Howdy Doody comforting.

Whatever life may be about, it's certainly interesting. Percussion stirs the air. A rhinoceros adorned in rubies stands in the Kenyan rain.

Ghosts bring us the soft light of other dimensions. Our speech thickens into wax, malleable transparencies that will sustain a small flame of listening cognition. Whatever consciousness is, it's been having a good swim in our heads. Our eyes shine all afternoon, renewed by the smell of rain.

The Whole Cloth And
Nothing But The Cloth

Pyrotechnics are the rhetoric of donkeys. There. I said it. And now we have a road on which to impose our impossible burdens. Thank you, donkey. Thank you, rhetoric. Thank you, chrysanthemum.

The lid on the Smucker's strawberry jam jar is plaid like a tablecloth. I maneuver the remaining jelly at the bottom with a butterknife. It comes easily, goopily to the edge, and I maneuver it onto a slice of toast. It's as if the universe were under my skin, and everything I did and saw and smelled and heard and lifted and touched were a continuous satori of enormous translucence. Where does this anguish come from? Is it something bubbling up from the unconscious? Maybe. It's a big planet. Here's what I think: the brain has been washed without harm. For this, and many other things, we should be grateful. The propaganda was only a crustacean, not an entire jaw of flapping ears.

Birds sing. The clouds mutter their therapies of rain. Loud red feathers stream behind my head.

Jesus. Why should so many artists be assholes? It doesn't devalue the art. It just makes it a little more difficult to diagnose.

Ok, I get it, you probably want your armchair to make sense. Well pass me the gin. I'll do something. I'll squirt blood at the ceiling. I'll mail a waterfall to Texas. Will that finally convince you that that I have big muscles? I could lift Chicago if I wanted. Until then, I'm going to clean the sink with a sponge and a Mel Gibson movie. The sun may break out into rags. Let's walk along the border and tell sad stories of the death of kings. Think of me as a response to cactus. The smell of life sparkles in our noses. And so it begins. Predicates and jackknives. It's about this time of night that my pants fall down. It's my way of saying hello.

It's all about tolerance this spring, acceptance and housewares. I feel suddenly graceful, like elevator doors opening and closing.

Life is mostly ooze, but sometimes it's also a nice warm towel.

NASA's Cassini spacecraft vaporized as it dove into Saturn's upper atmosphere this morning. It burned up in a patch of Saturn sky at 9.4 degrees north latitude and 53 degrees west longitude. Which reminds me. This morning, as I set my rocket down on the surface of a strange exotic planet, I heard the sound of my leather creak. A mysterious form of life lifted itself from the ground and peered in through the porthole. It was Samuel Johnson, holding a dictionary. It was then I realized that I had arrived on the Planet of Words.

Nothing is real on the Planet of Words, except words, and they go about their business creating lilies and hairdos. Words like these don't belong to me. They don't belong to anyone. They're just words. Words without socks when the foghorns blow. This wonderful chair. This lovely rocket upholstered in syntax. How can anything so imponderable pile so much darkness on our hands? It's easy: our hands are words, and therefore worlds.

This is your brain on words. Let's just get that out of the way. I like the idea of a hole. Pirate ships and mirrors. The philosophy of yourself. An X-ray and the light behind the X-ray.

Death is nothing. It just sits around watching goldfish explain a clam.

I feel pungent with airplanes. I'm willing to try anything. Even cloth. That's pretty much the story right there.

Wedding Reception

What happens when you use the same simile for stuff: you have eyes like a wedding reception. Today the hillside vineyards are like a wedding reception. He wrote madly, desperately, like a wedding reception. She gave me a haircut like a wedding reception. I love our new refrigerator it opens just like a wedding reception. He was poor, but he loved Paris, all the stalls along the Seine were like a wedding reception. Miles Davis's playing was introspective and lyrical like a wedding reception. The wedding reception was like a boiling bucket of paint, all smiles and tears and sudden quick emotions that flared into bitter controversy when John Ruskin discussed the role of art as a reflection of modern morality and the bride fell into a pool of champagne on the floor and the groom stomped away cursing like Charles Bukowski.

Pornographic Snowball

Words are the laxative the mind needs to liquefy and flow. Any time I have a fig newton in my hand I want to be the protoplasm I know I can be and further advance my biology with the immense natural beauty of the frog hopper ride. This is essentially a free fall ride, ascending and descending like the natural cycles of life itself, the tides of fortune coming and going like shock waves of stellar pulsation, or the formation of molecules in the primordial gas of the expanding universe.

I tend to favor style over content, but if you want to wear sweatpants go ahead. Forget the walls, just smile and wave at the penguins. You'll be glad you brought a chair.

Resilience is good. Try that. Try anything. Try cloth. Try crying. Try aluminum. Ride an elephant backward into Hamlet.

I think it's wonderful that things exist. That highways are asphalt and that there is a way out from the prison of selfhood. Just bring the narratives to their natural conclusion. Drop everything and run into the sky. Hope is a delegation from a future that doesn't exist. Don't go there.

I take balance very seriously. It's a gallant attempt to cope with life on life's own terms. We're all Philippe Petits. One way to get through this life is to become a rubbery substance, and bounce. Another is to not give a shit about anything. Which is hard. Most of the brain is a pornographic snowball. The rest just soaks up a lot of reality and twists it into augurs and tom toms.

Go, little liquid of my brain and become a drugstore awning. Show me the beauties of the universe. Something within the Goldilocks Zone. A habitable planet. Round, sweet, marbled and wet. Like Earth. But without the cars and prisons.

The Warm Sugar Of Bees

I feel the warm sugar of bees. I hold a cathedral in my hand: toast and honey. It lights up the mouth like a wad of antimatter. I feel the effulgent ball of a handspring rattle around in a woman's tear as a tiny head between her legs moves further into the world. These are just a few of my beautiful irritations. They make wonderful Mother's Day gifts. Although, you know, they don't. But if they did, they would revise our notions of birth and life and the meaningless pageantry of our existence. And how would they do that? I don't know. I just like the warm sugar of bees.

Spring Cleaning

My heart is clean. But my mind is dirty. I need to do some spring cleaning. What I need is a little soap, some Swiffer Sweeper Wet Mops, and a jukebox. One of those hydrogen jukeboxes filled with nitrous oxide. Little Richard. Bo Diddley. Chuck Berry. Jesus. Look at the size of that spider. The welder lifts his helmet and nods to the apparitions dancing on the walls.

Is life really just a simulacrum of sad, enigmatic objects with stories to be told? Or more like a hotel room?

Energy is eternal delight. It just assumes consciousness and starts smearing the air with drums. The self is a theatre for perceptions. Nothing is ever so near to us as the personal, physical feeling of our own being letting the world in. Everything feels like prepositions: over under sideways down. There is often the feeling that something is about to happen, something real, something exciting, something like cruise control on highway 61, or a puddle of sound in a lonely room in the south of Arkansas. The heart is a fist of lightning veined and red. The universe walks into your head and sits down. Night glitters in its empire. The horses jingle in their bells.

Mississippi Fred McDowell sits down and talks about the blues. He does not play rock and roll. I respect that. I does not play with words. Words play with me. It's why I don't like haircuts. The sentence is special when it's spatial and the parlor is remembered with its guns and piano. The TV expects us to watch it. The words get up and walk around creating chaos and misanthropy which is my favorite emotion. This is why the semantic rules of a language can be followed by angry little girls. The yearbooks will appear later wearing words like a person. Everything else is just rock and roll.

Coleridge visits me in my sleep. I'm on cruise control. I'm driving all night. Coleridge mumbles: "What if you slept, and what if in your sleep you dreamed, and what if in your dream you went to heaven and there plucked a strange and beautiful flower and what if when you awoke you had that flower in your hand. Ah, what then?"

I don't know, I said. I've got allergies. We stop for coffee and doughnuts in Laredo. It's pretty here. I see a lot of flowers. Oxblood Lily and Spiderwort. My nose gets weird. I sneeze. And sneeze. We're this sensation that keeps happening because we're alive and that's what happens when you're alive. You blow your nose on a napkin and wait for the check. You leave a tip. Later, a language comes along and take us the rest of the way to Xanadu.

The truth is not always reptiles. Sometimes it's streetlights. And sometimes jellyfish butter the truth with applause. I'm falling in love with a gooey tart. Listen to the words grow fat around the big idea. This is a moment of direct sunlight as Egypt steps into the Nile and shines. The eyes are lounges for the judgments of the brain, which are suspended in diplomacy. There is a movie in which Nicolas Cage is a suicidal alcoholic and a movie in which Ferdinand Pessoa gets trapped in a revolving door. Words don't happen by themselves. They need phosphorescence and tongs.

What does it mean to believe in something? I believe I can walk through a wall of granite, provided there is a hole. I believe people have lost touch with reality and that you cannot argue anyone out of a position using rational thought and facts. I wish I could believe that tattoos and smartphones will save us. Meanwhile I will continue hacking at reality with as many words as I can find lying around and put them here until the crowd grows restless and the identity wars heat up. I stopped making sense a long time ago. Who needs it? I say this in kisses and sweetness. For belief or no belief, this little lump of language is shaking in your eyeball and blazing with prose.

Where do all the vanished sentences go? The ones that never get written. I did spot a few words lying around sparkling, but they belonged to a different idea, a different theme altogether, and were calamities of poorly conceived meaning. They were no good. I had to let them go. It's strange being a writer in a post-literate world. Nobody likes to read. Nobody likes to think. What good is it to think about anything? Does thinking change anything? Does it change anyone's mind? Does anyone care what you're thinking? Pages of a book flap in the breeze as the Burlington Northern Santa Fe freight crashes and bangs under the Magnolia Bridge.

We look for fulfillment in different ways. I like books, movies, goldfish, and string. I can do all sorts of things with string. The following sentence is made of string. This is why it's thin and disheveled, like an unmade bed in Ibiza. I also like pillows, fig newtons, and clothes that are warm from the dryer, although I don't like to fold them. I believe gravity is a pleasure best understood by elephants and balloons. Today I want to forge a new objective based on imaginary ambitions. I'm too old for real ambitions. I just want to strive toward things I can achieve in the space of an afternoon. Go into a trance. Build a puppet show for words. Watch the pronouns dance.

Clouds float through my head like nothing matters. And it doesn't. That's why we have maps. They fit the distortions. I will verify my coordinates when I reach the summit of the next mountain. Meanwhile, let's just sit in the park and watch the evening sky grow dark.

Hope is a painter loading phenomena into a boat for a voyage across the River Styx. We see a passport dripping mosquitos. We hear a grasshopper fart. I will let this idea fall like an anchor and grab a downtown window. One must adapt to the world in the best way possible. Romance holds the petition of a wet feeling. Article one demands an end to fascism. Article two cries out for volleyball. Can we just leave it at that? I see the insects scatter. A thousand themes enliven the plains of Texas, but I don't know what any of them mean, and that makes the world beautiful.

When Language Was Tangible

Why does living on planet Earth hurt so much? Is it the planet, though, or is it society? Jobs, zombies, driving in heavy traffic, road rage, corruption and greed in politics, Columbus Day, arthritis, bursitis, appendicitis, conjunctivitis, are all a drag. But they don't add up to being a planet. Where am I going with this? I feel a need to get something out there, something abominably misanthropic to get my point across. But do I have a point? I just have questions.

Heidegger referred to the mind as a "cabinet of consciousness" as a false premise. Think about that. Pop a raisin in your mouth and chew it into the universe that is you. And ask yourself: who was Bob Denver, exactly? Was he Maynard G. Krebs, or Gilligan? I also have a theory about sagebrush, but I'm saving that for a Beatles concert. I live in the past. The rent is cheaper and the landlord is dead.

Words are always blurry. Take the unconscious: the unconscious is a reflection on a downtown window. I'm a ghost haunting a ghost haunting a reflection. Water walks through itself when I shave. A day will come when there is more to a chair than a chair. But until then, I'm going to keep dripping decoys. There's a door in my mind that keeps opening and closing. It must mean something. It's emblazoned with emblems of fire and empire. And sometimes I just sit and think. Welcome to the north. Welcome to the doors opening and closing. Notice the carpentry, how well the width of the jamb corresponds to the wall.

Good word: correspondence. Meaning connection, alliance, accord. Exchanging letters. One imagines an inkpot and a quill. The lone rider of a pony express. A guy like Charles Bukowski delivering the mail on a hot Los Angeles afternoon. It seems dated. Obsolete. People don't correspond anymore. Correspondence has gone the way of the dodo. I miss correspondence. I miss getting letters typed on paper. I could feel the letters. The impact of the typebar on the ribbon indented the paper. When you held a letter in your hand you could feel the impact on the other side of the paper. I could almost read them like braille. Language was tangible.

Words are packed in images because science is my favorite thermometer. Picasso leads a nebula of horses out of the barn. These words have produced a new reality. And you're in it. We're in this together. Surrounded by...shit I don't know. My head itches. The whole world crackles with poetry. And then it gets drunk. And then it writes itself. And then it walks around eating children and staring at the door. Nothing in mathematics is ever literal.

If something doesn't work, sprinkle a few vowels on it. Emotions grow out of vowels. Consonants give them dignity. Picture Denzel Washington taking a bite out of the heart of a deer. This proves that everything in life is sad and lonely. People are sometimes so introverted they pop open when you least expect it and fill the room with butterflies.

Perception doesn't always come in a box. Sometimes it comes as a female hormone. Snow falling on a staircase in the Ukraine. The pornography of headlights in a compound eye.

How might I describe this world? Is it a hell or a heaven? Purgatory? Limbo? None of the above? All of the above? The world is a big ball of stone circling a G-type main sequence star. Wildcats roam the cotton fields. There is the sparkle of literature everywhere. Consider the lilies. Lilies are wonderful and they don't need jobs, which is the essence of Christianity. If you believe in Christ you'll get lots of money. That was, after all, the central message? Right? In the end, the most important thing you can do for yourself is finish reading this sentence. My words are bleeding.

If you let me swim into your eyes I can explain everything. Language is an event, not a tropical drink. Music unbuttons the air. Death hunts for heirlooms. We feed it bones and revolutions. I flow beside the noise of history as thousands of jellyfish wash ashore. How do you describe vision to the blind? How do you describe a ball in the realm of the square? The waves come in. The waves go out. Life is mostly underwear, T-shirts, and socks.

I'm lost. What was the question again?

You can seduce the logic of the potato by leaning a broom toward the rear of the airplane. This will help relieve internal tensions and seat size.

Upon arriving in Minot, I disembarked and stretched my legs. It wasn't my original destination, but I'm happy the library was open and I could find a copy of Emily Dickinson on the table. "This is my letter to the world, that never wrote to me."

Dear Emily: I'm so sorry it's taken me all this time to write. Nobody feels the world turn and yet it is filled with silly tyrannies and secret recipes. You'd think the dirt around here would open up and talk. Oh well. I hope the food in heaven is good. People still clamor for the banquet of your poetry. As you yourself once said, Love's oven is always warm.

I can resolve almost any issue with a little puberty and bathroom tissue. Because if you think about blood you will come to realize that all the screaming of hell isn't some item that may be purchased on a CD at a gas station. Though it should be. No two experiences are ever exactly the same, but the chords have helped keep everything on my plate. What more can you ask for? We're in crisis. You do know that, right? Of course you do. Why else would anyone spend time in social media. We're all waiting for the other shoe to drop. Completely normal, I say. Completely normal to build a sentence of breath and sand and offer it to the ghosts of hypothesis. Together we can lift a sentence into the air and give it a push and watch it sail into redemption.

There's an asshole in all of us. I try not to let him out too often. Lately, that hasn't been working out well. I often wonder if it isn't better to be open about one's nastier predilections than try and keep it hidden. Is there anything creepier than people who keep disagreeable feelings buried inside? It's quite often what needs to be expressed the most. The most urgent. This is why I've nailed my voice to the wall. I want people to see it hanging there squirming, agitating, shaking its little fist. Watch as it ruptures into shadows. Gas station coffee and Windex and hot dogs. That kind of acrimony.

Go ahead. Jump into these words. Pump the juice right out of them. There's a shrine in the corner of the library. This is where sensations refine themselves into books active with sauerkraut. I could use this as an example, but it's already too sour. We should step away quietly and stand on the porch and listen to the rain. The buckets are carried by Buddhists. The glue is heavy. It's a sticky situation. Fortunately, most of the gas stations are open. They're full of introspection. It's not a gas, but it will do, until some actual thinking gets here.

The stars pour eternity on the world. The world continues to turn. Imagine a female movie star stumbling around backstage at a quiz show. If it can happen to rawhide it can happen to vaudeville. Hornets of the underworld wielding gumdrop vaginas. This is when an alibi stumbles into a garden for the rustle of taffeta in a Texas brothel. Intramural outlaw cookies are always radioactive. Witchcraft is for babies.

Fairy Kingdom

There's a fairy kingdom dancing around the big toe of my left foot. This is the one with the dusty entrails of a derelict explosion. It's an old story told by an emissary from the back of the bus. Hold the flashlight. I'm going to see if the undertaker is still alive. Can you hear it? The jelly of our eyes is nothing less than sanguine. The house is a sleeping disaster. There's always some discord in seeing a benevolent pope wave his hand over the crowds at Vatican City. This is why we need to carve some shapes out of the air. We need to make the invisible visible. You can't go wrong imitating snow. I just place the nouns where they're most needed and hope for the best.

A thing is metal when it's literal. No metal is metaphorical. Except tinfoil. It doesn't ring in the mouth like gold, but dazzles the eyes like God. Spinoza saw God as nature itself. He makes no mention of tinfoil. Why? Can it be he never made sandwiches? Just look at what I'm wearing. A tiara, a tutu, and a pair of dark leather gloves with a rabbit fur cuff. It must be obvious. I'm in love with concrete. Would you like anything? A glass of water? You've come this far. Let's finish this together. Here come the woodwinds. I can feel my needs evolve into scabbards and magnetism. I'm teetering on bobsleds, an irritation ransomed by ginger snaps.

If varnish isn't prominent in this sentence, then it must be barley, or the cornfields of Iowa. The kitchen sink is still alive. That's one clue. Another is the poultry humming next door. Can you hear it? It sounds like chickenpox. It's nice, but the reptiles are agitated, and the reservoir is dry. Stoicism can only go so far. This is why we need winks and nods. We need community. Let's walk the lava through the cathedral singing Neil Young songs. I never fully understood the Futurists. Is it sometimes emptier to say something when nothing needs to be said, or is it the overpowering fragrance of lavender that finally acquits us of our inarticulate demands? Listen to your heart. I'm guessing it sounds like a potato chip bag. The rest of this sentence is still boiling.

I know how to engage the world. What I haven't yet learned is how to disengage with the world. I know what it is to stand in a garden while the ganglions of one's brain hoist an idea of free will into cognition. Is there such a thing? Is it possible to powder the face and put on a wig and attend the ball without being recognized? Will anyone notice the look of Cubism on my face? Certain representative planets offer some good breakfast deals. Lolita's amnesia was due to anesthesia, not pizza. The doughnuts are perfectly fine. If you can eat enough of them, the result will give you power. The authority to occur at any time, postmarked and powdered in the morning light.

The coffee is acting silly. It crawls around in my mouth like a value. The hysteria smells pretty. I wonder what actual democracy looks like. I hear the eerie cry of a house fly overhead. Our cab is biased toward mingling. There's a story about this called "The Arthropod's Arthritis." It stars Robert De Niro and Jessica the Sorceress. Is this prismatic? Well, it should be. The mutiny is underway. We need every hand we can get, including back rubs. I can feel the metamorphosis about to begin. First the sentence turns almond, then a word sparkles with squirrels.

Peanut Butter Sandwich

Have you ever had a peanut butter sandwich so good that eating it felt almost sexual? I didn't even bother with a plate. I was so eager to get it into my mouth I ate it over the sink. It was like chewing porn. I may build a statue of Marcellus Gilmore Edson out of peanut butter and put it in the kitchen window like a shrine. Burn incense. Chant. Mouth full of bread and jam and peanut butter. It is a thing of might and beauty like the snow of the Himalayas or the rain of Cameroun. It's indecent and creamy and engorged with voluptuous jam. This may be the birth of a new feeling. Therefore be glad. I will meet you at the end of this sentence with a slice of description.

It's a little amazing when you come to discover you can still squeeze a little enjoyment out of all your old tissue. The cells are still functioning. The circuitry still sparks. Neurons twinkle. The spirits dance. My old hippie throat bends reflections around the moon. Some might see this as the behavior of a gargantuan angora bicycle. But it's just sugar. Really. I can handle a cookie or two. Or pretzels.

Candy impels the pungency of a moment of Martian reverie. Go ahead. Press it. Hold it against your ear. This is how thinking begins. There is an energy in the head manifesting itself as a flow of consciousness, whatever that is. I think it's some sort of feeling, a spirit of spontaneity, a dynamic of feathers and space. The skin of a balloon stuck to the ceiling. The bride stripped bare by her bachelors, even. Hanging upside down, like Dolly Parton on a Tennessee Tornado.

We are the door to ourselves. Moo if you have to navigate an inflated ego, like mine. All I need is one lousy pinprick and I'm done with this charade. It will feel like cold steel and encourage me to sit and meditate in a corner. Our galaxy roams through a cerebellum looking for odds and ends, something to rattle, like a broken taillight, or a piece of water.

Romania in the rain.

Here it is: an embryo. It's just what I was looking for. It's time I gave birth to something. A beautiful deformity would be nice, one in which all nothingness wiggles all its flippers and luxuriates in doodles of scrotum typography. But then it went wild in my hands and I lost it in the forest.

Sometimes I get something going on in my brain, something like an unfiltered perception, and I can't stop it, it becomes a thing. A phenomenon. Basically, a middle-aged woman standing in the rain in a leopard-skin bathrobe waiting for her dog to take a shit. Because, you know, who in this world doesn't occasionally have to relieve themselves? I don't mind a little melodrama now and then. It gets things out in the open. Bloody hell, as they say. Bloody this and bloody that. I've been aching to say that all day. And if the letters congeal in a certain way and the voice is strong and the spirit is willing, the sounds come flowing out, bright lucidities of thought, swollen and blue.

All these years I've tried avoiding pain when I should've just given it a home. A little wallpaper. A TV. A pot and a calliope and a big fur hat. A bed of topsoil and a load of compost and waited to see what could grow out of that. Piece of sod. Turn it over and look underneath. What's this, Chittagong? Pittsburgh? I realize that some of these words have lives of their own and might've done better in a bed of beets than this clumsy attempt at seaweed and sand. I'm not aiming here for an unmitigated realism. Just an acute sense of water on an infinite scale. Parrots and tuna held together by words. Sails billowing with wind. The pitch of a bow. The invention of clouds.

I'm beginning to get that feeling that words are about to interact with something huge and pervasive, mushrooms perhaps, or heartache. Drag the bicycle to the other side of the universe and ride it around a drawing.

A drawing of what?

I think it's a tug. A tug on the Thames with red smoke billowing from a white stack. Eye am my own Fauve clutter. Follow the words hunched together in venison. There's a version of this in Russian that evolves into coleslaw. I feel the power of Kazakhstan in my jaw. It's as if I yearned to grip breakfast with an ambush. Ask the spirits what I can soothe and if I can soothe it I will soothe it with backrubs and fungus. So, you see, words are important after all. They float here from England and swim through me like eels causing everything to shimmer like shag.

If you tap on the sky include geometry. Rocks and dolphins. The geometry of the lobster is an aesthetic of determination. The geometry of the sky is cruel, yes, but it is also beautiful and abstract, like the rain that comes falling out of it. I realize that some of these words have lives of their own and might do better in another sentence, one written with a little more care and delicacy, with two enormous claws raised in defense of its mandibles. My brain stirs with a thousand obscurities. One of them is gasoline. The others just rush around my head causing pumpernickel.

The mushrooms tell me I'm a spectral dispatch. We slither through a world that is partly perception, partly urban sprawl. And then I ask myself: why do I do this? Why do I search for other dimensions? I'm guess I'm just not satisfied with the current paradigms. I feel elemental. Maybe the Zen guys are right, there is no mind. Maybe there is only *mu*, non-existence, non-being, and muffins. In the meantime, we have Beowulf and New Brunswick. And the poetry of Frank O'Hara. Let's not forget that. It works as well as a gentle abrasive for cleaning the mind. You know? The one that isn't there. That doesn't exist. And weighs several tons.

I'm a mad little trumpet today a feeling disguised as a sharp bright noise. I didn't think the neurosis would've gotten this big and walked all over my nervous system in such heavy boots. Here's an interesting exhibit it's a string of domestic animals filling the space between my furloughs. Glass case with a perpendicular speech act and the face of Samuel Beckett at age 78. Lustrous horse and a gun made of goose bumps. It shoots real nibbles. This makes everything inglenook and perpetual, the way paper trembles under a load of words.

I feel the elephants heating the interior of the helicopter. And to think it's only Tuesday. My memory of your outskirts is a small organ at the front of the vulva. I hear the soft hand of darkness buttoning moonlight on a suit of ice. You can't walk away from an experience. They get inside you and become wind and time and horticulture. It all leads to welts and lingerie. I suck the iron teat of contrast. And return home to a rising tide of similarity. Get out. Get out now and walk to the other side where the dead are clawed into light. The slow drip of candle wax attests to the beauty of understatement. I don't think we're going to ride this one out. Hang on to your hat.

Perspective is everything. Blood wanders around my body murmuring dreams of happy momentum. I'm doing my best to understand the pornography of power. My favorite book is about an undercover jaywalker lost in a fairyland of rust. Jelly blooms in my hand like a sweatshirt. One day, I hope to explore space as a NASA eggplant. Though I would settle for being Superman and getting free coffee at Starbucks in exchange for saving planet Earth from being struck by a gigantic asteroid. I would ride that asteroid into Omaha and get a room at the Bored Bug Hotel. Even the bear comes down from the mountain when he's hungry.

Contemporary Matters

There comes a time when the news is too much. Too awful. Too demoralizing. Even the propaganda stinks. The duopoly is corrupt, income inequality is cruel and pharaonic and the algorithms won't leave you alone. Energy impels us to run. And so we run. Reality can go on like this all day. Structure is just the howl of ooze. Imagine a polymer. A compelling blob of elegance. Sew a face. Sputter into rock. Then invade Norway. Existence is largely presumption. My hands smell like an emergency room. Penitent, and intent. I don't want to force a discussion. But everything just dangles in the air like a burst of gunfire. And all the surgeons are drunk.

Call it what you will. Call it contemporary matters. Call it living in the 21st century. Call it surveillance. Call it totalitarianism. Call it dystopia. There are no panaceas, but there are choices. You can meditate, or do push-ups. You can mingle with the air. Each experience is unique. Each brain is a world and each world is a singularity. There is wisdom in the fin of a fish, cartilage in winter and warm words swarming around an ancient emotion. The zeitgeist needs a bath. I once had more expectations than I do now. I feel lost, helpless, sad. The arctic ice is vanishing. This is my Declaration of Symptoms. My shout to the spirits. My circus of words. My tribute to crows. The hardest need to fulfill is meaning. Language is always entertaining. Bring popcorn.

Solitude and society must come together and succeed one another, to be green, to get green, to become green. Because I don't know. I know what to do. Hold this sentence a minute while I finish it with words. The crust is language, but the inside is totally shiny. Life is a whisper. Take the car, for example: it has four wheels and an engine. This is what is known in phenomenology as Independence Day. That can have many meanings. But the elemental drift of it will sparkle like rails in the Mexican sun when the rattlesnake glides under a rock & solitude becomes aesthetic. Like that barn. The red one, with the horse in front. The mare with fire in her eyes.

The suppleness of meaning sleeps in the stones of the river. Nearby, we see cactus, which is a meaning awakening into itself. Rocks enter into definition with the melting of snow. Birds scatter. I sift through my memories to venerate the past. The mood becomes elegiac. I sharpen my jackknife. The autonomy of art requires seclusion. The fat of the thumb is a good place to start. Sand is the place where dirt acquires the language of water. I see in it the nothingness of mind. This is a resource. Insects swarm over the water. Words swarm in the hive of a paragraph. There is no interior, no exterior. There's only the blues, twilight hues and the gradual appearance of the stars. A universe sparkling at the edge of thought. Sneeze. And accelerate into oblivion.

Texture

Texture is a literature for the hands. It's touching. And gallant. Do you see this dust? That's a thought collapsing. The sticky resin of reason is a response to hot dogs. And watching TV, which can be splendid, as it empties the brain, and leaves you with an appetite for spontaneity and drugs. A woman's fingers running down your spine is a sensation. And a fine one. We call this poetical because it snaps into a place like a rubber band. Rubber was not a European invention. It was discovered by the Olmecs who used it in their ballgames. Me, I'm not much into sports. I prefer the vagaries of the sidewalk. I've never been to Louisiana, but I'm soaked in New Orleans.

This is the kind of convolution that leads to books. Remember books? They had life going on inside them fighting wars and boozing it up and staying disengaged from the petty realities of capitalism. That's what books do: they like being peripatetic. Nietzsche was right, don't catch the abyss looking back into you. That's a hard feeling to shake. Just start throwing words at it. When it bubbles to the surface it means there's a real universe beneath our clothes. It's silent and solid and relentlessly specific. Even the insects seem nervous.

I love the planetarium grounds. The attic runs away from my sadness, but that's ok. Bring a notebook. Write everything down. Hang out in the aftermath.

Raspberries trigger a dream of water. Evening in Cairo. The lightning behind an eyelid. I get dressed in the universe and put on a hat that drips with singularity.

Our heads are round so our thoughts can change direction, said Francis Picabia. Prepositions jump into the sentence and make it turn around and go under and sideways and arrive at the piano ready to blaze out of the fingers like Saskatchewan. Cool. We can let our hands hang in the water and continue our sewing later.

Immediate certainty, the thing in itself, is complicit in the construction of our experience. Who can look at a river and not feel that river moving through one's body? Every faucet has a mouth and every sentence has predicates clicking lyrics into the scenery of the mind. Writing is mostly sounds trapped in pearls. It makes Beings become Beings, words become words, and teeth become teeth. Sometimes it just feels good to have a pen in the hand and move it across a sheet of paper producing stout-bodied game birds warm ruminant thoughts vivid sensations phenomena crystalizing in the mind where squalls and angels stumble around looking for the right words with which to tell you that words don't happen by themselves. They need snow and limousines.

Religious practices are charming if they don't pinch too much or provoke guerrilla warfare. I get a bang out of cashmere. Perception is easy. It's also bugs. I'm coming toward you in ashes. It's exciting to see our minds come together in a sentence. Is this that sentence? They say the lake is garish and extroverted, but I found it hanging from a branch of words, braided and abstract, just like our conversation. Hey, here's a boat. This makes my grammar pink. Crinkled like a scrotum. I'm out on bail now. It's summer and the words in my mouth catch fire. Let's jump into the sky like God's spies, quiet and unassuming. It's not always the right word that counts, it's the parachute.

The Emperor Of Macaroni

Speed is aromatic when it becomes lightning. Who are you? Ribbon is one so-lution. Moccasins are another. Density is magnificent with mermaids. Think of this as a phenomenology of reaching and reading and reaching for some-thing to read. Of pianos and cockpits. Syncopation and garlic. Wax and honey, which are lieutenants of bric-a-brac, and dare to matter in a world of geeks and grossly inflated salaries. Even though, when you think about it, the sponge is every bit as brilliant as a whale, and a crisis such as this can loosen our frost-ing. I think it's wonderful that things exist. That the nose is naturally Zen and that one's chains are imaginary. Break them. Drop them. It's wonderful that magnesium can be a waitress and that the color gray can fall into the hands of a dwarf and televise the chlorophyll of a milkweed. That lips have their own brand of chivalry. That success can mean so many different things to so many different people. This hour will dissolve within the limits of another hour and various sensations will hatch out of that and become words in a sentence. Drop everything and run into the sky. Pasta is sensual because the streets are full of wasps, not because hope is cruel, and it takes courage to foster a load of despair. Hope is a delegation from a future that doesn't exist. Don't go there.

The Manufacture Of Dirt

The airs of the ants annoy my chest. The fat night goes askew in its myriad flashing. Traffic lights, headlights, moon. In the morning, it is dazzling to see the grain open to the rays of the sun. My hot attention flies with the wind. My marshy head begins humming its swamps. I see an empty parking lot and think, rocks are the panacea of Asia.

The vague prayers of my temperament sprawl in the air for my rescue. I feel the warm sugar of a gelatin knee. I hear the cry of a fork as the knife wiggles its plumage. The ruby indicates that the ocean is at ease. The garden swoons in the legs of the bees. I have twisted a nail in the wood of a splintered arena where enactments of semantic nebula fill the rapiers of tact. The coconuts of a complicated sky tumble to the ground in another paragraph.

Whose nomadic knee has furrowed the dirt for my trickle of thought? I hold a cathedral in my hand: four wings and an abdomen. It lights up like a refrigerator. Grape juice, mustard, painted ladies. The gentle spirit of yesterday hovers over tomorrow dropping parables and syntax. Audacity joins us at the table and swallows a chair. I like it that a spin of sheaves stirs in the muscle between my legs. Can I say that the beak of that sparrow churns with a providence that I'm not done rowing?

I have caused perception to open and lift the day into mending. The back door slams on the smells of the kitchen. The verdure favors the manufacture of dirt, not belt buckles, not tricky guitar strings. Just intentions. They're obvious. They're everywhere. But what's underneath them? Dirt. Every time I hear of a chance to rid myself of memories I shiver in the cold and need them back.

I get stormy sleep. My knee drinks the heat of the waves. I force an old dazzling temperament to tangle with theorems of disentanglement. The air gets up and hovers over a terrain of vagrants. Asian hay carpets seethe with the myths of catastrophe. I feel subversive. I relax control to stimulate the vagaries.

To examine antique realities.

A subtle velocity tints the seaweed surrounding my plough. I spread a soft light of memory in the tibia kitchen and the commas cry with the burning hot plop of a twinkle on the miasma of my inner humidity, which is entangled in mysteries of violence and space. Power to the regatta. Power to the pounce of the panther. Power to the empire of the light bulb. Power to the swirls of light in my pretty maelstrom of augurs and tom-toms. I'm willing to change direction at any time. There are samples of my flexibility on the edge of the soap. Help yourself.

Power to the saliva that drools from the mouth of reverie.

Swimming is divine. But walking is faster.

Power to walking. Power to swimming. Power to the follies of asphalt, which favor the charity of wheels. Power to the ideology of socks, which is soft with sequestration. Power to the tenderness of cork, which is porous, and to coffee, which has blends. Power to the theatre, which tends toward action. Power to humming, which accompanies strumming, and the ring of syllables, which are assimilable, and the blossoming of speech, which circulates in words. Power to the symmetries of structure and the enchantment of floating. Power to the oval, which is almost round, and to the ellipse, which is a generalization of the circle, and resembles a circle, but isn't a circle, and has eccentricity. Power to the jackknife, which folds and can go in a pocket, and to the shoebox, which is full of tissue, but mostly to trays, which carry glasses, and may be cleaned with a sponge, or a brush, and used again, which is a form of repetition, which is a form of rhythm, which is an element of music, which is a conveyance of value, which has to do with the worth of something, which is a proposal of what is good, and a proposal of what is bad, which is comparative to the understanding, which is a mental process, a charge of energy slopping around in the head, which chafes against the skull, and splashes against the rocks, which are also in the head, and are called images, which are pictures, dishes in the sink, mist rising from a river, or anything, really, which serves my purpose here, my mandate, if you want to call it that, which is how this got started, this thing, this momentum, this intuitive zone, this field of resonances, which is an amplification of something I feel, something I try to pedal, perturb into being, assert, coordinate, try to get across, squeeze into words, into an idea, a yo-yo, an imbroglio, anything I can work into further tumult, which is comprehensive and vague, and expansive like the ocean, which is wet, and deep, and full of strange and luminous fish.

There. I said it. And now I want to begin the sculpture. The gargoyle. The anatomy. The cabana.

I want to suggest an effulgent ball of nailing things. Sometimes a cricket speaks of agitations that offer a way to heat a problem gently to ashes and we begin to poke at time as if it operated by handspring and rattle. A tiny head appears in a woman's tear and creates sensations of adobe puppet. Our world is unrivalled in horses. There are movements that continue to signal ideas of botany for the briefcases we carry. Believe me. If I could accommodate your touch I would cradle it into milky action, so there. Let me see those nipples. I'm skulking now. You're right. These words need grease. Dwarf fever sprinkles lung nerves in a line of beautiful irritations. The poultry fulminates to black. Our carpet has scarlet reveries, and this makes us believe that apricots need arms. Although, you know, they don't. but if they did, they would revise our notions of fruit. Mutation is what it's all about, baby. That, and seamless cloudbursts.

The Gate Is Open

Sheaf of camber tar, it is a gallant attempt to cope with life with grace and prayer. Win a wasp. Writing is knots. Polar kick to the periphery where glass becomes heels. The crash in which I live is a sequel to the barn.

Become a substance, a wax or a vertebra. The storm palpates the mountains and thus acquires lightning. Help me explain the stunned warehouse affair. The streets of Paris, music, my room at midnight. An island in the mind for tomorrow's solitary coconut.

Toad book in which we wade with sweet monastery murmurs. We who seek the rhapsody of balance. We who have a locomotive to wear like a mushroom coat. The buttons are the thin dreams of sparrows. The pockets are filled with underground tunnels, and doors that elves oil with their frivolity.

Let me speak frankly. I have no power, and that makes me dangerous. A flash of lightning with ingots of ice. I hear the light bulb in its reverie of light. I see the hills climb into Saturday, and come back out on Monday carrying waves of grass.

The bra in the brain bath acts like a sponge, or terrain, it's gum, you know, a warm backstage full of foxes. A mass of library thunder. Unknown sewing. The Queen of Ears.

The weight of the pillow can live in pomegranate, but my caress will be an amenity for all time. Rowing a snowflake is a lush characteristic that familiarizes itself with detachment and is commendable in a strange way. The windows of the sugar hotel shine out with contempt as I throw my pants to ecstasy. Plaster ground of cinnabar and stone. Smoke all week as Canada burns down.

Barometer arena, marble hands of the inquisitive extending from a wall of mimosa, and on the table an alembic of bubbling migraines. We are in the era of mutation. Memory root of pure music. Go, little liquid of the flu awning and show me beauty, how it lives in subtlety and the universe is dead to money. There is a crash in the hardware, a man with cascading streams shivering out of him shouts advice to the spirits of Egypt, and the spirits come forward, gleaning little objects from the floor.

It's a complicated package, this life, this enormous pink lung, this Venus de Milo, glasses filled with porn queens. Chocolate has the force of commas made of ice. Even the lawn has to go buckle itself to a face when the world gets too big for horticulture. Forge drapery, be a genital to yourself for the sake of naiveté. The bell tower has a map to clean and the gate is open.

The Bingo Of Being

Pile the darkness in the climate of our hands. Our hands are warm. For the moment. This is how we do it. It's what we intend. We intend to feel at home. Scud through the house dropping trinkets. And hats.

Pass the syntax to the chocolate master to promote our sense of firmness. The chocolate master knows how to blaze into animation and melt. The smell of it sparkles in our noses. The roughness is chiseled out of tea. The rake re-frigerator has a bee sleep. There is a bean for the salvation of its fish and the honesty of its armchairs.

And so it begins.

The suppositions are ripped into stethoscopes. My pump is an idea I pumped from a well of language. It begins with a predicate and ends with a jackknife.

Deformations are heavy and visceral. I write so that I can shine and glide. But it backfires. I become sand. I reanimate veins of mad brilliant blood. It doesn't glide. It gives me resolution. I pull prepositions out of the air and empty them of radar so that they can be welded into carousels. Above, below, between and at go round and round and round. In is defined by out. Out is defined by in. On is defined by under. Under is defined by on. And on and on and on. Time is defined by wax. Space is defined by its desolation.

It's about this time of night that my pants fall down. It's my way of saying hello. We do this together. We do it with mushrooms. We do it with bingo. We do it with being. Being and bingo. The bingo of being.

Whatever happened to Melanie Safka? Girl about my own age. Old lady now. Sang "Lay Down (Candles in the Rain)" at Woodstock.

I continue to think about life on Mars. I know it's there. It's probably mi-crobial, not a creature with arms and legs or even tentacles, big head with bulg-ing veins and huge cat's eyes of outer space mysteries, but I don't care, life is life, even when it's invisible, or in my case, fucking up my gums.

The grape is classic, but the hive is chimerical. The simulacrum is haunted by its own similarities.

Am I an asshole? I've never hit anyone, but I've said a lot of regrettable things. I wish I could take them back. I would like to build a time machine and harvest all my stupidities. I could distill it, refine it, then market it as scintillating prose.

Sometimes I see a face on a branch or the trunk of a tree. Who is it? Martin Heidegger? Baruch Spinoza?

The eyes say consciousness is a fundamental property of matter, but the chin says abracadabra.

We are, as a matter of course, conscious of ourselves, but we do not, as a matter of course, know ourselves.

I think tin is a superior solution to oak when it comes to feeling the planets in my arm.

Stitches

The sun breaks the sky into rags. Let's walk along the border. My stick has a memory. The engine strains to get us over the hill. Don't worry. There are signs. Yesterday I saw a nose walking down the street. There was a head attached. It had ears and a mouth and a pair of eyes. Hair. Legs. Arms. Everything. Do you know what it is that I'm saying?

It was a woman with a turquoise bear on the middle finger of her left hand.

We are prisoners of our own ideas. Everyone needs a sense of the sublime. Otherwise life gets awkward and ugly. It's like holding a brandy snifter with a pair of boxing gloves on your feet.

For years, I caught the bus to the U-district in front of Jimmy Woo's Jade Pagoda. And then I didn't. I moved to a different hill. A different state of mind. A different picnic.

You can create a universe with your breath. Here is the filigree of my breath. Twist and shout. Plaster is plausible. Watch for falling rocks. Contrariety adorns the aching world. Do you sometimes feel like you're falling through yourself into a lost world?

It's more aromatic by the side of the road. Each species is an articulation of a new idea, a new adaptation. Conditions are always changing.

Don't talk to me about guilty pleasures. I know all about guilty pleasures. I really like watching Mel Gibson movies.

I'm adapting to the sheer nonsense of the United States of Nonsense.

Our bed is a condensation of paradise. The story of my life is just heating up. If I were part of a salvaging team I'd be in the deep looking for Prospero's book. Ocean swells moving in a symphony of engorgement and movement above me.

How much more insecure can you be than to lose an entire planet? The cactus is a response to aridity. I'm a response to cactus. Pain gets sloppy sometimes.

Planet Earth is losing its birds and bees to pesticide and constant wildfires. What can be done to save it? I'm not a king. I'm not a politician. I'm a wrestler. I'm a fool. I like sharp things. I like soft things. All I want to do is propagate the art of sewing, which is a rhapsody.

From Greek *rhapsōidia*, from *rhaptein* 'to stitch' + *ōidē*, 'song,' or ode.

The pelvis swivels according to the needs of the body. The conditions of life. I wish I could heal the look in your eyes. Think of me as a ball of molecules in an eccentric orbit. My glasses justify themselves by distinguishing reality from mirrors.

I don't belong here.

When was the last time you stopped at a motel without calling ahead and making a reservation?

Almost anything in language or done by words is an invention. I smell the filet of a dead chimera. All my jobs have been shit jobs. The power of Picasso is most evident in the nude. So please: don't touch my desk. My head is an arena of scars. Afterthought can be helpful but don't get lost in rumination. Rumination will ruin you. Ruin you with rumination. Eyeballs circling your head.

You can break anything you want but please don't break my heart.

A dragon acquires reality by spreading its wings. Jack Nicholson in a Cadillac. I set my rocket down on the surface of Titan. A mysterious form of life lifts itself from the ground and peers in through the porthole. Meanwhile, on earth the rice fields open to the rain. And the savage trumpets of estrangement play a funeral march in the brain of a cobra.

Abstraction heals the telephone. That happened in New Jersey, where I once played André Breton in a play about fertilizer.

I feel the timeless fire of language. I have dilated pupils and a textbook fog. My legs are allegories for the adventures of my arms. There's always a Friday buried somewhere in Monday. Every stitch of the fabric of time is a part of me. Silos. Insects. A flash of lightning to the south. What can one say about actuality that makes sense as a framework for your experience, as a sign that points beyond itself? We see a car. The shine of chrome, the rumble of an engine. And what then? We get in. We start it. We step on the accelerator. We accelerate. And we smile. Because it's not our car. And it's fifty miles to Tucson.

Time isn't always a chronology. Sometimes it's a tray of empty glasses. Old rusty nails in a slat of wood. An eye. A warm hand.

Zimbabwe, June 10th, 1887. 10:21 a.m. A rhinoceros breathes on the orbit of a bee. The bee goes about its business. The rhinoceros turns, and walks away.

Seattle, Washington, September 17th, 2017. The cat paws at the bedroom door, wanting in. Hurricane Maria is following Irma's path and getting stronger. Hamas agreed to dissolve its governing body in Gaza. NASA's Cassini spacecraft vaporized as it dove into Saturn's upper atmosphere this morning. It burned up in a patch of Saturn sky at 9.4 degrees north latitude and 53 degrees west longitude.

It is Samuel Johnson's birthday tomorrow. Take a dictionary out to dinner.

There are words that I haven't yet left here in the sentence, raked here like leaves. Here they are. The shimmering rapport of mercury prophesies churchyards of circumspect hairdos.

Words like these are residual. They don't belong to me. They don't belong to you. They've been painted to look like portable generators. But they don't. They look like escarole.

I'm not the captain of anybody's fate. I don't even know what fate is.

The fence embraces the backyard light, a bonfire in Polynesia. I catch the wind and take off.

Belief is a luxury for the inexperienced. Ambition is nothing without socks when the foghorns blow. Fasten your seatbelt. There's a blaze on the ridge of the mountain. It's time we got the hell out of Dodge.

I'll tell you what fate is: Mel Gibson at the wheel of a Mack truck.

Shadow On The Snow

A gleam below sleep has fangs. We cabbage mahogany beside nothing. I am not your wax. This mass enkindles above stirring. The hole murmurs clouds.

We know our cure turns tonic. It sprints across the buckle. We languish in faith below the elephant. I thicken in mints and crash into orchids. I linger in my umbrella and ponder the art of imitation.

Ok, I get it, you probably want your armchair to make sense. Well pass me the gin. I'll do something. I'll squirt blood at the ceiling. I'll steep myself in reading.

Here comes some death. We flip the search into ten pounds of philosophy. Please the winds. Gratify wood on water. It creaks under the weight of its own postulate.

I scurry into verticals and haunt a current. My penumbra rips into pull-ups. A reality plagues the Corot. I attract roads, too many roads if you ask me, but it helps to permit mutation. It is what I magnetize that causes the hills to thrill with nature.

What I need is string and paper, maybe a little tape, definitely some tape. I'm going to mail a waterfall to Texas. I want knobs on my muscles and a tan on my neck. I want invention and credit. I want nimble insults and a thousand alibis.

The bulb is at the light finding science. That's how it begins. We bubble out of our glass since snow exaggerates trees. Your Céret is not my Céret but a grapefruit house with green curtains. I sent a waterfall to Texas and it came back as a conversation.

The structural necessitates a club. This is so that the ripples narrate themselves as a form of water and not just another testicle. I mean to jingle the decorations and one day become a sentence impelled by real words. Until then, I'm going to clean the sink with a sponge and an old pair of oracles. Gonna rub-a-dub-dub until my neck is stars and the water is laughing and dusty.

Emotive rip diffused into throats and sent out into the world as a muscle. Tea is a rascal. It reflects the smell of swelling. I grapple with it and rise into being. The library is a jungle of imagery, most of it vines, rapiers, wars, storms and rhapsodies absorbed into words, into audacity, the boldness to say what is on your mind, to discharge cockatoos at a trapezoid.

Busy dimes of metamorphism are always hydrogen. Ablution is a conception of washing pounced on by spaniels. Oysters necessitate hibachi pumpkins. The grace to authorize cloth and heat a space with rocks. Furnish the tug with twigs and the butter is yours, my friend.

I crawl through the sentence searching for a pot of gold. Is that a propeller at the end of this moonbeam? No, but there's bratwurst and mashed potatoes in the universal flux of being. No autobiography is truly complete without a little flux.

Hope is nonsense. I don't like hope. It sets you up for disappointment. It swarms with purpose. I prefer aporia.

There are times, I think, when thinking makes things lumber. Planks of pine and oak in a drafty building. I think I'm a carpenter who builds things with adjectives.

Zipper in the snow. Photogenic plaster lingered by doing truth, which is a milieu of milieus, a tumble up the hill, somebody to love you, and a vascular vernacular of granular scapular scruples in doodled pupils of quadrupled noodle.

That said, the rest is easy. A banjo on the knee. Handles and milk. The experience of gauze. A gape, a grape and a shadow on the snow.

Lassitude Of Twisting Quintessence

Camel camaraderie away like bones in densely mixed tongues. Plop cat of chaos paint. Street on the roof of my shoulder where the pavement is speed. Body pins falling from an edge of morning. The weary emissary crosses the field. A church bell rings. Religious practices are charming if they don't pinch too much or provoke guerrilla warfare. Bob Kaufman crouches in my heart, a forgotten corner I didn't know I had until he stumbled into it, a brilliant maniac waiting to be loved.

I get a bang out of cashmere. Perception is easy. It's also bugs.

Grimace talk chair. Swarm and swirl and swirl and swarm and hold my eyes in this sentence long enough to read what is coming next which is blinding in its brightness. I am coming toward you in ashes. The beauty of ash is primordial. Support the rod of wandering. Thursday's salt, Friday's sheen. Heaven in a warehouse.

A snap plumps my heft into operation. I constrained an imponderable crack to say obstetrics to you and mean it. And I do I mean to stroll to the end and make another beginning out of moss. Innocence adapts to figures of speech. Metaphors set up camp in Romania.

I hear an identity chattering under my skin. It's exciting to see our minds come together in a sentence. Is this that sentence? Are we greenhorns in paradise?

I stand here in your café riveted to your definitions of sluice. The snow is an embodiment of heaven and I can understand its presence in the spoons, but the fugue that just went by was big as a truck and hinted at molybdenum as a possible resource in the future of our confusion.

Pile up the food of thought on pallets of mimosa butter. The stone makes the toad go up the mountain in a chivalry of popping thunder. Queen Mab in her greenery swarms the climbing she does with touch and artery. Flashing pins of complicated speed cause the manuscript to mimic a mustang and dive through the air on San Francisco hills. Later, after breakfast, the words convene in glass and I feel the obstinacy of the window when I photograph the turbulence of the aurora borealis as it existed three million years ago in an agate.

I'm writing an enigmatic mimosa, a mundane welcome ticket for the velvet hippopotamus of my congenial rage. I'm foggy, traveling in a misty state. Nothing is clear except wax. The wind climbs my capharnaüm. The introspection rivals the transcendence of a hinge.

The door opens and here we are.

I need the elf because the ice cracks. The caboose has a frog for rent, and a calm green moment that bubbles out of a floorboard. I'm visiting the barge right now and forcing myself to pray for the penumbral irritations I've managed to gather over a lifetime of irritations. The penumbral irritations are special because they exist in a timeless margin of funny brochures.

The locals say the skin of the Colorado River Toad makes a good hallucinogen, but my irritations assume a life of their own and continue as words, pulling images and thoughts behind them, forging new associations, new immensities of penumbral art, new irritations, new speculations, new fitting rooms for the mall, which is deserted, thanks to Amazon, and a dreadful economy. Hence, words, which have an exchange value of their own, I don't know what, bitcoins, recommendations, comments on Facebook, seesaws, patents, descriptions of pain, the strange behaviors of cats.

They say the lake is garish and extroverted, but I found it hanging from a branch of words, braided and abstract.

Lassitude of twisting quintessence. Sunset cloud sleeping in the orchard. The breath of the poem is a perusal of Eden floating in a fog of absence. Frankly, the handkerchief is not the panacea I thought it was but just another busy conception of dirt. The sky offers its sloth in a crate on the shore. We can use it to build our conversation.

Or not.

Hey, here's a boat. This makes my grammar pink. It does it to cinnamon and then crumbles into upheaval. Garments are often green but the pretzels weren't and that makes everything harked or something. Crinkled like a scrotum.

Packed with straw.

Children behave. That's what they say when we're together. Watch how you play.

I don't remember much after that. There was a knife on the bottom. I didn't know quite what to do, so I just flared into talk and added myriad subtleties of tone to my voice to confuse the crowd into thinking it was a form of invocation. You can tell them back home it didn't quite work. I'm out on bail now. It's spring, and that rusty old hook is still in me. I can't quite cut loose. Not just yet. There are still some things I need to do.

I want to magnify the magnetic air until the words in my mouth catch fire. You know? I'm not superstitious but there's going to come a time when I've got to spit them all out like chrome buckles on Attic Street. William Hurt hurries with a hurt back to a Paris taxi. They stop a few blocks later to pick up Geena Davis. This is a typical afternoon for me, my dazzling teeth gliding through an almanac of hope and despair while my shoulders brace for the next burden. This is the membrane of my sparkling world. See the needle nail in the wax man? It's the B side of the aforementioned membrane. The water shouts meaning at a revelation purged of cows and the scribbles in the sand murmur of impersonal pressures. The mind likes these things. Creosote and ice cream, the ocean rolling in and out.

It Must Be Love

Exultation is a blue saucepan. Bohemian planetarium in which a body rubs against leftist extraterrestrials. Poetry dares to weigh a head full of language. The red ecstasy of over-hoping comes to a boil in the plumage shirt. A Byzantium wax drools into snakes.

Dissonance worm on a crumbling path to better credit. Regatta dress sucking almonds is called flying. Drinking the lake is singular heading to the play about sons and daughters in a family of brawling acrobats. Stirring mixes our mixed maneuvers with twirls of curdled noise. The high raw honey of your eyes heats the words of the Bible.

And it all makes sense. The flow of it is bending to hear the story of the mechanical bear. The ease of blue has been denied the shovel and so the narrative continues as an intuition. The abandoned slip of the window plankton appoints a brassiere to the blurts of vertigo in a cockroach and everything gets nicely tractable. The far plumber mountain of circular strength tastes of lightning. But the aftertaste revolves in a mirror full of hideous laughter.

Shovel some honest pay my way. The smoke is adrift, the ash is a kindly whisper. Now glory glide up my leg and show me an escape. Here's the open garden gypsum scratch the energy approves. The silverware is shiny and radical on Wednesday. Everything else just seems to sleep unwritten or drift around my index finger.

It is to ecstasy that I want to believe in blinking. The sunset dwarf has a long barbiturate in his hand. Boil the slide and the tree will fence the wind. Needle a reason to hold what it wants. Dare breaking the food with the flexibility of a shattering beard.

My necessity whispers folds of air into prayer. The world was swallowed by a colossal, out-of-control capitalism. And then we imitated clay. A speed expands my outlook. This collides with Houston, but the sky is fiddlesticks, just pure fire.

I'm not a woman but I like to imagine what it would be like to make love to a thread. Flip the shout wiggle it into France. I know my stuff. My neck squirts out of me like a Roman Catholic. With a large open heart and a blast on Tuesday.

Come here baby, sit down on my knee.

We shook ourselves until the cows appeared in the balcony. I agree: space is a solution. But ablution, ablution calls for water. If you're feeling transcendental, I suggest climbing a mountain. Because if you don't climb the mountain the mountain will climb you, and then where will we be?

Boseman, I suspect.

Please tell me if I'm your Braque. Or am I just broke?

Dear pencil: your infantry of words is banging around in my acoustics. It must be love. It won't harm anything. Just let the highway go where it wants. Proximity is relative. Distance is more like probability, it's a feeling, a premonition, a ball tossed in the air, Cubism in the early 20th Century, sugar in a packet on a linoleum table, an operation being performed quietly in a hospital, hills remedied by strong afternoon light, roadside attractions, the dazzle of a new poem, the smell of a fired gun, a garden hose hemorrhaging water into a bed of jonquils.

Incommunicable

The substance of what I feel is incommunicable, and the more incommunicable it becomes, the more I feel the need to communicate it, communicate the incommunicable. Not because it's incommunicable, that would be too easy, too communicable, but because suffering often occurs in hotels where people sit solitary and glum in the nude, because dread, because vicissitude, because despair will sometimes try to invite the stars into its house but the stars aren't that easily fooled, because leaves without a wall will blow into the playground and brush the sand while fragments of a poem follow sleepers everywhere, especially in their sleep, where the dead reside, and there is no word for that. This is plain. But can we call it a substance? It is, after all, a feeling, and a feeling has no substance. It doesn't slop around in my body like water in a bathtub. It isn't grease, and it isn't the fluid that fills the interior of my eyes, aqueous humor. Not mockingbirds or the mirrors in the palace of Versailles. Nothing I can find in the trunk of a car. Not a black hole. Not a tank of propane shooting flame. Not the embrace of a woman or a man. The feeling of muscle, the feeling of hands on the wheel of a car speeding down the freeway to California, the time spent lingering at a table in a restaurant after the meal is done and the waiter has perfunctorily deposited the check in a leather check presenter, and you've been swept away by a daydream, a fantasy involving Patti Smith and a pirate ship, not that, but all these. The smell in the trunk of a car, the embrace of a woman, the mystery of black holes, the feeling of grease, warm water in a bathtub, mirrors in a palace, the light of chandeliers in the aqueous humor of my eyes.

I feel like a fisherman casting a net into the water hoping something will come up when I drag it back in, silvery bodies flip-flopping on the deck of my boat. But then I've never been fishing, not like that, not on a boat, I don't think I'd like it, I'd probably get sick. And so you see how easy it is to lose one's way when you're trying to define or describe the indescribable, the indefinable, the ineffable and strange.

The ineffable is linked with the sublime, whatever the sublime is. I know the sublime when I experience it. It's an intense feeling, a mixture of awe and fear and terribleness and sometimes, if I'm lucky, ecstasy. It can beautiful, but beauty is only a small part of it. There is something of the eternal in the sublime, the beatific rather than the beautiful, the boundless rather than the bountiful. "Whereas the beautiful is limited, the sublime is limitless, so that the mind in the presence of the sublime, attempting to imagine what it cannot, has pain in the failure but pleasure in contemplating the immensity of the attempt," wrote Immanuel Kant in his *Critique of Pure Reason.*

The immensity of the attempt is incommunicable. And so the argument becomes circular, goes round and round in my head making me dizzier and dizzier until I begin walking like a drunk and the world is a cuticle on the finger of eternity.

The more I try to define it, the slipperier it gets. Knowledge enters the arena gently, seeking to know what can be known and dissolving like sugar in that which is conjectural or wet. Neurons glimmer, exchanging impulses like sailors in a topless bar. Nothing is profane. The sacred imbues everything, every alley, every bar, every wharf and wharf rat and loin. Fascicles are off-putting and faults are fascinating. There is nothing in existence that doesn't ultimately fail the most sensitive equipment, the most supple language, the most agile violinist. It would take a Paganini to get even close to describing the scent of olives in southern Greece in late November, or the flight of a barn swallow just after the sun rises in Shoshoni, Wyoming.

Grief brings us close to the regions of the ineffable. When someone close dies, we feel the majesty of the sublime. And there are times forever after when everything feels just a little absurd, a little silly in how seriously some things are taken.

We pray to furnish our thoughts with the practices and skills of the bear, the great bear of the eastern sky who incarnates trigonometry, and is jeweled and reticent. The glaucous grammar of the chestnut causes buffalo to appear, and hot air balloons and sandwiches. The Renaissance walks in and sits down and begins talking about rope, the history of rope, the ins and outs of rope, the ontology of rope, the economics of rope. The recognition of rope, the unraveling of rope, is renewed, reborn, because rational discussion will do that. But what of the irrational? How do we corral the irrational? The behavior of the irrational is primordial as a typewriter, eccentric as spit.

Axle Shoe arrives on an axle, wearing shoes. Axle Shoe is wearing an oilskin coat and a pair of warm climates. Axle Shoe embraces a beautiful shape. It appears to be a duck, or pustule. It's all too mercurial to communicate with words or lips, and the greater the effort, the more elusive it becomes, until it is mist, and tingles on the skin, and Axle Shoe walks away, rolls away on an axle.

I'm doing a lousy job here because really, the incommunicable is fabulous and strains any attempt at faith or belief. Sometimes the ground cannot be negotiated because it's clay and it's been raining all day and there's no secure footing to be had anywhere. And the river below is raging and dark and turbulent. Which is how it is much of the time in the mind, in my mind, maybe your mind, I don't know, shall we put our minds together and see? I don't know what people mean by that. How do you put your mind together with the minds of other people?

And it occurs to me that we all share the same consciousness, roughly. Very roughly, I know. But if there is a copse of trees in our vision as we travel through Iowa everyone will see the same copse of trees. And that same copse of trees will trigger different memories and feelings about trees, but the facticity of the trees remains the same, they're poplars, and lean west with the wind.

I Have Answers For The Furniture

Shout a blatant sugar to the planet. The map is a drink of mountains and lakes, a tree swarming with pewter terrines and can-openers. Is this Puerto Rico? An armchair is a place for reflection. Chalk stitched together with icicles.

If I go away it's only because I have a pain in my heart that digs assault and I must mull it over in the parking lot with some purpose. The raggedness of hay awakens the stone of misnomer. I return home in time to see a philosophy give birth to a meatball. A sheet of paper lugs a knee across the room and deposits it in a ledger where everything morose and tattooed is given a description and a fork.

The bath salts rest in Hinduism.

Why is there no income for making glass spurs? Are there no glass cowboys? No glass horses?

There is exultation in lipstick. If I whisper equations to a Kentucky still I will win an absent metal by molding microcosms of spearmint and delta. This all takes place in a moccasin. The pamphlet said so. It came in the mail. It glittered. I plunged into it. I took a zoom lens and focused on the buffalo in the plaster. That's when my muscles gave me movement and the museum finally opened.

Buy a banana, my splatter dumpling, I said to no one in particular. Sell yourself. Bristle like an ombudsman on the shore of our understanding. Become a cosmetic for the sorrows of our language, a red engine translating the propane of transcendence into heaves of rapturous induction. I am the grammar that you worry about. I point my writing tools to a tricky purpose and let all hell break loose. I manage by an overflow of everything that the highway puts into emotion. I drive a long thermometer. I have a dog. His name is Hoax. You'll find a gun in the glovebox. It's loaded with truth.

There are moments of twisting a handkerchief into a prayer. Spread your eyes into the landscape and wish for mushrooms. Can I say something? Your éclairs are delicious. Other experiments have revealed that property is a property of property. And has properties.

There is a reason the refrigerator is in the garden. Spirits wear collar studs, you know. I have gleefully selected a very sexual float for tonight's entertainment. I can't tell you the weight of amber but I know how to eat a cookie. It begins with a stimulus and ends with a groan. A singular thought jangles into the paragraph like a rhinoceros dressed in rubies. I've seen this sort of thing before. It is generally the result of a longshoremen strike, but you never know. There might also be a festival later, one with heft and polish, like the stubble of the stratosphere on a good day in July.

The goldfish hit the pavement with everything they've got. It's an effective signal. Our ride is here. It's horizontal in the light, but oval in the shadows, where the enigmas bubble.

Were you expecting something different? An answer? A cure for language? A sack of carefully gathered mushrooms? A large granite rock glistening with moisture in the middle of a rainforest? I was, too, to be honest. But all I found was this Black and Decker drill. It's a 12 volt. Not a 20 volt. But I think it'll get the job done.

What was the job? Does anyone remember?

There is a certain resonance to the banjo that belies the spirit of the grapefruit. At least, that's the kind of spin I like to put on things. It smells of employment.

Are we together on this? Good. Let's get the convulsions going. I have answers for the furniture. Some of them fly, some of them don't. Some just diffuse into push-ups and chrome.

Chrome might look good on this car but the gasoline has no chin. Lightning bolts have been hurled forward to anticipate the unfettered behavior of children. Language returns to its imagery and the imagery returns to its trapeze.

And swings back and forth.

The greatest realities are usually the most obvious, which makes them hard to find. All the morbid disturbances of the intellect are due to coupons.

I have the skull and skill to know a skull is skillful. That a sponge takes on moisture and that a sink is a good place to do the dishes. That the breadboard makes a soft thud when a knife goes quickly through a loaf of bread and that a triangle is different from a delicatessen. That a certain amount of energy is necessary for being and that being is often sticky.

That the furrows in this soil mean that something has been planted. Or is about to be planted. That the dirt has been carefully tilled. That a part of each year's profit is regularly put into farm improvement, so that the hillsides show little or no signs of erosion, and the barns and silos are brightly painted structures of good proportions. That the rain smells good. And the mail arrives in the afternoon. But not always. The war continues, but the herbs help. The most everyday things here speak of things unheard. How do I know the true interpretation of a foghorn? I have a loud metallic ringing in my collarbone.

How The World Became Prose

Field of redemption where flakes whirling at the bottom have been translated into snow. I hope to have reflected a body of water. I hope to have backflipped over my own fluidity. If any of this is true, then the ceremony may begin. The blatant nobility of a bandage floating in a black powder is proof of agitation. Here is my clock fever hardware. Here is my logic and here is its lucid counterpart. Here is a blaze of swimming and here is a string of crack. The leather is almond. The windows are imparted by hoarding protozoans.

I don't know how to feel about that. I could feel thwarted, if that works, which it doesn't, and so I'll simply sit here and throb. Mass is not always a source of category. Sometimes the universe opens its mouth and says something green.

I like proportion. Explosions in deep space. Art and books. Apes. The crackle of twigs.

The soul is the body. The body is the soul. The soul favors pants with stars on them. The body likes to get winks. For this is the House of Sauce. The scrambling ink scolds a whispery claw of tumid junta. We sell splashes of cologne embalmed in quartz. The King of Calories holds a liquid wire and makes a bubo dance. The parameters expand into rims. The rhymes echo this with a pocketbook of tomboy hymns.

The scratches of my toes move to a crust of etiquette. I know. I'm complicated and I don't need to be. But I'm cold and Polynesia is so far from here. Meanwhile, I'm going to fly a yellow shoulder to a warehouse of coats for good measure, and because the emissary from Mars is here. We're aiming to hover over a more fruitful topic for the public tomorrow when the sailors arrive.

This poem deserves a better poet than me but for now I'll have to do. I'm the only one here. I feel massive and wet. That's got to be worth something. Can I squirt you? Savor it, my friend, this opportunity won't come again.

The radar pretends to be a dog. The hiker has a kick for pain. I feel raw. I roll a lung along and manage to break up lawn ornaments. It makes a crackling sound, something that I can hit with a shovel. The flavor of the sauce has nothing to do with pliers, but that doesn't stop us from strangling the turmoil created by mockingbirds. Afterwards comes silence, a soft strain of music explaining the rest of the day as a microphone.

If our charge of alchemy is rain I have little to say to the cogs. They're mostly eggs in my opinion. Picture that. Picture me doing push-ups. Picture a cake baked in forever. The frosting is timeless. The vermilion corresponds to prophecy. The taste is cruel. But the tinfoil is helpful. It has spirit.

My concern has more to do with fulfillment than the murkier ideas of roller skates. Circumference can happen to a snowball. I've seen it. My clutter is a more personal matter. There is nothing in this sentence but raw umber. I promise. If you see something else I didn't put it there. It happened by itself.

A cup of coffee is a moody excess, but what the hell. I don't care for tea. Tea is a bicycle. Coffee is a spaceship. Forget bourbon. That won't take you anywhere. At least that's my version of the story. It began with a voyage through the treetops and ended somewhere on Park Avenue. Jackson Pollock pissing in Peggy Guggenheim's fireplace.

If you want my opinion, poetry is mostly autumn. Then winter comes and turns the world into prose.

Here I Am

Everyone knows how life happens. It's over in a flash. Meanwhile, there's soup and mythology. Light gleaming on the Seine as it roams through Paris. Bombs and machine guns everywhere the U.S. claims empire. A woman in Rome bending over to pick up a beach ball. It's 7:27 p.m. November 14th and I'm sitting on a bed with a tuxedo cat reading *Persian Pony* by Michael McClure, "THE SOFT NEW SOUL / with its capsule of masks / tender and quivering / ascends into matter / and here I am." Fingers, fingernails, laptop, breath. A presence to myself until the absence I try to imagine occurs, and I cease to occur, hopefully before the arctic ice melts, and tens of millions of tons of methane are released into the already stressed and out-of-balance atmosphere. You can't stop extinction. You can't stop habitat loss. But you can focus on the present. The slippery, elusive present. Now it's here, and now it's gone. Here again, gone again.

And so some words walk around trying to be a pineapple. Let's let them. Welcome to smart investing. Welcome to the play of the concertina. Opinions shaved in the rain. Indigo octopi.

Curls, corkscrews, swirls, convolutions. Nothing in life is linear. It's waves and oscillations, embellishments and sleep. It's the weight of a dream, the murmur of wind in the trees. Cool water in a Peruvian jungle. A scratched Parisian angel. The mercurial spur of gossip, broken rain crumpled into gold. Theorems in serums. Sandstone arch in August heat.

We live in a world of flux. We *are* flux. Everything is soaked in phenomenology. Some say it's the singer not the song. I say it's elves riding on the backs of swans. Running over tree roots to avoid puddles. The opinions of a lotus. The force of subtlety in a drug taking effect. Truffles in the Dordogne. The thunder of giants punching eternity with improvisations of water.

Neon chrysanthemums. My bare feet resting on the blue sheep of a white blanket.

Eager fingers on a limestone ledge.

Puff on the seeds to be born into myth. The tongue is soaked in redemption. The stones of Iceland aren't there to glitter in idleness they're a punctuation of convergences, druid moons and Viking purgatories. Lug the pilgrim to the call of the lake. The singer of the song is unknown, but the song itself is exempt from agriculture, and paddles like a swan across a pond of belief.

Belief is a diversion. Agriculture was a mistake. Let us convene instead with the spirits.

Remember the spirits?

The spirits of water, the spirits of lingering, the spirits of sustenance and fever. Rosie and The Originals. Angel Baby.

I have a silver buckle and a hat of chaotic mahogany. Streams of consciousness percolate through the roots. A musician buys diamonds for his guitar. I talk about the problems of aging and mortality with a friend while a foreign melody gets dressed in a person with leprosy. I don't feel like ironing today.

I'm the Rembrandt of butter. Regret is a drawer in my skull. If I see the weirdness of wax drooling down the stick of a candle I want to paint it. There's a momentary pause in time that sometimes reveals itself as a pale morning sun. It's that moment of stillness right after the waitress has cleared and wiped the table and no one has been asked if they want more coffee yet.

Pains have personalities. Some of them emerge in music and some of them enter into Being like 150 pounds of pressure in a tire designed for 125 pounds of pressure. I like the ones that float in the air like astronauts looking down at Planet Earth weeping. The ones I don't like churn in the brain unendingly with no resolution. They're like the entanglement of vines in a blackberry bush, the insane repetitions of traffic around the Arc de Triomphe.

Rumination is a dead end. Time suspended in a cuckoo clock. A stuffed wildcat with its mouth open. Mickey Rourke gazing into a tank of rumble fish.

Think of chiaroscuro as an old man scrounging for change. The soul of white is black. Defining anything is a delicate process.

I've always loved the effects of darkness and light in Rembrandt's paintings. Among my favorites is *The Philosopher in Meditation*. An old man sits by a window through which a golden light diffuses its warmth. To the immediate right is a spiral staircase. And to the right of the staircase an old woman bends over to tend a fire in an open hearth. The philosopher is very calm, hands folded, head tilted slightly forward, as if with a weight of thought, or immersed in reverie. All around is darkness. It's the darkness that makes the light so voluminous and alive.

How does one get to the essence of something? We all want to see the interior of things. Interiority is a constant fascination. Everyone feels deceived on some level. Everyone seeks quiddity. The vital truth of a thing. A chair, a table, a crutch, a napkin.

Though perhaps not its essence so much as its whatness. Its presence as a thing in itself.

Time walks around in my head dropping memories. Some of them are long and delicate, and some of them are abrupt and brutal. A few are dopy. A lot of them are thematic. There is one in which I am crowned King of England and introduced to the dining room staff. I take long steps of introversion in a royal chamber of books and ledgers. Liquids bubble in tubes and flasks. I create a new velocity for the indecisions of purple. Malachite and jasper sparkle around my neck. A jet flies over a Fed Ex Office. I keep trying to write my way out of this world. Autonomy is a prompt solution. I use it carefully. But even that is a mistake. The train is a hymn of steel feeding on its own reverie.

Throw another log into the fire. The poem is ample that never loses its clarity. But you're not going to solve any riddles that way. What you need is a salute to nothingness, the superfluity of leaves blowing around in the wind. I can offer you a place to sprawl and dream. Do you feel the sting of a needle? Don't worry, it's just a spark from the foundry of apples.

The Three Most Exciting Sounds In The World

It is said that the three most exciting sounds in the world are the whistle of a train, an anchor chain, and the sound of an airplane engine. These sounds signal that adventure is coming. I don't have much to add to this, except, perhaps, the sound the air makes near my ear when a crow flies within inches of my head. It's not just a sound, it's a sensation, the sound of the air combined with the feeling of air. The crow flies ahead, makes a quick spin around and drops to the ground. I toss her a peanut and the peanut makes a small clicking sound on the sidewalk. I find that exciting. Though maybe not as exciting as the roar of a Saturn 5 rocket lifting into space at the Kennedy Space Center in Florida.

Or a mollusk daydreaming in the surf.

Or the boil of spaghetti noodles.

Or the little puffy sounds the plastic bottle makes when I squeeze it to get the last of the dishwater soap out of it.

I like to jingle when I walk. I also like the sound of adjectives in a forlorn attic.

I understand a chair by sitting in it. It creaks. It's a modest, peripheral sound, the sound wood makes after it has been occupied in being a chair for many years, and gets old, and has an old man sitting in it.

I feel the great chain of being in my syntax crashing around the soft breast of infinity.

I feel the lift of a powerful emotion. It sounds like the lowing of cattle in a dusty frontier town. There's been a gunfight. The curtains are drawn on the funeral home. The candles are burning aloud.

Death is a private affair. Grace and energy belong to the realm of the highway. A 300 ton telescope pivots atop its base, pointing in the direction of Altair, the brightest star in the southwest. I hear flames screaming like ghosts on the sun. All these sounds are in a tug-of-war with prison where all the sounds are metal and silence and men in thought.

Words are the wings of a multicellular fairies. Each time a word is released into the air a long trail of association follows. We can hear the meaning of this clanking behind a laboratory.

The Burlington Northern goes by at eight. That's when the coffee mugs rattle and the mirror swings back and forth. It's loud. And then it's quiet. And that's when the moon pours its silence on the world.

Other sounds include the rhythms of Bo Diddley, the drills of Black & Decker, the caprices of Niccolò Paganini & the Greek vase John Keats wrote about.

Which sounds like eternity. The pageant never dies because it is forever locked in marble. These marble men and women tease us out of thought in the same way eternity dazzles us out of ourselves and into the stars.

Which sound like the mind blossoming among its nerves.

This is why I wear blue jewelry to rock concerts and alarm clocks to roller rinks. There are few illusions in life as compelling as Pittsburgh. That's what hurts the most, the past rising out of a corner of the mouth. Even the drugstore awning is beaded with rain.

I feel better now. I can inform the moment that we're surrounded by language until it weighs like a voice on my eyes.

Art has no need to justify itself. The same snow falling on James Joyce's Dublin now falls as rain in Seattle. Sounds are impartial. They just happen. Sunlight on a fork, the wobble of a table, a waiter who vanishes into a kitchen, a garage door making weird springy sounds as it is pulled open.

The idea of content still exerts a tyrannical hegemony in the arts, but we're not going to let that happen here, no sir. This is about sound. And yet people continue to use leaf blowers and power-wash their driveways, which are not only sounds, they're shitty sounds. We should get rid of those and replace them with the silence of lions.

The tongue is an engine whose torrents are panoramic. What I cannot find in metaphysics I can find in sawdust. Just give me enough time to sort through the meanings of wood and what it intends to do with the embraces of the sky.

The answer, in a nutshell, is time sleeping behind the barn.

Life is messy, yes. And noisy. But I will use life to convey my sense of concertinas, the joy of narrow streets, and dabs of brown which we hurry along into chiaroscuro as if Rembrandt himself were looking over our shoulder and the world was newly informed by the sound of a brush on canvas moving paint, daubing paint, meditating in paint.

We are airports, you and I. Let our planes land. Let our words fill the air with convoys of joy. And let our sinews expand to embrace the accidental nod of radar in our excursions. Lean into the wind. Toss the seagulls a French fry. They sound hungry.

Coin Of The Realm

I want to eat a coconut on a scarlet capstan. I want to tangle with your conception of seraphim and pull a rumor out of the foundry. I want to drool my neck into the distant sky. I want to quarrel with philosophy in a Romanian kitchen and wear a faster plaster than Kyrgyzstan and button the shirt of a terrible crime. I want to twist these marshy chains of logistical positivism until they break and theorems spill forth in stirrups and paints and we can build a temperament together of heaving ocean waves that will make us pure and large in our understanding of one another.

Damascus is missing its carpenter. Hippopotamus and bear trigger the healing of a Mesopotamian river. I regret the mosaic that is causing the timid filigree to become a Danish padlock. Things could've been different. Things could've been fingers and sleds.

Instead of what? Instead of bugs. Instead of a storage bin stuffed with antlers and books. The pump by the stream that kept breaking until it finally became a pathos that led us to silk and now collects dust in a discarded spinal cord. No one could predict the senses we would evolve in order to get through a night of sleep, or the dreams that leave remnants of crabs and octopus on the walls.

What can explain the strange serendipity of our universe? That's easy: balloons. Would you like to be interested in my cinnabar sun hammer? Avoid knots and rocks when painting the body with magic symbols. I do, after all, have at least one tibia and the chair I pilot has fins of lava, which entitles me to some authority on the subject, the subject that keeps eluding me, I'll let you know as soon as it appears, as soon as I find it, or it finds me.

Ambient light enters a moment of varnish. The soap hammer twists in the mist and a handkerchief whispers an unknown air. I have a crude recollection of laughter, of a rhinoceros staggering through my nerves sparkling with rubies. It's all that frail sweetness sleeping in my fingers like sediment, that deep rich Mississippi silt that makes me feel so cool in the blues. I get drunk on flowers. Diamonds provide me with the foliage that I need for cradling the long gray premonition rattling in my bones, and the rest happens incidentally, in the periphery where the wrestlers meet with the Queen of Taste and bohemians sell trinkets of snow jelly.

Poetry happens around here in these days of late capitalism. I don't know why it does that. But it's like breathing, a natural process involving hills, bends in the river, weather-beaten hoists, clanging trolleys, strong coffee, books in brooks, sermons in stones, clean sheets, preposterous theories, grotesque calliopes and Rebekah Del Rio on YouTube. Why do I even bother to mention this? Essence is an ontological concern but the ties in the closet have something to say about garrulity and the incarnation of spruce.

And longing, there is always longing. As long as there has been life on earth there has been longing. Longing goes long into the caverns of the human heart. Sitka spruce grows chiefly in coastal areas, particularly in British Columbia, as does western hemlock. Colorado blue spruce favors more protected areas, such as gullies and canyons. But longing, longing grows in the Huckleberry Hills northwest of Rye, Colorado, where it becomes an ontological tension foregrounding the awareness of the role our linguistic categories play in the organization of the world into identifiable chunks, things like monuments and elbows, nebulas and spoons.

This position can be regarded as an amplification of Kant's thesis that mental concepts are responsible for determining the nature of reality. Or not. I mean, who knows, right? It's up to you, yeah you. Evolution shapes acceptable solutions, not optimal ones. You can have whole networks of arbitrary complexity, and that's the world.

Experiences are the real coin of the realm. That's where it all goes down, baby. Understanding makes glory of a parcel of rain. The face's natural laziness flows into ecstasies of hair. The swans are the signs of the swans, but desire in the mud is blunt, luxuriously so, and open to the fire, so that its signs are kisses and its consecrations are corks. Help these suggestions evolve into resin, the natural rubbers of a hypothetical shoe. We need to walk. The monograms are already ballads, and the telescope is trained on Saturn.

What was it, anyway, that I wanted to say to Peter Green? I can't remember, but if I could, it would be pillars of glass, tripods and shawls. It's important to enter a room with the assurance of your own authenticity, it's all in the way you hold the cue stick, the way you move to the side when the door opens, or the way you choose to approach the music of Beethoven. You should do it with a baton and a little blue flower, but I could be wrong, it might be time itself hungering for the very space it creates, life is so weird, what propels this boat, is it a battery or just plain anarchy? Here is a list of my demands: hummingbird bean foliage tunes. Button redemption. Knee that sparkles fire. A sack of regrets poured over the side of a bridge in Portugal.

As Water Is In Water

This sauce needs a snowball. I want to sugar the smell of your memory at this stage. To live in this mud is to deny to deepen to believe. Autumn is a heavy liquid that slips into winter. So knotty closer to you that your perfume opens my elevator.

Body embassy to the contrary I'm a reflection of surgical device. I have a franchise on candle wire. Embolden causes bone. Palpate flash of mimosa buttermilk. Troika fire. The quantum key breaking in my shoulder pin causes nothing but magnets.

The writing of the mollusk stings the gravity of convergence. The letter of the air acquires a puddle. I hang in the belief of doing water by swarming an apricot with the blue emissions of my inner pronoun, which shakes in its hooks. The mêlée that is nature has a thematic storm to railroad as the bandits vanish into the hills. The velour of sleep finishes its fingers in the sink.

I have shreds of Rocky Mountain moss and subtle pants. I have a drink to look for lazy sequels to busy days and slip toward catastrophes of grammar. I glean honest calories from stealing my shoes with walking. I write an aromatic sound to hit the flu into orbit. I see angels of rain swing down and flood the tamarind and dry river beds of Texas.

I've embarrassed myself before and I'll do it again. Pile up the forget book. I do ink in a foggy condition of philosophic sap. I have a stem of fabric for the verbal regattas splashing around in my tired brain. Nerves are an accidentally heated species of scrambled cat bath.

I drink a broom of emotion and am swept away. The noun is a hummingbird of nature's leg and is a steady precursor to the expansion of thought. Sawdust marks the place where the marble phenomenon of art hammers at the capharnaüm of life and awakens the sleep of scrap metal. The full articulation of a knuckle points to the flying ray of the windshield.

Catch a sturgeon from a muslin bee ray. It is to finish drinking to build a pleasure. It is to calculate a swampy dying sadness with harmonica twine. A tongue reflected on the virgin ceiling. Percussion of a sneaker's person moment.

Yesterday's scarlet is today's sorbet feeling. Small lashing of a lush clawing that drums the eyes into seeing. Head to the street where the damask whistles meringue. Picnic on Desire Mountain. Embolden the magnolia that it spreads its limbs to the stars and catches the universe in the lap of its theology.

There is nothing sadder than a naked heart. Cotton field in Mississippi heat. The blood of the thrush spelling its pleasures on a blue towel. A sorcerer gnaws a reverie while a man in a tinfoil mask dances with a blowtorch. The cottonmouth is slow but unpredictable.

This sleeve is a natural expansion of what there is to do about a spatula. There is a conception of height that weighs less than a pound and a coin of water immodest as wheels. It makes the lavender move closer. We need the perfume of it to pivot in blurry coalition and pay for the linen. There is a shadow in my hand wiggly as rhubarb and cagey as a sullen homunculus that demands expression in the totem of my caterwaul.

And so it shall be. That one day a depth will rise to the surface and cease to be a depth and be more like a season, an indigenous part of a spectral muskellunge, and leap into the air, and fill the eyes with spectacle. This is called looking, which is a form of seeing, which is a form of perception, which is a form of straining, an effort to be in the world, and take notice of things, and write them down, where they may become guitars or wool. For example, the little Blue Heron is white for its first year until it goes into its breeding season, when the plumage becomes a splotchy blue, and the man in the boat is alone and watchful, and mesmerized by the waves, their rhythm and form, which is an energy moving through the water, as energy moves through the brain, and becomes thought.

And the heron takes flight. The sky is a girl wandering the dead body of the moon. The garden introduces us to the poem of the stars. How much am I assuming here? I have a forehead and a pound of knowledge to trade for a fast car and a getaway plan, which is all I know at the moment, as things fall into place and the car starts, and the engine heats and the words take off for France, which is how I feel, and is both absurd and meaningless, but not so absurd it can't be verified or put in a bag and carried across the border.

Close Shave

A careless hue expresses dyeing. A beach bonfire crumbles in the lung kite. I go frisking past scratching my right leg. The wind is melting in an ebony crate. I'm floating in the weather of a bee making words come together.

Mechanical rain a dragon in my head. Neon money for a ruptured chocolate. I see a solitary radical ball that stuns the value of grease. The expansibility of shoe ash excites the senses like a swamp that jumps into an old New England spoon and begins varnishing oats. The lush spring of a streaming friend powers a tug of antique sugar as it journeys across space and time and so begins another rag with which to solace the groan of coupons burdened with impersonating raspberries in the butter Marie Laurencin spreads across this particular slice of bread.

Of course, when I say particular, I really mean bulky and round. You shouldn't have to think of this as surrealism. It's more like undressing a landscape of sage and smelling the sexuality of noon. Surrealism is for banquets and airports. This is more like lunch with a Q-tip. Anarchic chairs pondered in wild benediction. Fingers on an open G tuning.

It's almost irritating the way shaving lather keeps coming out of the can when I am sure it must be empty. But let's face it. Facial hair is intrinsic to the dominion of ivory. It's not like heresy, not entirely, despite some obvious resemblances. A beard must be worn as a portable device for heroic deeds.

Sometimes sitting in the garage chattering to the shelves about mutiny is the closest I can come to unbending the fizz of lacrosse.

This is where flirtatious 35-year old Charlotte (Laura Prepon) stumbles into the poem, explaining that she has a thing for older men, along with the poetry of Edna St. Vincent Millay.

I tell her she has the wrong poem and open the door to let her out.

My allegorical knee has a carpenter's scratch. I win everything by throwing chocolate at a bureau drawer and selling pineapples to a hoe. I attempt to do the same thing to an authoritarian tattoo. How cannot it not know what it is? Who doesn't like hats? The mission fails miserably and I console myself with ichthyology. I can always try to sputter a few opinions later when the meaning of being reawakens. I'm not going to argue with a menu built around augury.

Holes pause for an eon in a Mediterranean hamburger and the world gets sliced into turf. Nebulous and soft, I sift an obscure hill of dormant tinsel and thereby welcome butter, which is good to me, and simple like sleep. Later, when the proximities loom, luminous insects display their emotions in elevator eyebrows and an aromatic silverware creates a craze for openly indiscriminate music.

Which is the best kind of music. It dreams it's a cupboard with a canine tooth and plates crashed together and is the sage way to the salt beard. I am bitter about frozen agitation. I like the hint of flexibility on the street, the pendulum of tomorrow mingled with loops of iron like the crashing of words in a foundry. Anything else is just structure, a profession brought up on the hind legs of a uterus.

Cartoon Noises In
A Kitchen Sink

Cartoon noises in a kitchen sink. Metal crabs tap-dancing on a China plate. Water running. Two pieces of meat stuck to a spoon. What shall we do with this loaf of elevator? Give it a little baptism. The biology of a feeling, which is soon felt going chromosomal, like a rattlesnake chandelier, or a hymn to the speed bump. Everything in life sooner or later gets to feeling reptilian, or naked, the way a fork throws itself into space.

Words are sticks of meaning soaked in pain.

I stood on the stepladder trying to open a little plastic sack with two little screws in it for the ceiling light mount. It opened of a sudden and the screws went flying. That's how it always is. Just listen to Gregorio Allegri. Or the murmur of doctors focusing on a bone.

Breakfast explains nothing. I can hear the rustle of rain. It's early November. I can see a discarded bikini in the Hall of Mirrors. The pulse of a sawhorse wrapped in cloth. How many pounds are in the ghost of a hammer? I agree with my spine. The Renaissance is mostly about music. Science came later, blistered and stubborn, like language. Except language isn't very scientific. It's more like swans perched on the top of a barn. You can smell it as it gropes for a coat, or enters the parlor goofy as a traffic cone and sits down on a concertina. Oops.

Concentration is the essence of the concertina. The dreams of a halibut are different. The dreams of a halibut resemble the furniture of winter. The reason is obvious as cocoa.

I wouldn't characterize myself as jaunty. I fuss over the issue of subjectivity much of the time, but it leads nowhere testimonial. Nothing like an elephant, whose subjectivity is intellectual, and drinks experience from a waterhole of stillness and quiet, poised as a mosquito on a policeman's arm.

What does it mean to be ambitious? I'm not pleased by the taste of oysters. Never have been. I see a mockingbird on a barbed wire fence and think about the many unseen gears of the escalator. Let your eyes carry this sentence to the end of itself. When you arrive at the end, you will find an abyss. You will see ice and snow. Pain floating in the eyes of a stranger. And that stranger is you.

Or not. Maybe it's just another bend in the river, random and wide and full of reflection.

What do we mean when we speak of a music as "heavy metal?"

Consciousness is a rag of emotion, the crackle of feeling in a ball of thought. Stars in a jug of white lightning, the many doors to perception.

Did you forget to fall in love today? I didn't. I just now fell in love with a Dutch apple pie. Oats are easily made, but the many subtleties of sleep are not so easily described. I would like to further explore the idea of Sam Elliott's mustache. Has it been a boost to his career? Probably. Is it eloquent? Yes. Like a popped balloon, or a star hanging from a thread of music. Crystals sparkling in the arctic night.

My plan throughout life has been to evade too much planning. Stepladders make me angry. They never fold back up right. If I see puddles in a row I think of vertebrae. I think about singing in Montana. Belonging to a choir. I watch the cat as she rolls on the floor, exposing a white fur belly.

Can we bring some words into this sentence that usurp their own progression, that swirl back on themselves and duplicate the invasion of an eggplant? Sure. Why not. I don't want to get too fancy. Let's keep things simple and enjoy a sip of universe. It's calm tonight and my needs are congenial to the employment of various prepositions. Sometimes it takes a powerful drug to walk through a wall. And sometimes all you need is a few prepositions and a warped sense of oligarchy. A jug of conflict and a jar of argument. The heart is an armchair for feelings. So sit back, and let yourself float. The ugliness of time is remedied by oak. And the swans on the barn are quiet as Sam Elliott brushing his hair.

Not Yet Ready To Dye
My Jeans Goodbye

Life is a thematic snowball, a night of beautiful tar. It propagates by banjo. The book finishes its sweater and then achieves the glory of clutter, a bouquet of ignition for the gymnasium tea. The directions die openly in the map of the lake, which is a stork knee-deep in fiat, the ripple of legal tender. The canvas is smashed into color and a landscape emerges like rope from a stampede of specifications.

All of which fit cognition like the bone black sparkle of doing tickets.

We celebrate mass with gravity. The protons go wild. The particles are ticklish but thorough. This bums around from bikini to bikini until I'm nothing but adjectives and hairspray.

I use my fingers for some things and the tonic is fingered by roots.

The heat in the window grows into ginger. My bones are perfect examples of skiing. I'm a caphernaüm of bone, a buttermilk car in which a flock of music finds the velvet of velocity, and elects a pope by the sheer reverie induced by the motion of travel, which is sometimes a hum, sometimes a thumpity-thump-thump. I don't know why I said that because I'm not Catholic, except in my opinions, which are broad and universal, containing barges and almanacs, and the chemistry of speech, which comes to a boil, prayers and cats and revelations, an entire vocabulary of shape and shampoo.

Mass assumes the sting of habit where I wallow in laws that are entirely imaginary. A species of wind spins around in the virginity of my ash, which is in the future, and is not yet a memory, because it hasn't happened yet, I am not yet ash, despite the many urgings of the Neptune Society that come in the mail, and invite me to turn myself into ash at their behest, you don't want your loved ones stuck with you do you, your corpse, which we invite you to turn to ash, it's clean and simple, you'll love our product. I'm sure I will. When the times comes.

Dirty ratatouille you are my organ opened to dare to see it. This wrecking muck belonging to sugar. This loop propelling itself across the sentence. I'm a muscle for the puddle of night. I aim to feel everything I can feel, including the morning fog and the hair of the hummingbird.

The Danish body must be gentle. The drive through Copenhagen suggests frolic. But I ask you: is this how to obtain raspberries? I was told to whirl around in the cabbage while opening a foundry and splashing it with warmth and light. I was told it would be a solution. I was told not to linger. I was told to swirl open a drawer in the moon that is filled with spoons and jiggle it. I did this for some time. It made a sound like escalators breakdancing in an engagement ring.

People often ask if own a comb. I answer no, but I do have a brush. Then why don't you use it, they ask. And I shoot them.

I know why my pants are not a home. There is a snow bee that I support with all my hammers and it needs a book to find its money. The easel gets me started and then I find consonants for the sadness of all revolt and dip it in vowels. That makes it earth.

I'm warm in the legs with a kit to do morning. I hide myself from myself in a bed where sleep happens. When I get up the troika is beautiful. Being is what it is. A mind trapped in its ideas of tomorrow and trying to get away with flamenco. Shoot the month with pineapple and forge yourself. The weight of our dying makes it that reason must make fragments for the mouth to say.

Paper overflowing with Wednesday. The harpsichord is imaginary, a perfect instrument for becoming noble and tolerant of the annoyances of life, many of which are voices on the bus, and a few of which occur in art museums, assuming the form of limousines, hard black bodies of inhabited electricity. The paintings go on doing what paintings do, presenting illusions, representing life, flowers, senses, mountains and rain, the kind of things that excite you when you're dreaming.

What do you do with something imagined in your mind? Do you consider it an imbuement or a flavor? I consider the distant hips of the swans when they are at sea. I refuse to eat the hippopotamus. I clang like a bell. I shout at the books to get off of their shelves and do something about the puppets.

The storm slips over the elephants in a turbulent mass of mist and rain. This, too, becomes a lip.

Sling

Twenty-one days after dislocating my shoulder it still hurts. It heals very slow-ly. My body is old. My cells are probably wondering why they are being coaxed to repair damaged membrane. I'm too old to hunt for mastodon. It was my mission, as it is with all living things, to reproduce offspring. I didn't do that. I chose to make art instead. Whether this was of service to the future of human-ity that is for others to say, if they're still around. Things appear a little dicey. And my shoulder still hurts.

I was carrying a new laptop into the bedroom when Athena, our cat, can-nonballed between my legs, causing me to lose my balance and fall to the floor. I concentrated my attention on protecting the laptop and preventing it from dropping from my hand but did so at the peril of my right arm for which I had not prepared to catch my fall. I came down hard on it and felt the acromion (the bony tip of the scapula) separate from the clavicle. I could not move my arm. It had become a tree limb. The pain was excruciating. I went to the top of the bookshelf to get a spiral notebook in which the phone number to Rober-ta's bakery could be found. I thumbed through it as rapidly as I could, called Roberta, and within minutes she came home and drove me to the emergency room. Meanwhile, I'd managed to maneuver the arm back into place. We filled out a brief form and waiting in the lobby of the emergency room. The pain had subsided considerably but was still a shrill presence in my shoulder. A large man complained of bronchitis. He coughed continually. The receptionist, a middle-aged woman with long dark hair, asked if he could cover his mouth when he coughed. Indignant, he went outside.

X-rays were made and the doctor, an amiable, energetic man a few years younger than me, examined the X-rays and did not see anything fractured or damaged but did notice some arthritis. That made sense. My shoulder fre-quently hurts when I sit at the desktop computer moving a mouse around. I was given a sling made of some sort of silky material with a number of belts and fasteners and a pouch for my arm. I have to take it off to shower and eat dinner and we have a difficult time figuring out how to get it back on. It's a complicated device. When I have it on, I'm forced to do everything with my left arm, including signing things like credit card slips, which come out very badly. My name is barely recognizable.

Shampooing my hair is difficult. I can't lift my right arm, even without the sling. It's amazing how awkward my left hand is. What has it been doing all my life, just hanging at my side?

Well, yeah, pretty much.

It's like an understudy who never really expected to take over a part due to an emergency. None of the lines or choreography have been properly learned. Everything feels clumsy and dumb.

My right arm really likes being in a sling doing nothing while my left arm does all the work, handling cutlery, brushing my teeth, taking the garbage out, scooping the litter box, moving furniture, turning the radio on and off, opening cupboards and doors, wiping the table, brushing my hair.

My left arm is thinking of starting a union. It is, after all, my left arm, not my right arm, which has strong convictions and delusions of grandeur. My left arm believes in collective bargaining, free healthcare and Dunkin' Donuts. My right arm believes in free market capitalism, private property, and the right to bear arms. I give both arms a big hand.

My left arm is getting a little better at doing things. It sparkles with radius. It wants to increase its reach. I try teaching it how to bioluminesce like an octopus and frighten people. My right arm is getting jealous but prefers lying in the hammock that is my sling. My left arm is happy doing things. But it is still clumsy. I promise it a future of exoticism when my right arm returns to full activity. I will let it be a bayou, an arm of water that goes astray and languishes in cypress gloom, a world of orchids and Cajun jumbo. And really, the two arms work out pretty well together when I need to squeeze something like an accordion or an orthopedist. Chop wood. Carry water. Dance on a keyboard. Two arms, up in arms, armed with bravado and fingers.

Sleep Is The Other Side Of Life

Thought hefts impulse into courtesies where it might get sweaty in entreaty. Presently shovels share it. The garage is cold and smells of simulacrum. I moo toward space meaning bulbs that they burn brighter and creepiness from another planet has a door. This is that door.

It opens by chortle. Camaraderie leans against our experiments. The fugue is mostly furniture. The imagery of heaven rubs the pump until it brings up the water we thought belonged to the dead. The bubbles abandon necessity under the sentence of insoluble harmonicas.

Slap as doctrine waddle. Except New Jersey. A ramble baffles the savor of what I don't know, which is rubber, and a wide black shout. The cloud is suitably pineapple. Greenery exemplifies it like retail.

Those shoes are fast. Jellyfish don't have eyes but grace is literal when it varies. My car is a tap of nerve. I verify this form of despair by shopping and shaking little sacks of cough. It's easier to accept mutation than tailgating because the branches wiggle and sway like contact lenses.

There is a broken pool in which I like to swim. Dreams elude their own meaning. In the nude the body is grotesquely tabulated by the sea, a susurrus of waves existing outside of time, slipping in and out of the empirical world as if the words themselves ran out of a lyric, then ran back in to say something about those two little girls running toward the horizon. There are bird noises everywhere, but this is cinnamon, a crack at cinnamon, a simulation of cinnamon, not a blue supergiant in the Pleiades helping fusion to function like a fruit dish. Many of our former and current preoccupations could be oysters, a blue balloon full of helium, or drug paraphernalia hanging from a doorknob and the evening sun going down.

I say 'could be,' yes, but the fingers are obtained by age. You just grow into them, you know? Like a nostalgia visited in sunlight. Maturity diffuses into the hands and the veins and nails and stains appear to go all Rembrandt in contemplation. A burst pipe is thrilling blobs out of its umpteenth roll. And here it is Friday and all the alerts are implications of fish, the mind understanding its desires at last, even though the whole world is burning, and images form without regard to the laws of gravity.

The body dyes in darkness. The tendril exceeds its convenience. I get dressed once I get up and prepare for the thorns of day. The tar is in top shape. My pearls are floundering among the shoulders of a light turned soft with alphabets of fog.

Imagine the forehead of God. Imagine the blood circulating in the veins of a snowman. It's a tale told by a parrot in a paregoric attic of hungry stars and graveyard repose. The pungency we espouse is washed by tears. It all melts in the end and puddles in the street smell of omen.

The garden understates eternity. Shake it harder if it dribbles. Sometimes the early morning will stroll through a brain in a roll of oars. I'm doing a dimension that would permit hundreds of empty eyes to fill with bluestone. And then see Chappaquiddick porn.

This seems to work and then I realize that falling is laughing and respectable in its own way. It all depends on dust. Glass orchids gleaming like shins in a high school gym. There is a spot of grease on the ceiling how did it get there jump right ahead and get there get it down get it up get it going make it squirt. Sleep is the other side of life.

The Night Of The
Detached Embalmers

The expensive splash lights up a helicopter combing a beautiful bell that hangs from a black cloud of musical shirtsleeves. The world is swimming in its own narration. It's all I can do to rub myself in the shower and remember to pay my hair for the nice job it's doing. Sight slips through a showcase and falls on a country of knots, each knot hard as a sorbet in a lassitude of clocks. We found the water behind this utterance to be foolishly candid but sincere in its spare time. It was orange like my organs and made hormones look glazed like a glee club. The padlock made our feelings fall down. There was TV sausage everywhere and mud and conflagrations of cosmic pepper somersaulting in our mouths. We have silver mouths, like the gypsies, and when morning comes we turn mild as overalls in a sandpaper vagina. Some of these images may not entirely work, but I personally guarantee that the bank will honor this check I'm writing because it's sociable and scratchy, the way banks like it. Winter was stubbornly oceanic this year which means summer will be a dry rough carpet of ill-conceived sitcom sketches, some of them actual universes, including all the nails and bones of court stenography, which I am even now getting ready to fly like a kite above the world in order to catch the lightning of Melville's unwritten novels. Which I just now made up, and filled with sugar bowls and knobs, to make the ruby jelly of the turpentine beans undertake the full meaning of velvet, which is an apparatus for the fingers, as the imagery of mist was too late for the party, and so we used potato chips instead.

The Idea Of Being Water

If the wall swells I can feel it in the bacteria of life. I feel curiously explored by my own heart. A land of shadows squeezes out of the subtleties of the paragraph, snaps and airplanes, currents, drafts, tossing waves. The dream of life explains itself as a pulp, a soft moist mass of desire and drugstore awnings. Sometimes a little supposition is bent toward the howling of an animal in the darkness, followed by the smell of coffee in the morning, the merry ubiquities of birdsong, elephants, redwood, rolls of paper towels, apparitions still lingering in the brain.

Here, there, and everywhere in a Cupertino garage.

Life is a journey. Or so they say. I'd call it an odyssey. It's more like an odyssey. Swords and robes and tents on the Aegean, the sun of a new day striking on the ploughlands, rising out of the quiet water and the deep steam of the ocean to climb the sky, rung by rung, until the blue air is filled with light, and the oats sway in the wind, and the horses of wisdom stare at George Clooney as George Clooney stares back at them and a car at the bottom of the hill explodes.

Fuck, I'm tired of this imagery, filling the air with an arbitrary dream, I want a drill to fix the drywall, gently screw those screws in, get the heads nicely flush with the surface, then swab on some mud, add some tape, swab some more mud, and that's how it's done, how a hole in the wall is smoothed, integrated into the wall at large.

We still have imagery now that the hole is whole again.

The hole is a symbol of something.

Chimeras? Space probes? Yoga?

I hear the cat scratching at the wall. The painter withdraws from the canvas, squints his eyes, ponders it, then returns to add a little more yellow. Buffalo roam the hills. Thoughts strain to rupture the brain with a new epiphany. The paint is thick and yellow and creates a little light for Rembrandt's philosopher, there in the window, I don't know what to call that yellow, let's call it

Rembrandt yellow, philosopher yellow, the yellow of thought which is a quiet yellow, the yellow of acceptance, the yellow of endurance, the yellow of lilacs, the yellow of Amsterdam and breakfast and swirls of spirit.

There was a strong smell of bacon on 4th Avenue West today. That must mean something. I think it means bacon. Or that which is in itself and is conceived through itself and may be distinguished by its odor, which is penetrating, and is an epiphenomenon of morning activity, in this case breakfast, which is a contingency of bodies coming together.

Or spirit, which floats in the air, and is a thing of the air, and a motion of the mind, a thing that appears to the intellect, or intuition, and has a charm and a disposition.

The ghost of a pig, for example.

Or a winery on the Kitsap peninsula.

Aromas of rose petals, nutmeg and dark chocolate. Black licorice, plum, and a hint of sage. The world is a tapestry of energy concentrations. Much of it enters through the nose, which is a domain of nerves, receptors within the mucosa of the nasal cavity. The odor registers on the brain and becomes a search for understanding, a yearning, a pair of arms, and embraces immanence, the grand nature of the universe itself. And the universe loves this sort of thing. Don't agree? Fine. Go ask the universe.

The universe says yes, I will marry you. But you must be willing to kiss my stars, and crawl on the ground with your sisters and brothers the crocodile, and howl like a wolf in the middle of the night, and alarm the neighbors with the sudden reality of themselves, which Artaud called The Theatre of Cruelty.

The gist being that if you keep flapping those lips something eventually jars loose and reveals the blue hand of the screaming zebra.

The words in the hips of experience. The experience of air, of water, of fire and earth. The experience of banks. The experience of rungs on a ladder and gauze and waterfall and wax.

Especially wax.

The dribble of it, the wick of it, the fragrance of it. I want to be that. I want be something other than what I am. I want to be mercy and protein.

A comet. An icy lucidity. An open field. Invent new genres of being, a new sky of essences. To imagine oneself as being in the world, of living in the world, untangle phenomena and get at the bottom of things. The source. To emerge into the knowledge that my thoughts and the thoughts of others are woven into a single fabric of being. Life is the first certainty that life is inexplicable, that the permanent mobility of each minute diffuses into mist when it's falling from a rock. That the absence of a temperature is the absence of a word. That the substance of the world can only determine a form and not fulfill the binoculars of France.

Roughly speaking: objects are chopsticks.

I don't want innocence. Innocence is circular and sterile. I want a fan of lightning, silhouettes of gingko, and a neck of fable.

I want to be a river, a long moving magnitude of catfish and mud. I like the idea of being water. I like the idea of being an idea. I like the idea of being. I like the idea of flowing, meandering, divagation, opening my mouth and emptying into an ocean.

I want take a midnight bath and cruise its paraphernalia of tongues. I want to pull a silence from the other side of night and fill it with words. Make (as they say) something up. For the hell of it. For the fun of it. For the it of it.

There is a sky at the bottom of the ocean. It is made of churchyards and clouds. One day it will rise to the surface and assume its proper place high above the ground. It will spill its bags of moonlight. It will hang scriptures of lighting from the ribs of the void. It will obscure nothing, it will oppose nothing. It will reveal everything, then drop as rain and crawl back to the hard embrace of the ocean.

I will wait for you at the end of this sentence and show you that the ocean was really just a sink. And tear it out and give it to you in the form of a swan.

Feed it your wounds. It will enter you as an oscillating light. And when you fill a glass of water late at night, you may give it the freedom it craves, and I promise you, it won't end there.

The Hummingbird Of Gerunds

We harvest rubies in darkness, study our desires when inflammation is needed. Tongue shards make it soft. Percussion suggests the trumpets are burning, and the seismograph is fondled. Frog Woman shoots lightning at the void. I rub the faucets for fog. The velvet air puts itself into a pair of roasting pants and sifts the rafters for semantic assemblies of osteopathic snow. Thematic octane is the pell-mell of things. Alpine weather provided with bones and iron thinking.

Fold it pop pop. The box flirtation is also broke. Fingered incarnated fingerboard lumps. Subversive verse feelings on the finger of wavy nuts. I hold the world in my mouth. Energy fences of abandoned horses that arouse the luminous hills.

Raw brown arena supported by exultations of ginger. I feel the cosmetic drool of a shaken raft let's elect a hibiscus to be the queen of spring and eat a bag of onions. Supply me with an awning of squirting sherbet. I feel a storm is coming. I can see it in your eyes.

Here is an enigmatic Renaissance food dagger. It breathes with plausibility. It takes swirls of falling geometry to place a whistle on the snows of Pluto, but this is no whistle, this is a trickled ambience of pancake philosophy. Some things make better sense as a flutter of vanity. This is why I spend time with a handful of electrical indecisions while mechanical basement emotions crash into an agitated cauliflower chair. I come out shooting rays of sunshine and slide on a reverie of pure immodesty for the sheer hilarity of discovering the insistence of ice.

Afterwards, my life combs itself with a sea cruise.

I support alpine art with old offices. I wear hemoglobin to picnics and swoon in gnarled carpentries overflowing with correlatives. The roots rain mountains and the mountains rain roots. The gymnasium bathtub package certifies our sequoias. The benevolence of membranes respond to the nails and I hum with raw assumptions about the gloom of pottery.

The world is about anything, really, including itself and volleyball. I have fat medium teeth. The knife thinks it balances my arm. An embassy of fog makes brown look spread into lutes, and the colors that engulf the sewing of genitals reaffirms the complaints of the helicopter warehouse. The clocks gush their own shapes of time. The almanac rises into sorbet.

Thus, I lend my lungs to dropping off rhapsodies at the center for radical ear pants.

Plastic has strength for manufacturing attention, but not the rags of shadow that adorned the cast of Hamlet one day and then went their merry way into the open plains.

Correspondence is my hiking carpet and is opposite the meaning of spit. I undecidedly play at paradise. Matter is my tray of geometry, the great aromatic highway of undisclosed destinations. Plow, noodle, plow, for the dawn of astronomy is artless in its shirt of unsewn stars. Palpate this, my friend, and tell me it's not a capstan. This is bitter, but smoky like wood. I feel the mass of a nuclear face move over the prairie like a question.

But did I tell you? I have harpsichord work tomorrow. The dazzling hair of a placental rapture offers a perspective we can use later for the eggnog. Meanwhile, it's time to power up the forest thermostat and give the lawn the support of some crocodilian arteries. That's how flaky our eyes feel.

If I have the right materials I think I can complete what the ice started. My tongue is a moment of butter. Frenetic ink games and beauty with ears on purpose. I don't worry about the sorbet but I do worry that the birth of meaning will occur without me. I can taste the embarrassment of meat.

Cloud Tooth says his distress is drooling. Go, let the boiling south go swarming around its swamps, its orchids and keys. The horizon's benevolent kettle whistles on the stove of the turbulent sea. The distance undresses and whispers to the crickets. Our old Alpine silverware has been rolled into scorpions. We ask for a ticket to Australia and climb into our opinions of form.

Immense lightning and the memory of absence. The goodwill of the north with hills in the middle. The effulgent oil of sleep balanced in the understanding of wind. To lift the solitary is to grow satiated with poles. The hummingbird of gerunds is even now digging out its wings.

Proof

My emotions are wet and powerful. Do you need proof? The kettle spouts declarations of steam. The headland in the distance is fondled by euphorias of air. Indications suggest that there is a form of energy called hands that insist on sensation by pounding piano keys.

The result is sisters having a quiet drink.

Most of the time I don't know what to think.

They say the proof is in the pudding. But what proof do we have of pudding? Who is putting pudding forward as a matter of fact? Is pudding reliable?

Pudding is not reliable. But it is pudding. Pudding is pudding. It's not Jello and it's not steak.

God doesn't require proof. God is a word. God is the word. Take your pick.

One way or another, one day you will encounter pudding. It may be in a bowl. It will probably be in a bowl. One day you will encounter a bowl. And the bowl may have pudding in it. And the bowl may not have pudding in it. The bowl may have stew in it, or tomato juice, or bouillabaisse, or chowder, or macaroni, or a beautiful storm clearing its throat.

You may see your face in a broth. You may see both a broth and your face. If you see your face don't bother the broth. It's not your face. It's broth.

Traffic, meanwhile, was good today. It was surprising. The sun was out, although the humidity was high, 79%. It's that time of year (late March) when you don't know whether to leave the window up for warmth, or down because it's too warm. I did have to turn the heater on briefly, but mostly because the windows were fogged up. It didn't take long. I turned the heater off. And suddenly I realized: the trees are loaded with blossom and the air feels benign. Proof of spring.

Dinner will be good. Dinner will be rigatoni, which comes from Italian *rigatooni*, plural of *rigato*, past participle of *rigare*, "to draw a line, to make fluting," from *riga*, "line; something cut out." The noodles are, indeed, fluted.

Proof remained intuitive for two thousand years until Aristotle, eating a bowl of rigatoni, happened on the three proofs known as ethos, logos, and pathos. Ethos are the motivating beliefs and values that characterize a community, logos is the logic behind an argument, and pathos are my feelings about it, which are nervous and centrifugal, spinning outward, radial and panoramic, some you can see at a distance, curling into the sky like smoke, or sparks, others are more like vertebrae, causing the sentence to stand upright and nibble on leaves or study alchemy in a dark basement laboratory, flasks of liquids bubbling, some with bluish tints, some that are crimson and hectic with music.

Consider a stone being whirled round on a string: does a daguerreotype of Emily Dickinson matter to you as much as stepping out of a spacecraft into the zero gravity of space? If so, then I recommend jewelry by Victoire de Castellane, and in particular her Baudelairian extravaganza Fleurs d'Excès, which consists of ten floral jewels, each representing a woman in the ecstatic embrace of a different drug.

Drive Carefully

Pounce shout. Attract a trickle. Whispers stellar as cloud bulbs ride the proximity van with anarchic feathers agape. I want your attention. Please exchange your circle for a rocket.

Injuries are rarely discriminating. Run for your milk and use tattoos for running the machinery of the arm. Height is its own hook. Doing a glow amplifies the sanctity of push-ups. Sit beside the empty brown compliment brushing a milieu of animal.

It will whistle you. You must speculate on something. Tin ears are good for painting but questionable for pink shirts. Pink is not a necessity so much as a lingering idea of argyle. The world is only as large as its wheels and most solvents are flammable and create fire and stampeding jellyfish.

If I tell you something vital will you explode it into something wonderful? Salvation is for pilgrims. Phenomena is for string. I like to find wrinkles in bronze. That's why all my pencils are blue and lean every which way in simple modesty.

Algebra generates seaweed aloud. Nothing is quiet in Portugal. Examine the stew. Even the fish are walking. Think of me as an embryonic explosion of arms wading in a pool of words.

Drive carefully.

Drifting Into Infinity

I like sifting things, sifting through things, sifting. The sensation is soft, like buttoning a shirt. Emotions are huge and often confused. Try sifting that. But sift for what? What are we sifting for? I think I just like the sound it makes. Thoughts don't make sounds. Not unless we push them into our breath and shape them with our tongues and lips into carts and cargo, nets and knots, manifests and marlinspikes. Open sea. Lingua franca. Tentacles studded with photophores.

And as it is there, laying about, occupying podiums and gym floors to do this work, so the words break through to their sense. Phonetic elements and stress have varying psychological values, things like philosophy and heartache. This makes language show a number of rod-shaped particles of a brilliantly luminous matter embedded throughout the very delicate mass, candles at tables of people eating, bioluminescence in deep sunless seas. Camaraderie. Prom dress. The curious play of color after cephalopods are dead.

I am reminded of the sound that sugar makes when it is poured from a sack into a bowl or jar. It's a faint whisper. It's that sound. That whisper. Sugar.

Soft, like the feeling of a spider's legs on the skin of your hand.

Ants carrying grains of sugar into a hole.

Hilary Hahn performing Paganini's Caprice 24. The part where her fingers pluck the string. The bow isn't used. It's amazing. Soft swells in night's shadows.

Or daylight's maniacal glitter.

The world has always had a geometry, and sometimes we can hear it echoing in the abyss or the wings of flamencos in the swamps of the Yucatan peninsula. It's a simple geometry of oblongs and skulls, turtles and old moldy mattresses leaning on sad brick walls.

These things can be a dragon to mathematics and leave us with meaning. Wounds that whistle, wounds shooting hot sulfurous gases. Sad women who win the fat cold of Viennese furniture and find themselves face to face with pigment. Here comes Gypsum Face with his bottle of lightning soy sauce, theatre bandages and swirls of speedy stimulus. I know it has something to do with aluminum. Hamlet is somehow involved, and unfettered absorption.

Slapping people is an intriguing device but ultimately vain and universally discourteous. The cement just crackles. We continue to work and gratify ourselves with prophecies. There are those who say the motivations are broken and radiate Uruguay. This could be a plug, a form of outlet or philodendron. The spouts say the water is coming. The doors announce walls, the walls announce doors. The sun burns and burns and the work assumes new meanings, although some of us declare it to be nothing but a hollow blatant hill lugging and sliding with shoulders. I'm slow to say it, but building a nose is huge.

Which brings me back to sifting, to the soft filtration of the exterior into the interior, the confusions of the brain sloshed back and forth until something sparkles and rises to the surface like a bubble of description, the slop of representation, a homunculus painting the world in the brain, God and Adam on the ceiling of your skull, experience murmured with ripples and waves, the clay of rumination, which is a process, an intention similar to the drift of jellyfish, the play of resurrection, ambitions fondled amid the candles of Stuttgart.

Because really, who can take it all in at once? Imagine everything out there on the other side of your skin, your eyes and ears, your glands and agitations, all of it the whole universe flooding into you raw and unpasteurized. You could produce some pretty hot rock with that situation. You could flood your head with the Flathead National Forest and go medical and backward into the uproar of yourself. Wander alleys of Goth Pop spidery swagger spewing blaring melisma.

The world is a mess. It's chaos out there. Nobody can even get the news straight. What's real and what's fake, what's made up and what's actual, what's solid and what's treacherous.

I need time to digest things. Figure things out. Try to find answers. Unravel enigmas. It's navigation, is what it is. Making a map of your life. Identifying coasts and rivers, swamps and mountains, the whole geography of emotion, which is an ocean of its own, a deep full of strange luminosities, mouths and goggly eyes and long spindly antennae. Because there are worlds within worlds and the pinnacle of night is midnight, which is the crossing of an equator, traveling from one sphere to another, from the clarities of day to the soft obscurities of night. From the blunt morning telephone to the pillow where the head lies drifting into infinity.

Blackwork

I think we can all agree that sleep is a kind of knitting. Kiss the descent and watch the sparkle of knives. Flu sweat in the kitchen. Sullen troikas that fill the arena of the eye without causing conversation. These are phenomena that echo in prose with the tenacity of air-raid ulcers.

Inflammation is undoubtedly a more visible kind of achievement. One might infer here a gastric juice specially organized for life. Thinking is an activity but let's not exaggerate it with biology. A buckle of smoke completes the career of northern pans simmering in the ironworks of the mind, but it does so without a special diet. Instead, it uses E minor like a lullaby to a dying friend. The exultation of a tiger roars out of the night of science. We are at the mercy of our own understanding. A storm of the mind that wanders the head in a country of eyes.

The welder is hidden by sparks. The King of Oil recedes into the fog.

Carpentry causes the clocks to wander out of time and the carrot crickets are lazy as we pilot the birth of the sea. It is immense to speak and play at lavender. It is musical to walk the tarmac with a silver mustache. Amusing and graceful to help the cats catch fish on the opposite shore.

Does any of this shake the gum of vivacity? Do politics stick to the mouth? Is the moon a rock?

Yes, yes, and no. The moon is neither a rock nor a thing of rats and policemen. The moon is the moon. The moon is a torpor of dough on the glowing shore of a dangerous awakening. If the moon hits your eye like a big pizza pie, that's amore. If it does not, that is the reverse feeling hardened in the discipline of science.

Meaning particles are vibrations in the subatomic world. This makes the moon appear very large when it is standing next to you in the subway. For example, country music can manifest itself in a confusion of intentions depending on which way the wind is blowing, or the stars might be leaning down to kiss the mountain-tops at the very moment Mister Love stumbles out of the bar.

Every day I hammer at the daily material of canvases and time and the nuclei of Wyoming in order to make sense of the cathedral gently clawing at the door.

There is beauty and satisfaction when the roots of our memories are painted with chaos.

I crave a solitary puddle. If it creases, I am amazed. If it does not, it does not. The iron is only as good as its objective, which may go untreated until there is a general insurgency of older fowl.

But must I apologize? Adaptation is always a special concentration of effort. I have in my pocket a little context that will flex itself for the regatta pen. At the time of tunes and faucets the plumber swarms with a blue shirt, and this makes me certain that the poultry would like their freedom like anyone else. Vision bursts from the queen as she fills her clothes with meanings. "My hip is not a flying tiger but a casserole of bone," she shouts. The affairs of the gnarled are always a tale of knives.

It's an elastic and exquisite skill to make pills of exultation. Boil the whispers floating at the border of Iran and Afghanistan and the breath of a rogue will offer you the appearance of a bandaged face. This will further confirm that E-minor is a map of agitation combed with a winter horizon. The roots of this language go deep into the woods of Persia, where cinnabar and kiosk are joined by needle and thread.

Rumi once said "silence is the language of God, everything else is a poor translation."

This is thunderously true. Not even a translation. It is, in the place of silence, the fall of snow on the mountains of Afghanistan. The frayed edge of a neglected carpet, a drop of water on a mahogany table. And in the place of signs and omens, a hum in the bones, a woman with a golden voice, the weight of paradise in the tongue of a mute. We stand in a foundry trembling with a redeeming love, and wait for the metal to congeal into words.

There is a strange velocity in wishing for a road and then seeing that road and getting on that road and going wherever that road goes.

Be a windshield and shovel your thoughts into words. Make a sausage of words that is tenable to float in a paragraph of hands and pocket money. Pile the light against the sorbet. Thinking will harness these thoughts to a road in the woods and ride them into the moonlight like a team of mattresses.

Philosophy means living among ice and high mountains. It's different than, say, a quilt or a moment of road rage. It is here that our carriage acquires new meaning as a roller skate.

How much truth does a spirit dare to endure? Cemetery plot on a marble knee. Glorious thunderstorms in a swimming pool of the heart. A clock for translating time into mirrors. Green rake for the stomach of night. Agile toes on a crazy shore.

And This?

The autumn wasp acts as an airborne filigree, a mechanical pedestrian dressed in seaweed. What this tells us about cheese is sticky. Gold holds the soft roots of tonality, the élan that draws species into cabbage and bulldogs.

And this?

This is an aggression, a rubric of plumbing that comes to give us musk and music. Who knows this will place it where it belongs. I'm going to guess Colorado. The unknown sugar of life approves an arena of eggs and so opens the eye of the mountain. It makes sense. The humidity has muscle. It will lower the sky into our hearts where enough fog still lingers to climb into our pennies and exert a little sturgeon on our nerves.

Denver, meanwhile, sparkles at the base of the Rockies and chews the sun like a bas-relief on the side of a leavened dialogue.

With China.

Create an honest mimosa, my friend, and yesterday will sting on Wednesday. For this, it is necessary to overflow reality and steal the grimace of dark matter. The stars wear rubies. But music creates a space for scorpions and books.

Polar man kisses his girlfriend in the Hall of Coleslaw. The kiss is full of blood, as one might expect, considering the nature of grout and the difficulties of dark energy in an itchy sweater. We whistle at the Door of Light and put things in perspective when the hills shout their trees out of the ground. Structure is a rocking motion aroused by words. We pull ourselves into writing. We use binoculars. We use language and diesel. We tell timeless stories of regret and ejaculation. We foster the enigma of creation by waving fragments of gravity at a yo-yo. We deposit words in a greasy paragraph and participate in holes. Winning an organ is a cuddly banana if you can find suitable employment for it in a bubble bath. We have ears for the canary kit, but no nose for the analysis of exclusion. If you would like a sample of assimilation, intimate the unction of a buzzard in a tiny white felony. Please include your phone number, fallibilities, and a crystalline substance. You can find yourself in the auction over there by the barn. Look for the red wheelbarrow. The structure of cosmic voids is embedded in the silences of dirt. Ask for Worm.

Tired of shaving? Would you like a catastrophe to go with your coffee?

Here. Have a sheaf of sauerkraut for a wilder life of Friday enticements and a raw unsettling sandwich of Bavarian airplanes. The beverage of Polynesian bricks has arrived and it's already sparkling. We've put some thoughts on paper, potato catapults, broomstick bubbles, a dictionary of shivering sapphires and a junkyard goose, a sad wad of deduction, broken gods of cause and effect, close shaves with Toupee the Tornado and three hundred cathedrals flooded with infinity. The clouds float by beneath our feet. Listen. They sound swollen, like limousines with tinted windows and a gargantuan pulse. The hummingbird gum is cold with blinking. But the shore is a clean equation. Shake it little baby, shake it like a willow tree.

Pearls glitter in the membrane of a necktie as a pendulum swings back and forth in the package by the door, accompanied by a late night song. Think of this as a sample of cognition, the pollination of an idea of cheese by an errant quadrilateral. Not so much salt as a cardiovascular igloo immersed in thumps. How does one satisfy a craving like this? The propositional sign is a fact. The wall searches for an apricot, but cannot be expressed as a proposition unless it's coated with primer and then lightly sanded. A name has meaning only in the context of a delicatessen, or shoe store. We are tangled in one another's arena. The espadrille is tinted with the dreams of walking. Shadows sleep in abstraction. A layer of languorous dress floats in a kind of swimming pool in which a moss accomplishes an idea of birth. All this makes me feel a little extraordinary, like someone who writes with immoderation and memory sauce.

Can you blame me? The hours are in knots and the foundry caresses a moon overflowing with mist. I feel the wings of a dragon begin to lift the body of a paragraph above a bohemian melody. How to describe such feeling? With tourniquets and paper.

With sapphires and pipes. With toads and heat. With foliage and undulation. With anything that can become an actuality of muslin or oak and thoughts adrift in their own birth and development. If the paragraph is an embryo then Baudelaire is a gynecologist.

Said the postman just as he was leaving. The parcel has an electric mustache. This sometimes happens in the post. The mail begins as a treasure of possibility and commerce and ends as a badge of dusty resignation.

All things monstrous are eventually addressed as Mr. and Mrs. Outcome. The narrative is pushed forward by wildlife, elephants and cactus and squirrels. The cactus do most of the work. They use a form of telekinesis called needling. They needle and needle until something moves.

A logical picture of facts is a thought. A bottle of squirts is an interaction. The surf is ratified by drawing. Orchids grab the light and make it appealing, a juice in which colonnades of hosiery rupture with 12:30 p.m. and Ecuador finds a parking space in my heart.

It is essential to a thing that it can be a word, a group of words, or a small intestine at twilight. It's pretty hard to think of an object apart from its connection with other things. The highway arouses cruising. Feathers solicit flight. A blast of imagined dynamite reveals a face of amber. The shoal is a Möbius of brooding solidarity. Diamonds blaze in the glory of velvet.

So you see, if there is a picture, the elements of the picture will behave in a certain way with one another. The picture will walk out of its frame and shiver until someone drapes a blanket around it.

The silence is gorgeous. The indigo is providential. There is no snow. There is only fire. The wood spits sparks at the moon. The vertebrae of an engine of ice enlists drums of water. The water corresponds to the dictates of rain. The thinness of time in the streets of Paris make one's sneakers swell until the puddles become drawers full of push-ups and flirts. Ears wander the sounds of Mercury. The feathers are dry as ever at the scarf foundry. The sugar plow is available for viewing between 11:00 a.m. and posterity.

And so on, as if the general form of proposition had to face itself in a boxing match, and the fog rolled in and made everything a form of baptism, a renaissance dripping with sweat. Are opals gems, or hints of paradise? The nouns grapple for meaning, and the sentence pushes its words to the end, where they become Tuesday, and smell of benediction.

Life In The Imperative

Open time. Open it with a dent. Careless perspective. Vowel a gizzard in a window frame. Confess a grim speculation. Do it with flint. Do it with extraversion and pulleys and dramatically stubborn language stalks.

Seethe. Bronze the conversation with minnows.

When you hear rain at the window, do you elope with chlorophyll? Do you impel an easygoing, ebullient tumult of words? Words that will bounce across the brain, lightly, animating brooks and mutant serenades?

Translucency trumps the tuck of the basilica. There is tenderness and shrubbery. Freshwater groin of a noncommittal walk. This puts the proverbs within proximity of the airplanes and inspiration can begin with a root. Think potato. Shiver. Exude. Walk into the lotus. Krishna dreams of heaven and so heaven walks into heroin and the spirits touch us with their sleeves. We feel them strain. We feel them try to become granite.

The southern darling dares a chin and so begins the prunes of sorrow.

Inflate form with bursting calories of unzippered hibiscus. The musk of the mollusk figures its water among our friends. The ripples do as decoration, but the voices must be described as the whisper of crinoline.

Laughing hiking spouting scarlet. We buy the furniture later when the air becomes liquid with tales of the moon. And the wind rubs a wire and we begin to believe that the parables will pin us to the wood. I play an organ. Others drag memories out of the rain.

If you see death ride by on a white horse, create a gnarled ground of Gothic drapery. The dyeing wind eats to get by. Agitation sausage for the painter of abyssal toads. Mathematics flame for the crime of subtraction. Chewed paper for the outer space of a desk. Seeds in a wasteland saddle, seeds in a shamanic rattle. Dostoyevsky candor in a vinyl booth of elastic predication. We see them in bars all the time. These drunks, these old men propelled by engines of despair. Bombs of life explode into late night reflection, redemption by a window, listen to the rain, everything is going to be alright baby, because I feel you in my bones, and the rue d'Orsel is full of luminous stones.

Power is a crazy infatuation. But let's not get carried away. Awaken the flicker of allegory. The frail mat of helicopter pills. The brilliant forks of detachment. Rake the rhinoceros from the propagation of time. Then let the chamomile mouth its glorious confession.

I admire nature. Don't you? The action of waves on the sand. The dilation of soul in the shine of soup.

Now, where was I? The candle needs a silk handkerchief. It sneezes the light of a thousand grimacing skulls. I hear Peter Green in the fall of colors from a bulb oozing light at the edge of the universe. This is ratified by rags and volcanos and the flow of lava from a heart of crazy jewels. The enigma that is life is only an idea that camels carry on their backs across the desert at night. It's really just fishing around to hear the dunes sing scarlet songs to the stars.

Finding *Empfindung*

Ants in eccentric seaweed. Exultation in the waves. Thought furnished with burning winds. How many senses? Five? There must be more. Reconciliation in a car, old questions boiled into limestone. Knowledge is green. Sometimes beige.

A dry highway undertakes our eyes. Dazzling bandage of swamp art. Mahogany is a hard noble fact. Old agitations entangled in the unidentifiable substance that is music. Buoyant memories provided with lakes.

Others just sink.

Into oblivion. Or rise to the surface like methane and fill the night air with a beautiful blue glow that smells a little of something gone bad on the stove.

What am I doing? Where am I going? What am I writing? What is it that wants to come out? What is it that wants expression? What is it that wants to come alive in the sad starry snow of darkness?

And trudge forward like Frankenstein.

It is a subtle but not entirely clumsy refrigeration of time. The absence of Asia deepens Asia. This makes the nebulae of vague corresponding lights win catastrophes of space in our sleep. It is not surprising that poplar emboldens the honest. The veil undulates and thus helps the wind to realize oneself. And this is what nourishes the cure for percussion. It makes it thump with greater deliberation and less exposition, it crashes out of its own being and becomes the one activity in life that doesn't require explanation. It is swimming. It is talking. It is the ceaseless employment of sticks on a taut surface of paper.

Is everyone happy now?

Probably not. I don't know. Who is to know? Do you know?

Reanimating the dead is always a serious matter. But so is writing, which is driven by letters rather than body parts and lightning. But aren't they, when it comes down to it, the same? Writing, by its very existence, has an ideological aspect. In this respect, it is similar to money. Much of the inherent chaos and brutality of life has been rationalized by monetary exchange. The conversion of wealth into securities gives it a giddy insensitivity to the vagaries and sorrows of life. Meaning money isn't wealth. Money is a medium of exchange.

Securities are fungible, a cruel hoax. Real wealth is the loyalty of a friend, a good stand-up comic, and a shelter — however crude — to protect you from assholes and blasts of lightning. King Lear learned this lesson the hard way.

Real wealth is spirit. The strength to endure, and the means to do it. Art embodies what is wild and unmanageable. It reduces nominal wealth to the noxious and grotesque.

The ludicrous is what saves us. The comedic spirit is our best guarantee against authoritative sclerosis.

Which suggests that writing may not be as serious as we think.

Or I think. I can't think for you. I have enough trouble as it is thinking for myself. But hey, I'm not the one who invented language. Especially this language, with its funny pronouns and prepositions.

Where was I? Oh yeah, desire. When we can't quite reach what we want, we use words. Isn't that what they're for? Turning water to wine?

Nothing gets in the way of desire when it begins to objectify what it desires. Quite often we have it in hand already without realizing what we truly have.

Remember that scene in 2001? That really excited ape guy tossing the bone into the sky, which then becomes a spaceship docking with a space station to the music of Richard Strauss's *Thus Spake Zarathustra*? Who didn't enjoy a conflagration of ideas seeing that?

2001 turned out to be very different then the way we imagined it. Controlled demolition, ash billowing in the streets of lower Manhattan, people fleeing in panic, warrantless surveillance, ethnic profiling, indefinite military detention, torture, body scanners, the beginning of endless war.

No, the Big Lebowski did not come to our rescue.

But what am I saying? I always get lost as soon as I start using the royal 'we.'

Shall we turn to something more Gothic? Molecular squeaking on a library barge? Chains clanking, memories rubbing against the brainpan?

Juicy evening desires ignite the nerves. Scarves hang from a kite of Meissen porcelain. Niccolo Paganini does more for my head than cocaine ever did.

Beatitude is an elephant. But what's a diving board? Can a diving board be a symbol of something? And what's up with symbols, anyway? Are cymbals symbols? Are symbols an indication that everything has a transcendental aspect? Or are they just a convenient strategy for keeping the brain warm and occupied while empirical reality gambols about elsewhere?

The bones of the paragraph rest on a bed of paper. Meaning overflows with perfumes and rubies. Time leans against space. Space relies on gravity. Gravity walks through Egypt in a trance of opulence. The heart forgets its store of pain. Nails of carpentry tinkle in their bags as the searching winds of a blue neuron groan through the wood of a trembling abstraction.

Anything that deviates from the ruling consciousness is going to seem bizarre because it's trying to break free of a petrified reality. Or at least get out of doing the dishes.

Or not. I mean, is doing the dishes so bad? It can be soothing. The sound of running water sounds like the word 'essence.' Doesn't it? When you turn the faucet, do you hear essence? Someone else might say it sounds like dress, or stress, or evanescence. Dishes are their own truth content. Except for spoons. Spoons are magical.

Existence precedes essence, or is it the other way around? I always forget which is which. The motivation behind most objects is clear. I know why certain blues aficionados might have reservations about George Thorogood, he's a bit flashy, but I thoroughly like Thorogood, as I do the morning wind dancing on a puddle. The problem is precisely this: there is in everyday reality a sense that there is something else, power or divine undercurrent, that may or may not be related to a religious or mystical unknowable. What I do know is that we can find the embrace of being in ourselves, and most objects would congratulate us, if they had arms, and were in a cartoon.

My original solitude is beyond my reach. It exists on another plane. I may or may not find it in George Thorogood, but I will most definitely get a sense of it in John Lee Hooker's cover of "I Cover the Waterfront," a popular song and jazz standard composed by Johnny Green. I might also mention the noumenon behind Kant's *Empfindung*. Let's look there next time and see if we might also hear Bo Diddley.

It is in the past that I am what I am, but it is in the present that I am making progress toward the multitude that I might be, the warp and woof of weaving a moment together is rhythmically soothing, I must admit, but the pattern seems to be taking forever, and the cat wants to be fed, and I'm getting restless myself, maybe now isn't the time to go kicking an *Empfindung* down the street.

It is with more difficulty that the words are detached from the motherboard and tossed into whatever mutinous environment best suits them.

Articulation stubbornly extends an arm towards the border, and convulses with fields of lavender.

Everyday Cravings

I see adaptation in drinking chocolate. Temperament is a grass like you favor forks. I say these things not because the means are there but because the fabric of consciousness is romantic and vague and scratches at the thesis of ownership like an immigrant eager to come ashore and begin a new life as a rock musician, or forest. Chocolate is singular and therefore fulminates a kick. Neglect damask and meringue is the birth of legend.

Gelatin cabinet for archaic soap. Pillow craze slipping into Hume. The electric car includes buttons. Humming tibia of Rembrandt brown: the sting of the text is a pure can of everyday cravings. A blood vein propels the thunder of the onion to its destiny as a world of buried illumination.

And we are on our way.

Here: have some chicken in a lighter chair. The swirl of the plow drools earthly sod. The mushrooms leave their scarves. Harness the horses and load the propeller. The shade of an island is a percussion in the pool, the heaviness of time in a crude sample of logic distressed by the blush of the abyss, life curbed on a canvas of bleak thematic candor. When it bubbles to the surface it means that the plumber is done with his chaos and the camels are free to enter the fabric of our existence.

And yes, it's true, I like the word fabric.

I also like getting undressed. I like removing the burden of display. There is a real universe beneath my clothes. Tiny beings at work inside my cells (mitochondria, centrioles, organelles, symbiotic bacteria) weave a syntax of skin and bone that seems to fit me ok. Together they create a front of tenable subjectivity. I get traction in the world with these little brothers and sisters. We have festivals and events. Toothaches, headaches, heartaches. Life wouldn't be the same without them. Life wouldn't be life. I would go on non-existing as I non-existed before this mess I call an identity was pulled into this world. And what are any of us doing here? In a word: chocolate. I exist to eat chocolate.

You can improve the varnish of things by moving to a place of better varnish. The phenomena that is knees enjoys a certain closeness. Cartilage caressed by money. The shine of bodies after a shower. Agates in the rain. The marsh entangles its vines like letters written to the Black Angels of Austin. Equations tattooed on a shoulder of gold.

For example, the shear stress in a torque equation is perpendicular to the radius.

Radius of what? Let's say the rear axle of a Jeep Cherokee. Because that sounds good.

Rear. Axle. Of. A. Jeep. Cherokee. *Essieu arrière d'un Jeep Cherokee. Eje trasero de un Jeep Cherokee. Cùl aiseil de Jeep Cherokee.*

The camber of a melody in E minor suggests flagellation and lace. Rifles, ivory, nutmeg, and gum Arabic. Breath rising from a man awakened by language. Things float. Distant storms marble the far horizon. The genial regatta exults in chickens. Events occur everywhere agitation drinks its way toward disorientation, but they occur in a special light, they follow the wasps to the land of the Jeweled Canary. And at the junkyard is a sink filled with the dishes of a lonely man.

The improvement of a shade of beard depends on the amount of snowballs available to the armory of a radical subjectivity. Being lonely is a small part of that. The availability of snowballs is purely arbitrary, and therefore copper. Metaphors are generally trumpets, long bright scruples filled with Minnesota.

And yes, there are junkyards, and they are sad places, mournful destinations outside of town, old cars rusting in a dream of black interiors and torrential rains. It sometimes happens that people become strangers to themselves. There are drugs for this, and those for whom the threshold of sensation is suddenly gathered in a Shoshone chant, or a sudden light breeze across Lake Mead. There's also that first time you touch the warm skin of someone for whom you feel a strong, overwhelming desire to bring into your life.

The Sioux believe that the stone is the truest condition of creation. It is silent and solid and relentlessly specific. That which exists through itself is what is called meaning, Olson once scrawled on a blackboard in Berkeley, California.

Other beverages might include cherry soda, root beer, or gin.

To drink tea is to create drapery. The taste of squabbling that languishes in the bright lips of radar is modulated somewhere near the area of sailing in the mind of a Stoic. Saturday's rakes play at Saturday. The result is smoke. The willow by the river is moody, yes, but it also recommends propulsion as a source of rebellion, which is something to consider, given the status of Shakespeare's Hamlet, in which a young woman drowns. This is not a tender world. When sorrows come, they come not single spies, but in battalions. Adjustments will be required. Objectivity hardens into a mask and life becomes a defensive ritual. Eccentricity shimmers through an unreconciled life. Even the insects seem nervous.

A more thoughtful debauchery requires helicopters, but who can afford that?

Another thing sugar does is claw the unknown. Tomorrow we'll have jelly. Life on the lawn can be annoying without a few jars and spoons and something to maneuver on the table during conversation.

Leaves leave results of themselves in lacy decrepitude at the bottom of the creek. It is the substantives of the field that forget to incarnate description in the proper stratum of rocks when the terrain laughs and the hills accomplish the border between forgery and toad by a rapid broom of lightning. There is nothing anthropomorphic about a hill that hasn't already smiled upon the occurrence of noon at midnight. It is glorious when a full moon deposits samples of itself during an inundation of language and the nomads stop to gaze up at the sky.

And sometimes I'm so happy that a light comes on in the refrigerator when I open the door that I think of André Breton. Who said: we gaze at the unbelievable and believe it despite ourselves.

Amen.

Metallic Green Fruits

Marble hummingbirds calm the radio. I use this warp in the space/time continuum to dig through my obstinacy looking for the recent purchase of something that I can redirect towards liberation. I find a golf ball, a miniature Frisbee, and a thyroid gland. I liberate them. They become radio furniture.

I dare to believe that ink is capable of becoming diamonds. It's mostly just pretense, but that's ok. Rattlesnakes mostly hunt at night. Roast a chicken and what do you get? A roasted chicken.

But this isn't about roasted chickens. This is about fjords. Why do fjords tend to be forged in Norway? Are there fjords in Texas? What kind of clothes should one wear when visiting a fjord?

The answer to these questions can be found in rhubarb. The world is colder than it used to be. But rhubarb persists. They are like oysters chiseled in wood. It's never the appliance that needs to justify its existence but the watercolor that echoes the limits of our understanding that gives us the music-hall of the mollusk.

The rhubarb is a gimmick. It was never intended to liberate Moscow. It was all those sails that let the sky in on our plans and the winds that knocked some virtue into them that gave our crew something to do at last. Why didn't we think of that before? Sometimes the best answers come in the form of soap.

I like to sit in a chair and loaf. It makes me sad to think of veins. There's the sky above the cemetery and the sky as it exists in words, but which is the real sky? Remember bees? That's the real sky.

Whatever is round shows that geometry is present. Geometry is what happens when the zeppelins arrive with a supply of linen. The Theatre of Sensations opens its doors. The rainforests are deep and intermittently illumined. Snakes curl around branches of rubber trees and walking palm and multi-colored birds embroider the air with a deafening pandemonium.

This is what music looks like when it's assembling itself with catgut and camaraderie. A man carries words from one end of a sentence to another. Screams of murder complement the varnish of the sideboard. But these are not the words the man is carrying. These are the words that are carrying the man to a newly expanded rapport with all things hickory.

This is the way the mind chews things. Think of a shell then think of the meat in the shell. I see a blatant flexibility in the fire of sexuality that I would like to see in the need to say things about our life on this planet. This is precisely the kind of convolution that leads to genuflection. When we see the oasis ignite in the distance we will know that the planets are the darlings of a trigonometry invented on the backs of camels.

It never ends, does it? I mean life. We each personally conduct a life leaving behind books and art and children, but life itself is a hunger and a thirst that will never be fully understood. Even the end of life is the beginning of something new. These are the words that I was born to carry and lay them down here, one by one, so that they would rise and fulfill themselves in the metallic green fruits of another world.

Collections

I like collections. Amalgams. Goblets of gold & silver. Shields, swords, armor. Anything interconnected & multiple. Systems, compounds, compositions. Oysters, samovars, tugboats.

Words.

Words do command a powerful reality of their own. I have to remind myself that a rose by any other name is still a rose. The Dragon, a big tanker from Nassau, fills with grain at Pier 86. The day is sweet with leeway. This is what it means to describe things. Context is everything. When was the last time you fired a gun? Is there an art to enduring pain? Follow me. I will show you the effulgence of my head describe itself.

Think of me as a window. Can you tell me what this emotion is beating against my ribs? No? Me neither. My muscles revolve around my bones looking for something to do. Truth and intuition advance the evolution of the T-shirt. This is the place where the coyote stops and stares. What is the origin of art? We create it as much as it creates us. Who is the dreamer? You're the dreamer. I'm the dreamer. This is a dream. There is a swamp in my finger and a sample of daybreak burning in a stone lamp. Shakespeare's plume flirting with the puppets of human folly.

If I had alcohol in me right now I'd be singing out loud. I'd turn this boat around & turn it into a karaoke bar. Why is it even worth mentioning? This is why people gaze abstractedly at the ground. Ambition is thirty gallons of gas & a red Silverado. Wishing, on the other hand, occurs when desire doesn't take itself seriously. When desire takes itself seriously we call it Richard III. Trying singing Hamlet in a Wyoming bar. That's when the guns come out. Writing is feeling increasingly like that. You know? Like when somebody nabs you at a party to look at granite kitchen counter samples & all of Chekhov is happing in your head. This is what the spectrum of desire looks like from a human perspective. On the one hand soap. And on the other a gun.

The tongue is an engine whose noises produce strawberries. The rest is Costa Rica. What I cannot find in metaphysics I can find in sawdust. The answer, in a nutshell, is furniture. Everything else crawls to the door and bangs on it hard. Life is messy, yes. Our inner wealth comes from chiaroscuro. We're airports, you and I. Let our words fill the air with convoys of joy. What do you want me to tell you? That I met the Beatles? I didn't. The reality principle caught me off guard. Otherwise, life is just savage equations of rust and inter-play. The hum of neurons create impressions of a reality that pins a little fire in the stove. Creating anything is to go on talking. Philosophy is being a dog. You can smell shit and still think it's alright. We can work it out. It's at the cost of these very ruptures that there's a transcendent experience of self. And a jack and a spare tire in the trunk.

The Color Of Rain

Sometimes a beetle becomes firm in its resolve. Who isn't a slave to their own refrains? I want the Christmas trimming to drive into Easter carrying a load of dirt. If dirt isn't prominent in this sentence, then it must be a derelict explosion. It proves precisely nothing. Except that quarks are candlelight and our eyes are nothing if not sanguine. I never fully understood the Futurists. I just place the nouns where they're most needed and hope for the best. The carrot is a web of equations. This is a strange way to look at a carrot but I believe the quarks are delicious.

I like food. Who doesn't? What's not to like about food? Let's not talk about that. Let's talk about illusion. I love illusion. Though I also hate it a little, too.

Reality is too obvious to be true. Nothing is entirely explicit without becoming fiction. Everything, in Pataphysical terms, is a unique event with its own singular laws. It insists on a universe of exceptions. Homogenization cannot exist in such a universe. Imitation is quintessentially imaginary, and therefore impossible. Imitation cannot be imitated. The inimitable is illimitable.

Romance is a rascal. I see a haiku poking out of a book. And I scream. I smack the wall. I shove it down and dip into a little dream which solves itself with California. I find consistency in skin. And because it's generally soft, I find that violence doesn't work. Or does it? Does violence work? I'm often confused. I think I meant cherry pie. But I don't know why. Nipples are simpler. They express tenderness. And that's what I take with me to the party.

The future doesn't look good. But we'll see what we can do about bringing the saddles and bedrolls to the horses. If the hedonism is a success, the tarts will careen through our digestive tracts the way they're supposed to, and we can move on from there.

The importance of the Great Chain of Being in eighteenth-century thought is clanking across the floor like consonants at the end of a string. Who's pulling the string?

I guess I am. I must be feeling something paroxysmal and warm.

Nothing feels quite so good as clean sheets right out of the dryer. Or the first hot shower after having a cast on your leg removed. Nevada is larger than you can imagine. The garage door creaks open there sits Lou Reed in a lawn chair sipping coffee. I knew it. When thoughts enter the air they assume the color of rain.

Daub Of Blue

Calculus crawls into time and makes it twigs. If I had a jackknife, I would carve it into pharmaceuticals. Time lingers in an argument from yesterday and I wiggle it until it becomes cardboard mosquitoes. Nouns offer tranquility to the ceiling. The ceiling answers with refinement and water buffalo.

Sexual mushrooms cohere into eyes. The brightness is inconceivable. Hints of balance insinuate sinew. I'm not an astronaut but I know how to swim. I just get supple and grope.

Sometimes it just feels good to have a pen in the hand and put pressure on it on a sheet of paper and push it and pull words out of it by pushing it pushing it into words you didn't expect to see crystalizing in the air of the mind where the sky lives there in the nerves of your brain words crystallizing and falling slowly drifting as much as falling falling to the ground which is not in your mind or in your mind in a different way it's a sensation caused by gravity by mass which is the planet you're riding on through space the planet is round and teeming with human beings mammals that like to eat and reproduce and build things with their hands and eyes tall sparkly buildings shouting themselves into nowhere.

There are songs that make you want to buy a horse. Songs that make you want to fall in love and get hurt and drink impossible amounts of whiskey by rivers of rock and sand and water chuckling about its own silly directions. Songs that make you want to cry. Songs that make you want to disappear in the forest and eat trout and truffles at sundown. Toads go to the lake. They're listening to Bo Diddley. Not with their ears. It's in the blood. Thumps and thumpity thump thumps. That's it. The whole song and nothing but the song.

Pain opens space like a suitcase. We find a voice sleeping in an embryonic sock. When it awakens it plugs itself into a mouth and begins to embroider Uruguay with conversation. The voltage surrounding the bones is red. The mania is tinted with railroad ties.

The sock becomes a navy and defeats Bolivia. The suitcase is sold for a hundred Bolivianos. The voice moves to Scotland and inspires a movie starring Mel Gibson as the stratosphere of a duck. This proves that thought is a boat that appears at the shore whenever it wishes. Nobody thinks a thought, thought thinks us, and then it serves breakfast.

Or shows us how. How to break an egg so that the yolk doesn't run, how to slice a piece of bread evenly, how to wait patiently for the toaster to cough the bread up, how to slather it with jam and butter.

That lump of matter in which thought resides is the brain. The ego is something different. It's more like a dinghy. Free will is a charming concept. Thought enhances the experience. The rest of life is learning how to endure it.

We touch heaven at four in the afternoon. That's when heaven crawls out of its hiding place and becomes the afterlife we've all been waiting for. It's mostly blackberries and French wine. The cheese isn't bad either. But it's important to understand that heaven isn't the same for everyone. My concept of heaven is blue. Blue sky, blue oranges, blue stars, blue caribou. Everything soft and forgiving and deviant and strange. And blue. Buffalo Bill sits down to paint a hill and wiggles the easel. Then he applies a daub of blue.

Daub of blue, daub of blue, be my, be my, be my daub of blue.

Genesis

Jelly blooms in my hand like a sweatshirt. I'll pay my bills now. I'll pay them with corks and vignettes. I'll pay them with pretty little tales about my life and times as the captain of a shoe. There's a science to sparkling, and this leads me to think of pleasure as a class of fugitive sensation punctuated by hotels and minivans. The bills arrive later in the mail.

Money assumes strange forms. Sometimes it's cowrie shells. Sometimes it's a negotiable instrument and sometimes it's a cow. The Fula People of West Africa use coin belts. The Maori used pigs and potatoes.

Imagine pigs as loose change. Pockets stuffed with spuds. Imagine a language in which heaven and hell rub together like ravens and the words are in love with their own illusions.

Genesis is the name of the young woman in charge of housewares. She looks like Elsa Lanchester in *The Bride of Frankenstein*. People are afraid to go into the housewares department. Everything is dusty. Genesis stands in the center aisle between rows of pots and pans staring into space with blood-red eyes, electricity crackling around her body.

You can buy a good sauce pan for a pig if Genesis is in a good mood. Otherwise, money is just foolish and the impulse to buy anything is better kept as a secret. The work of our organs is the work of our organs. Immediate certainty, the thing in itself, be it a saucepan with a domed glass lid or a thermodynamic handshake with a heartwarming ohm, is interspersed with molecules whose component atoms justify their doodles in cheerful museums.

One day, I hope to explore space as a NASA astronaut. Though I would settle for being Superman and getting free coffee at Starbucks in exchange for saving planet Earth from being struck by a gigantic asteroid.

I would ride that asteroid into Omaha and get a room at the Bored Bug Hotel. Even the bear comes down from the mountain when he's hungry.

Have you had contact with the supernatural lately? Ghosts? Poltergeists? Snapping turtles? Yesterday a dark bank of clouds rolled up the Mississippi at about 11:00 a.m. A few minutes later it began raining heavily. The river swelled. The waters rose. When they receded, we were in Paris, floating down the Seine.

I'm not saying this was supernatural. I'm just saying that if we need to verify whether such and such a thing exists we need to examine our own complicity in the construction of our experience. Who can look at a river and not feel that river moving through their body? A thought may be nothing, nothing in itself, but if it's a thought about something, that something might be a vapor, or a Lincoln Continental, and invite our speculation further, so that it becomes a vowel or a story about a vowel, a tray of ice cubes in which a vowel might milk a consonant for its jewels.

When a representation about the world makes that world a world and not just another waiting room in a dentist's office, makes Beings become Beings, words become words, the pure gaze of the reader can be applied to its inventions without restriction to the world of an imperious grammar of Being, to nuclei of indecomposable meanings, webs of sticky hindsight.

I am implicit in these words. But I am not entirely within their compass either. I am at the periphery. I am in the margin, peering in. Floating among the reeds.

My Puppets Are Wet

Blood wanders my body murmuring being. It plays with my bones and glides into temperament. I feel its throats dip into pavement for crystal. Momentum does the rest. I grab some electricity from the clouds and throw it into a book.

A trance converges on socialism. A bump wanders my head looking for a home. Space is a sow drooling comets behind the sheriff. This corresponds to hawthorn. I'm doing my best to understand the pornography of power.

My experiences pull themselves into description. Power is a waterfall asleep on an ironing board. Or would that more properly be called potential? It is called by its true name, which is avocado. Power is the ability to fly a 240 ton cargo-aircraft through the eye of a needle.

And land in Guam. What does one do in Guam? Life is tangential to Guam which is also ribbons and seesaws. Perspective is everything. Including cracks.

There is a proverb in which are clothes are uncontrollable. And our ears reach into the garden for music. We have learned to better understand our knives by shipping them to high elevations and carving mountains out of the clouds. Or clouds out of the mountains. I once punched a stream of water and it blazed into reality as a brain.

My puppets are wet and infrared. Coals flash occasionally in the hibachi. A brain walks by dressed as a human being. I wave. The brain waves back.

My favorite book is a twinkle in the carousel. This involved three casualties, a carp, and an equally tall smack on the lips. If I told you it was raining would you believe me? It's raining. Cats and dogs.

Most of the phenomena around my legs grow into theorems that I can sift through shouts of eternity. This includes broken plates, accordions, doctrines, luminosities, and corn on the cob. I lead a full life of museums, fingers, and hectic abandon. There is a prominence on the rue d'Orsel that repeats its candy like a true buffalo. I see a bend in the road where we can end our turmoil in outer space.

And then some. You know? Like a real piccolo. I am adrift in a massive trembling that can only be music. My emotions feed it compliments and bones.

My intentions lean against the proboscis of a dead folk song. The new folk song will fling itself at the crowd like a bowl of coleslaw. It will appeal to their darkest instincts and mushroom into sirens. Empires will collapse. The human voice will be visceral as eels.

I know we'll have fun inventing a new movement. We haven't had a movement in a long time. Movements tend to come and go. This one will scud across the mind making libraries and ferns. Life will be different it will be more like rain than eviction.

Mongrel birds effect my toga. When the clarinetist is inside her instrument she has an international feeling. Her redemption of chrome walks into shouting and we paint ourselves into a corner with an old air of fairyland rust. Someone rides geometry bareback. The concluding elevation keeps on going until it's completely insoluble.

The Invention Of Clouds

If you tap on the sky include binoculars. The sky is a noun. Turn it over and look underneath. What do you see? The shine of brass, the trembling of feathers. The experiment isn't over until the paddles have been shellacked. This is often the case. I can feel the hum of distant horizons whenever solitude glides through the bones of an alpine lake and some patience is required to endure the full catastrophe of being. You can't always trust the weather, but I respect the solemnity of clouds. Even the wildcat must sleep.

My library includes volumes of radical vaccination. What can I say? I like to sleep. I like to eat. I like to let myself drift to the other side of this life. The zipper is enhanced by being a zipper. Even when the zipper sleeps, there is a potential for zipping. Unzip this carefully. Something might awaken.

The mountain sleeps in a bed of granite. The wind sleeps in the fog.

Here comes some now, drifting idly through the trees. You can hear the color of confession search for a mood to burn.

Geometry is the oldest jewel I have in the glaze of my momentum.

When geometry assumes the motions of life, it becomes a lobster. The lobster is quintessentially geometric. It does what it does based on a principle of longevity, dark habitats, and walking slowly on the floor of the sea. Having ten legs, two of which are claws, confers a certain majesty on the primal endurance of this persistent creature.

The geometry of the lobster is an aesthetic of symmetry & classical mechanics. It burrows under rocks. It feels its way with antennae. This is how geometry operates with an exoskeleton. The larger the lobster, the more energy is required to live. This is why the lobster looks so completely dedicated to being a lobster. The lobster honors its geometry with pluck and determination.

Geometry is cruel, yes, but it is also beautiful and abstract, like the triangle. Like the circle. Like pi. Like the lobster when it is walking through a sentence with its claws erect.

Oil and horns hurt the fifth emancipation of my pounding chest. I don't know why the harmonica is so ogled that its glare causes piety. As for the rest, let it pioneer controversy as I have, with two claws raised, with words coming out of my collar stud, a steady stream of mutant fireballs aimed at nothing but the bend of leather on a word of frantic sterling.

Vermilion roars at the incubation of space. Spasms of pink warp textures of rain.

I realize that some of these words have lives of their own and might do better in another sentence, one written with a little more care and delicacy, than this clumsy attempt at life, this monstrous light propelling itself through the furniture. What does it seek, this amber, this octagonal invention of forehead and volume? These shadows, these cities, these wharfs?

No, I don't mean you, whoever you are, whoever I am, all these pounds of tattoo, all this hockey and horns, mannerisms and cupcake, I mean the burdens we share, our encounters with one another, the suddenness and treachery of a rip tide, the drool of the moon when the ocean roars and the currents churn in the muck and seaweed and sand.

If I think of the ocean, I am in relation with the ocean. But which is the real ocean? The one in my mind, the one that I experience when I visit the shoreline, or the one that emerges when a lobster recoils, clumsily among the rocks, two enormous claws raised in defense of its being? What ocean is that? I'm not aiming, here, for an unjustified realism. Just an acute sense of water on an infinite scale. Parrots and tuna held together by words. Sails billowing with wind. The pitch of a bow. The invention of clouds.

Romania In The Rain

I trek into the wilderness after watching the spirits dance. My Parisian throat becomes lyrical if I languish in flax. I like to bend reflections around the moon. Some might see this as the behavior of a gargantuan vagrancy. I see it as a beautiful deformity in which all the garnishment overrides examination. It is as impersonal as space, yet intimate as an oasis.

Waves sparkle in deviation. Open lines echo the shouting of gnomes. Magic strains to break reality into oak. Nothingness wiggles a flipper.

Beauty is indefinable. We know that. But why does amber luxuriate in doodles of scrotum typography?

The rain continues to fall on the snow until the story ends. My seclusion is infrared. I have hidden the furrows of some freshly plowed stationary in the eggs of an angora bicycle. I don't know why. Maybe it had something to do with late winter, and the feel of the air on the way to the curb where we leave the bin for the compost to be picked up. Or the way the sheets folded this morning. They looked like sand dunes on the coast of an attitude. My attitude, to be more specific. It was round, like planet Earth, and light as a conception of Buddhism.

The swim path is cars if I shoal in interaction. My drink bleeds gauze. We are the door of ourselves. Some doors ripple. Some doors crackle. Some doors slam. Some doors emote.

This line jabbers beyond my ability to contain it. It's on the loose. I will regret this if it heaves itself into somebody's mind and becomes an image of Romania which I never intended.

I had hoped for an evocation a little more mutual.

But then it went wild in my hands and I lost it in the forest.

Of Romania.

This is stars if it crackles like a promise. This is stars if it doesn't. This is stars. This is sugar. But it's insufficient. So it's not stars. It's just sugar.

I can handle a boiling pot if I'm the only one in the kitchen. Moo if you have to navigate an inflated ego. If you pick up a perspective along the way you can incarnate a scruple. If you press an unrivalled noun to your forehead and it feels like the blade of a knife I can greet you at the end of this sentence with a slice of description.

It will feel like cold steel and encourage you to eat and meditate in your corner. Our galaxy roams through a robin. We think oars are involved. Or pretzels. Candy impels the pungency of mint. It is coins to the touch. It is pronouns for a body part and ripped apart. It is dreamy as a tibia and ticklish as a cerebellum. It's why I've called you here to come and look at it. Go ahead. Press it. Hold it against your ear. All of it. Romania. In the rain.

Romania in the rain.

The Twilight Zone

When you age, life does come to seem like a *Twilight Zone* episode. I can see Rod Serling off to the side making commentary: look where sits a lone man in a single room. A man surrounded by ghosts. A man nearing the end of his life, still seeking the grail of poetry, the epiphany to end all epiphanies. The drawer is overflowing with letters. Manuscripts. Submissions. Rejections. Proofs. There is no boundary that begins and ends at the human skull. A skull is just a skull. The stuff inside is amazing, but has its limits, until the limits dissolve, and the universe comes flooding in, and the division between the visible and the invisible dissolves as the golden light of the sun disappears and the first few stars appear in the sky. This is what we call The Twilight Zone.

They say the sun is a nuclear reactor fusing hydrogen atoms into helium. I have no reason to doubt that. But isn't the sun also a star? An angel of heat and light?

Helicopters and mollusks pursue different objectives, but are otherwise ideas based on dispersal, the erection of beams, the pouring of cement. Men in yellow helmets whistling, signaling, waving. It's a strange world, isn't it? Who knows how any of us came to be here. We just come out on the stage and say what we have to say and then make our exits with whatever grace and fortitude we can muster when the inevitable arrives.

I was a mollusk once. I flew a helicopter. No arms, no legs, no skill. I flew it because I created a sentence that said I flew it. One minute you're a mollusk, the next you're an angel. It's an endothermic change, a form of sublimation. Chemists use sublimation to purify a substance from its compounds. Poets use sublimation to volatilize the mundane into poetry and enjoy the luxury of detaching its energy from the impurities of a world obsessed with square footage and patio furniture.

It's simply a matter of will. Whether will is an actuality or not doesn't matter. If you believe you have will, you have will. You will will. You will it into being. Or at least a fiction, a credible proposition. You might not be able to save Planet Earth from an asteroid or abrupt climate change but you can change a lightbulb or bake some brownies. You surround it with a little narrative and voila! you've got the beginnings of a dialectic.

What is energy? Energy is a pile of dirt, fields of wheat rustling and waving in the hills of the Palouse. The landscape expands into buttes and canyons. And since the planet is a sphere, we pack our head with idle thoughts and plywood. With loops. And indirection. And life.

And like anything weird, life needs the endless treadmill of making a living.

Or not.

Making a living: what a strange phrase. As if life required a table saw and a hammer, a 60-volt drill and a bag of nails. All it really takes is a high-wire 1,000 feet above the ground and a T-shirt with a question mark. You'll make lots of friends. There will be feasts and ceremonies. And somewhere in the background will be a man named Rod Serling standing aloof and crepuscular with a knowing look and a martini.

The Answers Are Coming

We're lost. No one knows what to think anymore. We're awash in misinformation, propaganda, and fake news. Beliefs are hermetic. Subjectivity trumps objectivity.

It's hard to believe anything anymore. And this is dangerous, because it leads to totalitarianism.

I love that scene in *The Matrix* when Neo (Keanu Reeves), having just awakened to his actual body in a tub of slime and come unhooked by all the wires attached to his body gets flushed down the drain and resumes consciousness aboard the Nebuchadnezzar, his naked body bristling with electrodes, and asks "why do my eyes hurt?" To which Morpheus (Lawrence Fishburne) responds: "you've never used them before." "Rest, Neo, the answers are coming."

The tendency to question our reality — particularly our social and political reality — is the natural result of having a high level of cognition. My guess is that microbes and oysters don't question their reality much. But what do I know?

And that's the crux of the problem: what *do* I know? And how do I know it?

My world changed the day that my father told me that there is more space than lead in an ingot of lead.

Pythagoras held reality to be a mathematical code whose core structure was based on the number three. I picture all those numbers dribbling down like rain in *The Matrix*, especially at that critical moment when Neo reaches enlightenment.

That's probably not what Pythagoras had in mind, but Pythagoras didn't go to the movies.

"The world belongs to those who do not feel," writes Fernando Pessoa.

I'm not going to be very Buddhist about answering this. I'm going to be multi-layered and bubble up from the miasma. I like to put my fingers on the warm pages of a book and feel the world that way. Words have a greater presence when they're never satisfied. And the eye of an alligator appears on the surface of the water, infinitely watchful, infinitely alert.

In a word, sublime. Let's consider that. There are sensitivities that crave poetry in a society that cares only about commodity. Let's find something to feed them.

A Caesar salad. A hedge fund investor.

Our feeling of being unique and separate individuals is illusory. We can let them drift through our minds like clouds or haunt us like ghosts or lick our brains like Iggy Pop.

Every time that curtain of habit gets pulled back a real look at the universe can make you tremble with awe.

Large and Swollen and Blue

The arabesques of a fugue scurry before the windows of my eyes embodying the grace of persuasion sparkling in a blood stream. Basically, a middle-aged woman standing in the rain in a leopard-skin bathrobe waiting for her dog to take a shit.

Because, you know, who doesn't have a bloodstream? Blood pertains to everyone. It is our common denominator. More so than TV, or what is on TV, tits and dragons.

I get something going in my brain, something like blood, a bloodstream, and I can't stop it, it becomes a thing. A phenomenon. An entity that enters my consciousness and spins around until I give it more thought, which is what it wants, it wants thought, or is the blood itself the thought and I am the carrier of the thought, carrying the thought here, to this sentence, where it can slosh back and forth?

Bloody hell, as they say. Bloody this and bloody that.

If muscle is the horse blood is the spur. If blood is the spur bone is the ache. The concept of aching is important here. It swims in affiliation. It elevates grace.

I ache to play the glockenspiel. It is not enough to say the word. I do not own a glockenspiel. I do not know how to play a glockenspiel. And yet there exists a reality in which I might own and play a glockenspiel. So that by saying that I ache to play a glockenspiel I raise my antenna to the possibilities of playing a glockenspiel in order that they may be grasped as frequencies, which they most certainly are, waves and oscillations, vectors and fields, tuned keys and mallets, and understood to be hovering in the air in a hectic spectacle of play and plausibility.

There now, I said it, play and plausibility. I've been aching to say that all day.

I invoke a glockenspiel. I stand in the moleskin of a new reckoning. I knot the air with words. I hit slabs of shiny metal. I make music. I rehearse for a play that has not yet been written. A play in which a man and a glockenspiel are together in a room for the first time. And there is no regret. And there is no compulsion. The smell of a gargoyle turns vermilion and the larynx dilates to confess its diversions.

I sense the twirl of concern, the thrust of opinion. Concern is soft and green. Opinion is barbed and reckless. Concern is marinated, opinion is tossed. Opinion floats the myrrh of the market. The barter of suet, the murmur of silks. The souk is full of opinion. The man in the back sitting alone in the dark is full of concern.

If I find spots rattling with necessities of angelic fur, I murmur and sway in my iron steam. This is the result of propitiation, or hammers pounding the nails of persuasion.

The personality of a sound whispers its length to the drift of a towel. A word takes its time to form in the mouth and then crawls out of a paragraph triggering curvature and background.

The word is 'towel.' The meaning is wrapped inside. It will make an appeal to the warmth of your blood in a drone of fiber and shape. The skin receives the world on its surface. The world penetrates the skin in a reverie of nerve and constellation. Water drips to the floor. Reticence is discarded for a swirl of embroidery, the grasp of a hand, the pulse of a wrist.

And if the letters fall in a certain way, the frequencies stir, the sounds are bright lucidities of sensory wave, crested in white and rolling, rolling great distances, large and swollen and blue.

Crisis

Is there anything to say about art that hasn't been said already? It's possible that what needs to be said about art doesn't need to be said at all. No two experiences are ever exactly the same, but are like the chords harmonizing in the vibrations of space and time, the differences in pitch and timbre creating overtones of bone and boomerang. This is why I've nailed my voice to the wall. Watch as it ruptures into shadows. The need to crowd sounds together so that they spit and crackle. This is a chain of garlic, and this is a zone of wild speculation. Shake this medication and we can flame into pain back-flipping like experts on a Persian carpet.

The oysters have been stellar ever since gravity arrived and helped keep everything on my plate. What more can you ask for?

I've been feeling more than a little ungovernable lately. We're in crisis. You do know that, though, right? Of course you do.

We're all waiting for a wind to fill our sails and carry us somewhere distant, away from this mess.

Completely normal, I say. Completely normal to shout that the world drags me down.

I can resolve almost any issue with a little puberty and some tissue. A black wind intrinsic to impulse leans against Nevada pulling a spoon out of a bowl of adverbs. And none of us think this is strange. Because if you think about blood you don't need to read this. It will happen naturally, like an embroidered belt purchased at a gas station. The magazines will catch the light, the deodorants will be in the aisle next to the snacks and antacids, the colors will glitter, the air will smell of coffee and Windex and hot dogs, the shelves will be loaded with talcum powder and souvenirs, the clerk will ask if you've found everything, and you will say yes or no according your needs and disposition, the conversation will expand according to the vagaries of the situation, a recent robbery, the uptick in military helicopters or the crazy weather, the tornado that just decimated the adjacent town, the earthquakes in Italy, the price of gas, the floods and mudslides, the whims of the universe, signs and wonders, the fall of foreign governments, the wild luxuries of the rich, people lost in the mountains, the storm brewing to the east.

And that's how language works.

Iguanas push softly against our legs. The sky cracks open with thunder. The dust turns to mud. Mosquitoes. The stench of a tangible stupefaction.

What happened, America? What happened to that big adventure of life on the Mississippi? Delta catgut on an old guitar led wildly and crazily to the sideburns of a rock star in Vegas. You can't predict anything. Even death has gotten prodigal and sloppy.

Outside the glow of substitution soothes us with rumor. Ghosts of the former republic call out for circuses and metal.

You need to jump into these words, pump them into the light.

Who am I talking to?

I don't even know anymore.

The Hand of William Blake

I've tethered a willow to a mood of creamy premonition. Why a willow? The branches sway. Light wind. Humidity at 52%. You can unfold this pyramid at an altitude of 30,000 ft. You may also seduce the logic of cause and effect by leaning a broom toward the rear of the airplane.

I mourn the loss of my former feeling, which was convulsive with beauty and colorful as the Grand Canyon on a Wednesday morning. The new feeling is rhombohedral. Salty as a Martian's ear, insoluble as Gabriel's horn. Dark territory.

Upon arriving in Minot, I disembarked and stretched my legs. It wasn't my original destination, but I'm happy the library was open and I could find a copy of William Blake open on the table. "He who desires but acts not, breeds pestilence." "No bird soars too high, if he soars with his own wings." "What is now proved was once, only imagin'd."

I began searching for a magician. Didn't find one, no, but I can make a totem out of a conviction in wood and a little concentration.

Pronouns furnish us with different ways of feeling the push of identity in this world. We're united by feathers and fire. We shout at the artists to leap from their bones and bend the resignation of mourning into the glad rebellion of morning.

For the shadows of night are dead. And the shrewd signal of a whirling expansion hurries away into the distance.

The radio, meanwhile, shouts prophecy. The garden stumbles through itself creating raptures and odors. A crab moves laterally along a protuberance of words and mimicry. Some things cannot be imitated. You can't mimic verticality without at least standing up. You've got to begin somewhere. Let's say Toledo, Ohio. Population 287,208.

Why Toledo? Ok, Big Sandy, Montana. Bears Paw Mountains. Doesn't matter. Just begin. Resist what troubles you. Promote what gives you joy. Do what gives you release. Eject. Reject. Ejaculate. Be seminal. Be Seminole. Be incendiary. Sprinkle some words on a helmet.

I whisper tales of the Norsemen to the phantoms of my as yet unwritten novel.

The mountains confront us with the brutal serenity of granite. I have a primal need to accommodate my feelings as if they were actual wounds bleeding into the fabric of existence. The hives engorge with honey. The chemistry of love wanders through the blood eating coordinates.

I'm lost.

It's good to be lost.

Everyone knows you have to lose yourself to find yourself.

I look for signs in the moss and animals grazing on the hill. The positions of the moon and stars. The various proposals of evergreen and hawk.

If you need dispensation you have to assemble it with some mental arabesques and fancy patchwork. The palace is high and the gates are iron. The King sits down to a plate of lobster tart. The Queen is in her chamber tearing a letter apart. There's no forgiveness in a mirror. Just glass, and the farce of reflection.

But redemption?

Redemption is easy: just open your heart.

Nobody feels the world turn and yet it is filled with silly tyrannies and the stories of fools. You'd think by now the hallucinations would catch fire and burn into the oak cladding of reality. The gleaming chrome of its thorax.

The elegance of refusal argues against the stucco of complacency.

I crash through my walk rustling leaves. I've seen the ocean pinned to the moon. It surpassed anything masquerading as *kakemono*. It filled me with fire. It caused the cylinders of cognition to pump me into desire.

What am I waiting for? What do I expect? What do you expect? Does real science still exist? What happened to the empirical inquiries of the Enlightenment? Has it been once again swallowed up in superstition? Religious dogma? Is it truly the Dark Ages again?

We call our animals in and prepare for the winter.

I sparkle among the lions of rage. My reticence was carried away in a flood of recognition. I can feel something pulling me to the frontier, something intuitive and hazy. It feels warm. It feels light and angelic. Is it the spirit of the lake? Is it the hand of William Blake?

Mystery of the Golf Tee

I've galvanized the tonic in order to indicate the flow of kelp. The waves come in. The waves go out. Magic eludes its own tinsel. As my dives go deeper, the stones at the bottom become brighter. These hectic strains I've thrown at the canvas will make better sense once the mud begins to shine. The wind turns and skitters away. The hem of a gull argues with the stern of the boat. I find a whisper of reminiscence crying in the shadows. I smell destiny in the rattle of the east.

There's a trigger that I can pull, but that would lead to some nasty repercussions. The corollaries are violent enough. My fatigue is palpable. The words are vertical. I withdraw into coral and twinkle. The book embodies stratification. The geology is alive. My drum resembles a winter dance. I feel that there is a certain focus to be painted into neglect. Thought is kerosene. If I can swim into your eyes I can explain everything. A puddle is nothing like a hat but it will brake for children. No depth attains the surface without getting a little messy.

Language is an event, not a potato chip. If the ovation is thin it may also be extruded by a swarm of carbohydrates. For example, I go get the laundry out of the dryer. I pull it all out and feel its warmth and communion. It's mostly underwear, T-shirts, and socks. I find a little pointy plastic object. It's white and looks like a tiny rocket ship. I wonder what the hell it is. What does this thing have to do with clothes? Is it a pin, some sort of fastener? Should I toss it? We share the washer and dryer with three other units. What if it's important and someone comes asking for it? Should I put it somewhere where someone can see it and reclaim it? Where would that be? On top of the dryer? One of the shelves behind the sink? It's so small. I can't decide if this little doohickey is important or not. I can't decide if it's important or not because I don't know what it is. I bring it in with the clothes. My mind spins. What the fuck is this thing? I fold the clothes. Then I realize what it is: it's a golf tee. There are two golfers in the building. I toss it.

And so you see, this is how the world comes to be discovered. We find shapes, we define them by their function, and give them a name. Things without a function are harder to define. Some things aren't even things. They're ideas. Perceptions. Intuitions. Clues.

How do you describe vision to the blind?

How do you describe a ball in the realm of the square?

How do you know when something is music or just plain noise?

Music unbuttons the air. I can smell the invocations of Gilgamesh.

Death hunts for wrinkles. We feed it bones and revolutions. I try to unite examples of clothes and instinct. It amuses the sparrows to see versions of water blown by the wind. It's a big world with a lot of bananas and arguments on it. The blue tears of my sorrows are tilted to show the rotation of the planet. Sometimes my personality explodes out of my body. People get hurt. I try to make amends and decorate the future with French doors. The animals frolic. We sit and sew our clothes together.

I sense the grandeur of salt, whose events are peripheral to the elevation of taste. The recruitment of cantatas endures. The cylinders of the palace pump up and down. I flow beside the noise. Thousands of jellyfish wash ashore. The straw is sufficient unto itself. My faith burgeons before I can decide to linger in the wilderness or not. Faith in what I cannot say. All that I know is that if I gaze behind the curtains I may be able to identify what it is that keeps walking around in my blood looking for resolution.

The Debris of Pain

Words propagate like blood on my sleeve. Consider the hum that sleeps in the heart. Our chowder of insinuation. A magic belt of thin drawings is haunted by the grace of witness. I'm milked for falling. Heaven's dots chime through the centuries. I'm slammed into fireworks with sour folds of convolution. A paper constellation to occur must twinkle fields of description. Pleasure imagines pulling us into Baudelaire. Ok. I need a copy of my ears. I'm the rocks that hop into paper. Light is a monstrous sky. I bake with railroads. I wear indigo that a brain decorates in algebra. I carry fluttered raspberries. I'm tense like Byzantium. The radio fingernails cooked the ganglions of an apparition. I saw it all happen in my wrinkles. Idleness is a gift. Here I am painting by shoes. The weather sits beside me. I listen to a berry. It tells me meaning is delicate things. The interior is badly carried until the end of the day when it slops out of the door. I slapped it to happen. Velocity murders distance. This is how Iceland has its variations. When we're alone the sounds have a structure that might be called music. I think of kelp. A brass bell in a courtroom. The basement of a tattoo on somebody's arm. It enlarges in the sag of time. I'm learning to lean on banishment and not exclude it but magnetize it all the way to Wisconsin where I can fill it with pickles and watch it climb the walls and dance on the ceiling. A berry is so many things. It liberates cork. It bristles with thorns and is a cause of conversation. I'm a social being. Any day now a glamour will thud on my gloves and convince me that towels are cooperative. Don't worry. This is just imagery. The keys cry to say that copper is what my adjectives require if everything else continues to be Pythagorean and naked. Naked, yes, but naked in an abstract, Dubliner kind of way, drawing on the past and awakening syllables of fire in order to warm the room a little. Change in a blaze shatters into reality and is so appealing it energizes the consonants. I like to paper palpability. This is infinite in camaraderie. Thrust your eyes into this sentence. I do that every morning and it makes me cardboard. I gurgle anguish. Bubbles punctuate a house to powder and yardsticks perform by semantic obstetrics. We know that. We also know that to be a simple man isn't as easy as it seems. The climate confuses lightning with turnstiles. But I don't. I know a turnstile when I turn one. It's in squeezing your subtleties that I find the enticements of the hearth. Infinity dangles from your fingers. Corot drifts through a fly. I flip to expand it. Time collapses on life and bleeds sandstone. It granites our world as a hothouse gauze rides a beard to Scotland. The war ends. The castle climbs into itself. The emptinesses are filled at last. I saw this was going to happen and so I wrote it as consciousness culminated in mountains. Dishwashing does this. Writing is, after all, the debris of pain.

Spitting Planets on the Columbia River

Circulates furthers clay. The wind is itself the streets. My pump beside despair dissolved by barking. A cocoon broods on a dangled angle. A willow or punchdrunk I wear a tie like a hurricane. I'm doing what I'm writing. I'm writing. The thread considered the lake. Willingness is heavenly on a daub of red. The thumb across the sky. An idea plucked from the truth of dyes. Color into languor with Montmartre. Our shoes are all their own. The sidewalk in the excitement precedes the light of anarchy. A handspring means there is a strawberry. What is thinking? A violin concerto in B minor by Bela Bartok. What happens in the morning to the weight of an emotion is caused by syntax. Ghosts of ourselves tangled in the language of our drugs. Waves are an anonymous guide. The ocean is literal. I strain against the gust. Bag a stone in oboe sugar. Step toward the east singing. Wheels make it about the burlap. Your glue in the snow. The improbability of copper dripping water this is wealth. The chin is like a dive. Words describing their own event in motion and shape. Powder blue faster and faster among the stars. I remember prepositions and stir. I'm the ugly wars of my own perspective. I tilt toward Friday spitting out personalities. This is a sentence giving itself to a suggestion of itself on the tongue of a moment. Thought on a lip heats the sympathy which throws itself into straw. I worry that there can be a dragon to the skin and any phenomenon like a lunatic caboose. My impulse is gravel. Reading is gauze. I mean swimming. I can lift these words. There is some utility in paradise. This does birds by sitting down. The world boils. Bingo garlic pounds a lip. French happens by my philodendron. I think it's a tendency. My heart hurls itself into being moment by moment and when we reach the river we lean on the rain and writhe in soft chronologies. The problem is crawling. When that happens topaz is easy to do. Singing gets into the engine and drives everything forward until it becomes a play of cherries spitting planets on the Columbia river.

Murky Description

What a bumpy food hails to virtue is gathered by the baritones and doted on like glue. My smells sparkle. They do. But I worry about the caviar. There's little utility in tugging a picnic into this. I can still lift gauze. I can spin acceptance. I can boil pasta and make conversation. Sometimes bending in half will enhance my feelings about the garage. I can't speak for Neal Cassady but I can throw myself into the straw and watch the sweet light of dawn stream through the holes of the barn. Grab a pencil the weather is hemorrhaging words. I feel Missouri in the waves. A voice is literal but a dime in the hand is still a moment's reflection. I honor the truck. I drive it like an apparition gliding through a lip. If gravity draws me into the cafeteria I'll find a booth and sit down to think about it. Vinyl is what I feel, the squeak of vinyl and the glow of a jukebox and Del Shannon still singing about his runaway lover. And everything imbued with the smell of eggs and bacon. Outside there's a river. You don't need to see it you can feel it. It ignores time. It has its own time, the time of the river, which is meandering and hungry. The river in all of its deformations is a redemption of poor closeted life, a phenomenon of shine and stone suborning the linearity of narratives that crush our true sense of the world. You know? The stories that adhere to principles of causation, purpose, motivation, a false construction of cause and effect. It's true, much of life is a matter of causation. But there's nothing — nothing — like dogwood. My heart crumbles in images of the past. I get behind the past and push it into the future where it looks enduring and everyone loves the cello. We enjoy autumn. What I need is a dream of money to glide into the bank and heave its guts into my checking deposit. It often amazes me that whenever I become a large feeling with bones and hair I still can't play the accordion. The accordion eludes me. But hey, I can do this: I can shake the mighty currents of remorse and reflection like a river just after it leaves the city and continues flowing into the prairie. Singing is in me. It's bald as a participle. Clutch a poker and get the fire going. That's not a participle son, that's a correlation. I winched it with this sentence and brought it up and there it is, a dark thing moving slow and wavy like a giant catfish inventing itself in murky description.

Wild Einstein

My innocence has been pierced by deceit. Nothing new there, eh? I struggle with my scruples all the time. Who doesn't like going to bed? I mean, come on. If language is an hallucination, then cactus beards the desert sky as the philodendron fills the dendrites of a finger as it rises and falls.

Metaphors deform the sink. I'm ready for just about anything.

The Jolly Green Giant smashes a teacup in rage. The clitoris purrs and is properly deified. An arm moves. Jewelry clanks like a thermostat. The deeper angst of meaninglessness and bewilderment is transmuted into the desire to accomplish, to triumph over insipidity.

Bubbles of meaning flow from my fingers. I scatter the ashes of worry on the waves of enlightenment. I've got a reason now to like overalls.

Anguish blurs vision. Logic doesn't do that, but it doesn't go that far anyway. I want to name this wine Wild Einstein. It involves the immediacy of steam, the seductions of chocolate, the embrace of drama, the push toward dreams.

I sat on the bed with my left leg tucked under my right leg and listened to Bob Dylan sing "Not Dark Yet." "I ain't lookin' for nothin' in anyone's eyes. Sometimes my burden is more than I can bear. It's not dark yet, but it's gettin' there."

I'd like to visit Greece one day. I'd like to see the Parthenon at dusk. That philosophical mood in the air just as the sun beds down on the horizon, disappearing bit by bit until the stars brighten and the night brings its ideas of infinity to bear down on the sad cold ground of planet earth.

Nothing in mathematics is ever literal. The rock is literal, but the river is not. Whatever happened to the idea of virtue? Why is it always so dark in here? I say: the more pockets, the better. You can never have enough pockets. What if you find writing on a bone and have nowhere to put it? Pockets make us marsupial and friendly.

Envy is the bitter fruit of dissatisfaction. Certain things invite touch, others not so much.

I mounted my horse and mused under the Sonoran sun. Cactus relates the hidden resources of the desert. I can understand that. What I can't understand is twine. Is it string? Is it rope? What is it?

And please, tell me, whatever happened to the bill of rights? Habeas corpus? Free speech? Elvis Presley?

There's your democracy, crawling into a skull. The plot has been sliding toward punk rock. There's nothing quite so beautiful as the legendary mud disease. The theorem of plums stumbles out of a wild sorrow. All the clichés about old age are true. You get cranky. You don't understand things.

A capable individuality sometimes capsizes in outrage.

There's no formula for raw experience. Experience is experience. Hearing, seeing, touching, feeling. Mistakes occur. The buzzing we thought was coming from the Comcast box turned out to be my Gymboss Interval Timer vibrating on top of the bookcase.

The real basis of life is what? a blob of protoplasm? I would like to explore this jelly further. I can do that merely by living. Think of me as a blob of protoplasm with fingers and thumbs. Hair. Complexion. Feet. Walking from room to room. Opening and closing the refrigerator. What do we do for food if the economy collapses and food disappears from the grocery store and the dollars in my pocket are worthless paper? Life will be hard to support. But there will always be 7-11, right? 7-11 is as old as Rome. Did Julius Caesar shop at 7-11? Did Hannibal water his elephants at a 7-11 after he crossed the Alps?

The 7-11 closest to us closed up. Boarded its windows. That's not a good sign.

I grew a beard once. Nothing in my life changed significantly. I didn't become another person. I stayed the same person, but with a beard. Which I had to maintain with a pair of hedge clippers.

If something doesn't work, sprinkle a few vowels on it. I need emotion in order to say something. Emotion grows big out of vowels. Consonants give it dignity. Even when I had to get up in the middle of *The Magnificent Seven* I maintained my dignity and when I came back Denzel Washington was taking a bite out of the heart of a deer.

Morning blends with the river. A staircase walks through itself. Energy divided by the speed of light squared equals licorice. On the other hand the truth of the cruet is unassailable and definitive. No table should be without one. The table alone is impressive. Or should we toast the CD player? The harmonica holds a long blue note proving that everything is sad and lonely. People are sometimes so introverted they pop open when you least expect it and fill the room with butterflies.

If you cut a word in half, does a meaning spill out?

How might I describe this world? I would say it's the graffiti of a two-stringed guitar. A drawer full of socks. A young man named James Newel Osterberg growing up in a trailer park in Ypsilanti, Michigan. He insisted on being a musician. His father, a high school teacher, stood in the doorway, blocking his exit, then realizing the futility of it, moved aside and let James Newel Osterberg enter the world to become Iggy Pop.

Salvation doesn't always come in a box. The realities revealed in drama are more than emotional luxuries. They provide insights into our own dilemmas.

Which is one way to look at it.

Another is to follow the pornography of odor to its ultimate conclusion.

Snow falls on the fields of Minnesota. The ecstasies of the staircase result in pearls. Darkness lowers its tapestry of stars and headlights. The subtleties of life converse with a loaf of pumpernickel. They exist in order to teach us something. Something about compote, and compound eyes.

Folding laundry in Hollywood. The coagulation of blood. Fred Astaire sitting in a chair tapping his feet. The movement of snakes, the wetness of veins, the vertigo at the top of the tower.

The sound of salvation in the rocking trees.

Leave Your Stepping Stones Behind

Phenomena don't shake. The world is curled in your violin. Making clouds tokens grease in music. Describe a fork. I will do this to a blob and texture what a floor does. There's opium in my duty to rain. Henna is emphatic by chattering poetry. A wedge of ocean will light Spain. There are horses in me that soar through abstraction squirting tin. Joan Baez moos. A slice of cough creates a culture. Planets with crustaceans and desks shouting towns of thought. Language is the hallucination everyone expected but by the time it reached Minneapolis eternity tore it to shreds and there was nothing left but shadows and orchids and Karen Carpenter singing "Superstar." It's just the radio. Indeed. My favorite noun is flaming into recognition but I still can't sit down and write a letter without first removing the epilogue from the ear of a moccasin. Let secretion do its thing. Petition your glands with study. Graze these hills with strength and approximation. There's nothing in the asphalt except the indecent distances we associate with time. I'm not against contour but I do think it needs to get naked in somebody's house and explode into mischief. What this means is seltzer and an ugly towel for everybody. I dip my nerves into hypothesis to see what happens next. What happens next is drills and cradles. Thermometers and thumbs. Theorems and fog. The circle circles itself. The birds in my hair correspond roughly to the words with which I represent them. This makes me thirsty. It's rough work. A large blue feeling declares itself on a coat changer. Eyebrows, for instance, forest my forehead whenever I slouch into age and cultivate acceptance. I'm carving my escape out of midnight. I'm not really arguing with anyone I'm just letting the river know I'm in total agreement. You can't argue with divergence. That's what makes it diverge. Ok this is weird. I get it. But hey, if it ain't broke don't fix it. Just shout at the appliances until a lyric finally arrives on the strings of a guitar and someone drags a diphthong to the door. You know? Something proto-plasmic like a vowel. Something swollen. Something slippery like a pediculate fish. Something starry over the sky of Montmartre. Something hanging and peculiar. Something wet. Vitreous is all I want to do. Go and sit like a loaf of sparks creating a cadence of total expansion.

Take a Little Ride

Slop the halibut slash squat. It veers into atmospheric damask. Before I was a laccolith knee-deep in granite and now I'm a sponger chewing the haze of a Christmas rose. The glockenspiel is a mythology of bells arguing the glaze of a birch afternoon. Cab finger sparks abstractions and the spirit dances.

Denim punctuation coughs snow after the ultramarine romance peremptorily favors lake trout. The saga is equally mist. Instinctively, I draw your whatness in gallop glue. The noise of my skin broods performance. A tattooed slide accelerates shape. Motion's twigs curve into participles. The shade initiates shirts. I strain to please a tendency. It fits the distortions. The hoe chain hugs your puddle. It is there that we find glass. The jars contain morals. A trickle of words descends into the summer of 1966. Consciousness is powder blue for a day. Explicit as a birth. The details are passionate about ears.

The almond gives itself to the tongue of a moment. Medication enhances a corner of the granite door. What flutter at jabber urges lips. This solace is a cool jerk I can mean to say as much as glue.

I have tailored my farm to sympathize with cauliflowers. The nerves are birds bubbly and gyromagnetic. Depth and volume murmur our intuitive spinning. I experience require. By that I mean I require a point above contact that is both cool to the skin and slippery. If we apply algebra to the ovulation of hills the murder opens and no gold can sit down and parrot the softness of sewing.

I will be ferocious and growl.

Sound is equally alluring coming from a guitar.

The incendiary life is there if you want it. Shake it long. Shake it hard. Turn it around. Testify. Talk a whisper into abandoning the bazaar. We unite by bone. Autonomy hands its imagery down. None of it is dreamy and soft. You just feel like sitting down and grinning. Some arabesques break off from heaven and glide into the ears as music.

A cotton pocket gurgles parallels.

Try twanging a wilderness.

It feels good to be vague and malleable for a while. You should try it. Crumple something. Then blow into it. It will expand into ideas.

I word sink the unearthed crawl. A blaze happens by vague interaction with a ripened honor.

Honor. What is honor. Honor is stirring and heroic. It is nothing like cactus. It displays a long solace in translations of the moon by black conviction and throwing knives at a pizza.

This darkness is shattering the place. What are we going to do with the river? Let's take it with us. Give it bananas. I can already spot Thursday appearing above the horizon.

And finally, I have gulped Boston. My hinges make it greasy. I grant that I have pain. Yes. But what a beautiful havoc wears my abstractions at night when the gypsies arrive and rattle their castanets.

Burst

Burst. What did? Collar stud dusty personality muscle grapefruit I myriadly decipher.

Motion stretch. Honesty's rattle is a heavy throw. Call for an exterior angle. Something veering. See how a sensation is an acceptance study, a batch we expand into ears.

The swell thickens. The operation is on a roll.

Here I am pasting infinity's leather mutations to a trembling flavor of pathos. The rounded basket with the basset hounds medicates the combustion of preteens. Induces kindness. Welcomes birds. Pulverizes court plaster. The ladies at court all smile.

The abstract is this jingle I bells on a blue orchid. You know? It's a bit like a badge but more transcendent in its own diversions than a tangle of the mind or a grebe diving into the waters near Iceland.

This red light thing is only a mustache. I said it to build a monotonous tin chatter for a brown probability we can plunge into. Brown is an intellectual color and makes me reflect on boiling.

My act cures ten nobles of wishy washy Latin.

Fathom restoration then fight the barriers to partial differentiation. Trickle hinge subtleties. Your ceremony is a shade of language that I can engage in tailoring. Plough a slow theatre. Meditate paths. An ugly density converses with the ocean. My admonition is my door.

Sift structure.

The world pineapple spoon is its own abstraction.

I stir a burst grape to agree to impart a stimulation to the action behind the barn.

Tidepool spout.

Yell at your hair. A genie will appear and murder the mirror.

Ignite wealth. You do that by pushing money at a congress.

Go ahead. Bloom. The maple has a beard. The smooth it presses reaches geometry and folds. I cod swim there. I remembered to indulge. I've had time to think about it for a while. I touched the bump I mentally exceeded. Don't start the hermitage without me. The crack is a drug eating into the purity of goldfish.

Walk and eat. It's a solution. The split pea is our threshold. But the world is our halibut. This isn't a matter of hit songs so much as a plea for arabesques. I compliment the sparkle of your river. The sweet words that are never said but empower descriptions manipulated by hose.

The burst is a forehead drooling cement. It's all about prolonging the muffins. Forbearance is prayer. The paradigm vibrates its definitions but nobody gets the banishment. The weather at the end of this sentence has been seized by a shiny pain and carried to a woman on the dance floor. That's why we have maps. Perception is irritating. Proverbs induce grace. Go there. Go amplify a sound of feeling time consenting to change into mind on paper.

Impromptu

The hand is evidence of fingers. I always feel a trap of canvas the ooze articulates. The reflection is my dip into thought to ponder paper. My effervescent red palette trickles ocher on our willow. The forehead plays with mass just as words do when the salt claps. Cotton is to cloth what squeezing is to granite. Recruitment thickens with meat. And yet I can't help sell a trellis for a dollar at the local syntax committee.

It's time now for a little abstraction. The world doesn't get to be empirical all the time. How else can you appreciate someone like Neil Young? Transcendence flexes its muscle and does a back flip.

Age prolongs the sensation of touch. Some diseases stumble over their own symptoms. I think of filling a kiss with some structural integrity. It makes me feel bouncy, like Fred Astaire. Money comes with complications. It's better to evade the predictions and break out into imagery. Grammar is a muscle. All it requires is a little cooperation, a mattress, and a place to go.

The wind thuds into place but doesn't stick around very long. That's how wind is, you know? It blows. It twists into tornados and that has a kind of glamour until the towns are demolished. Then it becomes something else. Something no one pretends to understand.

Where was I in the summer of 1967? A garage, listening to the Velvet Underground and *Blonde on Blonde*.

Clouds and powwows float in my head like a world. So we went and bought a bathtub. We both like puddles. The opening of the mind can occur when you least expect it. Before the journey ends it helps to gnaw on a piece of wood. Some of us choose a saga of unfocussed rage and begin there. Others spread their wings in narration and effect a change of temperature which the garden accommodates like an elephant lying down in the shade of a baobab. And then nothing matters. Well, it does, but it doesn't, if you know what I mean.

Perception is a process. I need a good camel. I went to the well looking for divinity and found the sag of time. I leaned into the delectation of rock and mortar and felt good for a change. Water was near. It felt cool. It smelled cool. Cool and dark. Isn't that what we mean by the divine? Something mysterious, like mushrooms or baptism?

And why baptism?

And why not baptism?

Until then I'm just energy. I like ghosts and antiques. Those ruffled collars they wore in 17the century Europe and inglenooks and talking. Ted Berrigan's sonnets and walnuts and withdrawing into the house as soon as it begins to rain and you can smell the lightning before it strikes or thunders.

It's hard getting a strand of hair off of a piece of soap. The soap is slippery, the hair is stubborn. But lightning, you can't get lightning out of your blood once the storm has raged within, purging your being of NPR and Belgian waffles. Thus my being supports a mode of being of which it is not the source. The source is elsewhere. The source is a finger, a thumb, a finger and thumb maneuvering a piece of hair from a bar of soap. It is sitting on a bench in front of a keyboard. It is the interrelation between the external reality of soap and the inner reality of a piano that brings about a state of continuous propagation, note upon note pursuing a melody of fevered restlessness. Only if we created a piano made of soap could we pursue the smoother crescendos of a woman's leg.

It is within the realm of the simulacrum that we find metaphors for the spoon club. I will sometimes sit on the floor and beg the paper to come to me in a palace of candy. Ideas of movement and direction anticipate the flowering of a new sensation. Let's call it something. Let's call it bells. Let's call it singing, or equilibrium. I admire your willingness to read this far, and sit down by the river, and listen to the stones.

Who among us isn't under the influence? What matters is motion we make in order to locate a strawberry, or induce snowfall by way of our anguish, our sheer ability to rise and get dressed in a jacket of spectral green with ivory buttons.

The phrase "all hands on deck" attracts a crowd of astronauts and prostitutes. What is thinking, we ask ourselves, and use our biology to produce electricity, the poetry of electrons, the excitement inherent in a violin concerto. I can't think of a better way to put it: when the language of our hands hold the hunger of the universe, it's time to work the thumbs into opposition and assemble a pump. Scrape the bow across the strings in a hesitant, slow glide and create a mood that can sustain anything, including sports.

The Act Of Painting

The act of painting suspends time, then explodes it in jets of color. The move-
ment is played in one second, a flash of joy, the escort of hyaline nuclei. The
representation of noise really becomes noise and the grotesque assumes the
proportions of broken and chaotic sentences. This is painting in words, or
what might be called gurgling. Textured being, forge of luxuries, the total evo-
cation of the tactile. In this way, everything is organized and disorganized,
dismantled and mantled, each sound a symptom of chromatic brocade, the
effervescence of elaboration.

Sometimes it's really objective, the first white background. I take notes. In
fact, I aim for the perfection of gesture in the moment. The moment of paint-
ing is a spatio-temporal bubble. I watch the canvas that is a moment in time
slow down and realize itself, gel, inspissate in goop, separate from reality. Ges-
tate, beckon. Time doesn't matter anymore. The essential is a coincidence with
itself in a relationship blossoming into what the Greeks call *kairos*, a way of
seizing the opportunity when it presents itself. The experience is there. Here's
the creation: a back and forth between languor and lightning.

Beauty pants for a woman. The scientific lipstick languishes for expres-
sion. The shelf is glass. The friend of my character creaks into view. I become a
pterodactyl and begin sinking into darkness. Here is where painting becomes
a little flame pillow. My soft shoulder is a beard of foliage. My almanac behaves
like sleep. I'm frankly all for appliance, especially dishwashers, if they contrib-
ute a little intelligence to the sexual detergents of struggle. The tamarind has
been splendidly embalmed in Peru. Wednesday's business hangs out of the
window like a thesis of thirst, a radically gnarled lawn.

My car is in the sparrow cave. I have a poetry coupon that can be redeemed
at any gas station. It's a language of combustion. It helps me to understand
foreign realities. I can endure your odor, but please don't plug yourself into
another silly illusion. I can only take so much dementia. I need to comb my
body. The scorpions have been frightened from the shore. The parcel kisses
the music of the attic. I unpack the comforts of structure. I stroke the legs of
a blind hippopotamus and find something in my being that yearns for recog-

nition. This could be a music I can paint. The geometry of the hive affirms the journeys of the bees. The camel moves downstream on a barge. The painting becomes a crisis of sobbing revolt.

Shall we continue to regret the three-dimensional illusion in painting? There's more than one way to simplify the credibility of the ovoid. Space is there to be shaped, divided, enclosed, but not primped into a frizzy nimbus. The literal must not be allowed to stomp its way into calligraphy unless the weather calls for a flat and linear handling. Don't worry about the violent immediacy of the wallpaper. I think I know what it's doing. It's making itself more realistic by approximating a self-evident tautness for the sake of the public. We can relax it by academic softening. The plum is combing the helicopters. I've got a mixed feeling about the knife. Its intent is clear but the edge is scarily incisive. It's a little too intractable, a little too blatant to be brought within the scope of aesthetic purpose. But what would that be, exactly? A more immediate surface? Yes. Let's have more of that. The closet says a man is here. These are his sleeves and leather. Please, come see the eraser. It's a small thing to lift it to your lips. The crime knot makes a coconut tree. Gelatinous iconoclast. Mouth oozing suns.

I'm Glad The Brain Is Plastic

Memories are hives of strange honey. The human brain weighs three pounds. Imagine three pounds of honey or three pounds of salt or three pounds of anything, an ingot of gold or ostrich egg.

Imagine a brain full of honey and salt. Imagine the ghosts of the past sitting down at tables upon which are served haddocks and poached eggs and grilled plums with ricotta and honey, or arguments reheated in delicious resentment.

Memories weigh nothing, or have the weight of entire worlds. It depends on the memory. The same memory can weigh nothing at all one day and weigh as much as hurricane Irma the following afternoon, and come blowing out of your mouth in angry words.

Some memories are vivid, some are vague, and some are long sluggish wandering nights. The thing to remember is the plasticity. Plasticity is the word for the day.

Some of my more persistent memories concern trips to Europe, hitchhiking across France in the 70s, getting wickedly drunk night after night for several weeks in Lloret de Mar, a town on the Costa Brava of Spain's Catalonia.

Several accidents involving cars and motorcycles, the chaos, the kindness of strangers, insurance headaches.

Getting beat up in somebody's rec room when I was drunk at age 18, and experiments with LSD and amphetamine that same year, 1966, which did not end happily, but led prudently to the disuse of psychedelics and employment in Plant #2 of Boeing in Seattle, which also did not go well, I lasted six months and then quit.

What I mostly remember of 1967 is a friend's garage, listening to *Blonde on Blonde* over and over, and living in a bus for several months with three other guys until one morning the owner of the bus wouldn't let us into his house to use the bathroom and kitchen. There was a note stuck to the door urging us to leave which we read in the frosty air of December, towels and toothbrushes in our hands.

It would appear that I have an easier time remembering traumatic or catastrophic events more than happy events. Is that normal? I don't know.

But I'm glad the brain is plastic.

The Age Of Raisin

I have a craving for raisins. I have no reason to crave a raisin and yet I crave a raisin. The craving of a raisin craves a reason for having a raisin. I raise the craving to the sprawl of possibility. The possibility is everywhere possible except when it's impossible and then the impossible becomes possible and this possibility is the impossible undoing of impossibility. Impossibility is possible because possibility becomes an impossibility when impossibility becomes possible. The reasoning is circular, like a raisin. A dark wrinkled raisin. Each little raisin looks like the scrotum of a tiny elf. But a mound of raisins, a bunch of raisins, an agglomeration of raisins, is a meditation of matter, an imbroglio of the particular.

The need for sunlight is the reason why grapes are grown in the San Joaquin Valley. Sunlight pounds the valley like a hammer of radiant force. The grapes dry and their skin wrinkles into dark little kisses of light.

Reason pounds the irrational brain into tiny wrinkled raisins of scrotal scripture.

I love raisins. I like to scoop them up with a spoon and put them in my mouth. I put all my metaphors aside and appreciate them for what they are until they're swallowed and the metaphors come rushing back into my head and I have to do something about them.

The metaphors, that is. Not the raisins. The raisins have their own raisin d'être.

I have a reason to love raisins and the reason is reasonable and topaz. I don't know why it's topaz. I just like the word topaz. My reason for topaz is exonerating and vinyl. You can see where this is going.

A pair of pears glares among the dappled apples. Shinto potatoes tiptoe amid a dumb show of grapes agape in the landscape. Helen's melons gel in Helena. The swans in Ceylon feed on the lawn in the bygone chiffon of dawn. Hemmed in lemons persimmons summon the calmness of a psalmist in the juice of abuse. And the squash is awash with the slosh of the posh in the moonlight of our midnight appetite.

Clearly, the world is a place of things. Tables, chairs, pulleys, guitars, trees, rocks, hats, plugs, rugs, drugs and bugs. Heliotrope and fruit. Grapes and apes and drapes and crêpes. Figs and twigs and Buddha's hand.

I'm not separate from the world. Nobody is. When the world dies we die. Every atom belonging to me as good belongs to you said Whitman, who had a lot of atoms.

Heidegger referred to the mind as a "cabinet of consciousness" as a false premise. There's no separation between the mind and the world.

Think about that. Pop a raisin in your mouth and chew it into the universe that is you. And ask yourself: is what is in me and about me and around me one and the same? Yes and no. The body is host to the soul which is nowhere without the body and everywhere when the body goes.

What surrounds me, what surrounds you, is Umwelt.

That's what I'm putting out there today, right now. These are ideas. Just ideas. Perceptions hammered into words and vertices. Refreshments on the counter. Spring rain at the window. The blades of a fan. The sheen on the coffee table. The pain in my shoulder. The warmth in my hand. The pleasing reasoning in the taste of a raisin.

Savage Fragility

I'm feeling molecular today. I've got an atomic tibia and an electromagnetic eyebrow. My forehead is an event horizon and my hair travels across my scalp in probability waves. My whole existence is one quantum leap after another. I tremble with quarks. I'm a strong nuclear force full of spin. I walk on Planck units and get a Big Bang out of photons. Time dilates around my uncertainty principle. Wave-particle dualities dance on my toes at night, red-shifting from toe to toe like the superclusters of scooters in Rome on a Saturday night. Does it matter that I'm Boolean? Will my critical mass one day explode into water-color? Will I one day hang on a wall in a motel? Life is so strange. When will this dark energy become warmth and light and lead me into thermodynamic equilibrium? Who doesn't dream their life is a dream? Because it is. We are all interactive massive particles growing in variability until one day the universe sparkles at the end of the bed and space-time bends into a jewel of jubilant luminescence. Photons don't exist by themselves. We are all participants in a giant carnival of black holes and event horizons. Form is emptiness, emptiness is form. We've all heard this. But who can say what a wave function is, or the ways in which the mind can affect matter, like Keanu Reaves bending a spoon in *The Matrix*? I'm not that guy. I'm more like a cloud of mesons exchanging particles in an exquisite dance of positively charged ions. And I like that. It's not bad. It's better than being antimatter, better than being a weak interac-tion. But what do I call this accretion, this gathering of words, this *potentia*, this zone between possibility and reality? I will call it a conversation with ice. I will call it Caliban and order it to carry wood. I will call it a fez and put it on my head. It should be obvious. But is it? This is, after all, the world of the atom. The world of matter scattering in all directions. It's splendid to be details squirting out of a book. Writing is a form of reverie that sputters with its own private algebra, a lustrous sauté of improbable predication. Nothing as proprioceptive as Swedish massage but more like a savage fragility of su-perluminal quantum connectedness, a particle accelerator smashing itself into words. And for that I'm grateful, it's nice to have a mathematical foundation, an isotropic telephone and a place to hang my fez.

Scrambled Eggs

This is the peculiarity of scrambled eggs, that once scrambled eggs have become a habit of mind, this habit of mind converts everything that comes within its purview into the language of scrambled eggs. The territory of the scrambled is unlimited. The potential for scrambling is endless, each group of natural phenomena, each phase of social life, each stage of development past or present is matter for scrambling. Order and symmetry have their place, but too much order and symmetry deaden. They must be counteracted. They must be subject to scrambling. Without scrambling, there can be no eggs. Without eggs, there can be no scrambling of eggs. But there will be scrambling. Scrambling will occur. Scrambling cannot be restrained. Everyone strives to be scrambled. Scrambled in all the colors of distress, ecstasy, rapture, mortality, seminars, station wagons and office supplies. The essence of all scrambling is located in its method, not in its material. Sometimes shortcuts to scrambling may be found in books. Or amusement park rides. Bank robbers making breakfast. Jackson Pollock in a dance around a canvas making energy visible. The individual who sees relations in all things is a born scrambler. The facts may belong to the social statistics of our cities, to the atmospheres of the most distant planets, to the digestive organs of worms and cephalopods, to the quantum mechanics of the subatomic domain, but until they're scrambled, the facts are inert. The facts are dull and without life. It is not the facts themselves that form cognition, but the tumult in which they ignite.

Inimitable Thimbleful

Incendiary this walk on your hook. Creosote hugged there opposes a predicate with which I feel discursive and shortcake. Gloves it novels the chain. Butter this I tickle the grapple until fate summons a condolence. I grow my letters in Africa. The tin I grain to morning. Paddle punctuation if a house is about you. Enfold the echo that you are under the need for explosion. Wheel what treads the airplane across the tarmac. After you I flowed and swelled into my injury like a grapefruit. It was imprecise to disintegrate but the incandescence was superb. I occur among myself fencing a happy distance and deepening a raw sienna that I argue with below my suffering. I'm the painter of the compass I encompass in ensembles of wapiti. Infringe the sternum put the key into a monsoon. Corner the allegory in your breath since your hair is something awaited in cocoa. There I scatter where I endeavor to be the rain I walk through believing maidenhood to be a form of debut. The firmament runs on beginning and is manufactured by a glandular overshoot. It's deformed to construct the bobble we throb. I climb into death with my pounds of muskox. I'm a cloud to myself, a tableau of urges. I shine by a suitcase of garlic. If gravity lingers in this I will poke the technician into platinum. A cherry what? I dribble secretion when I shave don't ask why. This coordinates the thesis I'm yelling at a jilt. It happens that a frill swings from a veteran and makes it all wicker. And this is my banana.

The Creak Of Bedsprings

What divides the organic from the inorganic? Is it a mysterious Vital Force? Is it a chemical process? Is it Philadelphia?

Everything is a process. Moods are a process. Pressure is a process. Eyes are a process. Processions are a process.

The Fleetwood Mac of 1972 is vastly different from the Fleetwood Mac of 1977. *Future Games* is a very different album than *Rumours*. Clearly, a process was involved, an evolution including divorce and conflict and diamonds of sound. Romantic entanglement, emotional tumult and mountains of cocaine. Band members quit. Band members joined. Danny Kirwan's pre-Raphaelite reveries opened the way for Bob Welch's silky otherworldliness which blossomed into Stevie Nick's gypsy scarves. The band morphed from a serious blues band in the late 60s to a pop music salvo in the latter half of the 70s. You can't step into the same river twice. And the banks are muddy. Very, very muddy.

The organic is inherently messy. It's in a state of continuous transformation. Life is unceasing creation. Ergo, it's continuous variations are polymerizations of the long chain of being, accommodations to the humors of arousal and the warp of disproportion. We live in a volatile universe. The birth of stars. The death of stars. If you're alive, you're going to be wary. Living is easy, but staying alive is dicey. There is always worry. Apprehension. Unease.

Lately I've been subsisting on a steady diet of westerns, hypothesis, and cortisol. It all gets easier when you learn to let go. Letting go is half of the solution. The other half is getting it back.

We live on the edge of chaos, a region of bounded instability that engenders a constant dynamic interplay between order and disorder. If you don't believe me, just look under our bed.

Modification roars at the incubation of worry. The walls mediate the long slow odors of ceremony. The sculptor stands in his workshop caressing the transcendent form of the chisel.

There was a time I wanted to sound like Bob Dylan. It was an impetus. And then it became a puzzle. And then it became a mermaid. I learned how to make things go horizontally across the page rather than imperially like a physician's assistant. I was not in the business of taking anyone's pulse. I just wanted to break the sound barrier and create a phantasmagoria of breasts.

On Monday, we went for hamburgers. I noticed a painting on the wall above our booth, a mural by Myrna Yoder, who does all the murals for McMenamins.

Which is where we were: McMenamins.

There was a bowl of water with a goldfish in it. The water was non-existent. No attempt had been made to paint water. How do you paint water? The goldfish implied water. There was water by implication. That's all it took, a single goldfish to create the miracle that is water.

By implication.

Which is also a miracle.

The hamburgers, incidentally, were really good. Moist and flavorful.

The human mind is a compliment. You have to think of it as an epiphenomenon, a compilation of knotty pine and the exuberance of thingness. If the depiction of a goldfish is enough to suggest water, the human mind must be a category of gas, tending to expand indefinitely until the meal arrives.

Nothing soothes anxiety like food.

Or Xanax. That works pretty good, too.

Opium breaks Chicago in half.

Do you ever have feelings so powerful you can't share them with anyone? Anxiety is to fear what steam is to steel. One is vapory and moist and the other is a parable of heat and casting. Sparks fly. This process, known as smelting, is a form of extractive metallurgy, heating out impurities. Poetry does the same thing, but with less overhead. A man comes out and dissolves in a pool of emotion. The resulting extract hisses like a thousand snakes. Ropes of glowing metal create a ring of luminescence.

The mouth is a vagina in reverse.

I know you're out there somewhere. I can feel it. I can feel the way the dirt explains squash and the idea of roots finds expression in cotton and rhododendron. I can feel the way clothing forgets the body and becomes a whistle. I can feel the way a hot woman lingers by a piano in a dark room in Miami, fanning herself with a real estate brochure.

I raise my eyes and experience a sudden sharp sense of depth. The stars are stupefying. The mathematical order of things possesses a positive reality. If the shoe doesn't fit, I throw it at the president. This is how life repairs and rejuvenates itself. Climb into yourself and pepper your heart with the debris of heartache. Things viewed from a distance become pyrotechnic. I'm a little bit powder, a little bit water: shake me. I've always wanted to write a rock and roll of words. Philosophy borrows it from every day life. The energy of chaos, the beating of wings.

I apologize for the geometry. Let's boil these sounds into paradise. The spoon displays a distortion of trees. The air is an engine of liberation. I hold the sun in my hand. You can't film a feeling, but you can wander the Louvre in search of beauty. You can relax the tension in your body until the sense that is buried in the sounds becomes material. Becomes cartilage and bone.

Until then, there is process. There is gauze and hay. The horses describe the hills. The trails feed our imagination. Our education is unearthed from candlelight. It is time that puts a stick in the wheels. Living matter presents enough plasticity to take in turn such different forms as those of a fish, a reptile and a bird. The embryo of a bird or reptile is not initially that different from an elephant or human. It is in its development that it becomes a bird or a snake or a human.

A single cell accomplishes this by dividing. In this privileged case, what is the precise meaning of 'exist'? I pass from state to state. Sensations, volitions, feelings, ideas are the changes into which my existence is divided and which colors it in turns. Nothing is permanent. Everything is flux. I need a thousand wild horses to say a single meaningful thing. Something like the seed of a sequoia catching a little rain, or the quality of light in the skeleton of a whale on the beach. Something like this, like words, like the creak of bedsprings, like the resolution of a worry rattling around in my brain.

Reading fills the canvas of words with wind. I lean into life like rain.

The Death Of Gravity

The map of bamboo thrives in an exultation of steeples. There are roads one can take in life that go in truant sequence, like a rogue meow that declaims reality to be a valve, or marketplace. I see the avocados. But what are these? I believe they're students of hope. The vagaries of hope. The soaps and gropes and tropes of hope. The students bow in concentration. They weep. Their tears become patents. The patents are only valid if there is tip-toeing and multiplication. Otherwise, they're just nozzles walking around in a wooded area.

Hope is a Polynesia entangled in caresses of moonlight. I like drugs. But do drugs like me?

Drugs and hope go together like glands and augurs. Consider this pancreas. It rests in a bucket of ice controlled by two knights with lances. It was the prized possession of a great prince who lived in a palace of ice eating oysters and caviar and humming songs gathered from West Virginia. If there is a sleeveless one-piece dress in the closet you may put it on. You can wear it to the Ball of the Magic Pancreas. Do you have balls in your life? A life without balls is a life lived steamily amid jigsaws. Everything is a puzzle. Primeval traffic. Meaning encased in syntax. Sweet meringue scratched into existence with a blue rake and an effulgent cerebellum.

Imagine a propaganda based on punctuation. Make a bonfire on Saturday. Lend the pilot some gold. Nothing can come out of the breath but drapery. Everything else is satire.

Infinity's vines are for rent. This will make our exchanges important and bend them into scales. I think, therefore I struggle. Coffee storms into my gums at the small café on the corner of your attention. We see tables and chairs. We see encroachments and uniforms. The careless organs of a swan. A poem by Stéphane Mallarmé eating a stadium.

The ratatouille of time is shaking in its book. I have a pound of wind with which to build a narrative of shoals and yo-yos. The detached sumptuous foam of a howling storm inserts its literature into the fungus and scenery of an existential contusion. A reader's eyes move back and forth scraping meaning out of a page of hints and innuendoes. The leg of a cat drinks movement from a bird. The whole incident provokes a metallic tongue into making pencils of sound. We back away from the door just before a house comes crashing into real estate.

The buffalo were plugged into veins of Cubism. We plunged our minds into the problem of light. The answer brightened into unconsciousness. A few of us began to float. Some of us used oarlocks. Other used truisms. Everyone meanders. It's a fact of life. Even the eyes of the crocodile reveal a primordial reverie as they glimmer just above the surface of the bayou.

The constant drumming has made us thin and urgent. Any rhapsody can cure a claw but can a claw cure a rhapsody? The claw is just an excuse for genuflection. Spread the limestone on the bread and the landscape will precede its own hills in a trance of speculation. The crime universe was parked next to a satyr which made everything feverish and new. The tar package jumped into cognition, and this modernized my dignity into a young male horse, which was fast, and worrisome, and made of words. I felt, at last, the airplanes sell themselves to the death of gravity, and put my trust in voodoo.

Insoluble Solutions

Is there a philosophy of rejection? Ways to cope with rejection? Things to be learned from rejection? Is there anything to take the sting out of rejection? Is there a way to reject rejection?

I don't really have any answers. What I do have is a moment in time to sort out all my little operations. Various emotions trickle through my ribs. I wear a necklace of mastodons. If existence is wet, existence gets me wet. If existence is existential, existence makes me existential. If existence is a synonym for being there, I'm here, trying to solve life with a lubricant and a film projector.

Can I be personal for a moment? My eyebrows have a myriad conspicuous hairs corkscrewing out of my brow. This is how I describe reality. I see it as a diffusion of gradients. Then some gravity comes along and exaggerates the weight of morning. The gradients get squeezed into tangents, Yorkshire canaries and springs. Some become ridges and knolls. A few get stratified. They become laminated. They become glazed and delicious. Fortunately, we have forklifts for these things. And packaging and aisles and three-bean salad.

Not all gradients are granite. There are giraffes. There are greyhounds and Indiana. Goodbyes on the porch, obsessions on the road, discrepancies in road construction and drug sensitivity. Eggshell, ivory, and cream. Outer space, onyx, and midnight blue. Some gradients are ice and show necks of themselves floating in arctic water howling in preternatural silence to the indifferent stars.

What happened, exactly, in 1967? The world got weird and weirder and then it got cooked in various conversations. Conversation is what people used to do when they got together. They didn't have gadgets in their hands. Nothing to stare at but the lines in their hand, the hair on their wrist, the time on their watch. So they talked and shared experiences. The raw experience of life became tasty morsels of narrative.

And there's plenty of that to go around.

When one thinks of the infinite number of infinitesimal elements and infinitesimal causes that contribute to the genesis of a living being, and that the absence or deviation of any one of them can affect the stability of the overall evolution or result in an inflammation of musical notes that can humor a feeling into a public exhibition of tiny sea polyps and crackleware, the chandeliers of the unconscious burn a little brighter.

The world is largely imaginary. You can't see darkness with a torch. You have to experience the darkness in its natural state, which is a swimming pool late at night in the Hollywood hills imbued with underwater lights. The shimmer is hypnotic. But it's not my pool. It's an imagined pool. I imagined it for my imaginary life as a movie director. That life lasted for not quite a minute. Then I decided to become an astronaut. And now I'm 167 pounds of dark energy pounding images into a laptop screen.

Lately, I've been tossing peanuts to crows. They're among the few birds we have left. I want to make life a little easier for them. But I have to pay attention. Sometimes I wait to see if they go for the peanuts and trip over a tree root or irregularity in the sidewalk. I now have scabbed knees. I haven't had scabbed knees since I was nine.

I've never really learned to sew. But so what?

The paintings of Vermeer are spellbinding. The lucidity is stunning. Women read letters, pour milk, gaze affably at the viewer or focus on a piece of needlework. In *The Astronomer*, a man with extraordinarily long hair and wearing a large heavy robe is seated at a table. It is said that the man might be Antonie van Leeuwenhoek, the "Father of Microbiology." He leans forward in the light of a window with one hand on a globe, the other on a corner of the table. The scene is imbued with the spirit of inquiry.

Our past undresses in our emotions. Or is it the other way around? Our emotions undress in our past. No one can predict the future. That's good. Let's keep it that way. It's good to comb the fibers before spinning them, if you get my drift. It's ochre o'clock and the tide is beginning to walk onto the land and cover the mud with the dream that is water.

Conception grows by contrast and heat. For example, I need a flashlight to search in the closet for a bottle of white vinegar. If I find a rainforest instead, it's generally not a problem. What worries me is losing an entire planet. What kind of species destroys an entire planet?

It's not amusing to watch a society collapse. Do you believe in something greater than yourself? I don't believe I have a self. Not really. I think I'm a constellation of cells that evolved out of nature like anything else crawling or walking or slithering around looking for food and comfort.

Because it's all just a dream. And the clowns weep softly.

Gabby

We're hairless for the most part. There's a few of us with hair, bristly, fuzzy, shaggy, going clockwise in corkscrews or ethereal as halls of hallelujah in the summer picnic clouds, enough to appear mammalian, like a monkey, I think you get the picture. But mostly we're black and pink and various shades of brown and our skin is bare and tender and soft. The skin cuts easily. Bruises easily. And so we build shelters to prevent ourselves from bumping into one another, doors and windows and rooms to do things privately, unobtrusively, things like eat and shit, take showers, enjoy sex, watch TV, and keep from getting hurt, keep from getting shot or stabbed or stepped on or cut. That's pretty much it in a nutshell. And as we near extinction I have to wonder: will there one day evolve another species with enough curiosity and arms and fingers or appendages resembling arms and fingers, appendages with the suppleness and sensitivity to maneuver implements like shovels and trowels to come dig us up and reassemble our bones, put us back together like Humpy Dumpty and stick us in museums, position our anatomies in big display cases to do whatever it is the species taking our place imagines we might've been doing in those two-legged bodies with osteoblasts and osteocytes, little finger bones and big thigh bones and a big round skull to house and protect a squishy globular convoluted brain and tree-limb arms and beanpole legs and funny elegant bones of the feet. How do you walk on those?

We didn't just walk, we danced. Hard to believe. But there it is. A species that danced.

Will we be remembered? Will we have counted in the infinite reaches of space as a narrative of survival and civilization whose records indicate vertiginous odysseys of thought?

Or will we be forgotten, obliterated from the record, our bones reduced to atoms, our quirks reduced to quarks, our valentines crunched into neutrons? Was it all a charade? A masquerade? Does it matter? Not really.

And what am I doing? What's all this firefly chasing chimerical vermicelli?

I don't know. I'm trying to write it down. Life down. Put it in letters. Words. Sounds that make meaning. Sounds that make images appear in the brain. I don't know why. It's a compulsion. Amber beads strung together for a necklace. Why, I don't know. For decoration. Or more importantly conveyance. The conveyance of ribs. Drums. Fireworks. Emissions of truth, if you want to call it that. An attempt to be truthful.

Why? Why be truthful? Truth matters. I believe it does. And that's the truth. The truth for me.

I sound dark. I often do. It comes with age. It's hard to be buoyant when you're old. You cease developing and cultivating looks. A look is what you call an attitude. This would be poise and sunglasses. I did a lot of that when I was young. I tried looking cool. I looked at Miles Davis and thought, that's it. That's the look I want. How can I be cool like him? Like Miles Davis?

I don't know, but the end result was Gabby Hayes.

You'd have to be my age to know who Gabby Hayes was. Gabby Hayes was an American actor best known for his roles as a hairy sidekick, a goofy old guy with a wink and a howdy do. He starred alongside William Boyd as Windy Halliday, but then he got into a dispute with Paramount over his salary and went to Republic Pictures and changed his nickname to Gabby. He got a gig hosting the Quaker Oats Show. He'd sit on a bench whittling or sanding some little object, wearing a big black floppy hat, its brim gashed in several places, and speak in a creaky old man's voice about the sundry oddities and flaws of life, how he just couldn't remember what it was he was not supposed to forget and hold his hand up revealing a big black ribbon tied around his index finger. "Just look at that," he'd say, "now what have I got that doodad on my finger fur." He wasn't just a bedraggled clown of the windy old west, he had wit and fire, there was brimstone in him. He was handy with a gun. He hosted Quaker Oats for four years, 1950 to 1954, did a one-year stint with ABC in 1956, and then, in 1957, his wife died. He ended his days managing a ten-unit apartment building in North Hollywood.

Quintessence, some cosmologists say, is a hypothetical dark energy that is implicated in the accelerating expansion of the universe. It is fine-tuned to explain the cosmological constant problem. According to the cosmological constant, the universe is static. But it's not. The Hubble telescope showed that the universe is expanding more rapidly than expected. Astrophysical data shows that this sudden transition in the expansion history of the universe is marginally recent. That's a bit spooky. What's going on? Will any of us ever know, ever find out?

In real life, Gabby Hayes, whose real name was George Francis Hayes, was well-read, well-groomed, serious and highly philosophical.

There's more matter to matter than mass and density. There are also doodads and fur.

Glockenspiel Milk

Turpentine unites in sensation. The spirits split the paper into thinking. Thoughts are butter, just pull the string. I adjust to life as best as I can. I drink glockenspiel milk. I feel the seclusion of blue which is simultaneously reached by stumbling. I thrash around in bed each night looking for sleep in a hilly oblivion. I sweep the punches into a paper sack and go clanking around the house in the armor I welded by spark and anarchy. My buttons groan controlling opinions of my shirt. The thermometer trapped a temperature and ate it. Now it's cold in my sonnet and the lobsters adjust themselves to an ocean in the making, a basket of water charmed by correspondence. Can you hear the echoes of Spain? The airplane invents itself. The air endorses our injuries. If we linger among the clouds it's because there is a certain prominence in locating a friendly pie. We at the Théâtre Montmartre understand ourselves by speaking in metaphysical geographies, little smells like incense, big smells like grease in a motorcycle shop. I'm not responding to the liquor today because I didn't drink any. I'm too fond of glockenspiel milk. You squeeze the udders and pull. The rest is music. The delectation of sound in an aching expansion of logic.

A Good Hotel And
A Pair Of Dry Socks

Wrinkles explain the history of a face. They tell a tale of unappeased ambitions, weary compromise and popped bubbles of glistening illusion. But most of the time wrinkles just sit on your face and simmer and boil. They make you look soulful, weather-beaten, life-beaten, existence-beaten, hammered by ordeal but still standing, heart beating, eyes seeing through all the lies and prevarications hurled at you like curtains, blankets, wooly obfuscations. You get a face like Geronimo or Abraham Lincoln. This is good if you're male, not so good if you're female. If you're female, wrinkles aren't particularly a welcome feature, but they can give you a certain regal aura if you don't fight them too hard with makeup and denial. Denial generally doesn't do anyone any good, especially denial. Denial was born for better things than denial. The true impulse of denial is acceptance. It's just slow to get around to it.

Human anatomy begins at home. It begins at birth. Birth and home aren't necessarily synonymous, but they are in this case, because I'm imagining home as a planet with clouds and birds, and blood and mucus. Mucus is the music of the nose. But if you're going to describe my nose, please soften some adjectives first and apply a little science. There are sinuses to consider, and density. Density matters. Density throws a punch.

I ooze my veins forward to explain the movement of blood and illustrate the distance of milk. It helps me relax to think about sewing. I walk into a religious crack and talk to the ghosts using a mouth of rubber and a grammar like bees.

And suddenly another paragraph wants your attention. The fish are in full horizontal swing. The comb keeps groping for my hair. I suppose the thing to do is to let things be what they want to be and leave the rest to the distillery. I will leave the soft bark for later analysis. The mud languishes in its own essence compelling the stepladder to step forward and hurry into play. There's a drug that expands into odor and an odor that expands into steam. It may be understood as the consequence of an immense kitchen, and a mouth tossing itself into words.

What is most difficult in language is to render the tempo of its metabolism. There lurks beneath its decorum an animal thrashing in its cage. Long, difficult, hard, dangerous thoughts.

Yippee! I just discovered water. It was masquerading as a cushion.

I tease people by forgetting they're people. I try to convince them they're eyebrows. But the joke is on me. I'm the eyebrow. I'm all eyebrows. But a little of me is also fast food. I may look like a diving board but inside is a man with arms and legs and enough authority to carry this procession to the end of the sentence where it will leap into cotton and become hair.

The front door portfolio is fused to a space held in reserve by a perception. Like most perceptions, this perception seeks the gold of paradise. It's better to be awake than asleep when the generous reciprocity of the world awaits your basket of clouds. Sleep swallows itself while stirring in the bed. The harmonies of notoriety are not what they seem. Fame is a brocade that slams the door on anonymity. Never take anonymity for granted. Anonymity isn't anonymous for nothing. For each and every embryo there's an equal amount of chrome adjusting to the rigors of undersea exploration.

Is that what this is about? Beer?

Some of us prefer other beverages. I use the luminous puff moo to escape the spatial algebra of soccer. The tugboat drifts in the orange light of sunset. The hill across the bay translates the clouds as a Russian novel. Everyone insinuates knobs.

Hard to believe, but I noticed there's dust on the hairdryer. Has it been that long since we've used it? Apparently, I could also use a haircut. But is this what is meant by testimony? Am I a fool? Or just another kangaroo?

The imagination will make its prison explode. Whose prison? We know whose prison. The prison of ownership and string. The prison of anguish and paint.

Drop the property on the ground where it belongs. Write a story about face-lifts. Deform everything. The wizard's fanged envelope will arrive in the mail and offer a pretty bug. Saddle the bug. Ride to Paris. Enter Paris. Smile and wave. The mind is wild for resolution. A good hotel and a pair of dry socks.

Being Is A Feeling

Sunset is protected by distance. It can never be caught and put in a jar because it's always running away into the night. As soon as you think you're there you discover that you're not even close. Keep running after the sun fast enough and you'll find that one person's sunset is another person's morning.

The sun stumbles over the horizon in search of something to thaw. Thousands of snowmen melt. Definition arrives in a jeep. It's another lonely day. But not for everyone. For some it's a raw reckoning and a tight grip and for others it's a yodeling competition. Each jar is labeled, each aim is solid. Charcoal drinks the seclusion of rue.

Power is obtained by rope. Rope is obtained by thought. Thought is obtained by energy. Energy is obtained by sunlight. Pronouns are obtained by thumb and forefinger. I am the least interesting thing about me. And then comes wrestling. We must wrestle the thoughts that are the most literal. Metaphorical thoughts are matters of absorption. A paper towel is a metaphor. A worm is not. A worm is literal.

I think I see a feeling. Or does a feeling see me? Am I the feeling or is the feeling one of nature's divine prodigies still water skiing in my briefcase?

Is being a feeling?

Being is a feeling. It's also an occurrence. It feels mongrel and atmospheric and ticklish. It feels like being when being is a matter of struggling through life and mud as a worm.

Or not.

Worms live in dirt. Words live in spurts. Which is dirtier, dirt or dandruff? Dandruff isn't dirty. Dandruff is messy, but it's not dirty. It doesn't flash like a road sign. But it can be quite embarrassing at a dance club on a black sweater in a blue light.

It's the wild hour of allegory. Let's build a bonfire of buttermilk leaves. It takes heat to experience the power of language. The knee glue diver comes up with a chestnut chewed into birth. This makes everyone totemic.

Birth is a matter of perseverance, said the first lieutenant of sociability. Armies of sociability travel the night in search of the social. The social inhabits the jelly of affability. The debris of surrender flops down on a canvas and assumes a posture of divine hysteria. Everyone talks about Norway, how rocky it is, how rapturous in beauty, how topographic and blunt.

Outside of Oslo, I don't know of a single driveway that doesn't relish its being, its ontology of necessity and convenience locked in an embrace of imagery and wheel.

The control of cubes is occasionally brick. There's more than one way to wear a stream of water. My argument is bathed in milk, not description. I see a development of this theme that slithers across Cezanne seething with harps and oboes. I see another rolling into auburn creating diversions of pink and brown. I don't know which of them is authentic and which of them is arranged in pleats.

Or should be arranged in pleats.

Morality should be arranged in pleats. There are heights of the soul from which even tragedy ceases to look tragic. It looks more like fish. Thus the pleat, which is suffused with sunlight at a certain time in the afternoon, lingers in the mind as a form of overtone, an inflection of air if the window is left slightly open, a puff of palliative, a stirring of cotton, a bulging of fabric that reminds us — however haphazardly — of scallops. Cephalopods, gastropods, polyplacophorans. Elegy, laughter, Montmartre. We are alert to nuance. There are no polarities of yes and no. There are no clear answers. There is only the mania of milk-secreting glands and the pantomime of excuse.

In other words, communion.

No admonition is vexatious if it is made by a sad man on the corner of a street. Money isn't food. It isn't even pretty. It's a medium of exchange, like folklore, or power. It's in the sneeze of process that the dollars of heaven come raining down as potash.

The hour of sleep is upon us. The toad is welcome. Welcome to Being. Welcome to the garden. Welcome to squatting. Welcome to underbrush and description and flies.

The sediment of a word lifts the toad to our mouth and we say it as a refund. It's a mechanical maneuver, mostly, with a little pulp to incite it into category. The oyster is my comrade, but the pillow is my gym. My head is full of seashore. But the hay is easy by the lake. I will go there. This is the place where fingers exhort the palpability of rings to shine more energetically, as if syntax could mimic the properties of glass. The fresh spin of thought has been sewn together by insects. I know what shouting is. Shouting is solid and loud. The quiet simmer of language absorbs the light and fondles our elbows.

I'm sorry. Am I being obscure? I meant to be snow. I meant to be obvious and bones. I meant to push these luxuries forward where they might be seen by pilgrims. It's so nice to have a diversion. Bugs are signs. They rarely shine now. They stopped increasing and began decreasing. Autumn isn't what it used to be. Consciousness isn't what it used to be, either. It used to be rocks but now it's more like horses. All urgency and play, glistening and breath.

Yolk

Oppose the ablution wallet. Accept the absorption. Shove abhorrence. Reflection. Farm dabs. The stunned embrace of nails. We've trumpeted the metaphysics of crêpe within the tangling of violins and now the goldfish just keep dancing on my lips.

Engorge. Contact taproot. Buckles blaze with cartwheels. Furnish the extended treading.

Do you like your shoes? Bend your being to their eloquence.

Hallucinations crawl to the almond. A soft concept bends with gazing.

Assemble a pound of palette. Think brush. Forehead. Hunger. Blazing stars. Stick wheel climbing a waterfall. There is wrestling outdoors and bubbles. Flail the river with a ship. Turn the sculptures toward the east. Virtuosity is spicy. So is summer. Prominences percolate. Twitch the pepper. Aching is a treasure.

Do it with letters. Clatter. Float animals.

Paints in spots of abstract murmur echo the admonitions of the piano.

Rain.

Drink your travel. The novel is constrained to break. Lament tied by rope to the rattan. The battle is rescued by a convalescing pessimism.

Chrome potato. Energy tilted into canoes. Examples include migration and escape.

Engage the galaxy. String. Faith in brains.

Structure explains the grazing. Paper. Listen to ochre. Shovel the paradox roots. The hole that argues with its shape is called a personality. Push it out of the heartache. Cure it with talking. Appeal to the library. Let the clarinet pump its point. The details of the swan are embedded in yolk. Which is as it shall be and it shall be shiny.

A Minute Past Pink

The nipple has been washed without harm. For this, and many other things, are we thankful today. My ears are attuned to the evolution of viewpoints. Birds sing. The clouds mutter their therapies of rain. I wear a hat of stars and alligators. A piquant sunlight awakens thoughts of matter and density and points to the boiling of leaves during office hours. Gauze curtains blow inward where Fanny Brawne lies on a bed. I emerge into tolerance and drift toward summer. I climb into bubbles and perturb the statistics of a cornflake station wagon. Loud red feathers stream behind my head. The muse of torment gives me a dollar. I buy a cheap microphone and deliver a lovely jeremiad to no one in particular. If you want an audience for your reflections, look in a mirror. I guarantee that something about makeup will elongate into victory over the vagaries of nature. This is the instinctual part of the mind, its protocol and druids, theism and drums. I feel suddenly graceful, like elevator doors opening, or a leak in my chest revealing truant emotions. I need a lot of wool in order to say what I think. My sense of angels drops into empirical bombast. Worries tumble in my mind like the noisy temperatures of a dead clock. I swim among almonds. My name is tied to a jar of clay. It contains caviar. I hurry to wax the footstool most immediate to my perception. Apple blossoms pull libraries of thunder out of the air. The river considers itself red, but the clouds are a constant source of imprecision. The maple totem has succeeded at percussion. Beauty disrupts our voyage. Distance is an attitude, not a necessity. We go where the wind blows. We go where the snowshoes decipher the snow. Where the seven tigers of whoever and whatever convene in grooves of ancient music, and the reason for zeal is understanding, and understanding is understood as radar. If anything of this comes to a boil, I will end neurosis with a scowl and scramble the meaning of bricks with a few good protons and a parenthetical trowel.

Cow's Eye

Each big advance of the screwdriver opens our eyes to the fairy kingdom, which we have failed to see before, and makes new demands on our powers of observation. The first impulse is to back away from a volcano before it erupts and look down to consider the viability of our shoes. This extension of the visceral into the domain of the vocal causes the Vikings to reevaluate the diaphanous iridescences of trigonometry and jingle their bells in abject triumph. In brief, the dude abides.

Where am I going with this? I don't know.

The chemical constitution of stars is revealed through spectroscopy. But the chemical constitution of my afternoon is chiefly lopsided, or whatever floats around in the goldenrod. My telescope doesn't see as far as Babylon. But I can see the beach, which is only a mile away, and flavors my day with interaction, grains of sand employed in the business of yearning.

Today's poetry is brought to you by haircare. Just lean back and let the world fall over you. It will feel like alcohol. You will carve yourself out of a bar of soap. Your nose will be steep, but your eyes will be filled with spirit, and twinkle like little X-rays.

When the Greek surgeon Galen discovered the circulation of blood, he was chief physician to the gladiators in Pergamon. Think about that: a chest torn open by an opponent's blade, the heart still beating. My strategy is to not get too hung up on any idea but let the stigmas wallow in their own misperceptions and follow the flow of the river to its own natural conclusion.

I know that the truth lies in flashlights, and batteries, and that closets smell of old clothes and leather boots, and that bacteria thrive in the human gut, some of them good, some of them bad, and that a chief cause of Being is the irrefutable assembly of key chains. Key chains with gadgets, key chains with charms.

Key chains.

In a word, we should strive to attain the knowing of how little we know. It's a good place to begin. Abu Dhabi's new indoor amusement park doesn't open until July. We should not confuse the aestheticization of drum circles with graveyards. If my stove is engaged with fugues it's because circumference has the divinity of space.

And then there's the whole matter of mandrake. What is it, exactly? I never see it in the produce section at the grocery store, or as an ingredient in any health supplement. The plant has psychoactive properties and can induce frenzies, a state of divine madness. What the Greeks meant by madness was not a pathological state but a dramatic alteration of consciousness. I find that fascinating. Here in 21st century, there are very few shamanistic traditions to lead one out of the mundane and into the plazas where the mute become eloquent and the eloquent turn still.

But there was a time when the fungus was heard and the intonations of the trees stirred the humor of the imagination.

Mesopotamian cuneiform texts make frequent mention of a wine known as "cow's eye." This was a wine made with mandrake. One's pupils widened. Hence, "cow's eye." It's a rare plant, and its root is said to resemble a person.

Mighty River

Mighty river climbing into pique. Miscreant fiend sulking in jolts of fauna. Punctilious chocolate pleats. Checkerboard porthole crumbs. I'm the extension I wanted the ticks are naughty but the embarrassment is wadded in protons. This makes the nexus vanilla. I'm massive today in my pratfalls. Independent and soluble. I can lariat a grievance and bring it down into dust and cinch distaste into puppets. Gardenias of ruminant formaldehyde darn the unicorns with fingers, palms like palms, thumbs like psalms. The fabric I used to patrol the inseam is now a private rapture. The fez of the rival river has rivets of radiant champagne. There can be no metal without a brain that jets around in carnivals. Let this be the patriarch whose biases inflate with authority every time the misanthropes convene in division of themselves. Dextrose parquet or polar stumble, either way, the commas are restored to their natural ideals of blackberry and sage. A viscous discussion of Plato leads to horses, the pounding of hooves and the barking of dogs. The geology leaps onto my lap and breathes heavily like a cardboard upholsterer. Everybody knows the guide is a parakeet. But the fireplace pivots on a dormouse oinking in the rusted failure of our trilogy. Insinuation is often like that. It bubbles in its harness like a hairy asteroid and then is poured over pasta which makes the climate very close to being classified as a contest winner.

Panta Rhei

I feel lucid and sad, like a cold day. It's good to forget oneself. It's better to remember that one doesn't exist. Not in any true sense. That is to say, if non-existence is our ultimate destiny, life is sweeter and much more tolerable when this awareness penetrates consciousness and becomes a reality.

Diversions are visceral and ultramarine. They have my full endorsement.

Every day I feed crows. And wonder. What's it like to be a crow? Is it to be constantly hungry? To enjoy moments of total transcendence when spiraling in the air? Who's the man that brings us peanuts?

I always imagine thoughts in other animals that are similar to the thoughts that float through my head periodically. This is, no doubt, a mistake. Most of my thoughts are a brew of words. Ruminations assembled out of words. Narratives assembled out of words. Dramas assembled out of words.

Are there dramas without words? Yes. Of course. Many. Sunrise. Sunset. An owl swooping down on a mouse. The process of inquiry, the intent attention of intention. A man and a woman sitting in a car on a cold winter day, both searching for the right words, the sentence that will make everything right again.

Is calculus a garden? Is it a garden of convergences and infinite sequences? Yes. And much more. There are derivatives and infinitesimals. These are flowers of infinite abstraction. Flashes of insight and elegies and hammers.

There's not a single atom or molecule of my body that wasn't formed on this planet. Generated by this planet. Created by this planet. I am the planet. I'm a piece of the planet. An epiphenomenon of this planet. This whirl of feelings and thoughts I experience every minute of every day are the responses to phenomena to an entire universe of which I'm a part. Feelings and thoughts are waves, essentially, disturbances with no associated mass. Oscillations, vibrations, pulsations that transfer energy from one place to another. Or shape it into stems, bubbles, faces.

Or words. Words are waves. Vibrations. Sounds. Meanings. Images. Signals.

Everything.

Paint, oceans, nipples.

Nipples are signals. Railroads are different. Railroads differ from nipples in interesting ways. One is soft, the other is hard. One is totemic, the other is shovels. Just shovels. Ties and rocks. Steel and language. The shouts of men. Caustic tones of sweat and salt. The lowing of cows. Steers. Boxcars. The smell of shit. Clumsy actions. Frequencies of penumbral butter.

I prefer the spirit of the bohemian to that of the businessman. There are realities with no commercial value. To stick a commercial value on something is to effectively devalue it, to make it a part of exploitation, abuse, and structural violence. A number stapled to a cow's ear.

I have spent my entire life trying to live life to its fullest. Everyone does. Everyone who has adequate housing and access to water and food. This is a luxury in life, to worry whether one is living it as fully as possible, so that when one dies, there are fewer regrets. Because there's always that undercurrent. That anxiety. That life is fleeting, ungraspable, and deeply enigmatic. That life goes by fast and you need to hop on that train and experience it as fully as possible. That you may be one of the lucky ones to plummet its meaning and surface with epiphanies and insights and books to enlighten one's brothers and sisters. Unless, of course, you find yourself in a culture that no longer gives a shit. In which case your efforts will be for you and you alone and (if you're really lucky) one or two close friends, who are like-minded and react similarly to cemeteries and who chafe against the adjustments necessary to hold down a job and like to think outside the box. The proverbial box. The box that keeps us trapped in ignorance and comfort. A dubious comfort. The kind of comfort that rewards you for your subservience and good attitude. A good attitude is the attitude that you adopt to get along with the boss. That allows you to float gently through a life of comforting routine while beneath the planks and thwarts of your boat an ocean of nothingness festoons the horizon with an ellipsis of stars.

This is the condition into which we are born. The other animals don't appear to have this problem. This need to avoid feeling cheated. This need to explore one's interior complexities, one's moods and inner geography. Some people like to call it a journey. I like to call it a sneeze. There's a subtle but building irritation that culminates in an eruptive exhalation of air and saliva. That's life. A sudden involuntary expulsion of slobber and air.

And then wipe one's face with a Kleenex and stare at the rag draped over the kitchen faucet.

Is that satori? Is that living life to the fullest? Are there degrees of life? Gradations of life? How much of life is measurable and statistical and how much of life is changing bulbs and sweeping the floor and wondering who built the pyramids of Egypt?

Knowing and accepting death is a big one. The Egyptians had a definite idea about the afterlife. Osiris opened the door to the afterlife for everyone, which was called The Land of Two Fields. According to "Ancient Egypt for Kids," "You had to earn your way into your afterlife by doing good deeds while you were alive. The more good deeds you did, the lighter your heart became. If your heart was not light, you could not board Ra's board and sail away into your Afterlife. To avoid any chance of trickery, the goddess Maat weighed your heart after you died. If your heart was not light enough, you were stuck in your tomb forever. But once you were in, you were in. You only had to sail away in Ra's boat once. After that, you had a free pass, and your soul could come and go."

I like the come and go part. Well, think I'll take a spin around Milwaukee today. See what's up in Wisconsin. I'll be back later, in time for the all-you-can-eat-prawns night. Binge on a few episodes of *Breaking Bad*.

If anything like a soul persists after our body gives up the ghost (the ghost being us), what is it? A ball of energy? What would existence be like as a ball of energy? An amorphous, ectoplasmic blob bouncing off the walls. No arms, no hands, no fingers, no toes. No dick. No vagina. No ribs or snot or hair or skin. None of that stuff. Just energy. Energy is eternal delight, said Blake. I hope he's right.

We are currently facing the most historic event in the history of homo sapiens: extinction. But that's a whole other kettle of fish. Dead fish.

Let's focus on the now. The Now, capital 't' capitol 'n.' That fictional entity of continuous present tense. Which doesn't exist. How can it? As soon as it's now, it's gone, it's in the past. It's history. It's a word in this sentence. It's an insight that just got written down. And we're just in time. Here comes another one. Here comes another now. Oops. It was just here. Where'd it go?

Heraclitus got it right: life is flux. Everything flows. Panta Rhei (πάντα ῥεῖ) in ancient Greek. Meaning change is the ultimate reality. The current in the stream is the most real thing about the stream. Row, row, row your boat gently down the stream. Merrily, merrily, merrily for life is but a dream.

Shoes and Cookies

Lately, I've had trouble finding a good pair of running shoes. A pair I tried on not too long ago seemed to fit fine at the store but when I went running in them they proved to be too tight. I removed the insoles and cut off the tips, providing a little extra wiggle room for my toes. This little trick has worked in the past. It didn't this time. The shoes were too tight. And they felt funny: the heels felt much higher than the heels on the shoes I've worn in the past. This was a different brand, New Balance, and I usually get Saucony, which are often on sale at Big 5. The balance was indeed new: I felt like I was being tilted forward. I gave the new shoes to Goodwill and returned to the store to try on another pair. This time the shoes fit fine (I've learned over time to buy shoes two inches larger than my normal ten; either my feet have grown two inches larger, or measurements are not as standard as they once were), but the insole in the right foot has a tendency to creep up when I'm running. By the end of a short, three-mile run, half of the insole has moved to the rear of the shoe. I have to maneuver it back in.

Also, the fabric covering the toes began wearing out almost immediately. This has never happened before. A few more runs and my big toe will be nicely ventilated.

It may be time to go to a high-end running shoe boutique. But $200 bucks for running shoes? That's something I'll think about.

Meanwhile, I'll continue to make do with my creeping insole.

This afternoon I went on a longer run than usual. I've gained four pounds in the past several weeks. I don't know how this works metabolically, but somehow a two-ounce cookie translates immediately into sixteen ounces in my body. It's as if my metabolism exponentiated anything with sugar or carbohydrates in it.

When I got to the bottom of Queen Anne Hill on the far west side, there was a man smoking a cigarette in the alcove by the one of the back entrances to Magnolia Bridge Self-Storage. This seems to happen almost every time I go running down there now. That little alcove seems to have become an ad hoc smoker's lounge for the employees of the Seattle Park Department across the street. Unfortunately, that's the one side where the sidewalk happens to be. I kept to the other side to avoid cigarette smoke and negotiated the leviathan vehicles that pass for cars these days, hitting the side-view mirror of somebody's parked car with my shoulder. I hope I didn't knock the mirror out of position too much, or that the driver notices its altered position before driving too far.

There has been a definite uptick in cigarette smoking lately, which I find perplexing, considering the sorry state of the U.S. hellcare system. If pressed to provide a theory, I'd say it's due to despair, a bottomless pit of social malaise and opioid abuse.

I saw a seal in the water at Smith Cove, where the Foss Maritime Company keeps their tugs. I waved and shouted hello and the seal dove back under water. I didn't like seeing a seal there, as there is a sign warning people not to swim there due to the toxicity of the water. But what I was I going to do? Dive in, swim to the bottom, and whisper "get out of here" to the seal? He (or she) might take that the wrong way. And how do you whisper when you're underwater?

The tide was the highest I've ever seen it, almost flush with the piers, which normally have a clearance of twenty to thirty feet from the water.

The wind was up and there was a lot of wave action and water splashing up against the riprap on the shoreline.

I saw a flock of geese fly in V formation and several Pacific loons sitting on the water near the Pier 86 grain terminal.

I spent the rest of the day at home with R eating dinner and watching *The Messenger*, a disturbing 2015 documentary about the sharp decline of songbirds world-wide due to multiple factors, including pesticides, light pollution, noise pollution, habitat loss and cats.

Afterward, I answered some letters and read *Leo Frobenius On African History, Art and Culture an Anthology*, with a foreword by Léopold Sédar Senghor. I was greatly amused by the story of a disobedient son who — against the orders of his father — sets a trap for catching animals on the road to the village. He ends up catching various family members and then the road itself. He rolls the road up and puts it in a bag. He and his father get lost. Finally, admitting defeat, he puts the sack down. The road leaps out and father and son are able to return to the village. But the son catches the road again and decides to keep it. No one can use the road. It grows so sad that it dies.

Later that night, and shortly after going to bed, I listened to a conversation on YouTube between host Jeffrey Goldberg with author Kurt Andersen and his new book *Fantasyland: How America Went Haywire* at the Aspen Institute for Humanistic Studies about American tendencies to believe in almost anything, however divorced from reality it may be, its distrust of experts and cavalier disparagement of facts, and how this gullibility and subjectively inflated wishful thinking led to the election of Donald Trump. Andersen surmises that these tendencies find their root cause in the extreme religiosity of the early American puritans, but then later conflates this with the relativizing philosophies of French intellectuals such as Michel Foucault and Jean Baudrillard, and the spiritual cravings and explorations of the hippies in the 60s, and their stance against rationalism and anti-intuitive deductive reasoning as tools of social control, which I found grossly oversimplifying and crude. I completely agree with his theory about Calvinism and the maniacally despotic views of the Puritans, but find his conflation with hippies and French intellectuals to be completely bizarre and unfounded. He himself appears ready to invent the most ridiculous theories. He also seemed to squirm and express awkwardness over his simultaneous patriotism and pessimism over the future of the so-called "great American experiment." It was altogether a deeply disappointing, dishonest, and myopic talk.

The next day is rain, rain, rain. I love the sound of rain. Especially when it pelts the remaining leaves, those tender plates of chlorophyll stuck to the muddy wet ground.

The fact that it's raining rather than snowing is something to feel grateful for. I don't like ending sentences with prepositions but that's what the word for is for.

The Origin Of The World

The jabber at our table is useful. It collects our empty coordinates and gives them an echo amid the stains of time. We all have coordinates. Coordinates are things that you feed geometry to make it silky and otherworldly. Apothems, trapezoids, hot dogs. Giovanni Piranesi understood this. The cleavage of the rhombohedron is an aboriginal glimpse at the idiosyncrasies of life in an eyebrow, the way it is dreamed, and the way it is compounded into corkscrews of hair.

Do fat clothes make you look thinner? I don't think so. But nature abhors a vacuum and so I squirt bricks at a seesaw. This causes an immediate terracotta, a kind of cringe that teleports moods of amber to a nice quiet corner in the Louvre.

It should be obvious. I yearn to grow a neck as mighty as the potato. Nails aren't apparitions. Nor are they worlds. They're just nails, instruments for holding lumber together in a glorious cohesion. So yeah, I guess that does make them worlds of a sort. But what isn't a world? A dollar isn't a world. It's only a dollar. A million dollars is a world, but a very bad world. It's more of a milieu than a world, a place where orchids bloom in private conservatories and a hibachi rusts on the porch as a young woman weeps from a broken heart and a hairy lout and movie producer waters his grass during a drought.

I can make more than one noise. There is a pain on each page that thinks it's a boat.

I'm not against strikes. Far from it. I stand next to the potatoes with a bottle of nitroglycerin in one hand a prayer in the other. Life doesn't have to be sloppy, just sturdy. There is a way to articulate a grievance quite effectively with a few sparkling generalities sprinkled about the room and a little fanaticism to make it stick. You can go ahead and sag if you want, just lean back and let the jukebox selections wash over you.

But enough about fencing. What about happenings and such? Whatever happened to them? People squirming through inner tubes, or going for random walks in Amsterdam. I think I what I need right now is a little momentum and a big bowl of gravity.

Pretzels. Ocarinas. Waterfalls.

The arrival of spots expresses a break in the continuity of the climatological record. The grumble of bubbles arouses the shores of Denmark. A mermaid sits on a rock combing her hair. The fishing tackle crawls out of the dormitory clapping its signatures. We find a painter and the landscape begins to make sense as a form of analgesic, heroin or rainforest.

The knowledge of velvet is a difficult cage to open. That's what made the Fauves so crazy. How do you ad lib a vulva? Here it is, take a look. As you can see, the origin of the world alternates between convulsion and steam. Time may be ugly, but it's never trivial.

All those folds, all those membranes. Life evolves in so many interesting directions. Clams, camels, kangaroos, infusoria. Tiny aquatic animals and leopards prowling stealthily through the jungle. What is the color of ooze? Let's just call it henna and go on our way.

The thermometer does this all the time: clank by in its shadows, showing us temperatures that never existed until you scribbled the calculus of stucco on the blackboard. That made some sense, but it was too late to clink glasses with royalty. The army changed its clothes and became a crowd of individual shapes. And that's when everything else happened, and the enamel burst our expectations, causing Spanish and horseshoes.

The Truth Of Baking Soda

Start the day with absolute truth. If you can't find truth, try baking soda. Baking soda has an ontological foundation that makes it perfect for substitution, gentle exfoliation, and alleviating heartburn. When a proposition is true, it is identical to fact. What is a fact? A fact is grounded in further facts, which makes them abundant and public, like baking soda.

Is there a universe in which this makes sense? Yes. The universe of baking soda. In the universe of baking soda all one needs is a little conviction, a little butter, and enough energy to power a small frog.

There is no such thing as the absolute truth. Observation is a slippery animal. Perception is inherently amphibious, as it is ambiguous, and awkward. Observation may be unpacked in reflection, say in a hotel room, after going through your suitcase for some items pertaining to daily hygiene, such as toothpaste and mouthwash, or at least a credible action figure, Arnold Schwarzenegger as The Terminator, a cyborg assassin with a peculiar sense of humor.

Errors of judgment are inevitable in an art form that relies on putting words together. As soon as words are put together, they assume a life of their own. The next thing you know Arnold Schwarzenegger is breaking down your door and a magic black swan is carrying you away to Mars.

Why Mars? There are no vacancies on Venus, and Titan won't accept pets.

Balancing probabilities revives the milk from its effacement in coins. Start with this attitude in mind and you will end your day with singing. The song is up to you. But allow me to recommend *Miserere mei, Deus*, by Gregorio Allegri.

And for the sake of what it brings, this milk of humility is a precious gift. When to the sessions of sweet silent thought you summon up a lake and begin floating in it, the wrangling and unseemly disputes in your head will not help the serenity of the surface. Row quietly. Bring a book.

Today, for example, I poured some salt and baking soda into the drain of the bathtub and washed it down with a cup of vinegar and watched as it frothed and bubbled up out of the drain. I do this not only to clear the drain and quicken the flow of water into the drain and so on down the drain, but to amuse myself with philosophy, and the general flow of life, which leads to the cosmos, and diffusion among the stars.

And there is truth in this.

There will sometimes coexist a morbid sensitivity to fog. This may be performed by engines pumping steam into the air, or a chorus of female singers, sopranos with a flair for medicine as well as entomology.

In a majority of cases, forgiveness for one's failings may stray into stucco and become a blossom of rattling sportscasts. We must be ready, without fear or favor, to call into question our own experience, and let it slip into breakfast like an eyeball, and stare back at us, bubbling with amazement.

Pickled Ripples

Time to write simply now, simple like Beckett, Beckett in his elder years. I want Beckett's craggy old face, the eighty-something Beckett, a face of crags and crabs and wrinkles and runnels and ruts. The eyes of a hawk. The bristle of a thistle. Simple dimples. Pickled ripples. Giggly tinkles. Piano keys in olive sonatas, refractive galactic galvanic octaves, emotions in notes, phrases in stages. Words in herds. Herd heard by the ears in an acoustic chew stick. The ear of the seer is here to hear. The stick is to chew. The chew is to strew the stew to the throat. And what's a way to say swallow.

So much for keeping things simple. I don't know how he did it. It isn't simple to keep things simple. Each moment should be a haiku, an instant of stunning lucidity. Uncomplicated as a cat asleep on a blanket. A glass paperweight with a yellow flower frozen inside. All the morbid disturbances of the intellect crumpled up like a sheet of paper and tossed into a recycling bin. Detachment from circumstances. The mind like a puddle in which the limbs of a tree ride the shine of light on a misty winter day. Until time. And wind. And money and worry and anxiety for the future intervene.

How small. How vast. How if not boundless bounded. Whence the dim. Not now. Know better now. Unknow better now.

Time is a slime in the grime of a dime. A penny is plenty if you have more than twenty and a nickel to trickle into a meter when the cost of a space is softly and calmly valid. A salad of curb and chrome and asphalt and verb. A verb is either a noun phrase or a blaze of Motown. A verb is a word that expresses being and what does it do it does nothing if there's nothing to do. Otherwise a verb must work its way forward through a sentence undulating in the nudity of a moment. We're in a continual dialogue with the world. Can there be such a thing as an objectified subjectivity? Yes. I believe there are ways to objectify the sauce of my secrets, my secret sauces, which are bogs in a bag or a bag of bog, either way, a knob or a stratosphere. Weight, density, volume, heat. World haunted by cream. A subjectivity crammed with yolk.

Change is either something that alters or is a gob of metal in the hand.

The modern quarter is 75% copper and 25% nickel. The profile of George Washington is on the obverse. An eagle is on the reverse. E Pluribus Unum is inscribed above its head. Why an eagle? Why not a pigeon? A sparrow? A turkey? A robin? A crow? A·heron? A pterodactyl? A spondee? A trochee? An anapest?

I believe the image that best serves the object at hand is a dirigible. A fissionable pyramidal cetacean of the air. You might picture it as a hat, or a half sister named Render.

Or a ramble through the ways and trays of life as it throbs in utter effusion.

When the whisper is whispered the engine is in session.

I feel everything with a pair of eyes, a nose and a head of steam. I might also mention argyle. Argyle is a pattern. I trust patterns. I trust my senses. I trust the pattern of my senses. I choose not to argue with smells, sights and textures. But I am a little intrigued by dreams. Dreams are a fascinating way to experience alternate realities.

Is that what we want to call them? Alternate realities? Isn't there just the one giant reality of push-ups, thermometers and trying on new clothes? Isn't reality just an idea? A word? A mode? A way of being? As quantum mechanics says, reality is what you choose it to be. But that doesn't sound simple. Or real. It sounds like a glib and rather distorted view of quantum mechanics. Atoms are real. Quarks are real. They carry a fractional electric charge and come in six flavors: up, down, top, bottom, strange and charm. It's a mistake, however, to assign reality to something because it has matter. Are there realities without matter? Are there realities that don't matter? Aristotle would argue that motion, time, void, and change are all aspects of reality, as are mind, soul, intuition, imagination, potentiality, happiness, virtue and friendship. Nor is Aristotle alone among philosophers in believing ideas to be a fundamental ontological category of being.

"I am certain that I can have no knowledge of what is outside me except by means of the ideas I have within me," said Descarte in a letter to Guillaume Gibieuf dated January 19th, 1642.

I believe that whatever reality turns out to be it will include pickles. Tidepools perturb the mailbox. Junk mail anemones. Pins and needles. Ripples and pickles. Health insurance. Real estate. Invitations to cruise the Danube or the Rhine. This is it. This is not it. This is and isn't what reality is about. How could it be? Reality is the slipperiest eel in the bucket.

Beckett would, of course, express all this in much simpler terms. But the reality is, I'm not Beckett and have never been Beckett. My bucket isn't a Beckett bucket. My bucket is a plain bucket. A bucket bucket. Bucket of buckets. Pickles. A bucket of pickles.

A jar of pickles is a testament of age. Ripples of light. A lake in the mountains of China. A man guzzling a beer in Munich. A rapier on the wall. Chiaroscuro in a painting of devotion. A garden sent through the mail as sunlight. Anything preserved in the vinegar of words. The vigor of words. The veracity of words. The veneer and ventilation and adventure of words. Jiggle and swivel and ripple of words. Ripples in pickles. Pickles in ripples. Drizzle on a nickel on a nipple of tender human skin.

The Fallacy Of
Misplaced Concreteness

The mushrooms tell me I'm broken. I hop into a dream and peg a penumbra to the purge display. This helps tug a small round hill into place. I chop the invectives into a butterfly slap. Things proceed merrily. Even the rafters have a sheen of spectral dispatch. We slither through a world that is partly the invention of our perceptions and partly the harp of a towheaded python named Trinket the Mighty. And then I ask myself: why do I do this? Why do I constantly search for outer space? Why do I search for a semantic portal to another dimension? I'm guess I'm just not satisfied with the results of arbitration. The trade talks have collapsed into the basement releasing a colony of bats. Fortunately, I have two thumbs and a load of fingers that come in quite handy when it comes to grabbing things, or catching the weight of my body when I fall trying to grab things. Some things cannot be grasped by the hands. These would be invisible things, imponderable things, things like paradigms and summer vacations. It is what Alfred North Whitehead called the Fallacy of Misplaced Concreteness, though I prefer to call it a sandwich. I feel elemental at times like this, the vibration of electromagnetic forces creating a hotel for my mind. Your mind, my mind, makes no difference. Maybe there is no mind. Maybe there is only *mu*, non-existence, non-being, the original non-being from which being is produced, which is sometimes strangely sexual, sometimes strangely swollen. But thank you for sending the parrots, I appreciate it. The water in the bowl differs from the bowl, but the lamp oil burns cleanly and is superior to kerosene. I can hear the insoluble yell of chemistry as it walks beneath the muffins. I shall consider the abalone as a shout to communion, and will carry a bubbly insinuation wherever I go. If the ignition is dusty it is because the revival of classical culture is still blissfully incoherent. In the meantime, we have Beowulf and New Brunswick. Cooperation is a great asset for any team, but sometimes too much collaboration can get in the way of one's personal iridescence. I need to revisit the question of antennas, how they manage to interface between radio waves, bringing in sounds of the external world and sometimes emitting the chirps of a stubborn cricket, that thing I call a heart, and the poetry of Frank O'Hara. Once I understand a thing I will tell it to authorize a willow, or wallow in a willow the way the willow itself wallows in willowing. When we dream, feathers and wings lift us into a rain we cannot grasp and it is here that anguish is found, and the bristles of dogs and hairbrushes. You can take the world upside-down or sideways but one way or another you should fasten your seatbelt. It's a rough ride. Look how ravenous the crows are, how various bruises fly through the house looking for arms and legs to inhabit. We can pin this sleeve if we just find enough structure. Until then, I will pull as hard as I can on the wheel until this next swerve is over, and stop for some gas in Ukiah, which means "deep valley" in the Yuki language, and can be found along U.S. Route 101.

Spigot Trinket

The lake is shaving its form. The dazzling flu cuisine mirrors the tumble of belts in a drum of adults and this makes the lake both sad and subconscious. It's clearly a lake. What isn't clear are the perturbations and wrecks at the bottom. The many writhing figures, the columns of victory, the proportions and stools. What do we make of these things? Is this a moral universe, or just another truck stop along the way?

The heel of the universe drinks an ingot of Sunday's planet. The old tiger senses a thought in the throat and lets it out in the form of a hotel. What I'm trying to do here is ugly. It has to be. It has to be shaggy and weird and automatic or the arthropods won't dance and the curves in the eye will fail to transfer the images to the brain. The brain is constantly hungry for stories. It must be appeased by detachment. It's the only solution there is to the aggressive delicacies of tea.

A new parable emerges from my sleep. Our wall has been expecting it. I'll admit it. I was drunk. The spins were improved by electing a frontier to be my wife. I won't mention the secrecies of the garden and its many perversions. Let's just say that the new arena is good for inflating fingers, and the bar is a mailbox for the letters of the soul. But it's the infinite that borders our little shell of straw and violins.

This is a poem about Danny Kirwan. We will go right down to the sea. Bathing in light we will be free to wander. And we will find ourselves splattered by the sociability of surf.

I grow fat to start a franchise. The carrot has its molecular wilts and touches us with swallows. The sloth of the lazy ratatouille pulls a pound of kaolin into a dynamic eye that alters us with its visions. The tea strives to arrive. The heat perfumes Wednesday. I have to go and sew now. I have feathers for the cape and powder for my face.

I design the net away. The frail water likes to hike until it becomes an impala. The bickering words buy us some time. I maneuver the beautiful pendulum into horses. I want to go beyond suggesting perfume. I want to destroy time and resurrect it as life itself.

Life as a wide-eyed tug-of-war with existence at one end and fermentation at the other.

Life as an alarming gown of bugs and boats.

Pages upon pages of paradox. Bristling green moss on a concrete banister. A fashion model tripping on a divine hammer.

Bleed the mailboxes. Shake the pain to simmer a dream. The mint does its insects into growling fornication. I drink and think the pyramids are rascals of ancient empire. I generate knives by burning an experience with a fire in the rain.

I rub the vowels until a genie appears. I rub the genie until a vowel appears. I rub appearance until a genie howls vowels. The clumsy myth is screaming a cave into existence. The tickle is powered and accelerates our transactions. It's raining suns and collar studs. The rolls play a role and are an impenetrable bungle. The swan queen has chiseled a dance out of fire.

The New Planetarium

We love the new planetarium. Numberless stars produce a music that lifts us from our seats and causes us to float around the room. Nothing hangs in stark immobility. Everything moves in a vast perpetuity. The walls are invisible. Divisions are conveniently thin. Embarrassments unravel exciting optimism and children. Time and space undress and offer us a glimpse of elsewhere. Elsewhere is the place where you find yourself when the winter frost bicycles around a neon melody. A mechanical Tuesday sharpens its knives in the beautiful mud of your eyes. This annoys the nobility of lightning and splashes us with stories. We always have a lot to talk about. But we don't. The silence is too powerful to waste on conversation. A thundering paragraph rolls through the mind of a cricket. The cricket responds with a song in the key of D major. This creates a drawer of equations and tears. It helps to soak a sunflower in elucidation. Or place a metal horse in a hotel lobby. The armadillo lights the exaltation of snow. The subtle build of cosmetics does the rest. Every cloud has its peculiarities. And every planetarium has its contraptions. Some of them give us recipes. Others give us a diagnosis. This one gives us swallows. Max Jacob riding a giant turtle over a desert of raw sienna and broken chains.

When The Wood Dries

There's a private shine in my hammer. My indicative gaze cannot be explained by crawling. Our kitchen is full of mushrooms and pans. Some of the them are quite beautiful. They all shine. They all come into the foreground when the heat is on. I have, therefore, expanded my journey to include a lip or two. A tongue. An appetite for adventure. Mosquitos swarm around the pump. I compile shadows in order to describe the anatomy of the sky. I hope that the wine is good. We all have shadows. It's why we've painted the rattles red and created a door for the crustaceans to come and go at their pleasure. Life enhances its roots by flowering into vines and blackberries. Entanglements. Thorns. But the true treasures are in the appendix of the guidebook. This is where we find trails that have barely been used. They lead to grottos and the touch of moonlight. It was never my intention to pilot a brush through your hair. Each time I hear the flap of a flag I grab a shovel and start to dig. It's elementary to flex one's muscles. I do what I can. You do what you're good at. I've evolved mountain streams to startle the wandering gaze of grocery check-ers. No one expects a wet arm to punch the air into parenthetical pathos. The coupons reflect the density of autumn. Everything happens among words. I try to create a way to enter another dimension. A new perspective. Let's call it that. Embryonic sensations find full maturity in the drama of comparison. And sometimes they find expression in music. I suggest that the metamor-phosis of insects fluctuates between the ability to swim and the opacity of bluebells. I brush my hair with a crow. It's always respectable to find someone meditating. Emotions crash through my ribs seeking ecstasy. My eyes wander around a spoon. I fall to the ground and adapt to the eccentricities of my zip-per later. The catalogue omits the secrets of mink, and for good reason: the rags of morning offer the wisdom of shoes. I grabbed the lotus and ran. The mailbox gravy was in bas-relief, but the meanings inherent in the nimbleness of the tongue argued for more space and less gravity. Specifically, chisels. We'll get to them later, when the wood dries.

Formulary

There's cod below the cracked harness. I'm luminous to my shoes and eager to fly a button. I would like to discuss my gravity this autumn. It's a very weighted topic. I put the emphasis on a dollop of Wednesday, and swim toward the card game using a vocabulary of arms and feet. If I swamp the boat, turn the fireworks toward the symphony as they attempt to find their fugue. I spit shadows at a facsimile of bone. I'm not entirely reckless but I am open to spinning around with you. Let's assemble some reality with lines stolen from Dante. Look at the words glitter as they assume shapes of bubbling declension. Sweep the panic under a guitar twang. Later, when we unearth the pallet, we can envy Africa and its mighty flowers. It's never been like this before. That is to say, I'm haunted this year by a paper cow. I boil my words in a cauldron of verse. I curl into a towering seclusion and shave my reticence with a nebular cricket. The pulse of Céret is in its milk and cookies. The parlor pitches forward with conversation and Proust appears entangled in adjectives. Iron makes me happy. But it's oblivion that pays the rent. I feel hung up and I don't know why. I keep finding oars and oarlocks in my catch. I'm ordering some feathers from Oaxaca and committing myself to a bag of nails and a pack of Quetzalcoatl.

A Tender Button

He looked at a man in a straw hat on YouTube and thought "that could've been me, if I'd learned to play the guitar." He savored the wistfulness of the moment. The pluperfect always made him sad. But the conditional was almost too much to bear. Octopi were a charming puzzle. How did they slither around like that? No bones to impede their progress. The buoyancy of water. He could see a rattlesnake playing a guitar. That'd make a righteous tattoo. A creature with no arms wrapped around a Fender Strat with a maple fingerboard on his right arm. Or left. The left would be good. The arm he liked to use to roll a window down. Reach for a TV remote. Press a flyer to a telephone pole while stapling it with his right. There's nothing that a thought cannot do. Of course, thoughts don't really do anything. They create moods. Problems. Dramas. Resentments. Coordinates for travel. Wool caps for the head. Philosophical arguments to keep the brain warm. There's a million things that a thought cannot undo. Undoing is harder than doing. No thought can unmake a past mistake. It can just grill it. Listen to it sizzle. The meat of another remorseful morsel turning red over the coals of a glowing rumination.

When, exactly, did we lose the world, he thought. This was a big but empty thought. It was largely rhetorical. It had no answer. The story of Adam and Eve was compelling, but ultimately unbelievable. Unless taken in its truer sense, as a metaphor. Did we lose the world when science separated our minds from our bodies, or when topiary emerged in the gardens of Versailles? Were ExxonMobil and Coca Cola the ultimate seals of our division from all that was holy and sublime?

His parents had named him Wisconsin. He didn't know why. They'd never been to Wisconsin. They lived in Vermont. He slept in a room with curtains displaying nineteenth century men and women collecting sap from trees. The story went that he was conceived when his parents were high on LSD. He could see no relation between LSD and Wisconsin. What's in a name? Syllables. Sounds. Cows and cheese.

He lived in Anchorage and sold buttons. Glitter buttons, printed buttons, novelty buttons, holiday buttons, golf ball buttons, money buttons, tender buttons, angel buttons, skull buttons, Mona Lisa buttons, sheet music buttons, airplane buttons, butterfly buttons, scrimshaw buttons, two-hole polka-dotted striped buttons.

He liked the obscurity of the coffeehouse next door. He liked being lazy. He liked selling buttons. He liked staring into aquariums, sunlight diffusing in the transparency of a fin. Dreamy. He held the cry within. It wanted to come out. All the time. This cry. This shout. This plea for mercy. This limestone bee opening its memory of flowers in his mind. A button. A simple button. A world in ivory. Fishing nets in the mist. Wisconsin. Maybe one day he'd go to Wisconsin. A place of hills and lakes. Peaceful. Like a button. A tender button.

The Wildness Of Spoons

Wash the locomotive in Anchorage. Power the rattan in plywood. Hum pounds of gluttonous learning. My wallet extrudes flowers. Interior abstractions hustle my face to you. I'm the chowder inside the drum. Enrich the paraffin by incursion. Dachshund jar of adjectives. Harden the tumble taxi. Skim the abandoned steam. Throw and emerge and verify. Butter the nascent dream. Manipulate the crackle cream. Elegance sends its assembly. The myth of the jug stove is available to you in indiscriminate octaves. The moon rises congenial as papier collé. I mourn the wrap club. The sophisticated skidoodle dump. Shiver the slouch paint. I ship my mark in drops. I exclaim a public crack. My map explains the trek by pylons and cups. I spin the weather and burst. Choke and squeeze the strings to a resonance that we can remember. I need to feel to fit you. I grasp the hammer to amplify the probability of bolts. Tangle the details in glaze. Attract a climate and give it to a saga. Soliciting secretes you into building an argument and pioneering the new despair. Are you ready for the Hinduism ablution drill? I embark in chains and squirt. The red soubriquet velvet is my gift to translucence. I'm suitably clumsy and soothed by intercourse. The boat ripples with hunger. Pound the dollars into purchase. Events are the narrative stream. A block of power crashes through itself. The stimulus that is algebra has been approved by epoxy. Maturity grumbles in its pronouns. The buffalo are pungent and their poetry is flaming. I'm focused on a naked crowd of grass. I believe in the wildness of spoons. A whisper emerges and cuts the air into consonants. Vowels move them into fact.

The Music Of Elsewhere

The café is in twinkle mode. I infringe on nothing but my own assembly of smell. I linger in invention, which is a metaphysics of aching acceptance. My injuries require a museum, dioramas of Fauve pioneers, a Nebraska in which one's wallet charms the interior of a percolated airport. The thermometer reaches into its temperatures for a replica of paper. The pepper is an adjustment, but the salt is a sensation of mutual support, creating a bridge to the chronology of our buttons. Everyone swarms with opinion. It's anarchic to do otherwise. Even the crows approve. The shovel clanks against the concrete floor of the garage and the glockenspiel collects dust in the corner where the shadows stumble through the music of elsewhere. The animals spread into the hills. The hills spread into the afternoon. The afternoon squeezes the world with its fading light and lifts oblivion into its warmer emissions. We join the butter and pull the string. Baskets of fruit tumble on our heads. I can hear Istanbul in the distance. It sounds like a glass of milk spinning with lobsters. I can't control my opinions. I just let them wander around on paper until they become something I can throw over the wall and wait to hear them echo.

The Savor Of Postulation

Coordinates sizzle in the sewing kit. I know how our actions put words in the air, sew coherence amid chaos, cultivate flax, connect dots, unfold our architecture. Create dramas. Braid rope. Summon ghosts.

Neil Young enters the room with a guitar. He plays a few chords. The river moves gracefully into comprehension. A dead man floats out to sea.

The savor of postulation excites the blood. The purpose of it feels pearl. We tether the hammer until our arms stop flapping. We sell rain and buy shields. We ride a green dragon. We shop for shoes.

Shoes are shapes with tongues and laces. Therefore, our veins are mahogany. We stand by the window and muse.

The sphere is a gesture. It emerges from space as a planet or moon. You can write about such events as parables or freeways. We pass one another on the freeway knowing nothing about one another. And this serves as a form of civilization.

You can distance yourself from a definition, but will it alter ablution? You can swim in a metaphor, but will it duplicate the candor of Dakota topsoil? Dirt is the ultimate metaphor. It's where seeds take root. Where Being still speaks to us through the medium of wheat.

Sunflowers. Beans. Vincent Van Gogh.

The incision corresponds to your blade. I will exchange your smear for a towel. Not any towel, a bath towel, a very good towel, a thick towel, a towel soft as thought.

Haunted from within, and at the very peak of the solar eclipse, when the edge of the moon is singing with beads of light, we hop over a penumbra on the ground as it goes pulsing and undulating over a row of motorcycles.

What is Being? What is this clearing in the forests of time?

I can gather a chronology from a general abhorrence to neoliberalism and free market lust. But I won't. I prefer the non-linear invitations of space. I want to escape the sepia derelictions of a dying culture.

All the proverbs are bilingual. Even the rain is alive. I can see it in my sweat.

Indulge the bananas and walk toward the concentric and lost. I understand the perturbations of the garret and sew it together in a coincidence. I fold myself into a salon and pound the salt with my clocks.

It's black inside a whistle. Sunlight excites an entire excuse for living. The limestone is atmospheric with a stepladder. How would this all sound in a song? It would sound faraway.

The audacity of insects is semi-formal. Even the tuba has a pulse. The blisters arrive with the aquarium. I have the caboose of a clarinet in my pocket. That makes the valves warm and the melody stiffen into power.

I take a cough and cough it up with the spirit of a cod.

The flags continue to excite the delusional aspirations of youth. Who can say what a wave brings when it sprawls across the sand? It depends on the effacements of our names. When the void appears, the sun will burn brighter and our actions will assume the brilliance of exploration.

The clarinet is just a symbol for caffeine.

Who doesn't like coffee?

I wrap my conviviality in a joke. I disappear into the crowd and glue my emotions back together with words and fancy arabesques.

No. I'm not a comb. But I know what a bristle is. You've got to wear a hat on this planet. The winds all blow like crazy. I strain to understand sugar. I see sculptures. The oasis must be near. I like to flex my muscles, but not when I drive. I've got to keep my eyes on the road and my ears fully attuned to the silence of things carried free from the fire of my rage.

It isn't life that I hope to find. It's life that hopes to find me.

What is hope? Hope is a device for concealing the true nature of reality, which doesn't barter in terms of hope. Reality uses a far more ancient medium of exchange based on the generation of Oreo cookies.

What is destiny? Is destiny a reality? Or a fiction? I carry a basket of cherries and little by little the boats appear.

Snow Bump Whistle Burp

Personality is a limestone waddle. Piano keys in melodic thunder. Chiaroscuro morning. Turpentine. Catalogue sputter. Pathos hibachi propelled by sizzle. Exultation points wrapped in mass. The dark matter of a constitutional grain is manipulated by gremlins. We all seem curved. I turn infrared and find my muscles have all gulped Guyana.

Window cook. Coffee laughing at a map. I succeed at roots although the doctrine of bristles eludes me. I have rattan to murmur and I expect to be culminated in pink. The prominence of steel sticks to my secret humor, which is sideways, and huckleberry.

I'm bewildered by mimes. I pull my goals into kerosene and light them on fire. I endure by including emotion. The life of a cat is an office grouse. I saw my intestines in anarchic ecstasy and decided on burlap by counting the ruts in a nearby road. The incentive to fly deepens my respect for dreaming.

The door steers are an ensemble. Wisdom circulates the pigment thunder.

I float in syntax. I'm freely vital, but also a little roller skate. Orange is never vague. But it's baffling how the hairbrush is shoved across the head without stinging any sounds up there.

I explode into exhibition. Light hugs and a deep rub. Snow bump whistle burp.

I'm a lost chronological tonic of sparkly silt. The river moves over me I'm a catfish on the bottom of your attention. Unpredictable viscera whispering coalition. Heaven is an imponderable excursion through my leg. I'm all airplane. Wool's unseemly seamlessness in seesaw scrutiny. Roots finding themselves tangled in the cemetery transformations. A robin listening for worms.

If I increase my perspectives I get ghostly indentations in my lotus. I rip myself into appointments. I stray a little from the topic which was never quite established to begin with and anchor near Marseille. The caboose always greets the places its leaving.

And this is awakened by feather. The pulleys creak as we draw the sky closer. I feel the energy of sharing. Tugged. Jingled by the guests. I can see infinity in the curve of a spoon. Time in the tines of a fork. Sand. Mass is such a rascal. The thumb hangs from the hand indispensable and fun. We deepen our resources by leaving our doors open. And Cezanne gives space a theatre.

Hardball

The experience of being yourself is very difficult to grasp for two reasons. It is impossible to define *a priori* a "self" to which we would then try to correspond. This is a logical mistake, because you can't tell who you are before you've reached it, and it's not certain that what you find is really definable. It might be the convolutions of an ego hanging down from the ceiling fan like one of the twisting anacondas of hell's colorful aristocracy. Hardball is different. Hardballs are stitched by hand and have a round cushioned cork center. Let's be like that. Be a ball. Be a hardball. But don't be undernourished. Let the universe walk into your head and sit down.

At certain moments, we don't know WHO we are, but we know we ARE. How do you get there? Remember what the dormouse said: feed your head. The French beignets R brought home are exquisite. What does it mean to believe in something? I believe in the beauty of yeast. I believe texture is a literature for the hands and that the engineering of the human body is amazing. The brain alone is a phenomenal organ. And yet 100 billion neurons are not enough to get shitfaced on Gatorade. Is the mind separate from the body? No. Does the mind have reality? Yes, it contains 2,100 calories and a view of Earth from the bathroom. The Dutch call it an *Olijfput*.

Each individual has a polyphonic nature, and when we speak with ourselves, all the sources of culture resonate within. Most of our knowledge begins with Dead Sea mud while snakes and spiders are poured on our heads. One correct word and golden coins rain down. If death is simply non-existence, which is to say we simply cease to exist, and since there is no one to experience non-existence, who is to know? But if Swedenborg is right, I'm going to need a swimsuit and a bath towel. Mud likes to hang out in poetry because words are proteins and lipids and ribonucleic acid. Our true emotions are saucepans. Most feelings want you to do something. Shoot sparks or chip away at the edge of your life. Beliefs are sage at twilight. And this is a cause of igloos.

Through the erotic relationship, says Emmanuel Levinas, nudity, the giving of oneself to others, the caress, without the will of ultimate possession or fusion, opens an essential ethical field. What isn't erotic also varies, from wet kisses to poor hygiene. But what happens when we finally reach air, or atoms?

Is there a spirit that inhabits my body but is not my body, and is this spirit, which has a personality, the continuing narrative that is me, me? Cognition is mostly ants going off in all directions. We're all trapped in an illusion of choice. Here I go, leaping into space. I squeeze the morning sun. The horizon splits the day from night. I feel eloquent as a speed bump.

Joke String

Ground. Leave inquiry among the leaves. Endure a bashful temptation.

Symmetry produces my shoes, but my shoes are nuanced and ancient. The geometry smolders like a lawn sprinkler smeared with Gauss distribution, which is totally independent of the empirical subject and laced by two determined pairs of hands appearing out of the darkness.

There are signs that gravity is asymptotically safe. Fasten a flash to the nether end of a red giant and watch it flame into space like a busted guitar string. The wool is your point, even if it's a little theoretical. You can repair this goldfish. It's not a perception. It's a journey.

Jug clatter. Fill my murmur. Door that I believe. Folds. Eye rub. They fiddle a kiss who fountain scales. Twinkle like a lip.

With a word on it.

The appeal of mindfulness is in its complete highway, an umbrella in the backseat. This is where the trance meets the current. A whistle churns the spirits.

Rattle. Joke string. Accommodate your swallow. The skull has a life in it. Technicolor glockenspiel baby.

Cocoon. Dusty artist. Painter dirt freely exploded.

Fathom. Gleaming pain. Greet it organically.

Picasso lobster piano nailed beyond the convoy. Music in a metal. I'm sending you an alchemy. Plays. Infantry figures. Dribble perception and dig. Chemicals diffusing in demurral. A club clatter a wheel with effective sounds on the gravel. Motorcycles. Lights. Crumpled beer cans.

Virtue. World spout. Red flickered to ochre. Stroll. Drum gravy. Sophisticated snow chair. Abalone finger which an opinion explains to be a platform for the enactment of steam.

Fish before fish crush the distortion.

I feel bronze. Meat during science gets scraped to gristle. And then a mitten is written into space. Break a fast and rob a pratfall. Falling in love is a new pavement for the engines of groan.

Great music has to be scraped out of the air. Or pumped.

Coaxed, cajoled, rubbed, persuaded, magnetized, pleaded, begged, beguiled, chiseled.

Delegations of pearl undertake the lassitude of ash. If space is within space, then spatiality must have something to do with *Le Palais Idéal du Facteur Cheval*.

This is my electric yellow pin. I'm licking the power that is nature. I smell sweet from my locomotive breakfast. Causation causes itself by eating the glitter of enigma.

A cricket singing from a high edge of involvement exclaims nothingness, which is now a nail in the two-by-four of a sentence cycling around a man's tongue.

String theory states that all matter in the universe is composed of tiny vibrating strings of energy and in the long run will redeem us from the old ideals, which were beginning to smell like icebergs. Locke believed that makers have property rights.

What a joke.

Nobody has property rights. All we have is one another. Pluck that G string, and sing a tune of dark blistering energy.

Foodstuff

We have a small refrigerator. You can only put small items in it. Five women standing in front of a door. Tomatoes, lettuce, that odd feeling you get when you go underwater for the first time after going a long time without swimming. Never underestimate the fertility of one's own existence. Can a pain be ugly or beautiful? Here's a smear of poetry on a glass side: little microbial words create sugar. A sweetness for the mind. String theory & loop quantum gravity. It's delicious, & goes with anything. Horsepower, weekends, the hills of West Virginia. Do you see? Each word is a palimpsest, cold meat diffusing the sun's heat. But enough of that. Let's eat.

Let's eat the sky at midnight and cough it back up at dawn. Tyrants and derelicts alike rise to touch the gown of morning, brush their teeth and do what they do, go where they go.

A door opens to another dimension. I'm wearing a finger of ice, a necklace of tin soldiers. If we have enough salt we can assemble a star in a garden of nerves. We have seclusion in a farmhouse. And except for the onions, it's easy enough to endure one's personality. Throw yourself into it. Don't be shy. Walk out of yourself and tell everyone what time is. Tell them that time is nothing more than a little upholstery, something to soften the steam of intuition at noon when the guano changes color and the innocent come forward to be initiated in espresso. That it talks to us in a forward-driven story and ends with a monolith humming "Twinkle Twinkle Little Star."

Grenadine adds propulsion. Sticks of meaning carry me forward. A melee of sugar reveals the shiver of camaraderie. The grog has a northern shine and the clock wags its glass, the story of pearls behind my knee is a species of cognition, a distant matter for the gallantry of the moment. If you look closely at a Viking ship you will immediately notice the magnitude of grace in the sweep of its lines. This might be used as an example of thought. The brain alone is a phenomenal organ. And yet 100 billion neurons are not enough to get the world to stop burning up.

The important thing is that Montaigne, as he writes to Madame de Duras, wants to "form his life" and "exist elsewhere than on paper," to become fully himself. I know just how he feels. I dip my pen in the ink of sleep and write my name in water. I mean, you know, words. It's what we do. We make them do things. Inflate the sun with your breath. Paint mosquitos with your Costco antlers. Reality is just another rattle in the elbow of electricity. This beard is my grandfather. Even now, there are winds shaping my indigestion. How is it possible for one mind to know another? Let's explain it with binoculars as we watch an insect cycle around an apple. Thank you for coming.

Imaginary Solution

The pharmaceutical garden gnomes handspring through my brain. Despite the clatter I believe the dirt. The grip of cognition verifies the twinkle of paraphernalia. I greet the joke beneath the gleam of its smile. A prowling acceptance folds itself into Liverpool.

Bingo in a nipple which my gravity neglects. We accept the virtue of my eating. I drum beside the artist's sag. Sift the jingles in your sternum if you want to find the satori of the thyroid. It's indicative of scorn to cry along the exploration of our inner gardenia.

The texture of my aim was rough before I had intuition. I oppose nothing. I jug the studio in blue. I chronicle birds and change what I can. My chew is the kiss and shout of all things perpendicular and walking. Wall the idea in a wild disarray and it will validate the polo in a trickle of inseam.

I'm enthralled to have pinned this argument to an abalone. England will carry our history into the future. If there is a future. They're doing to the fiddle what the fiddle did to Paganini. I mean to touch the firmament when the steam rises from the flash of my nerves.

The thickening of my succotash allows the evasion of my hurry. No balloon requires an insinuation. I sing the speed that so intrigues our realism. This wheel on the ground this bone black engine this spout of opium are all the rationale I need to sit by a brook and think. I thunder reality.

Gothic water intake valve. Sauerkraut book on a warm blue chair. I'm a whispering gun. A month of amphetamine in Vermont. An open flame of consciousness throwing language at an imaginary solution.

Chuckle Buckle Prawn Guffaw

There are hundreds of ways to learn the guitar, but writing poetry isn't one of them. I will one day be an octogenarian. Will that help? Probably not.

I agree with limestone. The world is a tease. Headland drool. Sagebrush fields and basalt rocks.

What ugly leaves this tree is forming. I can't explain my eyebrows. I'm traveling along a line of clatter cluttered with hundreds of brilliant dahlias. I have the emotive locomotive pulse of propane in the rain. I'm all roots and words. Everything is a hustle including this guide to the screams of the local chateau. I'm out to prove the worth of writing in a postmodern culture. I do that by drifting, like clouds. Sobbing does the rest. Hills like white elixirs.

I'm on a path to glory. I can feel that now. I'm in revolt. I dig your camaraderie. Welcome to the oasis. Here's a sandwich of pineapple, lettuce and ham. Here's a pair of aesthetic shoes with stars on them. You will need them for the hike into the stratosphere.

I feel at home on paper. I have a nice plump duchy and ten pounds of thinking churning in my blood. The process is a matter of brocade. This is done by working a supplementary weft into the weave, creating the illusion that segments have been embossed into the fabric of my life, or embroidered on top of it, like the sparkle of hypothetical butter.

I dangle my panic over the dots conversing in comic books. Winter expands my sense of black, especially that bone black of Rembrandt's paintings, which he got from the charring of animal bones or waste ivory in a closed crucible, and used it to clothe his subjects with the somber facts of life.

And what, pray tell, are the somber facts of life?

Mortality. Hard-to-get-at elbow joints. The rumble of the stomach during group meditation. Sticky fingers, seborrheic dermatitis, the taste of grass when you're grazing on a mohair dish of monster eyeball. The weight and movement of the world, which is constantly in rotation, constantly changing, constantly demanding that you change with it.

Or suffer the consequences, which wallop our heads with history.

I'm breaking free of my chains. I'm no longer in this world I'm looking at tourists. I'm adrift in rivers of reverie. Nocturnal discharge. The smell of the sea.

Electricity is timeless. Galvanized bucket with the sternum of Marie Laurencin. Attend to this strain, Peter Green on guitar, I'm there at last, a bag of nails, a discarded TV. My eyebrows are soft pink stars.

Let's build a slide. Let me take you into a time warp.

I'm healed by exploration. I have the enhanced luggage of a lobster tap-dancing on a picnic table next to a hole in the rain. I feel the wet of the universe like two sweaty wrestlers. My address is a canker sore. A dragonfly flutters and darts around my head.

Drink this and call me in the morning.

What is it? It's the interior of a good idea. Perception walks in dirty water. My head is a nebula of hair and thought in a milieu of rogue elevators. Rattlesnake nutmeg. The city of Houston lost in vapor. Whatever you feel right now don't force it let it be.

Age is a son-of-a-bitch.

This is the André Breton room. Eat this sentence. It will make you strong and beautiful. Eat it all, ganglions and tongue.

I'm enthralled with the predicate embedded in this brocade. Portugal materializes like a tug out on the sound. Language pumps an income to the surface of an unemployed poem. Thousands celebrate the invention of the metaphor, which stirs in the mouth of the sky creating thunder.

I like to flirt with apples. I have a jungle in my breath. I have a Cubist elbow and a smear of meaning on my hands. This is me pumping on a concertina. And this is me sitting in an office, gazing out of a window, sprinkling the air with prepositions. Lift this sentence with your eyes: ramble the amble to bramble and scramble, my only son, and you will one day find nuance in the indeterminate and mastery in the dead.

When will I ever be done?

Done with what? Oh you know. Circulating. Hauling soubriquets of meaning across the desert in the middle of a cuticle. Then going to sleep. Entering that other world. The one whose proposals are solace to the holes in my head.

A Sad Opacity

Currently, the sensory neurons in the olfactory epithelium are responding to the scent of frangipani. In and of itself it means nothing, but accompanied by valentines, it could mean a visit from the pope is imminent, or that ideas like icicles invite pillow ticking. The chains belong to yesterday. They were good chains, serviceable chains, but sooner or later one must break loose, one must flourish, one must prosper by being showered by hail, blasted by winds, bombarded by interviews. Life is a sadness that can be hard to maintain by hitting a tambourine all day by the side of the road.

Sometimes a melody will give rise to a cosmic broom and I will sweep the floor until I am soaked with sweat and deputized for mayhem. I get undressed and the sky undresses with me. The effulgent music of mushrooms craves a certain kind of movement, a certain kind of shampoo that makes the hair yearn to be lustrous and young. Scratch the chameleon whose chest is a foundry of infinite pewter. The ribs are boleros of welcome fire.

Let's choose a song and then not sing it. Let's think about singing it, imagine singing it, and then not sing it. Sometimes words are best left alone resting quietly on paper, waiting for a pair of eyes to awaken them, bring them to life. And the words get up and walk around and lick the walls of a hypothetical limit imposed on language until everything bursts open and the mind tastes the glory of the logos in a gown of orange taffeta, sighing, breathing heavily, dancing circles around the piano.

This is not a happy planet. Bagpipes syncopate into pratfalls. Injuries go unnoticed. Rattlesnakes coil and hiss. Bellicosity goes unrewarded.

There is much to be said about chalk. I will sometimes see someone guest on a TV show about books and their shirt will be untucked, as if to say something evocative about Henri Bergson and intuition. Relics confuse history with French fries and the result is unwholesome. We need to be more oceanic, more penetrating in our sagas.

A muscular banana deserves a diamond, at least. Maybe three or four. Who am I to decide? If I'm annoyed I squeak. The whole affair of the curtain gave birth to a scooter that would have remained dormant had it not been for the barn and its numerous rolls of twine.

The body is a theater of blood and sweat. Even the king has a body. The king and queen both have bodies. Who does not have a body? Ghosts. Ghosts don't have bodies, ghosts have memories. The ghost of the king is a memory. The ghost of the queen is a water fountain on *La Plaza de Gaudi* in Barcelona.

The body is an amalgam of earth and water. Millions of molecules convening in skin. Millions of molecules aggregating in bone. Millions of molecules assembling in blood.

I am, roughly, a constellation of 37.2 trillion cells. Mitochondria, centrioles, endoplasmic reticulum.

Linked in a protein chain, an amino acid is called a residue. This particular residue is getting up to get the laundry out of the dryer. This residue that I call home (the home which is me, whatever 'me' is) wears clothes. The residue that is my wife wears clothes. The residue of black and white fur lying on the bed is called a cat. She does not wear clothes. She has fur.

Why don't I have fur? If I had fur I would not need to wear clothes.

I do have hair. That's something. Hair is something. Hair is assembled methodically by the Elves of Music, who are bald, and who play instruments made of string and bone.

We are but the sad opacity of our future specters, said Mallarmé.

I remember the packed earth during an Indian sweat lodge ceremony. How good it felt. The heat was so intense I thought I would become a bucket of oracles. I dripped islands of laughter.

There is the blurring of the window ablaze with lightning, glass veined with beads of drooling water. The exultation of a flannel panacea gives me the light of an inner eye. The border of pure tone in the climate of your skin makes me giddy with dissolution, thorns in a handkerchief I found lying in a cricket. A conflagration jumps from root to root in an ingot of clouds, serving the realm of desire with symbols and rain.

Can language get any thicker than nine inch nails? Yes, it can. It can get perpetual and purr. It can become an escalator whose buttons serenade the fingers on a single touch, and rise in the sky to visit the angels as they sit at their desks pondering the beauty of mahogany, and shuffle papers for the feeling it produces, which is breezy and theoretical, phenomenology in a moment of luscious distraction, or descend into the basement where a row of telephones offers assistance to the subterranean realm.

It's all signals and codes, you know? Stews and stems, stars and stenography. Gaudy Gaudi. Tears of a willow by the gurgle of a brook. Brook of a gurgle by the willow of a tear.

Nothing adds up. It never does in the end. Most of everything goes unstated, or vacillates between utterance and mermaid, conferring on the fabulous without consulting an orthopedist, or restoring the sputter of incense to the nozzle of a cashew.

There are feelings that tabulate our sense of certitude, make it a haze of unstrung leaves, a vague and wonderful ocean that resides in our medication, our dresser drawer, and rock out in our personal auditoriums, everyone has one, a stage on which the Beatles play all night and day, and frogs in platform shoes fly helicopters around our insignia.

It's a sad opacity that calls me crying, who are you, who am I, what are we doing, never mind, I'll call back later. Because opacity is like that. Opacity is a few minutes of black genius making records in an electrifying wig, a pink sexuality maniacal as science. It's the specter of our future selves banging away on a piano, hidden fires looking over our shoulders.

Singing In Silence

Every injury has a moment in which to swallow an egg of knowledge and create a sound for the silence of a shoe, the backdrop of a snowflake, the plumage of a duck, and make it rock, make it rattle, make it talk. A scarf weighs the light and subtlety aspires to the solidity of the hammer. I feel strangely detached from everything chained to simulation. Artifice steals our rope, our ribbon, our presence. The fullness of our wheels, the portent of our steam. The kettle whistles making a grapefruit of the kitchen. I've got rubies and gold but none of it sticks to the religion I'm trying to describe with a little glue, a few feathers and a block of stone.

Not to worry: there's a theater in my skin and a dragon in the garage. Being is all about antifreeze, the eye of the beholder, the crack in the truth of moonlight. Currents of science fiction blossom at the periphery. The only real remedy for distance is the trajectory of remorse, which goes to Borneo and back, bubbling along like a hideous sweater with Darth Vader on it.

Conflagrations at sea. A foundry swallowing men at dawn. These are the things that make sense of a convulsion, that make an assembly of fully mature adults get up and applaud. Think of it as a healthful rupture, a weave, a wave, a yolk in the shamrock of acceptance.

I always get lost looking for a reason, a logic, a rationale for the revelatory gold of Byzantium. It's always swampy where our suggestions are magnified by crystals and magic. It's not easy finding burlap when the cuts are sharp and the fabric is fully spread. There are all these holes to consider, little tears and colors assembled in a casual glide through our vowels, qualities of almond in consonants like tongs.

A troika is loaded with pineapples and salt sprinkled near the hill of a sleeping giant. There's a soft blue light sleeping in a hard blue rock and a history written by footprint in the ooze by the side of the river. A plough splits the earth and flames leap out. The chimera puts on her ski boots. I think it's time to rent a trailer and rip the sky into little pieces of sport.

The salt coincides with the light hiding in the pineapples. Everything seems linked to an idea of itself, just like a can of shaving cream: the sublime is longer when it lingers in the hand, soft and white and moist, like a kiss of ambiguity, or the tutelage of twilight. This is called flannel, or how to resolve the problem of agriculture.

The past stumbles into a paperweight and liberates a cloud of words. A sheet of paper catches everything nebulous and allusive and tossed by the side of the road. The fuller development of our dreams offers us the savor of mushrooms and melts it into calculus. Thursday turns out to be significantly larger than the chameleon crawling on my hand, which invites further speculation, struts and wings and a meridional imagery that I can use later to describe a collarbone.

I hope the manure doesn't ruin our appreciation of apricots. Is it any less thematic to enter a café and order a cup of reminiscence and drag it across the sacrament of eating? In a word, yes. The hammer eventually persuades the nail to enter the wood. And the vertebrae charm the pants off of a xylophone. It's how everything redeems the neon of alternative and provokes reverie. I know whereof I speak. Ebony supports the significance presumed living in the barometer. Contrariety rattles down the road and the barge awaiting us in the canal is magnificent. And we walk toward it, singing in total silence.

Burrito

The sounds are teeming in leaves. The muffin I faucet has pluck. I take the time
to fulfill a copperplate there and wax a shoe. It glues pleasure to the images I
wife. We organize exploration by hunger. We explore hunger as hunger ex-
plores us. This is the stethoscope I prefer. It murmurs with swans, which guide
a lonely power through the painting of life in a library. Appliances are watched
by ducks. The pool is a languorous dream. It's effervescent to extend summer
under the skin. If structure pokes me I find a bikini and sift it for waterfalls.
The idea's peculiarities make it an orchard whose fruit are the mosaic of books
and whose enjoyments are sucked by addicts in attics. It's prodigal to laugh,
crucial to keep the silverware cool at night. Tiger our art at a trouble. Tube
this plummet and show our snakes. Glasses it cuts there to cook a vocabulary
until it smolders with the pneuma of the dead as they gather around a roar-
ing bonfire. Your knife begs to attack a pimple. Discharge a gratitude then
hit escape. My bingo falls and I slap it. Your wings perpetuate inquiry, thus
proving the theorem of anomalistical semantics, that a poinsettia is welcome
at the horizon, and there will be rent for a feather if the wind is from the east
and the feather is from a goose. The right angle is the wrong angle if the hy-
potenuse rolls through a funhouse germinating conversation. The sparkle at
the press teases tweezers into books. The sentence has to be lifted carefully.
The lightening underneath it is convulsing with headlines. There's sand in the
parable and dust in your sweater. This is why Pythagoras dreams of ovals and
the mathematics is the very sauce of darkness whose fingers uphold the moon.
It goes with the groove of the universe undertaking the utterances of electric
men. Jimi Hendrix sitting on a stool with an acoustic crowbar. It seems a little
nugatory but the equation fulfills the requirements of the radio, which is just
now busy with water. The body speeds through its music. The breath carries
meaning like a thunderstorm cradled in time. How funny that there's a plumb-
er on the shore. Is this truly radio or a box of migrant consciousness? I think
it's mainly all about making a difference and appearing before judges dressed
as a cypress and ignoring the ramifications. If a poem doesn't come as natural
as leaves to a tree, it's better fry it up and eat it as a burrito.

The Field Of Variegated Winds

The rock is a circus of limestone. Therefore, I'm feeling glass. The distance to this emotion is rolling toward its pennies like an oyster shaking its face with a genuine agitation. My life is spread out on the floor. There's a murder on my lip and it just seems usual, like an encyclopedia. And yes, there's an afterlife. It's an oasis delivered by elves at midnight. Other than that, everything is pleasant as lipstick and there's a bird in the staircase, shifting about in icicles and sherry.

The light is incidental to the convulsion as the magenta is healing a book with its old stick and philosophy. No desire is without its pound of blob and passion aswirl in the blood, a loop in the birth of an apricot, any available orchard where the moonlight completes its shine on the memory kettle.

This passage is my next bitumen. I'm abandoning the pipes. The emotion is Pythagorean that seeds birch by the asphalt. I twinkle at the shale. My hand is there, reaching for altitude. I say this with chrome in my heart and a song in my popcorn. We all have problems. It's that mine seem, I don't know, cuddly when I hug them with all eight tentacles.

The sky is our bean, our metal swelled into purity. This is where the air flows, where the foghorn blows, where the agates become toupees for the heads of the carpenters, all of them ghostly in their hairpin gloom.

The reason for plywood is obvious: the bandages in Bohemia are sewn by haberdashery malcontents and need a little extra adhesion. It all turns banana eventually. I like enkindling relationships with a kind look and a chisel. The pickle within is a radical approach to winter. A development has been treading here all along, its shadow punched into meaning like a cramp. We can get through this together. But if we don't, take an enigma with you.

A wrestler has only so many curls. You can't waste your trousers on a scrutiny, not when your brain is about to burst into garrulity. I think I'll let the prepositions occur naturally, beside the old-timey phonograph, a jabbering of words provided with enough melody to make a text get wet with the high sticks of indecision and the short sticks of sugar.

The wild stems of the pillow start a forest in my head. I find pearls for the chicken whistles and undertake an acute way to swim the upcoming channels, the field of variegated winds, where all the conversations happen, and the laughter is frank by the fire.

Weave of the Dream King is JOHN OLSON's tenth collection of prose poetry. He is also the author of five novels, including *Souls of Wind* which was short-listed for a Believer Book Award in 2008, *The Seeing Machine, The Nothing That Is, In Advance of the Broken Justy,* and *Mingled Yarn,* an autobiographical novel. In 2004, Seattle's popular weekly *The Stranger* awarded Olson its annual Genius Award for literature and in 2012 he was one of eight finalists for Washington State's Innovator Award.

BLACK WIDOW PRESS POETRY IN TRANSLATION

BLACK WIDOW PRESS MODERN POETRY SERIES

WILLIS BARNSTONE
ABC of Translation
African Bestiary (forthcoming)

DAVE BRINKS
The Caveat Onus
The Secret Brain: Selected Poems 1995–2012

RUXANDRA CESEREANU
Crusader-Woman. Translated by Adam J. Sorkin.
    Introduction by Andrei Codrescu.
Forgiven Submarine by Ruxandra Cesereanu and
    Andrei Codrescu.

CLAYTON ESHLEMAN
An Alchemist with One Eye on Fire
Anticline
Archaic Design
Clayton Eshleman/The Essential Poetry: 1960–2015
Grindstone of Rapport: A Clayton Eshleman Reader
Penetralia
Pollen Aria
The Price of Experience
Endure: Poems by Bei Dao. Translated by Clayton
    Eshleman and Lucas Klein.
Curdled Skulls: Poems of Bernard Bador. Translated
    by Bernard Bador with Clayton Eshleman.

PIERRE JORIS
Barzakh (Poems 2000–2012)
Exile Is My Trade: A Habib Tengour Reader

MARILYN KALLET
How Our Bodies Learned
The Love That Moves Me
Packing Light: New and Selected Poems
Disenchanted City (La ville désenchantée) by Chantal
    Bizzini. Translated by J. Bradford Anderson,
    Darren Jackson, and Marilyn Kallet.

ROBERT KELLY
Fire Exit
The Hexagon

STEPHEN KESSLER
Garage Elegies
Last Call (forthcoming)

BILL LAVENDER
Memory Wing

HELLER LEVINSON
from stone this running
LinguaQuake
Lurk
Seep
Tenebraed
Un-
Wrack Lariat

JOHN OLSON
Backscatter: New and Selected Poems
Dada Budapest
Larynx Galaxy
Weave of the Dream King

NIYI OSUNDARE
City Without People: The Katrina Poems

MEBANE ROBERTSON
An American Unconscious
Signal from Draco: New and Selected Poems

JEROME ROTHENBERG
Concealments and Caprichos
Eye of Witness: A Jerome Rothenberg Reader.
    Edited with commentaries by Heriberto
    Yepez & Jerome Rothenberg.
The President of Desolation & Other Poems

AMINA SAÏD
The Present Tense of the World: Poems 2000–2009.
    Translated with an introduction by Marilyn Hacker.

ANIS SHIVANI
Soraya (Sonnets)

JERRY W. WARD, JR.
Fractal Song

ANTHOLOGIES / BIOGRAPHIES

*Barbaric Vast & Wild: A Gathering of Outside and
    Subterranean Poetry* (Poems for the Millennium,
    vol. 5). Editors: Jerome Rothenberg and John
    Bloomberg-Rissman

Clayton Eshleman: The Whole Art by Stuart Kendall

Revolution of the Mind: The Life of André Breton by
    Mark Polizzotti